Programming Scala

Programming Scala

Dean Wampler and Alex Payne

O'REILLY®

Beijing · Cambridge · Farnham · Köln · Sebastopol · Taipei · Tokyo

Programming Scala

by Dean Wampler and Alex Payne

Copyright © 2009 Dean Wampler and Alex Payne. All rights reserved.
Printed in the United States of America.

Published by O'Reilly Media, Inc., 1005 Gravenstein Highway North, Sebastopol, CA 95472.

O'Reilly books may be purchased for educational, business, or sales promotional use. Online editions
are also available for most titles (*http://my.safaribooksonline.com*). For more information, contact our
corporate/institutional sales department: 800-998-9938 or *corporate@oreilly.com*.

Editor: Mike Loukides	**Indexer:** Ellen Troutman Zaig
Production Editor: Sarah Schneider	**Cover Designer:** Karen Montgomery
Proofreader: Sarah Schneider	**Interior Designer:** David Futato
	Illustrator: Robert Romano

Printing History:

    September 2009:   First Edition.

O'Reilly and the O'Reilly logo are registered trademarks of O'Reilly Media, Inc. *Programming Scala*, the
image of a Malayan tapir, and related trade dress are trademarks of O'Reilly Media, Inc.

Many of the designations used by manufacturers and sellers to distinguish their products are claimed as
trademarks. Where those designations appear in this book, and O'Reilly Media, Inc. was aware of a
trademark claim, the designations have been printed in caps or initial caps.

While every precaution has been taken in the preparation of this book, the publisher and authors assume
no responsibility for errors or omissions, or for damages resulting from the use of the information contained herein. This work has been released under the Creative Commons Attribution-Noncommercial
license (*http://creativecommons.org/licenses/by-nc/3.0/*).

ISBN: 978-0-596-15595-7

[M]

1252091290

To Dad and Mom, who always believed in me.

To Ann, who was always there for me.

—Dean

To my mother, who gave me an appreciation for good writing and the accompanying intellectual tools with which to attempt to produce it.

To Kristen, for her unending patience, love, and kindness.

—Alex

Table of Contents

Foreword

If there has been a common theme throughout my career as a programmer, it has been the quest for better abstractions and better tools to support the craft of writing software. Over the years, I have come to value one trait more than any other: composability. If one can write code with good composability, it usually means that other traits we software developers value—such as orthogonality, loose coupling, and high cohesion—are already present. It is all connected.

When I discovered Scala some years ago, the thing that made the biggest impression on me was its composability. Through some very elegant design choices and simple yet powerful abstractions that were taken from the object-oriented and functional programming worlds, Martin Odersky has managed to create a language with high cohesion and orthogonal, deep abstractions that invites composability in all dimensions of software design. Scala is truly a SCAlable LAnguage that scales with usage, from scripting all the way up to large-scale enterprise applications and middleware. Scala was born out of academia, but it has grown into a pragmatic and practical language that is very much ready for real-world production use.

What excites me most about this book is that it's so practical. Dean and Alex have done a fantastic job, not only by explaining the language through interesting discussions and samples, but also by putting it in the context of the real world. It's written for the programmer who wants to get things done. I had the pleasure of getting to know Dean some years ago when we were both part of the aspect-oriented programming community. Dean holds a rare mix of deep analytical academic thinking and a pragmatic, get-things-done kind of mentality. Alex, whom I've had the pleasure to meet once, is leading the API team at Twitter, Inc. Alex has played a leading role in moving Twitter's code and infrastructure to Scala, making it one on the first companies to successfully deploy Scala in production.

You are about to learn how to write reusable components using mixin and function composition; how to write concurrent applications using Scala's Actors; how to make effective use of Scala's XML/XPath support; how to utilize Scala's rich, flexible, and expressive syntax to build Domain-Specific Languages; how to effectively test your Scala code; how to use Scala with popular frameworks such as Spring, Hadoop, and Terracotta; and much, much more. Enjoy the ride. I sure did.

—Jonas Bonér

Independent Consultant, Scalable Solutions AB

August, 2009

Preface

Programming Scala introduces an exciting new language that offers all the benefits of a modern object model, functional programming, and an advanced type system. Packed with code examples, this comprehensive book teaches you how to be productive with Scala quickly, and explains what makes this language ideal for today's scalable, distributed, component-based applications that support concurrency and distribution. You'll also learn how Scala takes advantage of the advanced Java Virtual Machine as a platform for programming languages.

Learn more at *http://programmingscala.com* or at the book's catalog page (*http://oreilly .com/catalog/9780596155957/*).

Welcome to Programming Scala

Programming languages become popular for many reasons. Sometimes, programmers on a given platform prefer a particular language, or one is institutionalized by a vendor. Most Mac OS programmers use Objective-C. Most Windows programmers use C++ and .NET languages. Most embedded-systems developers use C and C++.

Sometimes, popularity derived from technical merit gives way to fashion and fanaticism. C++, Java, and Ruby have been the objects of fanatical devotion among programmers.

Sometimes, a language becomes popular because it fits the needs of its era. Java was initially seen as a perfect fit for browser-based, rich client applications. Smalltalk captured the essence of object-oriented programming (OOP) as that model of programming entered the mainstream.

Today, concurrency, heterogeneity, always-on services, and ever-shrinking development schedules are driving interest in functional programming (FP). It appears that the dominance of object-oriented programming may be over. Mixing paradigms is becoming popular, even necessary.

We gravitated to Scala from other languages because Scala embodies many of the optimal qualities we want in a general-purpose programming language for the kinds of applications we build today: reliable, high-performance, highly concurrent Internet and enterprise applications.

Scala is a multi-paradigm language, supporting both object-oriented and functional programming approaches. Scala is scalable, suitable for everything from short scripts up to large-scale, component-based applications. Scala is sophisticated, incorporating state-of-the-art ideas from the halls of computer science departments worldwide. Yet Scala is practical. Its creator, Martin Odersky, participated in the development of Java for years and understands the needs of professional developers.

Both of us were seduced by Scala, by its concise, elegant, and expressive syntax and by the breadth of tools it put at our disposal. In this book, we strive to demonstrate why all these qualities make Scala a compelling and indispensable programming language.

If you are an experienced developer who wants a fast, thorough introduction to Scala, this book is for you. You may be evaluating Scala as a replacement for or complement to your current languages. Maybe you have already decided to use Scala, and you need to learn its features and how to use it well. Either way, we hope to illuminate this powerful language for you in an accessible way.

We assume that you are well versed in object-oriented programming, but we don't assume that you have prior exposure to functional programming. We assume that you are experienced in one or more other programming languages. We draw parallels to features in Java, C#, Ruby, and other languages. If you know any of these languages, we'll point out similar features in Scala, as well as many features that are new.

Whether you come from an object-oriented or functional programming background, you will see how Scala elegantly combines both paradigms, demonstrating their complementary nature. Based on many examples, you will understand how and when to apply OOP and FP techniques to many different design problems.

In the end, we hope that you too will be seduced by Scala. Even if Scala does not end up becoming your day-to-day language, we hope you will gain insights that you can apply regardless of which language you are using.

Conventions Used in This Book

The following typographical conventions are used in this book:

Italic

> Indicates new terms, URLs, email addresses, file names, and file extensions. Many italicized terms are defined in the Glossary on page 393.

`Constant width`

> Used for program listings, as well as within paragraphs to refer to program elements such as variable or function names, databases, data types, environment variables, statements, and keywords.

Constant width bold

Shows commands or other text that should be typed literally by the user.

Constant width italic

Shows text that should be replaced with user-supplied values or by values determined by context.

 This icon signifies a tip, suggestion, or general note.

 This icon indicates a warning or caution.

Using Code Examples

This book is here to help you get your job done. In general, you may use the code in this book in your programs and documentation. You do not need to contact us for permission unless you're reproducing a significant portion of the code. For example, writing a program that uses several chunks of code from this book does not require permission. Selling or distributing a CD-ROM of examples from O'Reilly books does require permission. Answering a question by citing this book and quoting example code does not require permission. Incorporating a significant amount of example code from this book into your product's documentation does require permission.

We appreciate, but do not require, attribution. An attribution usually includes the title, author, publisher, and ISBN. For example: "*Programming Scala* by Dean Wampler and Alex Payne. Copyright 2009 Dean Wampler and Alex Payne, 978-0-596-15595-7."

If you feel your use of code examples falls outside fair use or the permission given above, feel free to contact us at *permissions@oreilly.com*.

Getting the Code Examples

You can download the code examples from *http://examples.oreilly.com/9780596155964/*. Unzip the files to a convenient location. See the *README.txt* file in the distribution for instructions on building and using the examples.

Some of the example files can be run as scripts using the `scala` command. Others must be compiled into class files. Some files contain deliberate errors and won't compile. We have adopted a file naming convention to indicate each of these cases, although as you learn Scala it should become obvious from the contents of the files, in most cases:

-script.scala

Files that end in *-script.scala* can be run on a command line using `scala`, e.g., `scala foo-script.scala`. You can also start `scala` in the interpreter mode (when you don't specify a script file) and load any script file in the interpreter using the `:load filename` command.

-wont-compile.scala

Files that end in *-wont-compile.scala* contain deliberate errors that will cause them to fail to compile. We use this naming convention, along with one or more embedded comments about the errors, so it will be clear that they are invalid. Also, these files are skipped by the build process for the examples.

sake.scala

Files named *sake.scala* are used by our build tool, called `sake`. The *README.txt* file describes this tool.

*.scala

All other Scala files must be compiled using `scalac`. In the distribution, they are used either by other compiled or script files, such as tests, not all of which are listed in this book.

Safari® Books Online

Safari Books Online is an on-demand digital library that lets you easily search over 7,500 technology and creative reference books and videos to find the answers you need quickly.

With a subscription, you can read any page and watch any video from our library online. Read books on your cell phone and mobile devices. Access new titles before they are available for print, and get exclusive access to manuscripts in development and post feedback for the authors. Copy and paste code samples, organize your favorites, download chapters, bookmark key sections, create notes, print out pages, and benefit from tons of other time-saving features.

O'Reilly Media has uploaded this book to the Safari Books Online service. To have full digital access to this book and others on similar topics from O'Reilly and other publishers, sign up for free at *http://my.safaribooksonline.com*.

How to Contact Us

Please address comments and questions concerning this book to the publisher:

O'Reilly Media, Inc.
1005 Gravenstein Highway North
Sebastopol, CA 95472
800-998-9938 (in the United States or Canada)

707-829-0515 (international or local)
707-829-0104 (fax)

We have a web page for this book, where we list errata, examples, and any additional information. You can access this page at:

http://oreilly.com/catalog/9780596155957/

To comment or ask technical questions about this book, send email to:

bookquestions@oreilly.com

For more information about our books, conferences, Resource Centers, and the O'Reilly Network, see our website at:

http://oreilly.com

Acknowledgments

As we developed this book, many people read early drafts and suggested numerous improvements to the text, for which we are eternally grateful. We are especially grateful to Steve Jensen, Ramnivas Laddad, Marcel Molina, Bill Venners, and Jonas Bonér for their extensive feedback.

Much of the feedback we received came through the Safari Rough Cuts releases and the online edition available at *http://programmingscala.com*. We are grateful for the feedback provided by (in no particular order) Iulian Dragos, Nikolaj Lindberg, Matt Hellige, David Vydra, Ricky Clarkson, Alex Cruise, Josh Cronemeyer, Tyler Jennings, Alan Supynuk, Tony Hillerson, Roger Vaughn, Arbi Sookazian, Bruce Leidl, Daniel Sobral, Eder Andres Avila, Marek Kubica, Henrik Huttunen, Bhaskar Maddala, Ged Byrne, Derek Mahar, Geoffrey Wiseman, Peter Rawsthorne, Geoffrey Wiseman, Joe Bowbeer, Alexander Battisti, Rob Dickens, Tim MacEachern, Jason Harris, Steven Grady, Bob Follek, Ariel Ortiz, Parth Malwankar, Reid Hochstedler, Jason Zaugg, Jon Hanson, Mario Gleichmann, David Gates, Zef Hemel, Michael Yee, Marius Kreis, Martin Süsskraut, Javier Vegas, Tobias Hauth, Francesco Bochicchio, Stephen Duncan Jr., Patrik Dudits, Jan Niehusmann, Bill Burdick, David Holbrook, Shalom Deitch, Jesper Nordenberg, Esa Laine, Gleb Frank, Simon Andersson, Patrik Dudits, Chris Lewis, Julian Howarth, Dirk Kuzemczak, Henri Gerrits, John Heintz, Stuart Roebuck, and Jungho Kim. Many other readers for whom we only have usernames also provided feedback. We wish to thank Zack, JoshG, ewilligers, abcoates, brad, teto, pjcj, mkleint, dandoyon, Arek, rue, acangiano, vkelman, bryanl, Jeff, mbaxter, pjb3, kxen, hipertracker, ctran, Ram R., cody, Nolan, Joshua, Ajay, Joe, and anonymous contributors. We apologize if we have overlooked anyone!

Our editor, Mike Loukides, knows how to push and prod gentle. He's been a great help throughout this crazy process. Many other people at O'Reilly were always there to answer our questions and help us move forward.

We thank Jonas Bonér for writing the Foreword for the book. Jonas is a longtime friend and collaborator from the aspect-oriented programming (AOP) community. For years, he has done pioneering work in the Java community. Now he is applying his energies to promoting Scala and growing that community.

Bill Venners graciously provided the quote on the back cover. The first published book on Scala, *Programming in Scala* (Artima), that he cowrote with Martin Odersky and Lex Spoon, is indispensable for the Scala developer. Bill has also created the wonderful ScalaTest library.

We have learned a lot from fellow developers around the world. Besides Jonas and Bill, Debasish Ghosh, James Iry, Daniel Spiewak, David Pollack, Paul Snively, Ola Bini, Daniel Sobral, Josh Suereth, Robey Pointer, Nathan Hamblen, Jorge Ortiz, and others have illuminated dark corners with their blog entries, forum discussions, and personal conversations.

Dean thanks his colleagues at Object Mentor and several developers at client sites for many stimulating discussions on languages, software design, and the pragmatic issues facing developers in industry. The members of the Chicago Area Scala Enthusiasts (CASE) group have also been a source of valuable feedback and inspiration.

Alex thanks his colleagues at Twitter for their encouragement and superb work in demonstrating Scala's effectiveness as a language. He also thanks the Bay Area Scala Enthusiasts (BASE) for their motivation and community.

Most of all, we thank Martin Odersky and his team for creating Scala.

CHAPTER 1

Zero to Sixty: Introducing Scala

Why Scala?

Today's enterprise and Internet applications must balance a number of concerns. They must be implemented quickly and reliably. New features must be added in short, incremental cycles. Beyond simply providing business logic, applications must support secure access, persistence of data, transactional behavior, and other advanced features. Applications must be highly available and scalable, requiring designs that support concurrency and distribution. Applications are networked and provide interfaces for both people and other applications to use.

To meet these challenges, many developers are looking for new languages and tools. Venerable standbys like Java, C#, and C++ are no longer optimal for developing the next generation of applications.

If You Are a Java Programmer...

Java was officially introduced by Sun Microsystems in May of 1995, at the advent of widespread interest in the Internet. Java was immediately hailed as an ideal language for writing browser-based applets, where a secure, portable, and developer-friendly application language was needed. The reigning language of the day, C++, was not suitable for this domain.

Today, Java is more often used for server-side applications. It is one of the most popular languages in use for the development of web and enterprise applications.

However, Java was a child of its time. Now it shows its age. In 1995, Java provided a syntax similar enough to C++ to entice C++ developers, while avoiding many of that language's deficiencies and "sharp edges." Java adopted the most useful ideas for the development problems of its era, such as object-oriented programming (OOP), while discarding more troublesome techniques, such as manual memory management. These design choices struck an excellent balance that minimized complexity and maximized developer productivity, while trading-off performance compared to natively compiled code. While Java has evolved since its birth, many people believe it has grown too complex without adequately addressing some newer development challenges.

Developers want languages that are more succinct and flexible to improve their productivity. This is one reason why so-called scripting languages like Ruby and Python have become more popular recently.

The never-ending need to scale is driving architectures toward pervasive concurrency. However, Java's concurrency model, which is based on synchronized access to shared, mutable state, results in complex and error-prone programs.

While the Java language is showing its age, the Java Virtual Machine (JVM) on which it runs continues to shine. The optimizations performed by today's JVM are extraordinary, allowing byte code to outperform natively compiled code in many cases. Today, many developers believe that using the JVM with new languages is the path forward. Sun is embracing this trend by employing many of the lead developers of JRuby and Jython, which are JVM ports of Ruby and Python, respectively.

The appeal of Scala for the Java developer is that it gives you a newer, more modern language, while leveraging the JVM's amazing performance and the wealth of Java libraries that have been developed for over a decade.

If You Are a Ruby, Python, etc. Programmer...

Dynamically typed languages like Ruby, Python, Groovy, JavaScript, and Smalltalk offer very high productivity due to their flexibility, powerful metaprogramming, and elegance.

Statically Typed Versus Dynamically Typed Languages

One of the fundamental language design choices is *static versus dynamic* typing.

The word "typing" is used in many contexts in software. The following is a "plausible" definition that is useful for our purposes.

> A type system is a tractable syntactic method for preserving the absence of certain program behaviors by classifying phrases according to the kinds of values they compute.
>
> —Benjamin C. Pierce, *Types and Programming Languages* (MIT Press, 2002)

Note the emphasis on how a type system allows reasoning about what a system *excludes* from happening. That's generally easier than trying to determine the set of all allowed possibilities. A type system is used to catch various errors, like unsupported operations on particular data structures, attempting to combine data in an undefined way (e.g., trying to add an integer to a string), breaking abstractions, etc.

Informally, in static typing, a *variable* is bound to a particular type for its lifetime. Its type can't be changed and it can only reference type-compatible instances. That is, if a variable refers to a value of type A, you can't assign a value of a different type B to it, unless B is a subtype of A, for some reasonable definition of "subtype."

In dynamic typing, the type is bound to the *value*, not the *variable*. So, a variable might refer to a value of type A, then be reassigned later to a value of an unrelated type X.

The term *dynamically typed* is used because the type of a *variable* is evaluated when it is used during runtime, while in a statically typed language the type is evaluated at parse time.

This may seem like a small distinction, but it has a pervasive impact on the philosophy, design, and implementation of a language. We'll explore some of these implications as we go through the book.

Scala and Java are statically typed languages, whereas Ruby, Python, Groovy, Java-Script, and Smalltalk are dynamically typed languages.

For simplicity, we will often use the terms *static language* and *dynamic language* as shorthands for *statically typed language* and *dynamically typed language*, respectively.

An *orthogonal* design consideration is *strong versus weak* typing. In strong typing, every variable (for static typing) or value (for dynamic typing) must have an unambiguous type. In weak typing, a specific type is not required. While most languages allow some mixture of strong versus weak typing, Scala, Java, and Ruby are *predominantly* strongly typed languages. Some languages, like C and Perl, are more weakly typed.

Despite their productivity advantages, *dynamic* languages may not be the best choices for all applications, particularly for very large code bases and high-performance applications. There is a longstanding, spirited debate in the programming community about the relative merits of dynamic versus static typing. Many of the points of comparison are somewhat subjective. We won't go through all the arguments here, but we will offer a few thoughts for consideration.

Optimizing the performance of a dynamic language is more challenging than for a static language. In a static language, optimizers can exploit the type information to make decisions. In a dynamic language, fewer such clues are available for the optimizer, making optimization choices harder. While recent advancements in optimizations for dynamic languages are promising, they lag behind the state of the art for static languages. So, if you require very high performance, static languages are probably a safer choice.

Static languages can also benefit the development process. Integrated development environment (IDE) features like *autocompletion* (sometimes called *code sense*) are easier to implement for static languages, again because of the extra type information available. The more explicit type information in static code promotes better "self-documentation," which can be important for communicating intent among developers, especially as a project grows.

When using a static language, you have to think about appropriate type choices more often, which forces you to weigh design choices more carefully. While this may slow down daily design decisions, thinking through the types in the application can result in a more coherent design over time.

Another small benefit of static languages is the extra checking the compiler performs. We think this advantage is often oversold, as type mismatch errors are a small fraction of the runtime errors you typically see. The compiler can't find *logic* errors, which are far more significant. Only a comprehensive, automated test suite can find logic errors. For dynamically typed languages, the tests must cover possible type errors, too. If you are coming from a dynamically typed language, you may find that your test suites are a little smaller as a result, but not *that* much smaller.

Many developers who find static languages too verbose often blame static typing for the verbosity when the real problem is a lack of *type inference*. In type inference, the compiler infers the types of values based on the context. For example, the compiler will recognize that x = 1 + 3 means that x must be an integer. Type inference reduces verbosity significantly, making the code feel more like code written in a dynamic language.

We have worked with both static and dynamic languages, at various times. We find both kinds of languages compelling for different reasons. We believe the modern software developer must master a range of languages and tools. Sometimes, a dynamic language will be the right tool for the job. At other times, a static language like Scala is just what you need.

Introducing Scala

Scala is a language that addresses the major needs of the modern developer. It is a statically typed, mixed-paradigm, JVM language with a succinct, elegant, and flexible syntax, a sophisticated type system, and idioms that promote scalability from small, interpreted scripts to large, sophisticated applications. That's a mouthful, so let's look at each of those ideas in more detail:

Statically typed
    As we described in the previous section, a statically typed language binds the type to a *variable* for the lifetime of that variable. In contrast, *dynamically typed* languages bind the type to the actual *value* referenced by a variable, meaning that the type of a *variable* can change along with the value it references.

    Of the set of newer JVM languages, Scala is one of the few that is statically typed, and it is the best known among them.

Mixed paradigm—object-oriented programming
    Scala fully supports *object-oriented programming* (OOP). Scala improves upon Java's support for OOP with the addition of *traits*, a clean way of implementing classes using *mixin composition*. Scala's traits work much like Ruby's *modules*. If you're a Java programmer, think of traits as unifying interfaces with their implementations.

    In Scala, everything is *really* an object. Scala does not have primitive types, like Java. Instead, all numeric types are true objects. However, for optimal performance, Scala uses the underlying primitives types of the runtime whenever possible. Also, Scala does not support "static" or class-level members of types, since they are not associated with an actual instance. Instead, Scala supports a singleton object construct to support those cases where exactly one instance of a type is needed.

Mixed paradigm—functional programming

Scala fully supports *functional programming* (FP). FP is a programming paradigm that is older than OOP, but it has been sheltered in the ivory towers of academia until recently. Interest in FP is increasing because of the ways it simplifies certain design problems, especially concurrency. "Pure" functional languages don't allow for any mutable state, thereby avoiding the need for synchronization on shared access to mutable state. Instead, programs written in pure functional languages communicate by passing messages between concurrent, autonomous processes. Scala supports this model with its Actors library, but it allows for both mutable and immutable variables.

Functions are "first-class" citizens in FP, meaning they can be assigned to variables, passed to other functions, etc., just like other values. This feature promotes composition of advanced behavior using primitive operations. Because Scala adheres to the dictum that *everything is an object*, functions are themselves objects in Scala.

Scala also offers *closures*, a feature that dynamic languages like Python and Ruby have adopted from the functional programming world, and one sadly absent from recent versions of Java. Closures are functions that reference variables from the scope enclosing the function definition. That is, the variables aren't passed in as arguments or defined as local variables within the function. A closure "closes around" these references, so the function invocation can safely refer to the variables even when the variables have gone out of scope! Closures are such a powerful abstraction that object systems and fundamental control structures are often implemented using them.

A JVM and .NET language

While Scala is primarily known as a JVM language, meaning that Scala generates JVM byte code, a .NET version of Scala that generates Common Language Runtime (CLR) byte code is also under development. When we refer to the underlying "runtime," we will usually discuss the JVM, but most of what we will say applies equally to both runtimes. When we discuss JVM-specific details, they generalize to the .NET version, except where noted.

The Scala compiler uses clever techniques to map Scala extensions to valid byte code idioms. From Scala, you can easily invoke byte code that originated as Java source (for the JVM) or C# source (for .NET). Conversely, you can invoke Scala code from Java, C#, etc. Running on the JVM and CLR allows the Scala developer to leverage available libraries and to interoperate with other languages hosted on those runtimes.

A succinct, elegant, and flexible syntax

Java syntax can be verbose. Scala uses a number of techniques to minimize unnecessary syntax, making Scala code as succinct as code in most dynamically typed languages. *Type inference* minimizes the need for explicit type information in many contexts. Declarations of types and functions are very concise.

Scala allows function names to include non-alphanumeric characters. Combined with some syntactic sugar, this feature permits the user to define methods that look and behave like operators. As a result, libraries outside the core of the language can feel "native" to users.

A sophisticated type system

Scala extends the type system of Java with more flexible generics and a number of more advanced typing constructs. The type system can be intimidating at first, but most of the time you won't need to worry about the advanced constructs. Type inference helps by automatically inferring type signatures, so that the user doesn't have to provide trivial type information manually. When you need them, though, the advanced type features provide you with greater flexibility for solving design problems in a type-safe way.

Scalable—architectures

Scala is designed to scale from small, interpreted scripts to large, distributed applications. Scala provides four language mechanisms that promote scalable composition of systems: 1) explicit *self types*; 2) abstract type members and generics; 3) nested classes; and 4) *mixin* composition using *traits*.

No other language provides all these mechanisms. Together, they allow applications to be constructed from reusable "components" in a type-safe and succinct manner. As we will see, many common design patterns and architectural techniques like dependency injection are easy to implement in Scala without the boilerplate code or lengthy XML configuration files that can make Java development tedious.

Scalable—performance

Because Scala code runs on the JVM and the CLR, it benefits from all the performance optimizations provided by those runtimes and all the third-party tools that support performance and scalability, such as profilers, distributed cache libraries, clustering mechanisms, etc. If you trust Java's and C#'s performance, you can trust Scala's performance. Of course, some particular constructs in the language and some parts of the library may perform significantly better or worse than alternative options in other languages. As always, you should profile your code and optimize it when necessary.

It might appear that OOP and FP are incompatible. In fact, a design philosophy of Scala is that OOP and FP are more synergistic than opposed. The features of one approach can enhance the other.

In FP, functions have no side effects and variables are immutable, while in OOP, mutable state and side effects are common, even encouraged. Scala lets you choose the approach that best fits your design problems. Functional programming is especially useful for concurrency, since it eliminates the need to synchronize access to mutable state. However, "pure" FP can be restrictive. Some design problems are easier to solve with mutable objects.

The name *Scala* is a contraction of the words *scalable language*. While this suggests that the pronunciation should be *scale-ah*, the creators of Scala actually pronounce it *scah-lah*, like the Italian word for "stairs." The two "a"s are pronounced the same.

Scala was started by Martin Odersky in 2001. Martin is a professor in the School of Computer and Communication Sciences at the Ecole Polytechnique Fédérale de Lausanne (EPFL). He spent his graduate years working in the group headed by Niklaus Wirth, of Pascal fame. Martin worked on Pizza, an early functional language on the JVM. He later worked on GJ, a prototype of what later became Generics in Java, with Philip Wadler of Haskell fame. Martin was hired by Sun Microsystems to produce the reference implementation of `javac`, the Java compiler that ships with the Java Developer Kit (JDK) today.

Martin Odersky's background and experience are evident in the language. As you learn Scala, you come to understand that it is the product of carefully considered design decisions, exploiting the state of the art in type theory, OOP, and FP. Martin's experience with the JVM is evident in Scala's elegant integration with that platform. The synthesis it creates between OOP and FP is an excellent "best of both worlds" solution.

The Seductions of Scala

Today, our industry is fortunate to have a wide variety of language options. The power, flexibility, and elegance of dynamically typed languages have made them very popular again. Yet the wealth of Java and .NET libraries and the performance of the JVM and CLR meet many practical needs for enterprise and Internet projects.

Scala is compelling because it feels like a dynamically typed scripting language, due to its succinct syntax and type inference. Yet Scala gives you all the benefits of static typing, a modern object model, functional programming, and an advanced type system. These tools let you build scalable, modular applications that can reuse legacy Java and .NET APIs and leverage the performance of the JVM and CLR.

Scala is a language for *professional* developers. Compared to languages like Java and Ruby, Scala is a more difficult language to master because it requires competency with OOP, FP, and static typing to use it most effectively. It is tempting to prefer the relative simplicity of dynamically typed languages. Yet this simplicity can be deceptive. In a dynamically typed language, it is often necessary to use metaprogramming features to implement advanced designs. While metaprogramming is powerful, using it well takes experience and the resulting code tends to be hard to understand, maintain, and debug.

In Scala, many of the same design goals can be achieved in a type-safe manner by exploiting its type system and mixin composition through *traits*.

We feel that the extra effort required day to day to use Scala will promote more careful reflection about your designs. Over time, this discipline will yield more coherent, modular, and maintainable applications. Fortunately, you don't need all of the sophistication of Scala all of the time. Much of your code will have the simplicity and clarity of code written in your favorite dynamically typed language.

An alternative strategy is to combine several, simpler languages, e.g., Java for object-oriented code and Erlang for functional, concurrent code. Such a decomposition can work, but only if your system decomposes cleanly into such discrete parts and your team can manage a heterogeneous environment. Scala is attractive for situations in which a single, all-in-one language is preferred. That said, Scala code can happily co-exist with other languages, especially on the JVM or .NET.

Installing Scala

To get up and running as quickly as possible, this section describes how to install the command-line tools for Scala, which are all you need to work with the examples in the book. For details on using Scala in various editors and IDEs, see "Integration with IDEs" on page 353. The examples used in this book were written and compiled using Scala version 2.7.5.final, the latest release at the time of this writing, and "nightly builds" of Scala version 2.8.0, which may be finalized by the time you read this.

 Version 2.8 introduces many new features, which we will highlight throughout the book.

We will work with the JVM version of Scala in this book. First, you must have Java 1.4 or greater installed (1.5 or greater is recommended). If you need to install Java, go to *http://www.java.com/en/download/manual.jsp* and follow the instructions to install Java on your machine.

The official Scala website is *http://www.scala-lang.org/*. To install Scala, go to the downloads page (*http://www.scala-lang.org/downloads*). Download the installer for your environment and follow the instructions on the downloads page.

The easiest cross-platform installer is the *IzPack* installer. Download the Scala JAR file, either *scala-2.7.5.final-installer.jar* or *scala-2.8.0.N-installer.jar*, where *N* is the latest release of the 2.8.0 version. Go to the download directory in a terminal window, and install Scala with the `java` command. Assuming you downloaded *scala-2.8.0.final-installer.jar*, run the following command, which will guide you through the process:

```
java -jar scala-2.8.0.final-installer.jar
```

On Mac OS X, the easiest route to a working Scala installation is via MacPorts. Follow the installation instructions at *http://www.macports .org/*, then `sudo port install scala`. You'll be up and running in a few minutes.

Throughout this book, we will use the symbol *scala-home* to refer to the "root" directory of your Scala installation.

 On Unix, Linux, and Mac OS X systems, you will need to run this command as the **root** user or using the **sudo** command if you want to install Scala under a system directory, e.g., *scala-home* = */usr/local/ scala-2.8.0.final*.

As an alternative, you can download and expand the compressed TAR file (e.g., *scala-2.8.0.final.tgz*) or ZIP file (*scala-2.8.0.final.zip*). On Unix-like systems, expand the compressed file into a location of your choosing. Afterward, add the *scala-home/ bin* subdirectory in the new directory to your PATH. For example, if you installed into */usr/local/scala-2.8.0.final*, then add */usr/local/scala-2.8.0.final/bin* to your PATH.

To test your installation, run the following command on the command line:

```
scala -version
```

We'll learn more about the `scala` command-line tool later. You should get something like the following output:

```
Scala code runner version 2.8.0.final -- Copyright 2002-2009, LAMP/EPFL
```

Of course, the version number you see will be different if you installed a different release. From now on, when we show command output that contains the version number, we'll show it as `version 2.8.0.final`.

Congratulations, you have installed Scala! If you get an error message along the lines of `scala: command not found`, make sure your environment's PATH is set properly to include the correct *bin* directory.

 Scala versions 2.7.X and earlier are compatible with JDK 1.4 and later. Scala version 2.8 drops 1.4 compatibility. Note that Scala uses many JDK classes as its own, for example, the `String` class. On .NET, Scala uses the corresponding .NET classes.

You can also find downloads for the API documentation and the sources for Scala itself on the same downloads page.

For More Information

As you explore Scala, you will find other useful resources that are available on *http://scala-lang.org*. You will find links for development support tools and libraries, tutorials, the language specification [ScalaSpec2009], and academic papers that describe features of the language.

The documentation for the Scala tools and APIs are especially useful. You can browse the API at *http://www.scala-lang.org/docu/files/api/index.html*. This documentation was generated using the `scaladoc` tool, analogous to Java's `javadoc` tool. See "The scaladoc Command-Line Tool" on page 352 for more information.

You can also download a compressed file of the API documentation for local browsing using the appropriate link on the downloads page (*http://www.scala-lang.org/downloads*), or you can install it with the `sbaz` package tool, as follows:

```
sbaz install scala-devel-docs
```

`sbaz` is installed in the same *bin* directory as the `scala` and `scalac` command-line tools. The installed documentation also includes details on the scala tool chain (including `sbaz`) and code examples. For more information on the Scala command-line tools and other resources, see Chapter 14.

A Taste of Scala

It's time to whet your appetite with some real Scala code. In the following examples, we'll describe just enough of the details so you understand what's going on. The goal is to give you a sense of what programming in Scala is like. We'll explore the details of the features in subsequent chapters.

For our first example, you could run it one of two ways: interactively, or as a "script."

Let's start with the interactive mode. Start the scala interpreter by typing `scala` and the return key on your command line. You'll see the following output. (Some of the version numbers may vary.)

```
Welcome to Scala version 2.8.0.final (Java ...).
Type in expressions to have them evaluated.
Type :help for more information.

scala>
```

The last line is the prompt that is waiting for your input. The interactive mode of the `scala` command is very convenient for experimentation (see "The scala Command-Line Tool" on page 345 for more details). An interactive interpreter like this is called a REPL: *Read, Evaluate, Print, Loop.*

Type in the following two lines of code:

```
val book = "Programming Scala"
println(book)
```

The actual input and output should look like the following:

```
scala> val book = "Programming Scala"
book: java.lang.String = Programming Scala

scala> println(book)
Programming Scala

scala>
```

The first line uses the **val** keyword to declare a read-only variable named **book**. Note that the output returned from the interpreter shows you the type and value of **book**. This can be very handy for understanding complex declarations. The second line prints the value of **book**, which is "Programming Scala".

 Experimenting with the **scala** command in the interactive mode (REPL) is a great way to learn the details of Scala.

Many of the examples in this book can be executed in the interpreter like this. However, it's often more convenient to use the second option we mentioned, writing Scala scripts in a text editor or IDE and executing them with the same **scala** command. We'll do that for most of the remaining examples in this chapter.

In your text editor of choice, save the Scala code in the following example to a file named *upper1-script.scala* in a directory of your choosing:

```
// code-examples/IntroducingScala/upper1-script.scala

class Upper {
  def upper(strings: String*): Seq[String] = {
    strings.map((s:String) => s.toUpperCase())
  }
}

val up = new Upper
Console.println(up.upper("A", "First", "Scala", "Program"))
```

This Scala script converts strings to uppercase.

By the way, that's a comment on the first line (with the name of the source file for the code example). Scala follows the same comment conventions as Java, C#, C++, etc. A // *comment* goes to the end of a line, while a /* *comment* */ can cross line boundaries.

To run this script, go to a command window, change to the same directory, and run the following command:

```
scala upper1-script.scala
```

The file is interpreted, meaning it is compiled and executed in one step. You should get the following output:

```
Array(A, FIRST, SCALA, PROGRAM)
```

Interpreting Versus Compiling and Running Scala Code

To summarize, if you type `scala` on the command line without a file argument, the interpreter runs in interactive mode. You type in definitions and statements that are evaluated on the fly. If you give the command a scala source file argument, it compiles and runs the file as a script, as in our `scala upper1-script.scala` example. Finally, you can compile Scala files separately and execute the `class` file, as long as it has a `main` method, just as you would normally do with the `java` command. (We'll show an example shortly.)

There are some subtleties you'll need to understand about the limitations of using the interpreter modes versus separate compilation and execution steps. We discuss these subtleties in "Command-Line Tools" on page 343.

Whenever we refer to *executing a script*, we mean running a Scala source file with the `scala` command.

In the current example, the `upper` method in the `Upper` class (no pun intended) converts the input strings to uppercase and returns them in an array. The last line in the example converts four strings and prints the resulting `Array`.

Let's examine the code in detail, so we can begin to learn Scala syntax. There are a lot of details in just six lines of code! We'll explain the general ideas here. All the ideas used in this example will be explained more thoroughly in later sections of the book.

In the example, the `Upper` class begins with the `class` keyword. The class body is inside the outermost curly braces (`{...}`).

The `upper` method definition begins on the second line with the `def` keyword, followed by the method name and an argument list, the return type of the method, an equals sign (=), and then the method body.

The argument list in parentheses is actually a *variable-length argument list* of `String`s, indicated by the `String*` type following the colon. That is, you can pass in as many comma-separated strings as you want (including an empty list). These strings are stored in a parameter named `strings`. Inside the method, `strings` is actually an `Array`.

When explicit type information for variables is written in the code, these *type annotations* follow the colon after the item name (i.e., Pascal-like syntax). Why doesn't Scala follow Java conventions? Recall that type information is often *inferred* in Scala (unlike Java), meaning we don't always show type annotations explicitly. Compared to Java's `type item` convention, the `item: type` convention is easier for the compiler to analyze unambiguously when you omit the colon and the type annotation and just write `item`.

The method return type appears after the argument list. In this case, the return type is `Seq[String]`, where `Seq` ("sequence") is a particular kind of collection. It is a *parameterized type* (like a *generic* type in Java), parameterized here with `String`. Note that Scala uses square brackets (`[...]`) for parameterized types, whereas Java uses angle brackets (`<...>`).

Scala allows angle brackets to be used in method names, e.g., naming a "less than" method `<` is common. So, to avoid ambiguities, Scala uses square brackets instead for parameterized types. They can't be used in method names. Allowing `<` and `>` in method names is why Scala doesn't follow Java's convention for angle brackets.

The body of the `upper` method comes after the equals sign (`=`). Why an equals sign? Why not just curly braces (`{...}`), like in Java? Because semicolons, function return types, method arguments lists, and even the curly braces are sometimes omitted, using an equals sign prevents several possible parsing ambiguities. Using an equals sign also reminds us that even functions are values in Scala, which is consistent with Scala's support of *functional programming*, described in more detail in Chapter 8.

The method body calls the `map` method on the `strings` array, which takes a *function literal* as an argument. Function literals are "anonymous" functions. They are similar to *lambdas*, *closures*, *blocks*, or *procs* in other languages. In Java, you would have to use an anonymous inner class here that implements a method defined by an interface, etc.

In this case, we passed in the following function literal:

```
(s:String) => s.toUpperCase()
```

It takes an argument list with a single `String` argument named `s`. The body of the function literal is after the "arrow," `=>`. It calls `toUpperCase()` on `s`. The result of this call is returned by the function literal. In Scala, the last *expression* in a function is the return value, although you can have `return` statements elsewhere, too. The `return` keyword is optional here and is rarely used, except when returning out of the middle of a block (e.g., in an `if` statement).

The value of the last expression is the default return value of a function. No **return** is required.

So, **map** passes each **String** in **strings** to the function literal and builds up a new collection with the results returned by the function literal.

To exercise the code, we create a new **Upper** instance and assign it to a variable named up. As in Java, C#, and similar languages, the syntax **new Upper** creates a new instance. The **up** variable is declared as a read-only "value" using the **val** keyword.

Finally, we call the **upper** method on a list of strings, and print out the result with **Console.println(...)**, which is equivalent to Java's **System.out.println(...)**.

We can actually simplify our script even further. Consider this simplified version of the script:

```
// code-examples/IntroducingScala/upper2-script.scala

object Upper {
  def upper(strings: String*) = strings.map(_.toUpperCase())
}

println(Upper.upper("A", "First", "Scala", "Program"))
```

This code does exactly the same thing, but with a third fewer characters.

On the first line, **Upper** is now declared as an **object**, which is a *singleton*. We are declaring a class, but the Scala runtime will only ever create one instance of **Upper**. (You can't write **new Upper**, for example.) Scala uses **objects** for situations where other languages would use "class-level" members, like **static**s in Java. We don't really need more than one *instance* here, so a singleton is fine.

Why doesn't Scala support **static**s? Since *everything* is an object in Scala, the **object** construct keeps this policy consistent. Java's **static** methods and fields are not tied to an actual instance.

Note that this code is fully thread-safe. We don't declare any variables that might cause thread-safety issues. The API methods we use are also thread-safe. Therefore, we don't need multiple instances. A singleton **object** works fine.

The implementation of **upper** on the second line is also simpler. Scala can usually infer the return type of the method (but not the types of the method arguments), so we drop the explicit declaration. Also, because there is only one expression in the method body, we drop the braces and put the entire method definition on one line. The equals sign before the method body tells the compiler, as well as the human reader, where the method body begins.

We have also exploited a shorthand for the function literal. Previously we wrote it as follows:

```
(s:String) => s.toUpperCase()
```

We can shorten it to the following expression:

```
_.toUpperCase()
```

Because map takes one argument, a function, we can use the "placeholder" indicator _ instead of a named parameter. That is, the _ acts like an anonymous variable, to which each string will be assigned before toUpperCase is called. Note that the String type is inferred for us, too. As we will see, Scala uses _ as a "wildcard" in several contexts.

You can also use this shorthand syntax in some more complex function literals, as we will see in Chapter 3.

On the last line, using an object rather than a class simplifies the code. Instead of creating an instance with new Upper, we can just call the upper method on the Upper object directly (note how this looks like the syntax you would use when calling static methods in a Java class).

Finally, Scala automatically imports many methods for I/O, like println, so we don't need to call Console.println(). We can just use println by itself. (See "The Predef Object" on page 145 for details on the types and methods that are automatically imported or defined.)

Let's do one last *refactoring*. Convert the script into a compiled, command-line tool:

```
// code-examples/IntroducingScala/upper3.scala

object Upper {
  def main(args: Array[String]) = {
    args.map(_.toUpperCase()).foreach(printf("%s ",_))
    println("")
  }
}
```

Now the upper method has been renamed main. Because Upper is an object, this main method works exactly like a static main method in a Java class. It is the entry point to the Upper *application*.

 In Scala, main must be a method in an object. (In Java, main must be a static method in a class.) The command-line arguments for the application are passed to main in an array of strings, e.g., args: Array[String].

The first line inside the main method uses the same shorthand notation for map that we just examined:

```
args.map(_.toUpperCase())...
```

The call to `map` returns a new collection. We iterate through it with `foreach`. We use a `_` placeholder shortcut again in another *function literal* that we pass to `foreach`. In this case, each string in the collection is passed as an argument to `printf`:

```
...foreach(printf("%s ",_))
```

To be clear, these two uses of `_` are completely independent of each other. Method chaining and function-literal shorthands, as in this example, can take some getting used to, but once you are comfortable with them, they yield very readable code with minimal use of temporary variables.

The last line in `main` adds a final line feed to the output.

This time, you must first compile the code to a JVM .*class* file using `scalac`:

```
scalac upper3.scala
```

You should now have a file named *Upper.class*, just as if you had just compiled a Java class.

You may have noticed that the compiler did not complain when the file was named *upper3.scala* and the `object` was named `Upper`. Unlike Java, the file name doesn't have to match the name of the type with `public` scope. (We'll explore the visibility rules in "Visibility Rules" on page 96.) In fact, unlike Java, you can have as many public types in a single file as you want. Furthermore, the directory location of a file doesn't have to match the package declaration. However, you can certainly follow the Java conventions, if you want to.

Now, you can execute this command for any list of strings. Here is an example:

```
scala -cp . Upper Hello World!
```

The `-cp .` option adds the current directory to the search "class path." You should get the following output:

```
HELLO WORLD!
```

Therefore, we have met the requirement that a programming language book must start with a "hello world" program.

A Taste of Concurrency

There are many reasons to be seduced by Scala. One reason is the Actors API included in the Scala library, which is based on the robust Actors concurrency model built into Erlang (see [Haller2007]). Here is an example to whet your appetite.

In the Actor model of concurrency ([Agha1987]), independent software entities called *Actors* share no state information with each other. Instead, they communicate by exchanging messages. By eliminating the need to synchronize access to shared, mutable state, it is far easier to write robust, concurrent applications.

In this example, instances in a geometric **Shape** hierarchy are sent to an Actor for drawing on a display. Imagine a scenario where a rendering "farm" generates scenes in an animation. As the rendering of a scene is completed, the shape "primitives" that are part of the scene are sent to an Actor for a display subsystem.

To begin, we define a **Shape** class hierarchy:

```
// code-examples/IntroducingScala/shapes.scala

package shapes {
  class Point(val x: Double, val y: Double) {
    override def toString() = "Point(" + x + "," + y + ")"
  }

  abstract class Shape() {
    def draw(): Unit
  }

  class Circle(val center: Point, val radius: Double) extends Shape {
    def draw() = println("Circle.draw: " + this)
    override def toString() = "Circle(" + center + "," + radius + ")"
  }

  class Rectangle(val lowerLeft: Point, val height: Double, val width: Double)
      extends Shape {
    def draw() = println("Rectangle.draw: " + this)
    override def toString() =
      "Rectangle(" + lowerLeft + "," + height + "," + width + ")"
  }

  class Triangle(val point1: Point, val point2: Point, val point3: Point)
      extends Shape {
    def draw() = println("Triangle.draw: " + this)
    override def toString() =
      "Triangle(" + point1 + "," + point2 + "," + point3 + ")"
  }
}
```

The **Shape** class hierarchy is defined in a **shapes** package. You can declare the package using Java syntax, but Scala also supports a syntax similar to C#'s "namespace" syntax, where the entire declaration is scoped using curly braces, as used here. The Java-style package declaration syntax is far more commonly used, however, being both compact and readable.

The **Point** class represents a two-dimensional point on a plane. Note the argument list after the class name. Those are constructor parameters. In Scala, the *whole* class body is the constructor, so you list the arguments for the *primary* constructor after the class name and before the class body. (We'll see how to define auxiliary constructors in "Constructors in Scala" on page 91.) Because we put the **val** keyword before each parameter declaration, they are automatically converted to read-only fields with the same names with public reader methods of the same name. That is, when you instantiate a `Point` instance, e.g., `point`, you can read the fields using `point.x` and `point.y`. If you want *mutable* fields, then use the keyword `var`. We'll explore variable declarations and the `val` and `var` keywords in "Variable Declarations" on page 24.

The body of `Point` defines one method, an *override* of the familiar `toString` method in Java (like `ToString` in C#). Note that Scala, like C#, requires the `override` keyword whenever you override a concrete method. Unlike C#, you don't have to use a `virtual` keyword on the original concrete method. In fact, there is no `virtual` keyword in Scala. As before, we omit the curly braces (`{...}`) around the body of `toString`, since it has only one expression.

`Shape` is an abstract class. Abstract classes in Scala are similar to those in Java and C#. We can't instantiate instances of abstract classes, even when all their field and method members are concrete.

In this case, Shape declares an *abstract* `draw` method. We know it is abstract because it has no body. No `abstract` keyword is required on the method. Abstract methods in Scala are just like abstract methods in Java and C#. (See "Overriding Members of Classes and Traits" on page 111 for more details.)

The `draw` method returns `Unit`, which is a type that is roughly equivalent to `void` in C-derived languages like Java, etc. (See "The Scala Type Hierarchy" on page 155 for more details.)

`Circle` is declared as a concrete subclass of `Shape`. It defines the `draw` method to simply print a message to the console. `Circle` also overrides `toString`.

`Rectangle` is also a concrete subclass of `Shape` that defines `draw` and overrides `toString`. For simplicity, we assume it is not rotated relative to the *x* and *y* axes. Hence, all we need is one point, the lower lefthand point will do, and the height and width of the rectangle.

`Triangle` follows the same pattern. It takes three `Points` as its constructor arguments.

Both `draw` methods in `Circle`, `Rectangle`, and `Triangle` use `this`. As in Java and C#, `this` is how an instance refers to itself. In this context, where `this` is the righthand side of a String concatenation expression (using the plus sign), `this.toString` is invoked implicitly.

 Of course, in a real application, you would not implement drawing in "domain model" classes like this, since the implementations would depend on details like the operating system platform, graphics API, etc. We will see a better design approach when we discuss *traits* in Chapter 4.

Now that we have defined our shapes types, let's return to Actors. We define an Actor that receives "messages" that are shapes to draw:

```
// code-examples/IntroducingScala/shapes-actor.scala

package shapes {
  import scala.actors._
  import scala.actors.Actor._

  object ShapeDrawingActor extends Actor {
    def act() {
      loop {
        receive {
          case s: Shape => s.draw()
          case "exit"   => println("exiting..."); exit
          case x: Any   => println("Error: Unknown message! " + x)
        }
      }
    }
  }
}
```

The Actor is declared to be part of the **shapes** package. Next, we have two import statements.

The first import statement imports all the types in the **scala.actors** package. In Scala, the underscore _ is used the way the star * is used in Java.

 Because * is a valid character for a function name, it can't be used as the import wildcard. Instead, _ is reserved for this purpose.

All the methods and public fields from **Actor** are imported by the second **import**. These are not **static** imports from the **Actor** type, as they would be in Java. Rather, they are imported from an **object** that is also named **Actor**. The **class** and **object** can have the same name, as we will see in "Companion Objects" on page 126.

Our Actor class definition, **ShapeDrawingActor**, is an **object** that extends **Actor** (the type, not the **object**). The **act** method is overridden to do the unique work of the Actor. Because **act** is an abstract method, we don't need to explicitly override it with the **override** keyword. Our Actor loops indefinitely, waiting for incoming messages.

During each pass in the loop, the **receive** method is called. It blocks until a new message arrives. Why is the code after **receive** enclosed in curly braces {...} and not parentheses (...)? We will learn later that there are cases where this substitution is allowed and is quite useful (see Chapter 3). For now, what you need to know is that the expressions inside the braces constitute a single *function literal* that is passed to **receive**. This function literal does a *pattern match* on the message instance to decide how to handle the message. Because of the **case** clauses, it looks like a typical switch statement in Java, for example, and the behavior is very similar.

The first case does a type comparison with the message. (There is no explicit variable for the message instance in the code; it is inferred.) If the message is of type Shape, the first case matches. The message instance is cast to a Shape and assigned to the variable s, and then the draw method is called on it.

If the message is not a Shape, the second case is tried. If the message is the string "exit", the Actor prints a message and terminates execution. Actors should usually have a way to exit gracefully!

The last case clause handles any other message instance, thereby functioning as the *default* case. The Actor reports an error and then drops the message. Any is the parent of all types in the Scala type hierarchy, like Object is the root type in Java and other languages. Hence, this case clause will match any message of any type. Pattern matching is eager; we have to put this case clause at the end, so it doesn't consume the messages we are expecting!

Recall that we declared draw as an abstract method in Shape and we implemented draw in the concrete subclasses. Hence, the code in the first case statement invokes a polymorphic operation.

Pattern Matching Versus Polymorphism

Pattern matching plays a central role in functional programming just as polymorphism plays a central role in object-oriented programming. Functional pattern matching is much more important and sophisticated than the corresponding switch/case statements found in most *imperative* languages, like Java. We will examine Scala's support for pattern matching in more detail in Chapter 8. In our example here, we can begin to see that joining functional-style pattern matching with object-oriented polymorphic dispatching is a powerful combination that is a benefit of mixed paradigm languages like Scala.

Finally, here is a script that uses the ShapeDrawingActor Actor:

```
// code-examples/IntroducingScala/shapes-actor-script.scala

import shapes._

ShapeDrawingActor.start()

ShapeDrawingActor ! new Circle(new Point(0.0,0.0), 1.0)
ShapeDrawingActor ! new Rectangle(new Point(0.0,0.0), 2, 5)
ShapeDrawingActor ! new Triangle(new Point(0.0,0.0),
                                 new Point(1.0,0.0),
                                 new Point(0.0,1.0))
ShapeDrawingActor ! 3.14159

ShapeDrawingActor ! "exit"
```

The shapes in the shapes package are imported.

The ShapeDrawingActor Actor is started. By default, it runs in its own thread (there are alternatives we will discuss in Chapter 9), waiting for messages.

Five messages are sent to the Actor, using the syntax actor ! message. The first message sends a Circle instance. The Actor "draws" the circle. The second message sends a Rectangle message. The Actor "draws" the rectangle. The third message does the same thing for a Triangle. The fourth message sends a Double that is approximately equal to *Pi*. This is an unknown message for the Actor, so it just prints an error message. The final message sends an "exit" string, which causes the Actor to terminate.

To try out the Actor example, start by compiling the first two files. You can get the sources from the O'Reilly download site (*http://examples.oreilly.com/ 9780596155964/*) (see "Getting the Code Examples" on page xix for details), or you can create them yourself.

Use the following command to compile the files:

```
scalac shapes.scala shapes-actor.scala
```

While the source file names and locations don't have to match the file contents, you will notice that the generated class files are written to a *shapes* directory and there is one class file for each class we defined. The class file names and locations must conform to the JVM requirements.

Now you can run the script to see the Actor in action:

```
scala -cp . shapes-actor-script.scala
```

You should see the following output:

```
Circle.draw: Circle(Point(0.0,0.0),1.0)
Rectangle.draw: Rectangle(Point(0.0,0.0),2.0,5.0)
Triangle.draw: Triangle(Point(0.0,0.0),Point(1.0,0.0),Point(0.0,1.0))
Error: Unknown message! 3.14159
exiting...
```

For more on Actors, see Chapter 9.

Recap and What's Next

We made the case for Scala and got you started with two sample Scala programs, one of which gave you a taste of Scala's Actors library for concurrency. Next, we'll dive into more Scala syntax, emphasizing various keystroke-economical ways of getting lots of work done.

CHAPTER 2

Type Less, Do More

In This Chapter

We ended the previous chapter with a few "teaser" examples of Scala code. This chapter discusses uses of Scala that promote succinct, flexible code. We'll discuss organization of files and packages, importing other types, variable declarations, miscellaneous syntax conventions, and a few other concepts. We'll emphasize how the concise syntax of Scala helps you work better and faster.

Scala's syntax is especially useful when writing scripts. Separate compile and run steps aren't required for simple programs that have few dependencies on libraries outside of what Scala provides. You compile and run such programs in one shot with the `scala` command. If you've downloaded the example code for this book, many of the smaller examples can be run using the `scala` command, e.g., `scala` *filename*`.scala`. See the *README.txt* files in each chapter's code examples for more details. See also "Command-Line Tools" on page 343 for more information about using the `scala` command.

Semicolons

You may have already noticed that there were very few semicolons in the code examples in the previous chapter. You can use semicolons to separate statements and expressions, as in Java, C, PHP, and similar languages. In most cases, though, Scala behaves like many scripting languages in treating the end of the line as the end of a statement or an expression. When a statement or expression is too long for one line, Scala can usually infer when you are continuing on to the next line, as shown in this example:

```
// code-examples/TypeLessDoMore/semicolon-example-script.scala

// Trailing equals sign indicates more code on next line
def equalsign = {
  val reallySuperLongValueNameThatGoesOnForeverSoYouNeedANewLine =
    "wow that was a long value name"

  println(reallySuperLongValueNameThatGoesOnForeverSoYouNeedANewLine)
```

```
}

// Trailing opening curly brace indicates more code on next line
def equalsign2(s: String) = {
  println("equalsign2: " + s)
}

// Trailing comma, operator, etc. indicates more code on next line
def commas(s1: String,
           s2: String) = {
  println("comma: " + s1 +
          ", " + s2)
}
```

When you want to put multiple statements or expressions on the same line, you can use semicolons to separate them. We used this technique in the **ShapeDrawingActor** example in "A Taste of Concurrency" on page 16:

```
case "exit" => println("exiting..."); exit
```

This code could also be written as follows:

```
...
case "exit" =>
      println("exiting...")
      exit
...
```

You might wonder why you don't need curly braces ({...}) around the two statements after the **case** ... => line. You can put them in if you want, but the compiler knows when you've reached the end of the "block" when it finds the next **case** clause or the curly brace (}) that ends the enclosing block for all the **case** clauses.

Omitting optional semicolons means fewer characters to type and fewer characters to clutter your code. Breaking separate statements onto their own lines increases your code's readability.

Variable Declarations

Scala allows you to decide whether a variable is immutable (read-only) or not (read-write) when you declare it. An immutable "variable" is declared with the keyword **val** (think *value object*):

```
val array: Array[String] = new Array(5)
```

To be more precise, the **array** reference cannot be changed to point to a different **Array**, but the array itself can be modified, as shown in the following **scala** session:

```
scala> val array: Array[String] = new Array(5)
array: Array[String] = Array(null, null, null, null, null)

scala> array = new Array(2)
<console>:5: error: reassignment to val
```

```
    array = new Array(2)
          ^

scala> array(0) = "Hello"

scala> array
res3: Array[String] = Array(Hello, null, null, null, null)

scala>
```

An immutable `val` must be initialized—that is, defined—when it is declared.

A mutable variable is declared with the keyword `var`:

```
scala> var stockPrice: Double = 100.
stockPrice: Double = 100.0

scala> stockPrice = 10.
stockPrice: Double = 10.0

scala>
```

Scala also requires you to initialize a `var` when it is declared. You can assign a new value to a `var` as often as you want. Again, to be precise, the `stockPrice` reference can be changed to point to a different `Double` object (e.g., `10.`). In this case, the object that `stockPrice` refers to can't be changed, because `Doubles` in Scala are immutable.

There are a few exceptions to the rule that you must initialize `vals` and `vars` when they are declared. Both keywords can be used with constructor parameters. When used as constructor parameters, the mutable or immutable variables specified will be initialized when an object is instantiated. Both keywords can be used to declare "abstract" (uninitialized) variables in abstract types. Also, derived types can override `vals` declared inside parent types. We'll discuss these exceptions in Chapter 5.

Scala encourages you to use immutable values whenever possible. As we will see, this promotes better object-oriented design and is consistent with the principles of "pure" functional programming. It may take some getting used to, but you'll find a newfound confidence in your code when it is written in an immutable style.

 The `var` and `val` keywords only specify whether the reference can be changed to refer to a different object (`var`) or not (`val`). They don't specify whether or not the object they reference is mutable.

Method Declarations

In Chapter 1 we saw several examples of how to define *methods*, which are functions that are members of a class. Method *definitions* start with the `def` keyword, followed by optional argument lists, a colon character (`:`) and the return type of the method, an equals sign (=), and finally the method body. Methods are implicitly *declared* "abstract" if you leave off the equals sign and method body. The enclosing type is then itself abstract. We'll discuss abstract types in more detail in Chapter 5.

We said "optional argument lists," meaning more than one. Scala lets you define more than one argument list for a method. This is required for *currying* methods, which we'll discuss in "Currying" on page 184. It is also very useful for defining your own Domain-Specific Languages (DSLs), as we'll see in Chapter 11. Note that each argument list is surrounded by parentheses and the arguments are separated by commas.

If a method body has more than one expression, you must surround it with curly braces ({...}). You can omit the braces if the method body has just one expression.

Method Default and Named Arguments (Scala Version 2.8)

Many languages let you define default values for some or all of the arguments to a method. Consider the following script with a StringUtil object that lets you join a list of strings with a user-specified separator:

```
// code-examples/TypeLessDoMore/string-util-v1-script.scala
// Version 1 of "StringUtil".

object StringUtil {
  def joiner(strings: List[String], separator: String): String =
    strings.mkString(separator)

  def joiner(strings: List[String]): String = joiner(strings, " ")
}
import StringUtil._    // Import the joiner methods.

println( joiner(List("Programming", "Scala")) )
```

There are actually two, "overloaded" joiner methods. The second one uses a single space as the "default" separator. Having two methods seems a bit wasteful. It would be nice if we could eliminate the second joiner method and declare that the separator argument in the first joiner has a default value. In fact, in Scala version 2.8, you can now do this:

```
// code-examples/TypeLessDoMore/string-util-v2-v28-script.scala
// Version 2 of "StringUtil" for Scala v2.8 only.

object StringUtil {
  def joiner(strings: List[String], separator: String = " "): String =
    strings.mkString(separator)
}
import StringUtil._    // Import the joiner methods.

println(joiner(List("Programming", "Scala")))
```

There is another alternative for earlier versions of Scala. You can use *implicit* arguments, which we will discuss in "Implicit Function Parameters" on page 188.

Scala version 2.8 offers another enhancement for method argument lists, *named arguments*. We could actually write the last line of the previous example in several ways. All of the following println statements are functionally equivalent:

```
println(joiner(List("Programming", "Scala")))
println(joiner(strings = List("Programming", "Scala")))
println(joiner(List("Programming", "Scala"), " "))    // #1
println(joiner(List("Programming", "Scala"), separator = " ")) // #2
println(joiner(strings = List("Programming", "Scala"), separator = " "))
```

Why is this useful? First, if you choose good names for the method arguments, then your calls to those methods document each argument with a name. For example, compare the two lines with comments #1 and #2. In the first line, it may not be obvious what the second " " argument is for. In the second case, we supply the name separator, which suggests the purpose of the argument.

The second benefit is that you can specify the parameters in any order when you specify them by name. Combined with default values, you can write code like the following:

```
// code-examples/TypeLessDoMore/user-profile-v28-script.scala
// Scala v2.8 only.

object OptionalUserProfileInfo {
  val UnknownLocation = ""
  val UnknownAge = -1
  val UnknownWebSite = ""
}

class OptionalUserProfileInfo(
  location: String = OptionalUserProfileInfo.UnknownLocation,
  age: Int        = OptionalUserProfileInfo.UnknownAge,
  webSite: String = OptionalUserProfileInfo.UnknownWebSite)

println( new OptionalUserProfileInfo )
println( new OptionalUserProfileInfo(age = 29) )
println( new OptionalUserProfileInfo(age = 29, location="Earth") )
```

OptionalUserProfileInfo represents all the "optional" user profile data in your next Web 2.0 social networking site. It defines default values for all its fields. The script creates instances with zero or more named parameters. The order of those parameters is arbitrary.

The examples we have shown use constant values as the defaults. Most languages with default argument values only allow constants or other values that can be determined at parse time. However, in Scala, any expression can be used as the default, as long as it can compile where used. For example, an expression could not refer to an instance field that will be computed inside the class or object body, but it could invoke a method on a singleton object.

A related limitation is that a default expression for one parameter can't refer to another parameter in the list, unless the parameter that is referenced appears earlier in the list *and* the parameters are *curried*, a concept we'll discuss in "Currying" on page 184.

Finally, another constraint on named parameters is that once you provide a name for a parameter in a method invocation, the rest of the parameters appearing after it must also be named. For example, `new OptionalUserProfileInfo(age = 29, "Earth")` would not compile because the second argument is not invoked by name.

We'll see another useful example of named and default arguments when we discuss *case classes* in "Case Classes" on page 136.

Nesting Method Definitions

Method definitions can also be nested. Here is an implementation of a factorial calculator, where we use a conventional technique of calling a second, nested method to do the work:

```
// code-examples/TypeLessDoMore/factorial-script.scala

def factorial(i: Int): Int = {
  def fact(i: Int, accumulator: Int): Int = {
    if (i <= 1)
      accumulator
    else
      fact(i - 1, i * accumulator)
  }

  fact(i, 1)
}

println( factorial(0) )
println( factorial(1) )
println( factorial(2) )
println( factorial(3) )
println( factorial(4) )
println( factorial(5) )
```

The second method calls itself recursively, passing an `accumulator` parameter, where the result of the calculation is "accumulated." Note that we return the accumulated value when the counter `i` reaches 1. (We're ignoring invalid negative integers. The function actually returns 1 for `i` < 0.) After the definition of the nested method, `factorial` calls it with the passed-in value `i` and the initial accumulator value of 1.

Like a local variable declaration in many languages, a nested method is only visible inside the enclosing method. If you try to call `fact` outside of `factorial`, you will get a compiler error.

Did you notice that we use `i` as a parameter name twice, first in the `factorial` method and again in the nested `fact` method? As in many languages, the use of `i` as a parameter name for `fact` "shadows" the outer use of `i` as a parameter name for `factorial`. This is fine, because we don't need the outer value of `i` inside `fact`. We only use it the first time we call `fact`, at the end of `factorial`.

What if we need to use a variable that is defined outside a nested function? Consider this contrived example:

```
// code-examples/TypeLessDoMore/count-to-script.scala

def countTo(n: Int):Unit = {
  def count(i: Int): Unit = {
    if (i <= n) {
      println(i)
      count(i + 1)
    }
  }
  count(1)
}

countTo(5)
```

Note that the nested count method uses the n value that is passed as a parameter to countTo. There is no need to pass n as an argument to count. Because count is nested inside countTo, n is visible to it.

The declaration of a field (member variable) can be prefixed with keywords indicating the *visibility*, just as in languages like Java and C#. Similarly the declaration of a non-nested method can be prefixed with the same keywords. We will discuss the visibility rules and keywords in "Visibility Rules" on page 96.

Inferring Type Information

Statically typed languages can be very verbose. Consider this typical declaration in Java:

```
import java.util.Map;
import java.util.HashMap;
...
Map<Integer, String> intToStringMap = new HashMap<Integer, String>();
```

We have to specify the type parameters <Integer, String> twice. (Scala uses the term *type annotations* for explicit type declarations like HashMap<Integer, String>.)

Scala supports *type inference* (see, for example, [TypeInference] and [Pierce2002]). The language's compiler can discern quite a bit of type information from the context, without explicit type annotations. Here's the same declaration rewritten in Scala, with inferred type information:

```
import java.util.Map
import java.util.HashMap
...
val intToStringMap: Map[Integer, String] = new HashMap
```

Recall from Chapter 1 that Scala uses square brackets ([...]) for generic type parameters. We specify Map[Integer, String] on the lefthand side of the equals sign. (We are sticking with Java types for the example.) On the righthand side, we instantiate the actual type we want, a HashMap, but we don't have to repeat the type parameters.

For completeness, suppose we don't actually care if the instance is of type `Map` (the Java interface type). It can be of type `HashMap` for all we care:

```
import java.util.Map
import java.util.HashMap
...
val intToStringMap2 = new HashMap[Integer, String]
```

This declaration requires no type annotations on the lefthand side because all of the type information needed is on the righthand side. The compiler automatically makes `intToStringMap2` a `HashMap[Integer,String]`.

Type inference is used for methods, too. In most cases, the return type of the method can be inferred, so the : and return type can be omitted. However, type annotations are required for all method parameters.

Pure functional languages like Haskell (see, e.g., [O'Sullivan2009]) use type inference algorithms like *Hindley-Milner* (see [Spiewak2008] for an easily digested explanation). Code written in these languages require type annotations less often than in Scala, because Scala's type inference algorithm has to support object-oriented typing as well as functional typing. So, Scala requires more type annotations than languages like Haskell. Here is a summary of the rules for when explicit type annotations are required in Scala.

When Explicit Type Annotations Are Required

In practical terms, you have to provide explicit type annotations for the following situations:

1. A variable declaration, unless you assign a value to the variable (e.g., `val name = "Programming Scala"`)
2. All method parameters (e.g., `def deposit(amount: Money)...`)
3. Method return values in the following cases:
   a. When you explicitly call `return` in a method (even at the end)
   b. When a method is recursive
   c. When a method is overloaded and one of the methods calls another; the *calling* method needs a return type annotation
   d. When the inferred return type would be more general than you intended, e.g., `Any`

The `Any` type is the root of the Scala type hierarchy (see "The Scala Type Hierarchy" on page 155 for more details). If a block of code returns a value of type `Any` unexpectedly, chances are good that the type inferencer couldn't figure out what type to return, so it chose the most generic type possible.

Let's look at examples where explicit declarations of method return types are required. In the following script, the upCase method has a conditional return statement for zero-length strings:

```
// code-examples/TypeLessDoMore/method-nested-return-script.scala
// ERROR: Won't compile until you put a String return type on upCase.

def upCase(s: String) = {
  if (s.length == 0)
    return s
  else
    s.toUpperCase()
}

println( upCase("") )
println( upCase("Hello") )
```

Running this script gives you the following error:

```
... 6: error: method upCase has return statement; needs result type
      return s
      ^
```

You can fix this error by changing the first line of the method to the following:

```
def upCase(s: String): String = {
```

Actually, for this particular script, an alternative fix is to remove the **return** keyword from the line. It is not needed for the code to work properly, but it illustrates our point.

Recursive methods also require an explicit return type. Recall our **factorial** method in "Nesting Method Definitions" on page 28. Let's remove the : Int return type on the nested **fact** method:

```
// code-examples/TypeLessDoMore/method-recursive-return-script.scala
// ERROR: Won't compile until you put an Int return type on "fact".

def factorial(i: Int) = {
  def fact(i: Int, accumulator: Int) = {
    if (i <= 1)
      accumulator
    else
      fact(i - 1, i * accumulator)
  }

  fact(i, 1)
}
```

Now it fails to compile:

```
... 9: error: recursive method fact needs result type
          fact(i - 1, i * accumulator)
          ^
```

Overloaded methods can sometimes require an explicit return type. When one such method calls another, we have to add a return type to the one doing the calling, as in this example:

```
// code-examples/TypeLessDoMore/method-overloaded-return-script.scala
// Version 1 of "StringUtil" (with a compilation error).
// ERROR: Won't compile: needs a String return type on the second "joiner".

object StringUtil {
  def joiner(strings: List[String], separator: String): String =
    strings.mkString(separator)

  def joiner(strings: List[String]) = joiner(strings, " ")
}
import StringUtil._    // Import the joiner methods.

println( joiner(List("Programming", "Scala")) )
```

The two `joiner` methods concatenate a `List` of strings together. The first method also takes an argument for the separator string. The second method calls the first with a "default" separator of a single space.

If you run this script, you get the following error:

```
... 9: error: overloaded method joiner needs result type
    def joiner(strings: List[String]) = joiner(strings, "")
                                         ^
```

Since the *second* `joiner` method calls the first, it requires an explicit `String` return type. It should look like this:

```
    def joiner(strings: List[String]): String = joiner(strings, " ")
```

The final scenario can be subtle, when a more general return type is inferred than what you expected. You usually see this error when you assign a value returned from a function to a variable with a more specific type. For example, you were expecting a `String`, but the function inferred an `Any` for the returned object. Let's see a contrived example that reflects a bug where this scenario can occur:

```
// code-examples/TypeLessDoMore/method-broad-inference-return-script.scala
// ERROR: Won't compile; needs a String return type on the second "joiner".

def makeList(strings: String*) = {
  if (strings.length == 0)
    List(0)  // #1
  else
    strings.toList
}

val list: List[String] = makeList()
```

Running this script returns the following error:

```
...11: error: type mismatch;
 found    : List[Any]
 required: List[String]
```

```
val list: List[String] = makeList()
                         ^
```

We intended for makeList to return a List[String], but when strings.length equals zero, we returned List(0), incorrectly "assuming" that this expression is the correct way to create an empty list. In fact, we returned a List[Int] with one element, 0. We should have returned List(). Since the else expression returns a List[String], the result of strings.toList, the inferred return type for the method is the closest common supertype of List[Int] and List[String], which is List[Any]. Note that the compilation error doesn't occur in the function definition. We only see it when we attempt to assign the value returned from makeList to a List[String] variable.

In this case, fixing the bug is the solution. Alternatively, when there isn't a bug, it may be that the compiler just needs the "help" of an explicit return type declaration. Investigate the method that appears to return the unexpected type. In our experience, you often find that you modified that method (or another one in the call path) in such a way that the compiler now infers a more general return type than necessary. Add the explicit return type in this case.

Another way to prevent these problems is to always declare return types for methods, especially when defining methods for a public API. Let's revisit our StringUtil example and see why explicit declarations are a good idea (adapted from [Smith2009a]).

Here is our StringUtil "API" again with a new method, toCollection:

```
// code-examples/TypeLessDoMore/string-util-v3.scala
// Version 3 of "StringUtil" (for all versions of Scala).

object StringUtil {
  def joiner(strings: List[String], separator: String): String =
    strings.mkString(separator)

  def joiner(strings: List[String]): String = strings.mkString(" ")

  def toCollection(string: String) = string.split(' ')
}
```

The toCollection method splits a string on spaces and returns an Array containing the substrings. The return type is inferred, which is a potential problem, as we will see. The method is somewhat contrived, but it will illustrate our point. Here is a client of StringUtil that uses this method:

```
// code-examples/TypeLessDoMore/string-util-client.scala

import StringUtil._

object StringUtilClient {
  def main(args: Array[String]) = {
    args foreach { s => toCollection(s).foreach { x => println(x) } }
  }
}
```

If you compile these files with scala, you can run the client as follows:

```
$ scala -cp ... StringUtilClient "Programming Scala"
Programming
Scala
```

 For the -cp ... class path argument, use the directory where scalac wrote the class files, which defaults to the current directory (i.e., use -cp .). If you used the build process in the downloaded code examples, the class files are written to the *build* directory (using scalac -d build ...). In this case, use -cp build.

Everything is fine at this point, but now imagine that the code base has grown. StringUtil and its clients are now built separately and bundled into different JARs. Imagine also that the maintainers of StringUtil decide to return a List instead of the default:

```
object StringUtil {
  ...

  def toCollection(string: String) = string.split(' ').toList  // changed!
}
```

The only difference is the final call to toList that converts the computed Array to a List. You recompile StringUtil and redeploy its JAR. Then you run the same client, *without* recompiling it first:

```
$ scala -cp ... StringUtilClient "Programming Scala"
java.lang.NoSuchMethodError: StringUtil$.toCollection(...
    at StringUtilClient$$anonfun$main$1.apply(string-util-client.scala:6)
    at StringUtilClient$$anonfun$main$1.apply(string-util-client.scala:6)
...
```

What happened? When the client was compiled, StringUtil.toCollection returned an Array. Then toCollection was changed to return List. In both versions, the method return value was inferred. Therefore, the client should have been recompiled, too.

However, had an explicit return type of Seq been declared, which is a parent for both Array and List, then the implementation change would not have forced a recompilation of the client.

 When developing APIs that are built separately from their clients, declare method return types explicitly and use the most general return type you can. This is especially important when APIs declare *abstract* methods (see, e.g., Chapter 4).

There is another scenario to watch for when using declarations of collections like val map = Map(), as in the following example:

```
val map = Map()

map.update("book", "Programming Scala")

... 3: error: type mismatch;
 found    : java.lang.String("book")
 required: Nothing
map.update("book", "Programming Scala")
        ^
```

What happened? The *type parameters* of the generic type `Map` were inferred as
[Nothing,Nothing] when the map was created. (We'll discuss `Nothing` in "The Scala
Type Hierarchy" on page 155, but its name is suggestive!) We attempted to insert an
incompatible key-value pair of types `String` and `String`. Call it a `Map` to nowhere! The
solution is to parameterize the initial map declaration, e.g., `val map = Map[String,
String]()`, or to specify initial values so that the map parameters are inferred, e.g., `val
map = Map("Programming" → "Scala")`.

Finally, there is a subtle behavior with inferred return types that can cause unexpected
and baffling results (see [ScalaTips]). Consider the following example `scala` session:

```
scala> def double(i: Int) { 2 * i }
double: (Int)Unit

scala> println(double(2))
()
```

Why did the second command print () instead of 4? Look carefully at what the `scala`
interpreter said the first command returned: `double (Int)Unit`. We defined a method
named `double` that takes an `Int` argument and returns `Unit`. The method doesn't return
an `Int` as we would expect.

The cause of this unexpected behavior is a missing equals sign in the method definition.
Here is the definition we actually intended:

```
scala> def double(i: Int) = { 2 * i }
double: (Int)Int

scala> println(double(2))
4
```

Note the equals sign before the body of `double`. Now, the output says we have defined
`double` to return an `Int` and the second command does what we expect it to do.

There is a reason for this behavior. Scala regards a method with the equals sign before
the body as a function definition and a function always returns a value in functional
programming. On the other hand, when Scala sees a method body without the leading
equals sign, it assumes the programmer intended the method to be a "procedure"
definition, meant for performing side effects only with the return value `Unit`. In practice,
it is more likely that the programmer simply forgot to insert the equals sign!

When the return type of a method is inferred and you don't use an equals sign before the opening parenthesis for the method body, Scala infers a Unit return type, even when the last expression in the method is a value of another type.

By the way, where did that () come from that was printed before we fixed the bug? It is actually the real name of the *singleton* instance of the Unit type! (This name is a functional programming convention.)

Literals

Often, a new object is initialized with a *literal* value, such as val book = "Programming Scala". Let's discuss the kinds of literal values supported by Scala. Here, we'll limit ourselves to lexical syntax literals. We'll cover literal syntax for functions (used as *values*, not member methods), tuples, and certain types like Lists and Maps as we come to them.

Integer Literals

Integer literals can be expressed in decimal, hexadecimal, or octal. The details are summarized in Table 2-1.

Table 2-1. Integer literals

Kind	Format	Examples
Decimal	0 *or* a nonzero digit followed by zero or more digits (0–9)	0, 1, 321
Hexadecimal	0x followed by one or more hexadecimal digits (0–9, A–F, a–f)	0xFF, 0x1a3b
Octal	0 followed by one or more octal digits (0–7)	013, 077

For Long literals, it is necessary to append the L or l character at the end of the literal. Otherwise, an Int is used. The valid values for an integer literal are bounded by the type of the variable to which the value will be assigned. Table 2-2 defines the limits, which are inclusive.

Table 2-2. Ranges of allowed values for integer literals (boundaries are inclusive)

Target type	Minimum (inclusive)	Maximum (inclusive)
Long	-2^{63}	$2^{63} - 1$
Int	-2^{31}	$2^{31} - 1$
Short	-2^{15}	$2^{15} - 1$
Char	0	$2^{16} - 1$
Byte	-2^{7}	$2^{7} - 1$

A compile-time error occurs if an integer literal number is specified that is outside these ranges, as in the following examples:

```
scala > val i = 12345678901234567890
<console>:1: error: integer number too large
        val i = 12345678901234567890
scala> val b: Byte = 128
<console>:4: error: type mismatch;
 found   : Int(128)
 required: Byte
        val b: Byte = 128
                      ^

scala> val b: Byte = 127
b: Byte = 127
```

Floating-Point Literals

Floating-point literals are expressions with zero or more digits, followed by a period (.), followed by zero or more digits. If there are no digits before the period, i.e., the number is less than 1.0, then there must be one or more digits after the period. For Float literals, append the F or f character at the end of the literal. Otherwise, a Double is assumed. You can optionally append a D or d for a Double.

Floating-point literals can be expressed with or without exponentials. The format of the exponential part is e or E, followed by an optional + or -, followed by one or more digits.

Here are some example floating-point literals:

```
0.
.0
0.0
3.
3.14
.14
0.14
3e5
3E5
3.E5
3.e5
3.e+5
3.e-5
3.14e-5
3.14e-5f
3.14e-5F
3.14e-5d
3.14e-5D
```

Float consists of all IEEE 754 32-bit, single-precision binary floating-point values. Double consists of all IEEE 754 64-bit, double-precision binary floating-point values.

To avoid parsing ambiguities, you must have at least one space after a floating-point literal, if it is followed by a token that starts with a letter. Also, the expression 1.toString returns the integer value 1 as a string, while 1. toString uses the *operator notation* to invoke toString on the floating-point literal 1..

Boolean Literals

The boolean literals are true and false. The type of the variable to which they are assigned will be inferred to be Boolean:

```
scala> val b1 = true
b1: Boolean = true

scala> val b2 = false
b2: Boolean = false
```

Character Literals

A character literal is either a printable Unicode character or an escape sequence, written between single quotes. A character with a Unicode value between 0 and 255 may also be represented by an octal escape, i.e., a backslash (\) followed by a sequence of up to three octal characters. It is a compile-time error if a backslash character in a character or string literal does not start a valid escape sequence.

Here are some examples:

```
'A'
'\u0041'  // 'A' in Unicode
'\n'
'\012'    // '\n' in octal
'\t'
```

The valid escape sequences are shown in Table 2-3.

Table 2-3. Character escape sequences

Sequence	Unicode	Meaning
\b	\u0008	Backspace (BS)
\t	\u0009	Horizontal tab (HT)
\n	\u000a	Line feed (LF)
\f	\u000c	Form feed (FF)
\r	\u000d	Carriage return (CR)
\"	\u0022	Double quote (")
\'	\u0027	Single quote (')
\\	\u0009	Backslash (\)

String Literals

A string literal is a sequence of characters enclosed in double quotes or *triples* of double quotes, i.e., `"""..."""`.

For string literals in double quotes, the allowed characters are the same as the character literals. However, if a double quote `"` character appears in the string, it must be "escaped" with a `\` character. Here are some examples:

```
"Programming\nScala"
"He exclaimed, \"Scala is great!\""
"First\tSecond"
```

The string literals bounded by triples of double quotes are also called *multi-line* string literals. These strings can cover several lines; the line feeds will be part of the string. They can include any characters, including one or two double quotes together, but not three together. They are useful for strings with `\` characters that don't form valid Unicode or escape sequences, like the valid sequences listed in Table 2-3. Regular expressions are a typical example, which we'll discuss in Chapter 3. However, if escape sequences appear, they aren't interpreted.

Here are three example strings:

```
"""Programming\nScala"""
"""He exclaimed, "Scala is great!" """
"""First line\n
Second line\t

Fourth line"""
```

Note that we had to add a space before the trailing `"""` in the second example to prevent a parse error. Trying to escape the second `"` that ends the `Scala is great!` quote, i.e., `"Scala is great!\"`, doesn't work.

Copy and paste these strings into the `scala` interpreter. Do the same for the previous string examples. How are they interpreted differently?

Symbol Literals

Scala supports symbols, which are *interned* strings, meaning that two symbols with the same "name" (i.e., the same character sequence) will actually refer to the same object in memory. Symbols are used less often in Scala than in some other languages, like Ruby, Smalltalk, and Lisp. They are useful as map keys instead of strings.

A symbol literal is a single quote (`'`), followed by a letter, followed by zero or more digits and letters. Note that an expression like `'1` is invalid, because the compiler thinks it is an incomplete character literal.

A symbol literal `'id` is a shorthand for the expression `scala.Symbol("id")`.

If you want to create a symbol that contains whitespace, use e.g., `scala.Symbol(" Programming Scala ")`. All the whitespace is preserved.

Tuples

How many times have you wanted to return *two* or more values from a method? In many languages, like Java, you only have a few options, none of which is very appealing. You could pass in parameters to the method that will be modified for all or some of the "return" values, which is ugly. Or you could declare some small "structural" class that holds the two or more values, then return an instance of that class.

Scala, supports *tuples*, a grouping of two or more items, usually created with the literal syntax of a comma-separated list of the items inside parentheses, e.g., `(x1, x2, ...)`. The types of the x_i elements are unrelated to each other; you can mix and match types. These literal "groupings" are instantiated as `scala.TupleN` instances, where `N` is the number of items in the tuple. The Scala API defines separate `TupleN` classes for `N` between 1 and 22, inclusive. Tuple instances are immutable, *first-class* values, so you can assign them to variables, pass them as values, and return them from methods.

The following example demonstrates the use of tuples:

```
// code-examples/TypeLessDoMore/tuple-example-script.scala

def tupleator(x1: Any, x2: Any, x3: Any) = (x1, x2, x3)

val t = tupleator("Hello", 1, 2.3)
println( "Print the whole tuple: " + t )
println( "Print the first item:  " + t._1 )
println( "Print the second item: " + t._2 )
println( "Print the third item:  " + t._3 )

val (t1, t2, t3) = tupleator("World", '!', 0x22)
println( t1 + " " + t2 + " " + t3 )
```

Running this script with `scala` produces the following output:

```
Print the whole tuple: (Hello,1,2.3)
Print the first item:  Hello
Print the second item: 1
Print the third item:  2.3
World ! 34
```

The `tupleator` method simply returns a "3-tuple" with the input arguments. The first statement that uses this method assigns the returned tuple to a single variable `t`. The next four statements print `t` in various ways. The first print statement calls `Tuple3.toString`, which wraps parentheses around the item list. The following three statements print each item in `t` separately. The expression `t._N` retrieves the `N` item, starting at 1, *not* 0 (this choice follows functional programming conventions).

The last two lines show that we can use a tuple expression on the lefthand side of the assignment. We declare three vals—t1, t2, and t3—to hold the individual items in the tuple. In essence, the tuple items are extracted automatically.

Notice how we mixed types in the tuples. You can see the types more clearly if you use the interactive mode of the scala command, which we introduced in Chapter 1.

Invoke the scala command with no script argument. At the scala> prompt, enter val t = ("Hello",1,2.3) and see that you get the following result, which shows you the type of each element in the tuple:

```
scala> val t = ("Hello",1,2.3)
t: (java.lang.String, Int, Double) = (Hello,1,2.3)
```

It's worth noting that there's more than one way to define a tuple. We've been using the more common parenthesized syntax, but you can also use the arrow operator between two values, as well as special factory methods on the tuple-related classes:

```
scala> 1 -> 2
res0: (Int, Int) = (1,2)

scala> Tuple2(1, 2)
res1: (Int, Int) = (1,2)

scala> Pair(1, 2)
res2: (Int, Int) = (1,2)
```

Option, Some, and None: Avoiding nulls

We'll discuss the standard type hierarchy for Scala in "The Scala Type Hierarchy" on page 155. However, three useful classes to understand now are the Option class and its two subclasses, Some and None.

Most languages have a special keyword or object that's assigned to reference variables when there's nothing else for them to refer to. In Java, this is null; in Ruby, it's nil. In Java, null is a keyword, not an object, and thus it's illegal to call any methods on it. But this is a confusing choice on the language designer's part. Why return a keyword when the programmer expects an object?

To be more consistent with the goal of making everything an object, as well as to conform with functional programming conventions, Scala encourages you to use the Option type for variables and function return values when they may or may not refer to a value. When there is no value, use None, an object that is a subclass of Option. When there is a value, use Some, which wraps the value. Some is also a subclass of Option.

 None is declared as an object, not a class, because we really only need one instance of it. In that sense, it's like the null keyword, but it is a real object with methods.

You can see `Option`, `Some`, and `None` in action in the following example, where we create a map of state capitals in the United States:

```
// code-examples/TypeLessDoMore/state-capitals-subset-script.scala

val stateCapitals = Map(
  "Alabama" -> "Montgomery",
  "Alaska"  -> "Juneau",
  // ...
  "Wyoming" -> "Cheyenne")

println( "Get the capitals wrapped in Options:" )
println( "Alabama: " + stateCapitals.get("Alabama") )
println( "Wyoming: " + stateCapitals.get("Wyoming") )
println( "Unknown: " + stateCapitals.get("Unknown") )

println( "Get the capitals themselves out of the Options:" )
println( "Alabama: " + stateCapitals.get("Alabama").get )
println( "Wyoming: " + stateCapitals.get("Wyoming").getOrElse("Oops!") )
println( "Unknown: " + stateCapitals.get("Unknown").getOrElse("Oops2!") )
```

The convenient `->` syntax for defining name-value pairs to initialize a `Map` will be discussed in "The Predef Object" on page 145. For now, we want to focus on the two groups of `println` statements, where we show what happens when you retrieve the values from the map. If you run this script with the `scala` command, you'll get the following output:

```
Get the capitals wrapped in Options:
Alabama: Some(Montgomery)
Wyoming: Some(Cheyenne)
Unknown: None
Get the capitals themselves out of the Options:
Alabama: Montgomery
Wyoming: Cheyenne
Unknown: Oops2!
```

The first group of `println` statements invoke `toString` implicitly on the instances returned by `get`. We are calling `toString` on `Some` or `None` instances because the values returned by `Map.get` are automatically wrapped in a `Some`, when there is a value in the map for the specified key. Note that the Scala library doesn't store the `Some` in the map; it wraps the value in a `Some` upon retrieval. Conversely, when we ask for a map entry that doesn't exist, the `None` object is returned, rather than `null`. This occurred in the last `println` of the three.

The second group of `println` statements goes a step further. After calling `Map.get`, they call `get` or `getOrElse` on each `Option` instance to retrieve the value it contains. `Option.get` requires that the `Option` is not empty—that is, the `Option` instance must actually be a `Some`. In this case, `get` returns the value wrapped by the `Some`, as demonstrated in the `println` where we print the capital of Alabama. However, if the `Option` is actually `None`, then `None.get` throws a `NoSuchElementException`.

We also show the alternative method, getOrElse, in the last two `println` statements. This method returns either the value in the Option, if it is a Some instance, or it returns the second argument we passed to getOrElse, if it is a None instance. In other words, the second argument to getOrElse functions as the default return value.

So, getOrElse is the more defensive of the two methods. It avoids a potential thrown exception. We'll discuss the merits of alternatives like get versus getOrElse in "Exceptions and the Alternatives" on page 311.

Note that because the `Map.get` method returns an Option, it automatically documents the fact that there may not be an item matching the specified key. The map handles this situation by returning a None. Most languages would return null (or the equivalent) when there is no "real" value to return. You learn from experience to expect a possible null. Using Option makes the behavior more explicit in the method signature, so it's more self-documenting.

Also, thanks to Scala's static typing, you can't make the mistake of attempting to call a method on a value that might actually be null. While this mistake is easy to do in Java, it won't compile in Scala because you must first extract the value from the Option. So, the use of Option strongly encourages more resilient programming.

Because Scala runs on the JVM and .NET and because it must interoperate with other libraries, Scala has to support null. Still, you should avoid using null in your code. Tony Hoare, who invented the null reference in 1965 while working on an object-oriented language called ALGOL W, called its invention his "billion dollar mistake" (see [Hoare2009]). Don't contribute to that figure.

So, how would you write a method that returns an Option? Here is a possible implementation of get that could be used by a concrete subclass of Map (`Map.get` itself is *abstract*). For a more sophisticated version, see the implementation of get in `scala.collection.immutable.HashMap` in the Scala library source code distribution:

```
def get(key: A): Option[B] = {
  if (contains(key))
    new Some(getValue(key))
  else
    None
}
```

The `contains` method is also defined for Map. It returns `true` if the map contains a value for the specified key. The getValue method is intended to be an internal method that retrieves the value from the underlying storage, whatever it is.

Note how the value returned by getValue is wrapped in a Some[B], where the type B is inferred. However, if the call to contains(key) returns `false`, then the `object` None is returned.

You can use this same idiom when your methods return an Option. We'll explore other uses for Option in subsequent sections. Its pervasive use in Scala code makes it an important concept to grasp.

Organizing Code in Files and Namespaces

Scala adopts the package concept that Java uses for namespaces, but Scala offers a more flexible syntax. Just as file names don't have to match the type names, the package structure does not have to match the directory structure. So, you can define packages in files independent of their "physical" location.

The following example defines a class `MyClass` in a package `com.example.mypkg` using the conventional Java syntax:

```
// code-examples/TypeLessDoMore/package-example1.scala

package com.example.mypkg

class MyClass {
  // ...
}
```

The next example shows a contrived example that defines packages using the nested package syntax in Scala, which is similar to the `namespace` syntax in C# and the use of `modules` as namespaces in Ruby:

```
// code-examples/TypeLessDoMore/package-example2.scala

package com {
  package example {
    package pkg1 {
      class Class11 {
        def m = "m11"
      }
      class Class12 {
        def m = "m12"
      }
    }

    package pkg2 {
      class Class21 {
        def m = "m21"
        def makeClass11 = {
          new pkg1.Class11
        }
        def makeClass12 = {
          new pkg1.Class12
        }
      }
    }

    package pkg3.pkg31.pkg311 {
      class Class311 {
        def m = "m21"
      }
    }
  }
}
```

Two packages, pkg1 and pkg2, are defined under the com.example package. A total of three classes are defined between the two packages. The makeClass11 and makeClass12 methods in Class21 illustrate how to reference a type in the "sibling" package, pkg1. You can also reference these classes by their full paths, com.example.pkg1.Class11 and com.example.pkg1.Class12, respectively.

The package pkg3.pkg31.pkg311 shows that you can "chain" several packages together in one clause. It is not necessary to use a separate package clause for each package.

Following the conventions of Java, the root package for Scala's library classes is named scala.

 Scala does not allow package declarations in scripts that are executed directly with the scala interpreter. The reason has to do with the way the interpreter converts statements in scripts to valid Scala code before compiling to byte code. See "The scala Command-Line Tool" on page 345 for more details.

Importing Types and Their Members

To use declarations in packages, you have to import them, just as you do in Java and similarly for other languages. However, compared to Java, Scala greatly expands your options. The following example illustrates several ways to import Java types:

```
// code-examples/TypeLessDoMore/import-example1.scala

import java.awt._
import java.io.File
import java.io.File._
import java.util.{Map, HashMap}
```

You can import all types in a package, using the underscore (_) as a wildcard, as shown on the first line. You can also import individual Scala or Java types, as shown on the second line.

Java uses the "star" character (*) as the wildcard for matching all types in a package or all static members of a type when doing "static imports." In Scala, this character is allowed in method names, so _ is used as a wildcard, as we saw previously.

As shown on the third line, you can import all the static methods and fields in Java types. If java.io.File were actually a Scala object, as discussed previously, then this line would import the fields and methods from the object.

Finally, you can selectively import just the types you care about. On the fourth line, we import just the java.util.Map and java.util.HashMap types from the java.util package. Compare this one-line import statement with the two-line import statements we used in our first example in "Inferring Type Information" on page 29. They are functionally equivalent.

The next example shows more advanced options for import statements:

```
// code-examples/TypeLessDoMore/import-example2-script.scala

def writeAboutBigInteger() = {

  import java.math.BigInteger.{
    ONE => _,
    TEN,
    ZERO => JAVAZERO }

  // ONE is effectively undefined
  // println( "ONE: "+ONE )
  println( "TEN: "+TEN )
  println( "ZERO: "+JAVAZERO )
}

writeAboutBigInteger()
```

This example demonstrates two features. First, we can put import statements almost anywhere we want, not just at the top of the file, as required by Java. This feature allows us to scope the imports more narrowly. For example, we can't reference the imported BigInteger definitions outside the scope of the method. Another advantage of this feature is that it puts an import statement closer to where the imported items are actually used.

The second feature shown is the ability to *rename* imported items. First, the java.math.BigInteger.ONE constant is renamed to the underscore wildcard. This effectively makes it invisible and unavailable to the importing scope. This is a useful technique when you want to import everything *except* a few particular items.

Next, the java.math.BigInteger.TEN constant is imported without renaming, so it can be referenced simply as TEN.

Finally, the java.math.BigInteger.ZERO constant is given the "alias" JAVAZERO.

Aliasing is useful if you want to give the item a more convenient name or you want to avoid ambiguities with other items in scope that have the same name.

Imports are Relative

There's one other important thing to know about imports: they are *relative*. Note the comments for the following imports:

```
// code-examples/TypeLessDoMore/relative-imports.scala
import scala.collection.mutable._
import collection.immutable._         // Since "scala" is already imported
import _root_.scala.collection.jcl._  // full path from real "root"
package scala.actors {
  import remote._                      // We're in the scope of "scala.actors"
}
```

Note that the last import statement nested in the `scala.actor` package scope is relative to that scope.

The [ScalaWiki] has other examples at *http://scala.sygneca.com/faqs/language#how-do -i-import*.

It's fairly rare that you'll have problems with relative imports, but the problem with this convention is that they sometimes cause surprises, especially if you are accustomed to languages like Java, where imports are absolute. If you get a mystifying compiler error that a package wasn't found, check that the statement is properly relative to the last import statement or add the `_root_.` prefix. Also, you might see an IDE or other tool insert an `import _root_...` statement in your code. Now you know what it means.

 Remember that import statements are relative, not absolute. To create an absolute path, start with `_root_`.

Abstract Types And Parameterized Types

We mentioned in "A Taste of Scala" on page 10 that Scala supports *parameterized types*, which are very similar to *generics* in Java. (We could use the two terms interchangeably, but it's more common to use "parameterized types" in the Scala community and "generics" in the Java community.) The most obvious difference is in the syntax, where Scala uses square brackets (`[...]`), while Java uses angle brackets (`<...>`).

For example, a list of strings would be declared as follows:

```
val languages: List[String] = ...
```

There are other important differences with Java's generics, which we'll explore in "Understanding Parameterized Types" on page 249.

For now, we'll mention one other useful detail that you'll encounter before we can explain it in depth in Chapter 12. If you look at the declaration of `scala.List` in the Scaladocs, you'll see that the declaration is written as `... class List[+A]`. The `+` in front of the `A` means that `List[B]` is a *subtype* of `List[A]` for any `B` that is a subtype of `A`. If there is a `-` in front of a type parameter, then the relationship goes the other way; `Foo[B]` would be a *supertype* of `Foo[A]`, if the declaration is `Foo[-A]`.

Scala supports another type abstraction mechanism called *abstract types*, used in many *functional programming* languages, such as Haskell. Abstract types were also considered for inclusion in Java when generics were adopted. We want to introduce them now because you'll see many examples of them before we dive into their details in Chapter 12. For a very detailed comparison of these two mechanisms, see [Bruce1998].

Abstract types can be applied to many of the same design problems for which parameterized types are used. However, while the two mechanisms overlap, they are not redundant. Each has strengths and weaknesses for certain design problems.

Here is an example that uses an abstract type:

```scala
// code-examples/TypeLessDoMore/abstract-types-script.scala

import java.io._

abstract class BulkReader {
  type In
  val source: In
  def read: String
}

class StringBulkReader(val source: String) extends BulkReader {
  type In = String
  def read = source
}

class FileBulkReader(val source: File) extends BulkReader {
  type In = File
  def read = {
    val in = new BufferedInputStream(new FileInputStream(source))
    val numBytes = in.available()
    val bytes = new Array[Byte](numBytes)
    in.read(bytes, 0, numBytes)
    new String(bytes)
  }
}

println( new StringBulkReader("Hello Scala!").read )
println( new FileBulkReader(new File("abstract-types-script.scala")).read )
```

Running this script with scala produces the following output:

```
Hello Scala!
import java.io._

abstract class BulkReader {
...
```

The BulkReader *abstract* class declares three abstract members: a type named In, a val field source, and a read method. As in Java, instances in Scala can only be created from *concrete* classes, which must have definitions for all members.

The derived classes, StringBulkReader and FileBulkReader, provide concrete definitions for these abstract members. We'll cover the details of class declarations in Chapter 5 and the particulars of overriding member declarations in "Overriding Members of Classes and Traits" on page 111 in Chapter 6.

For now, note that the type field works very much like a type parameter in a parameterized type. In fact, we could rewrite this example as follows, where we show only what would be different:

```scala
abstract class BulkReader[In] {
  val source: In
  ...
```

```
}

class StringBulkReader(val source: String) extends BulkReader[String] {...}

class FileBulkReader(val source: File) extends BulkReader[File] {...}
```

Just as for parameterized types, if we define the In type to be String, then the source field must also be defined as a String. Note that the StringBulkReader's read method simply returns the source field, while the FileBulkReader's read method reads the contents of the file.

As demonstrated by [Bruce1998], parameterized types tend to be best for collections, which is how they are most often used in Java code, whereas abstract types are most useful for type "families" and other type scenarios.

We'll explore the details of Scala's abstract types in Chapter 12. For example, we'll see how to constrain the possible concrete types that can be used.

Reserved Words

Table 2-4 lists the reserved words in Scala, which we sometimes call "keywords," and briefly describes how they are used (see [ScalaSpec2009]).

Table 2-4. Reserved words

Word	Description	See ...
abstract	Makes a declaration abstract. Unlike Java, the keyword is usually not required for abstract members.	"Class and Object Basics" on page 89
case	Start a case clause in a match expression.	"Pattern Matching" on page 63
catch	Start a clause for catching thrown exceptions.	"Using try, catch, and finally Clauses" on page 70
class	Start a class declaration.	"Class and Object Basics" on page 89
def	Start a method declaration.	"Method Declarations" on page 25
do	Start a do...while loop.	"Other Looping Constructs" on page 61
else	Start an else clause for an if clause.	"Scala if Statements" on page 58
extends	Indicates that the class or trait that follows is the parent type of the class or trait being declared.	"Parent Classes" on page 91
false	Boolean *false*.	"The Scala Type Hierarchy" on page 155
final	Applied to a class or trait to prohibit deriving child types from it. Applied to a member to prohibit overriding it in a derived class or trait.	"Attempting to Override final Declarations" on page 112
finally	Start a clause that is executed after the corresponding try clause, whether or not an exception is thrown by the try clause.	"Using try, catch, and finally Clauses" on page 70

Word	Description	See ...
for	Start a for comprehension (loop).	"Scala for Comprehensions" on page 59
forSome	Used in *existential type* declarations to constrain the allowed concrete types that can be used.	"Existential Types" on page 284
if	Start an if clause.	"Scala if Statements" on page 58
implicit	Marks a method as eligible to be used as an *implicit* type converter. Marks a method parameter as optional, as long as a type-compatible substitute object is in the scope where the method is called.	"Implicit Conversions" on page 186
import	Import one or more types or members of types into the current scope.	"Importing Types and Their Members" on page 45
lazy	Defer evaluation of a val.	"Lazy Vals" on page 190
match	Start a pattern matching clause.	"Pattern Matching" on page 63
new	Create a new instance of a class.	"Class and Object Basics" on page 89
null	Value of a reference variable that has not been assigned a value.	"The Scala Type Hierarchy" on page 155
object	Start a *singleton* declaration: a class with only one instance.	"Classes and Objects: Where Are the Statics?" on page 148
override	Override a *concrete* member of a class or trait, as long as the original is not marked final.	"Overriding Members of Classes and Traits" on page 111
package	Start a package scope declaration.	"Organizing Code in Files and Namespaces" on page 44
private	Restrict visibility of a declaration.	"Visibility Rules" on page 96
protected	Restrict visibility of a declaration.	"Visibility Rules" on page 96
requires	Deprecated. Was used for *self typing*.	"The Scala Type Hierarchy" on page 155
return	Return from a function.	"A Taste of Scala" on page 10
sealed	Applied to a parent class to require all directly derived classes to be declared in the same source file.	"Case Classes" on page 136
super	Analogous to this, but binds to the parent type.	"Overriding Abstract and Concrete Methods" on page 112
this	How an object refers to itself. The method name for *auxiliary constructors*.	"Class and Object Basics" on page 89
throw	Throw an exception.	"Using try, catch, and finally Clauses" on page 70
trait	A *mixin module* that adds additional state and behavior to an instance of a class.	Chapter 4
try	Start a block that may throw an exception.	"Using try, catch, and finally Clauses" on page 70

Word	Description	See ...
true	Boolean *true*.	"The Scala Type Hierarchy" on page 155
type	Start a *type* declaration.	"Abstract Types And Parameterized Types" on page 47
val	Start a read-only "variable" declaration.	"Variable Declarations" on page 24
var	Start a read-write variable declaration.	"Variable Declarations" on page 24
while	Start a while loop.	"Other Looping Constructs" on page 61
with	Include the trait that follows in the class being declared or the object being instantiated.	Chapter 4
yield	Return an element in a for comprehension that becomes part of a sequence.	"Yielding" on page 60
_	A placeholder, used in imports, function literals, etc.	*Many*
:	Separator between identifiers and type annotations.	"A Taste of Scala" on page 10
=	Assignment.	"A Taste of Scala" on page 10
=>	Used in *function literals* to separate the argument list from the function body.	"Function Literals and Closures" on page 169
<-	Used in for comprehensions in *generator* expressions.	"Scala for Comprehensions" on page 59
<:	Used in *parameterized* and *abstract type* declarations to constrain the allowed types.	"Type Bounds" on page 259
<%	Used in *parameterized* and *abstract type* "view bounds" declarations.	"Type Bounds" on page 259
>:	Used in *parameterized* and *abstract type* declarations to constrain the allowed types.	"Type Bounds" on page 259
#	Used in *type projections*.	"Path-Dependent Types" on page 272
@	Marks an *annotation*.	"Annotations" on page 289
⇒	(Unicode \u21D2) Same as =>.	"Function Literals and Closures" on page 169
←	(Unicode \u2190) Same as <-.	"Scala for Comprehensions" on page 59

Notice that break and continue are not listed. These control keywords don't exist in Scala. Instead, Scala encourages you to use functional programming idioms that are usually more succinct and less error-prone. We'll discuss alternative approaches when we discuss for loops (see "Generator Expressions" on page 62).

Some Java methods use names that are reserved by Scala, for example, java.util.Scanner.match. To avoid a compilation error, surround the name with single back quotes, e.g., java.util.Scanner.`match`.

Recap and What's Next

We covered several ways that Scala's syntax is concise, flexible, and productive. We also described many Scala features. In the next chapter, we will round out some Scala essentials before we dive into Scala's support for object-oriented programming and functional programming.

CHAPTER 3

Rounding Out the Essentials

Before we dive into Scala's support for object-oriented and functional programming, let's finish our discussion of the essential features you'll use in most of your programs.

Operator? Operator?

An important fundamental concept in Scala is that all operators are actually methods. Consider this most basic of examples:

```
// code-examples/Rounding/one-plus-two-script.scala

1 + 2
```

That plus sign between the numbers? It's a method. First, Scala allows non-alphanumeric method names. You can call methods +, -, $, or whatever you desire. Second, this expression is identical to 1 .+(2). (We put a space after the 1 because 1. would be interpreted as a Double.) When a method takes one argument, Scala lets you drop both the period and the parentheses, so the method invocation looks like an operator invocation. This is called "infix" notation, where the operator is between the instance and the argument. We'll find out more about this shortly.

Similarly, a method with no arguments can be invoked without the period. This is called "postfix" notation.

Ruby and Smalltalk programmers should now feel right at home. As users of those languages know, these simple rules have far-reaching benefits when it comes to creating programs that flow naturally and elegantly.

So, what characters can you use in identifiers? Here is a summary of the rules for identifiers, used for method and type names, variables, etc. For the precise details, see [ScalaSpec2009]. Scala allows all the printable ASCII characters, such as letters, digits, the underscore (_), and the dollar sign ($), with the exceptions of the "parenthetical" characters—(,), [,], {, and }—and the "delimiter" characters—`, ', ', ", ., ;, and ,. Scala allows the other characters between \u0020–\u007F that are not in the sets just shown, such as mathematical symbols and "other" symbols. These remaining characters are called *operator characters*, and they include characters such as /, <, etc.

Reserved words can't be used

As in most languages, you can't reuse reserved words for identifiers. We listed the reserved words in "Reserved Words" on page 49. Recall that some of them are combinations of operator and punctuation characters. For example, a single underscore (_) is a reserved word!

Plain identifiers—combinations of letters, digits, $, _, and operators

Like Java and many languages, a *plain identifier* can begin with a letter or underscore, followed by more letters, digits, underscores, and dollar signs. Unicode-equivalent characters are also allowed. However, like Java, Scala reserves the dollar sign for internal use, so you shouldn't use it in your own identifiers. After an underscore, you can have either letters and digits *or* a sequence of operator characters. The underscore is important. It tells the compiler to treat all the characters up to the next whitespace as part of the identifier. For example, `val xyz_++= = 1` assigns the variable `xyz_++=` the value `1`, while the expression `val xyz++= = 1` won't compile because the "identifier" could also be interpreted as `xyz ++=`, which looks like an attempt to append something to `xyz`. Similarly, if you have operator characters after the underscore, you can't mix them with letters and digits. This restriction prevents ambiguous expressions like this: `abc_=123`. Is that an identifier `abc_=123` or an assignment of the value `123` to `abc_`?

Plain identifiers—operators

If an identifier begins with an operator character, the rest of the characters must be operator characters.

"Back-quote" literals

An identifier can also be an arbitrary string (subject to platform limitations) between two back quote characters, e.g., `val `this is a valid identifier` = "Hello World!"`. Recall that this syntax is also the way to invoke a method on a Java or .NET class when the method's name is identical to a Scala reserved word, e.g., `java.net.Proxy.`type`()`.

Pattern matching identifiers

In pattern matching expressions, tokens that begin with a lowercase letter are parsed as *variable identifiers*, while tokens that begin with an uppercase letter are parsed as *constant identifiers*. This restriction prevents some ambiguities because of the very succinct variable syntax that is used, e.g., no `val` keyword is present.

Syntactic Sugar

Once you know that all operators are methods, it's easier to reason about unfamiliar Scala code. You don't have to worry about special cases when you see new operators. When working with Actors in "A Taste of Concurrency" on page 16, you may have noticed that we used an exclamation point (!) to send a message to an Actor. Now you know that the ! is just another method, as are the other handy shortcut operators you can use to talk to Actors. Similarly, Scala's XML library provides the \ and \\ operators to dive into document structures. These are just methods on the scala.xml.NodeSeq class.

This flexible method naming gives you the power to write libraries that feel like a natural extension of Scala itself. You could write a new math library with numeric types that accept all the usual mathematical operators, like addition and subtraction. You could write a new concurrent messaging layer that behaves just like Actors. The possibilities are constrained only by Scala's method naming limitations.

Just because you *can* doesn't mean you *should*. When designing your own libraries and APIs in Scala, keep in mind that obscure punctuational operators are hard for programmers to remember. Overuse of these can contribute a "line noise" quality of unreadability to your code. Stick to conventions and err on the side of spelling method names out when a shortcut doesn't come readily to mind.

Methods Without Parentheses and Dots

To facilitate a variety of readable programming styles, Scala is flexible about the use of parentheses in methods. If a method takes no parameters, you can define it without parentheses. Callers must invoke the method without parentheses. If you add empty parentheses, then callers may optionally add parentheses. For example, the size method for List has no parentheses, so you write List(1, 2, 3).size. If you try List(1, 2, 3).size(), you'll get an error. However, the length method for java.lang.String does have parentheses in its definition, but Scala lets you write both "hello".length() and "hello".length.

The convention in the Scala community is to omit parentheses when calling a method that has no *side effects*. So, asking for the size of a sequence is fine without parentheses, but defining a method that transforms the elements in the sequence should be written with parentheses. This convention signals a potentially tricky method for users of your code.

It's also possible to omit the dot (period) when calling a parameterless method or one that takes only one argument. With this in mind, our List(1, 2, 3).size example could be written as:

```
// code-examples/Rounding/no-dot-script.scala

List(1, 2, 3) size
```

Neat, but confusing. When does this syntactical flexibility become useful? When chaining method calls together into expressive, self-explanatory "sentences" of code:

```
// code-examples/Rounding/no-dot-better-script.scala

def isEven(n: Int) = (n % 2) == 0

List(1, 2, 3, 4) filter isEven foreach println
```

As you might guess, running this produces the following output:

```
2
4
```

Scala's liberal approach to parentheses and dots on methods provides one building block for writing *Domain-Specific Languages*. We'll learn more about them after a brief discussion of operator precedence.

Precedence Rules

So, if an expression like 2.0 * 4.0 / 3.0 * 5.0 is actually a series of method calls on Doubles, what are the *operator precedence* rules? Here they are in order from lowest to highest precedence (see [ScalaSpec2009]):

1. *All letters*
2. |
3. ^
4. &
5. < >
6. = !
7. :
8. + -
9. * / %
10. *All other special characters*

Characters on the same line have the same precedence. An exception is = when used for assignment, when it has the lowest precedence.

Since * and / have the same precedence, the two lines in the following scala session behave the same:

```
scala> 2.0 * 4.0 / 3.0 * 5.0
res2: Double = 13.333333333333332

scala> (((2.0 * 4.0) / 3.0) * 5.0)
res3: Double = 13.333333333333332
```

In a sequence of left-associative method invocations, they simply bind in left-to-right order. "Left-associative" you say? In Scala, any method with a name that ends with a colon : actually binds to the *right*, while all other methods bind to the left. For example, you can prepend an element to a `List` using the `::` method (called "cons," short for "constructor"):

```
scala> val list = List('b', 'c', 'd')
list: List[Char] = List(b, c, d)

scala> 'a' :: list
res4: List[Char] = List(a, b, c, d)
```

The second expression is equivalent to `list.::(a)`. In a sequence of right-associative method invocations, they bind from right to left. What about a mixture of left-binding and right-binding expressions?

```
scala> 'a' :: list ++ List('e', 'f')
res5: List[Char] = List(a, b, c, d, e, f)
```

(The `++` method appends two lists.) In this case, `list` is added to the `List(e, f)`, then *a* is prepended to create the final list. It's usually better to add parentheses to remove any potential uncertainty.

 Any method whose name ends with a `:` binds to the *right*, not the *left*.

Finally, note that when you use the `scala` command, either interactively or with scripts, it may appear that you can define "global" variables and methods outside of types. This is actually an illusion; the interpreter wraps all definitions in an anonymous type before generating JVM or .NET CLR byte code.

Domain-Specific Languages

Domain-Specific Languages, or DSLs, provide a convenient syntactical means for expressing goals in a given problem domain. For example, SQL provides just enough of a programming language to handle the problems of working with databases, making it a Domain-Specific Language.

While some DSLs like SQL are self-contained, it's become popular to implement DSLs as subsets of full-fledged programming languages. This allows programmers to leverage the entirety of the host language for edge cases that the DSL does not cover, and saves the work of writing lexers, parsers, and the other building blocks of a language.

Scala's rich, flexible syntax makes writing DSLs a breeze. Consider this example of a style of test writing called *Behavior-Driven Development* (see [BDD]) using the Specs library (see "Specs" on page 363):

```
// code-examples/Rounding/specs-script.scala

"nerd finder" should {
```

```
"identify nerds from a List" in {
  val actors = List("Rick Moranis", "James Dean", "Woody Allen")
  val finder = new NerdFinder(actors)
  finder.findNerds mustEqual List("Rick Moranis", "Woody Allen")
}
}
```

Notice how much this code reads like English: "This should test that in the following scenario," "This value must equal that value," and so forth. This example uses the superb Specs library, which effectively provides a DSL for the Behavior-Driven Development testing and engineering methodology. By making maximum use of Scala's liberal syntax and rich methods, Specs test suites are readable even by non-developers.

This is just a taste of the power of DSLs in Scala. We'll see other examples later and learn how to write our own as we get more advanced (see Chapter 11).

Scala if Statements

Even the most familiar language features are supercharged in Scala. Let's have a look at the lowly if statement. As in most every language, Scala's if evaluates a conditional expression, then proceeds to a block if the result is true, or branches to an alternate block if the result is false. A simple example:

```
// code-examples/Rounding/if-script.scala

if (2 + 2 == 5) {
  println("Hello from 1984.")
} else if (2 + 2 == 3) {
    println("Hello from Remedial Math class?")
} else {
  println("Hello from a non-Orwellian future.")
}
```

What's different in Scala is that if and almost all other statements are actually expressions themselves. So, we can assign the result of an if expression, as shown here:

```
// code-examples/Rounding/assigned-if-script.scala

val configFile = new java.io.File("~/.myapprc")

val configFilePath = if (configFile.exists()) {
  configFile.getAbsolutePath()
} else {
  configFile.createNewFile()
  configFile.getAbsolutePath()
}
```

Note that if statements are expressions, meaning they have values. In this example, the value configFilePath is the result of an if expression that handles the case of a configuration file not existing internally, then returns the absolute path to that file. This value can now be reused throughout an application, and the if expression won't be reevaluated when the value is used.

Because `if` statements are expressions in Scala, there is no need for the special-case ternary conditional expressions that exist in C-derived languages. You won't see x ? doThis() : doThat() in Scala. Scala provides a mechanism that's just as powerful and more readable.

What if we omit the `else` clause in the previous example? Typing the code in the `scala` interpreter will tell us what happens:

```
scala> val configFile = new java.io.File("~/.myapprc")
configFile: java.io.File = ~/.myapprc

scala> val configFilePath = if (configFile.exists()) {
     |     configFile.getAbsolutePath()
     | }
configFilePath: Unit = ()

scala>
```

Note that `configFilePath` is now `Unit`. (It was `String` before.) The type inference picks a type that works for all outcomes of the `if` expression. `Unit` is the only possibility, since no value is one possible outcome.

Scala for Comprehensions

Another familiar control structure that's particularly feature-rich in Scala is the **for** loop, referred to in the Scala community as a **for** *comprehension* or **for** *expression*. This corner of the language deserves at least one fancy name, because it can do some great party tricks.

Actually, the term `comprehension` comes from functional programming. It expresses the idea that we are traversing a set of some kind, "comprehending" what we find, and computing something new from it.

A Dog-Simple Example

Let's start with a basic **for** expression:

```
// code-examples/Rounding/basic-for-script.scala

val dogBreeds = List("Doberman", "Yorkshire Terrier", "Dachshund",
                     "Scottish Terrier", "Great Dane", "Portuguese Water Dog")

for (breed <- dogBreeds)
  println(breed)
```

As you might guess, this code says, "For every element in the list `dogBreeds`, create a temporary variable called `breed` with the value of that element, then print it." Think of the <- operator as an arrow directing elements of a collection, one by one, to the scoped variable by which we'll refer to them inside the **for** expression. The left-arrow operator is called a *generator*, so named because it's *generating* individual values from a collection for use in an expression.

Filtering

What if we want to get more granular? Scala's for expressions allow for *filters* that let us specify which elements of a collection we want to work with. So to find all terriers in our list of dog breeds, we could modify the previous example to the following:

```
// code-examples/Rounding/filtered-for-script.scala

for (breed <- dogBreeds
  if breed.contains("Terrier")
) println(breed)
```

To add more than one filter to a for expression, separate the filters with semicolons:

```
// code-examples/Rounding/double-filtered-for-script.scala

for (breed <- dogBreeds
  if breed.contains("Terrier");
  if !breed.startsWith("Yorkshire")
) println(breed)
```

You've now found all the terriers that don't hail from Yorkshire, and hopefully learned just how useful filters can be in the process.

Yielding

What if, rather than printing your filtered collection, you needed to hand it off to another part of your program? The yield keyword is your ticket to generating new collections with for expressions. In the following example, note that we're wrapping up the for expression in curly braces, as we would when defining any block:

```
// code-examples/Rounding/yielding-for-script.scala

val filteredBreeds = for {
  breed <- dogBreeds
  if breed.contains("Terrier")
  if !breed.startsWith("Yorkshire")
} yield breed
```

 for expressions may be defined with parentheses or curly braces, but using curly braces means you don't have to separate your filters with semicolons. Most of the time, you'll prefer using curly braces when you have more than one filter, assignment, etc.

Every time through the for expression, the filtered result is yielded as a value named breed. These results accumulate with every run, and the resulting collection is assigned to the value filteredBreeds (as we did with if statements earlier). The type of the collection resulting from a for-yield expression is inferred from the type of the collection being iterated over. In this case, filteredBreeds is of type List[String], since it is a subset of the dogBreeds list, which is also of type List[String].

Expanded Scope

One final useful feature of Scala's for comprehensions is the ability to define variables inside the first part of your for expressions that can be used in the latter part. This is best illustrated with an example:

```
// code-examples/Rounding/scoped-for-script.scala

for {
  breed <- dogBreeds
  upcasedBreed = breed.toUpperCase()
} println(upcasedBreed)
```

Note that without declaring upcasedBreed as a val, you can reuse it within the body of your for expression. This approach is ideal for transforming elements in a collection as you loop through them.

Finally, in "Options and for Comprehensions" on page 308, we'll see how using Options with for comprehensions can greatly reduce code size by eliminating unnecessary "null" and "missing" checks.

Other Looping Constructs

Scala provides several other looping constructs.

Scala while Loops

Familiar in many languages, the while loop executes a block of code as long as a condition is true. For example, the following code prints out a complaint once a day until the next Friday the 13th has arrived:

```
// code-examples/Rounding/while-script.scala
// WARNING: This script runs for a LOOOONG time!

import java.util.Calendar

def isFridayThirteen(cal: Calendar): Boolean = {
  val dayOfWeek = cal.get(Calendar.DAY_OF_WEEK)
  val dayOfMonth = cal.get(Calendar.DAY_OF_MONTH)

  // Scala returns the result of the last expression in a method
  (dayOfWeek == Calendar.FRIDAY) && (dayOfMonth == 13)
}

while (!isFridayThirteen(Calendar.getInstance())) {
  println("Today isn't Friday the 13th. Lame.")
```

```
  // sleep for a day
  Thread.sleep(86400000)
}
```

Table 3-1 later in this chapter shows the conditional operators that work in `while` loops.

Scala do-while Loops

Like the `while` loop, a `do-while` loop executes some code while a conditional expression is true. The only difference that a `do-while` checks to see if the condition is true *after* running the block. To count up to 10, we could write this:

```
// code-examples/Rounding/do-while-script.scala

var count = 0

do {
  count += 1
  println(count)
} while (count < 10)
```

As it turns out, there's a more elegant way to loop through collections in Scala, as we'll see in the next section.

Generator Expressions

Remember the arrow operator (`<-`) from the discussion about `for` loops? We can put it to work here, too. Let's clean up the `do-while` example just shown:

```
// code-examples/Rounding/generator-script.scala

for (i <- 1 to 10) println(i)
```

Yup, that's all that's necessary. This clean one-liner is possible because of Scala's `RichInt` class. An *implicit conversion* is invoked by the compiler to convert the `1`, an `Int`, into a `RichInt`. (We'll discuss these conversions in "The Scala Type Hierarchy" on page 155 and in "Implicit Conversions" on page 186.) `RichInt` defines a `to` method that takes another integer and returns an instance of `Range.Inclusive`. That is, `Inclusive` is a nested class in the `Range` *companion object* (a concept we introduced briefly in Chapter 1; see Chapter 6 for details). This subclass of the *class* `Range` inherits a number of methods for working with sequences and iterable data structures, including those necessary to use it in a `for` loop.

By the way, if you wanted to count from 1 up to but not including 10, you could use `until` instead of `to`. For example: `for (i <- 0 until 10)`.

This should paint a clearer picture of how Scala's internal libraries compose to form easy-to-use language constructs.

When working with loops in most languages, you can **break** out of a loop or **continue** the iterations. Scala doesn't have either of these statements, but when writing idiomatic Scala code, they're not necessary. Use conditional expressions to test if a loop should continue, or make use of recursion. Better yet, filter your collections ahead of time to eliminate complex conditions within your loops. However, because of demand for it, Scala version 2.8 includes support for **break**, implemented as a library method, rather than a built-in **break** keyword.

Conditional Operators

Scala borrows most of the conditional operators from Java and its predecessors. You'll find the ones listed in Table 3-1 in **if** statements, **while** loops, and everywhere else conditions apply.

Table 3-1. Conditional operators

Operator	Operation	Description
&&	and	The values on the left and right of the operator are true. The righthand side is *only* evaluated if the lefthand side is *true*.
||	or	At least one of the values on the left or right is true. The righthand side is *only* evaluated if the lefthand side is *false*.
>	greater than	The value on the left is greater than the value on the right.
>=	greater than or equals	The value on the left is greater than or equal to the value on the right.
<	less than	The value on the left is less than the value on the right.
<=	less than or equals	The value on the left is less than or equal to the value on the right.
==	equals	The value on the left is the same as the value on the right.
!=	not equal	The value on the left is not the same as the value on the right.

Note that **&&** and **||** are "short-circuiting" operators. They stop evaluating expressions as soon as the answer is known.

We'll discuss object equality in more detail in "Equality of Objects" on page 142. For example, we'll see that **==** has a different meaning in Scala versus Java. Otherwise, these operators should all be familiar, so let's move on to something new and exciting.

Pattern Matching

An idea borrowed from functional languages, *pattern matching* is a powerful yet concise way to make a programmatic choice between multiple conditions. Pattern matching is the familiar **case** statement from your favorite C-like language, but on steroids. In the typical case statement you're limited to matching against values of ordinal types, yielding trivial expressions like this: "In the case that i is 5, print a message; in the case that i is 6, exit the program." With Scala's pattern matching, your cases can include types, wildcards, sequences, regular expressions, and even deep inspections of an object's variables.

A Simple Match

To begin with, let's simulate flipping a coin by matching the value of a boolean:

```
// code-examples/Rounding/match-boolean-script.scala

val bools = List(true, false)

for (bool <- bools) {
  bool match {
    case true => println("heads")
    case false => println("tails")
    case _ => println("something other than heads or tails (yikes!)")
  }
}
```

It looks just like a C-style case statement, right? The only difference is the last case with the underscore (_) wildcard. It matches anything not defined in the cases above it, so it serves the same purpose as the default keyword in Java and C# switch statements.

Pattern matching is *eager*; the first match wins. So, if you try to put a case _ clause before any other case clauses, the compiler will throw an "unreachable code" error on the next clause, because nothing will get past the default clause!

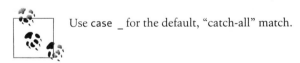 Use case _ for the default, "catch-all" match.

What if we want to work with matches as variables?

Variables in Matches

In the following example, we assign the wildcard case to a variable called other Number, then print it in the subsequent expression. If we generate a 7, we'll extol that number's virtues. Otherwise, we'll curse fate for making us suffer an unlucky number:

```
// code-examples/Rounding/match-variable-script.scala

import scala.util.Random

val randomInt = new Random().nextInt(10)

randomInt match {
```

```
    case 7 => println("lucky seven!")
    case otherNumber => println("boo, got boring ol' " + otherNumber)
}
```

Matching on Type

These simple examples don't even begin to scratch the surface of Scala's pattern matching features. Let's try matching based on type:

```
// code-examples/Rounding/match-type-script.scala

val sundries = List(23, "Hello", 8.5, 'q')

for (sundry <- sundries) {
  sundry match {
    case i: Int => println("got an Integer: " + i)
    case s: String => println("got a String: " + s)
    case f: Double => println("got a Double: " + f)
    case other => println("got something else: " + other)
  }
}
```

Here we pull each element out of a List of Any type of element, in this case containing a String, a Double, an Int, and a Char. For the first three of those types, we let the user know specifically which type we got and what the value was. When we get something else (the Char), we just let the user know the value. We could add further elements to the list of other types and they'd be caught by the other wildcard case.

Matching on Sequences

Since working in Scala often means working with sequences, wouldn't it be handy to be able to match against the length and contents of lists and arrays? The following example does just that, testing two lists to see if they contain four elements, the second of which is the integer 3:

```
// code-examples/Rounding/match-seq-script.scala

val willWork = List(1, 3, 23, 90)
val willNotWork = List(4, 18, 52)
val empty = List()

for (l <- List(willWork, willNotWork, empty)) {
  l match {
    case List(_, 3, _, _) => println("Four elements, with the 2nd being '3'.")
    case List(_*) => println("Any other list with 0 or more elements.")
  }
}
```

In the second case we've used a special wildcard pattern to match a List of any size, even zero elements, and any element values. You can use this pattern at the end of any sequence match to remove length as a condition.

Recall that we mentioned the "cons" method for List, ::. The expression a :: list prepends a to a list. You can also use this operator to extract the head and tail of a list:

```
// code-examples/Rounding/match-list-script.scala

val willWork = List(1, 3, 23, 90)
val willNotWork = List(4, 18, 52)
val empty = List()

def processList(l: List[Any]): Unit = l match {
  case head :: tail =>
    format("%s ", head)
    processList(tail)
  case Nil => println("")
}

for (l <- List(willWork, willNotWork, empty)) {
  print("List: ")
  processList(l)
}
```

The processList method matches on the List argument l. It may look strange to start the method definition like the following:

```
def processList(l: List[Any]): Unit = l match {
  ...
}
```

Hopefully hiding the details with the ellipsis makes the meaning a little clearer. The processList method is actually one statement that crosses several lines.

It first matches on head :: tail, where head will be assigned the first element in the list and tail will be assigned the rest of the list. That is, we're extracting the head and tail from the list using ::. When this case matches, it prints the head and calls process List recursively to process the tail.

The second case matches the empty list, Nil. It prints an end of line and terminates the recursion.

Matching on Tuples (and Guards)

Alternately, if we just wanted to test that we have a tuple of two items, we could do a tuple match:

```
// code-examples/Rounding/match-tuple-script.scala

val tupA = ("Good", "Morning!")
val tupB = ("Guten", "Tag!")

for (tup <- List(tupA, tupB)) {
  tup match {
    case (thingOne, thingTwo) if thingOne == "Good" =>
        println("A two-tuple starting with 'Good'.")
    case (thingOne, thingTwo) =>
```

```
            println("This has two things: " + thingOne + " and " + thingTwo)
        }
    }
```

In the second `case` in this example, we've extracted the values inside the tuple to scoped variables, then reused these variables in the resulting expression.

In the first case we've added a new concept: *guards*. The `if` condition after the tuple is a guard. The guard is evaluated when matching, but only extracting any variables in the preceding part of the case. Guards provide additional granularity when constructing cases. In this example, the only difference between the two patterns is the guard expression, but that's enough for the compiler to differentiate them.

 Recall that the cases in a pattern match are evaluated in order. For example, if your first case is broader than your second case, the second case will never be reached. (Unreachable cases will cause a compiler error.) You may include a "default" case at the end of a pattern match, either using the underscore wildcard character or a meaningfully named variable. When using a variable, it should have no explicit type or it should be declared as **Any**, so it can match anything. On the other hand, try to design your code to avoid a catch-all clause by ensuring it only receives specific items that are expected.

Matching on Case Classes

Let's try a *deep match*, examining the contents of objects in our pattern match:

```scala
// code-examples/Rounding/match-deep-script.scala

case class Person(name: String, age: Int)

val alice   = new Person("Alice", 25)
val bob     = new Person("Bob", 32)
val charlie = new Person("Charlie", 32)

for (person <- List(alice, bob, charlie)) {
  person match {
    case Person("Alice", 25) => println("Hi Alice!")
    case Person("Bob", 32) => println("Hi Bob!")
    case Person(name, age) =>
      println("Who are you, " + age + " year-old person named " + name + "?")
  }
}
```

Poor Charlie gets the cold shoulder, as we can see in the output:

```
Hi Alice!
Hi Bob!
Who are you, 32 year-old person named Charlie?
```

We first define a *case class*, a special type of class that we'll learn more about in "Case Classes" on page 136. For now, it will suffice to say that a case class allows for very terse construction of simple objects with some predefined methods. Our pattern match then looks for Alice and Bob by inspecting the values passed to the constructor of the `Person` case class. Charlie falls through to the catch-all case; even though he has the same `age` value as Bob, we're matching on the `name` property as well.

This type of pattern match becomes extremely useful when working with Actors, as we'll see later on. Case classes are frequently sent to Actors as messages, and deep pattern matching on an object's contents is a convenient way to "parse" those messages.

Matching on Regular Expressions

Regular expressions are convenient for extracting data from strings that have an informal structure, but are not "structured data" (that is, in a format like XML or JSON, for example). Commonly referred to as *regexes*, regular expressions are a feature of nearly all modern programming languages. They provide a terse syntax for specifying complex matches, one that is typically translated into a state machine behind the scenes for optimum performance.

Regexes in Scala should contain no surprises if you've used them in other programming languages. Let's see an example:

```
// code-examples/Rounding/match-regex-script.scala

val BookExtractorRE = """Book: title=([^,]+),\s+authors=(.+)""".r
val MagazineExtractorRE = """Magazine: title=([^,]+),\s+issue=(.+)""".r

val catalog = List(
  "Book: title=Programming Scala, authors=Dean Wampler, Alex Payne",
  "Magazine: title=The New Yorker, issue=January 2009",
  "Book: title=War and Peace, authors=Leo Tolstoy",
  "Magazine: title=The Atlantic, issue=February 2009",
  "BadData: text=Who put this here??"
)

for (item <- catalog) {
  item match {
    case BookExtractorRE(title, authors) =>
      println("Book \"" + title + "\", written by " + authors)
    case MagazineExtractorRE(title, issue) =>
      println("Magazine \"" + title + "\", issue " + issue)
    case entry => println("Unrecognized entry: " + entry)
  }
}
```

We start with two regular expressions, one for records of books and another for records of magazines. Calling `.r` on a string turns it into a regular expression; we use raw (triple-quoted) strings here to avoid having to double-escape backslashes. Should you find the `.r` transformation method on strings unclear, you can also define regexes by creating new instances of the `Regex` class, as in: `new Regex("""\W""")`.

Notice that each of our regexes defines two *capture groups*, connoted by parentheses. Each group captures the value of a single field in the record, such as a book's title or author. Regexes in Scala translate those capture groups to *extractors*. Every match sets a field to the captured result; every miss is set to `null`.

What does this mean in practice? If the text fed to the regular expression matches, `case BookExtractorRE(title, authors)` will assign the first capture group to `title` and the second to `authors`. We can then use those values on the righthand side of the `case` clause, as we have in the previous example. The variable names `title` and `author` within the extractor are arbitrary; matches from capture groups are simply assigned from left to right, and you can call them whatever you'd like.

That's regexes in Scala in nutshell. The `scala.util.matching.Regex` class supplies several handy methods for finding and replacing matches in strings, both all occurrences of a match and just the first occurrence, so be sure to make use of them.

What we won't cover in this section is the details of writing regular expressions. Scala's `Regex` class uses the underlying platform's regular expression APIs (that is, Java's or .NET's). Consult references on those APIs for the hairy details, as they may be subtly different from the regex support in your language of choice.

Binding Nested Variables in Case Clauses

Sometimes you want to bind a variable to an object enclosed in a match, where you are also specifying match criteria on the nested object. Suppose we modify a previous example so we're matching on the key-value pairs from a map. We'll store our same `Person` objects as the values and use an employee ID as the key. We'll also add another attribute to `Person`, a `role` field that points to an instance from a type hierarchy:

```
// code-examples/Rounding/match-deep-pair-script.scala

class Role
case object Manager extends Role
case object Developer extends Role

case class Person(name: String, age: Int, role: Role)

val alice = new Person("Alice", 25, Developer)
val bob = new Person("Bob", 32, Manager)
val charlie = new Person("Charlie", 32, Developer)

for (item <- Map(1 -> alice, 2 -> bob, 3 -> charlie)) {
  item match {
    case (id, p @ Person(_, _, Manager)) => format("%s is overpaid.\n", p)
    case (id, p @ Person(_, _, _)) => format("%s is underpaid.\n", p)
  }
}
```

The `case objects` are just singleton objects like we've seen before, but with the special `case` behavior. We're most interested in the embedded `p @ Person(...)` inside the case clause. We're matching on particular kinds of `Person` objects inside the enclosing tuple. We also want to assign the `Person` to a variable `p`, so we can use it for printing:

```
Person(Alice,25,Developer) is underpaid.
Person(Bob,32,Manager) is overpaid.
Person(Charlie,32,Developer) is underpaid.
```

If we weren't using matching criteria in `Person` itself, we could just write `p: Person`. For example, the previous `match` clause could be written this way:

```
item match {
  case (id, p: Person) => p.role match {
    case Manager => format("%s is overpaid.\n", p)
    case _ => format("%s is underpaid.\n", p)
  }
}
```

Note that the `p @ Person(...)` syntax gives us a way to flatten this nesting of match statements into one statement. It is analogous to using "capture groups" in a regular expression to pull out substrings we want, instead of splitting the string in several successive steps to extract the substrings we want. Use whichever technique you prefer.

Using try, catch, and finally Clauses

Through its use of functional constructs and strong typing, Scala encourages a coding style that lessens the need for exceptions and exception handling. But where Scala interacts with Java, exceptions are still prevalent.

 Scala does not have checked exceptions, like Java. Even Java's checked exceptions are treated as unchecked by Scala. There is also no `throws` clause on method declarations. However, there is a `@throws` annotation that is useful for Java interoperability. See the section "Annotations" on page 289.

Thankfully, Scala treats exception handling as just another pattern match, allowing us to make smart choices when presented with a multiplicity of potential exceptions. Let's see this in action:

```
// code-examples/Rounding/try-catch-script.scala

import java.util.Calendar

val then = null
val now = Calendar.getInstance()

try {
  now.compareTo(then)
} catch {
```

```
  case e: NullPointerException => println("One was null!"); System.exit(-1)
  case unknown => println("Unknown exception " + unknown); System.exit(-1)
} finally {
  println("It all worked out.")
  System.exit(0)
}
```

In this example, we explicitly catch the `NullPointerException` thrown when trying to compare a `Calendar` instance with `null`. We also define `unknown` as a catch-all case, just to be safe. If we weren't hardcoding this program to fail, the `finally` block would be reached and the user would be informed that everything worked out just fine.

 You can use an underscore (Scala's standard wildcard character) as a placeholder to catch any type of exception (really, to match any case in a pattern matching expression). However, you won't be able to refer to the exception in the subsequent expression. Name the exception variable if you need it; for example, if you need to print the exception as we do in the catch-all case of the previous example.

Pattern matching aside, Scala's treatment of exception handling should be familiar to those fluent in Java, Ruby, Python, and most other mainstream languages. And yes, you throw an exception by writing `throw new MyBadException(...)`. That's all there is to it.

Concluding Remarks on Pattern Matching

Pattern matching is a powerful and elegant way of extracting information from objects, when used appropriately. Recall from Chapter 1 that we highlighted the synergy between pattern matching and polymorphism. Most of the time, you want to avoid the problems of "switch" statements that know a class hierarchy, because they have to be modified every time the hierarchy is changed.

In our drawing Actor example, we used pattern matching to separate different "categories" of messages, but we used polymorphism to draw the shapes sent to it. We could change the `Shape` hierarchy and the Actor code would not require changes.

Pattern matching is also useful for the design problem where you need to get at data inside an object, but only in special circumstances. One of the unintended consequences of the *JavaBeans* (see [JavaBeansSpec]) specification was that it encouraged people to expose fields in their objects through getters and setters. This should *never* be a default decision. Access to "state information" should be encapsulated and exposed only in ways that make logical sense for the type, as viewed from the abstraction it exposes.

Instead, consider using pattern matching for those "rare" times when you need to extract information in a controlled way. As we will see in "Unapply" on page 129, the pattern matching examples we have shown use `unapply` methods defined to extract information from instances. These methods let you extract that information while hiding the implementation details. In fact, the information returned by unapply might be a transformation of the actual information in the type.

Finally, when designing pattern matching statements, be wary of relying on a default case clause. Under what circumstances would "none of the above" be the correct answer? It may indicate that the design should be refined so you know more precisely all the possible matches that might occur. We'll learn one technique that helps when we discuss *sealed* class hierarchies in "Sealed Class Hierarchies" on page 151.

Enumerations

Remember our examples involving various breeds of dog? In thinking about the types in these programs, we might want a top-level Breed type that keeps track of a number of breeds. Such a type is called an *enumerated type*, and the values it contains are called *enumerations*.

While enumerations are a built-in part of many programming languages, Scala takes a different route and implements them as a class in its standard library. This means there is no special syntax for enumerations in Scala, as in Java and C#. Instead, you just define an object that extends the Enumeration class. Hence, at the byte code level, there is no connection between Scala enumerations and the enum constructs in Java and C#.

Here is an example:

```
// code-examples/Rounding/enumeration-script.scala

object Breed extends Enumeration {
  val doberman = Value("Doberman Pinscher")
  val yorkie = Value("Yorkshire Terrier")
  val scottie = Value("Scottish Terrier")
  val dane = Value("Great Dane")
  val portie = Value("Portuguese Water Dog")
}

// print a list of breeds and their IDs
println("ID\tBreed")
for (breed <- Breed) println(breed.id + "\t" + breed)

// print a list of Terrier breeds
println("\nJust Terriers:")
Breed.filter(_.toString.endsWith("Terrier")).foreach(println)
```

When run, you'll get the following output:

```
ID      Breed
0       Doberman Pinscher
1       Yorkshire Terrier
2       Scottish Terrier
3       Great Dane
4       Portuguese Water Dog
```

```
Just Terriers:
Yorkshire Terrier
Scottish Terrier
```

We can see that our `Breed` enumerated type contains several variables of type `Value`, as in the following example:

```
val doberman = Value("Doberman Pinscher")
```

Each declaration is actually calling a method named `Value` that takes a string argument. We use this method to assign a long-form breed name to each enumeration value, which is what the `Value.toString` method returned in the output.

Note that there is no namespace collision between the type and method that both have the name `Value`. There are other overloaded versions of the `Value` method. One of them takes no arguments, another takes an `Int` ID value, and another takes both an `Int` and `String`. These `Value` methods return a `Value` object, and they add the value to the enumeration's collection of values.

In fact, Scala's `Enumeration` class supports the usual methods for working with collections, so we can easily iterate through the breeds with a `for` loop and `filter` them by name. The output above also demonstrated that every `Value` in an enumeration is automatically assigned a numeric identifier, unless you call one of the `Value` methods where you specify your own ID value explicitly.

You'll often want to give your enumeration values human-readable names, as we did here. However, sometimes you may not need them. Here's another enumeration example adapted from the Scaladoc entry for `Enumeration`:

```
// code-examples/Rounding/days-enumeration-script.scala

object WeekDay extends Enumeration {
  type WeekDay = Value
  val Mon, Tue, Wed, Thu, Fri, Sat, Sun = Value
}
import WeekDay._

def isWorkingDay(d: WeekDay) = ! (d == Sat || d == Sun)

WeekDay filter isWorkingDay foreach println
```

Running this script with `scala` yields the following output:

```
Main$$anon$1$WeekDay(0)
Main$$anon$1$WeekDay(1)
Main$$anon$1$WeekDay(2)
Main$$anon$1$WeekDay(3)
Main$$anon$1$WeekDay(4)
```

When a name isn't assigned using one of the `Value` methods that takes a `String` argument, `Value.toString` prints the name of the type that is synthesized by the compiler, along with the ID value that was generated automatically.

Note that we imported `WeekDay._`. This made each enumeration value (`Mon`, `Tues`, etc.) in scope. Otherwise, you would have to write `WeekDay.Mon`, `WeekDay.Tues`, etc.

Also, the import made the *type alias*, `type Weekday = Value`, in scope, which we used as the type for the argument for the `isWorkingDay` method. If you don't define a type alias like this, then you would declare the method as `def isWorkingDay(d: Week Day.Value)`.

Since Scala enumerations are just regular objects, you could use any object with `vals` to indicate different "enumeration values." However, extending `Enumeration` has several advantages. It automatically manages the values as a collection that you can iterate over, etc., as in our examples. It also automatically assigns unique integer IDs to each value.

Case classes (see "Case Classes" on page 136) are often used instead of enumerations in Scala because the "use case" for them often involves pattern matching. We'll revisit this topic in "Enumerations Versus Pattern Matching" on page 300.

Recap and What's Next

We've covered a lot of ground in this chapter. We learned how flexible Scala's syntax can be, and how it facilitates the creation of Domain-Specific Languages. Then we explored Scala's enhancements to looping constructs and conditional expressions. We experimented with different uses for pattern matching, a powerful improvement on the familiar `case-switch` statement. Finally, we learned how to encapsulate values in enumerations.

You should now be prepared to read a fair bit of Scala code, but there's plenty more about the language to put in your tool belt. In the next four chapters, we'll explore Scala's approach to object-oriented programming, starting with *traits*.

CHAPTER 4

Traits

Introducing Traits

Before we dive into object-oriented programming, there's one more essential feature of Scala that you should get acquainted with: *traits*. Understanding the value of this feature requires a little backstory.

In Java, a class can implement an arbitrary number of *interfaces*. This model is very useful for declaring that a class exposes multiple abstractions. Unfortunately, it has one major drawback.

For many interfaces, much of the functionality can be implemented with boilerplate code that will be valid for all classes that use the interface. Java provides no built-in mechanism for defining and using such reusable code. Instead, Java programmers must use ad hoc conventions to reuse implementation code for a given interface. In the worst case, the developer just copies and pastes the same code into every class that needs it.

Often, the implementation of an interface has members that are unrelated ("orthogonal") to the rest of the instance's members. The term *mixin* is often used for such focused and potentially reusable parts of an instance that could be independently maintained.

Have a look at the following code for a button in a graphical user interface, which uses callbacks for "clicks":

```
// code-examples/Traits/ui/button-callbacks.scala

package ui

class ButtonWithCallbacks(val label: String,
    val clickedCallbacks: List[() => Unit]) extends Widget {

  require(clickedCallbacks != null, "Callback list can't be null!")

  def this(label: String, clickedCallback: () => Unit) =
    this(label, List(clickedCallback))

  def this(label: String) = {
```

```
    this(label, Nil)
    println("Warning: button has no click callbacks!")
  }

  def click() = {
    // ... logic to give the appearance of clicking a physical button ...
    clickedCallbacks.foreach(f => f())
  }
}
```

There's a lot going on here. The primary constructor takes a `label` argument and a list of `callbacks` that are invoked when the button's `click` method is invoked. We'll explore this class in greater detail in Chapter 5. For now, we want to focus on one particular problem. Not only does `ButtonWithCallbacks` handle behaviors essential to buttons (like clicking), it also handles notification of click events by invoking the callback functions. This goes against the *Single Responsibility Principle* (see [Martin2003]), a means to the design goal of *separation of concerns*. We would like to separate the button-specific logic from the callback logic, such that each logical component becomes simpler, more modular, and more reusable. The callback logic is a good example of a *mixin*.

This separation is difficult to do in Java, even if we define an interface for the callback behavior. We still have to embed the implementation code in the class somehow, compromising modularity. The only other alternative is to use a specialized tool like *aspect-oriented programming* (AOP; see [AOSD]), as implemented by AspectJ (see [AspectJ]), an extension of Java. AOP is primarily designed to separate the implementations of "pervasive" concerns that are repeated throughout an application. It seeks to modularize these concerns, yet enable the fine-grained "mixing" of their behaviors with other concerns, including the core domain logic of the application, either at build or runtime.

Traits As Mixins

Scala provides a complete mixin solution, called *traits*. In our example, we can define the callback *abstraction* in a trait, as in a Java interface, but we can also implement the abstraction in the trait (or a derived trait). We can declare classes that "mix in" the trait, much the way you can declare classes that implement an interface in Java. However, in Scala we can even mix in traits at the same time we create instances. That is, we don't have to declare a class first that mixes in all the traits we want. So, Scala traits preserve separation of concerns while giving us the ability to compose behavior on demand.

If you come from a Java background, you can think of traits as interfaces with optional implementations. Or, if you prefer, you can think of traits as a "constrained" form of multiple inheritance. Other languages provide constructs that are similar to traits, such as *modules* in Ruby, for example.

Let's use a trait to separate the callback handling from the button logic. We'll generalize our approach a little bit. Callbacks are really a special case of the *Observer Pattern* (see

[GOF1995]). So, let's create a trait that implements this pattern, and then use it to handle callback behavior. To simplify things, we'll start with a single callback that counts the number of button clicks.

First, let's define a simple `Button` class:

```
// code-examples/Traits/ui/button.scala

package ui

class Button(val label: String) extends Widget {
  def click() = {
    // Logic to give the appearance of clicking a button...
  }
}
```

Here is the parent class, `Widget`:

```
// code-examples/Traits/ui/widget.scala

package ui

abstract class Widget
```

The logic for managing callbacks (i.e., the `clickedCallbacks` list) is omitted, as are the two auxiliary constructors. Only the button's `label` field and `click` method remain. The `click` method now only cares about the visual appearance of a "physical" button being clicked. `Button` has only one concern, handling the "essence" of being a button.

Here is a trait that implements the logic of the *Observer Pattern*:

```
// code-examples/Traits/observer/observer.scala

package observer

trait Subject {
  type Observer = { def receiveUpdate(subject: Any) }

  private var observers = List[Observer]()
  def addObserver(observer:Observer) = observers ::= observer
  def notifyObservers = observers foreach (_.receiveUpdate(this))
}
```

Except for the `trait` keyword, `Subject` looks like a normal class. `Subject` defines all the members it declares. Traits can declare *abstract* members, *concrete* members, or both, just as classes can (see "Overriding Members of Classes and Traits" on page 111 for more details). Also like classes, traits can contain nested trait and class definitions, and classes can contain nested trait definitions.

The first line defines a `type` for an `Observer`. This is a *structural type* of the form `{ def receiveUpdate(subject:Any) }`. Structural types specify only the structure a type must support; you could think of them as "anonymous" types.

In this case, the structural type is defined by a method with a particular signature. Any type that has a method with this signature can be used as an observer. We'll learn more about structural types in Chapter 12. If you're wondering why we didn't use Subject as the type of the argument, instead of Any, we'll revisit that issue in "Self-Type Annotations and Abstract Type Members" on page 317.

The main thing to notice for now is how this structural type minimizes the coupling between the Subject trait and any potential users of the trait.

 Subject is still coupled by the name of the method in Observer through the structural type, i.e., to a method named receiveUpdate. There are several ways we can reduce this remaining coupling. We'll see how in "Overriding Abstract Types" on page 120.

Next, we declare a list of observers. We make it a var, rather than a val, because List is immutable, so we must create a new list when an observer is added using the addObserver method.

We'll discuss Scala Lists more in "The Scala Type Hierarchy" on page 155 and also in Chapter 8. For now, notice that addObserver uses the list cons "operator" method (::) to *prepend* an observer to the list of observers. The scala compiler is smart enough to turn the following statement:

```
observers ::= observer
```

into this statement:

```
observers = observer :: observers
```

Note that we wrote observer :: observers, with the existing observers list on the *right*hand side. Recall that any method that ends with : binds to the *right*. So, the previous statement is equivalent to the following statement:

```
observers = observers.::(observer)
```

The notifyObservers method iterates through the observers, using the foreach method and calls receiveUpdate on each one. (Note that we are using the "infix" operator notation instead of observers.foreach.) We use the placeholder _ to shorten the following expression:

```
(obs) => obs.receiveUpdate(this)
```

into this expression:

```
_.receiveUpdate(this)
```

This expression is actually the body of an "anonymous function," called a *function literal* in Scala. This is similar to a *lambda* and like constructs used in many other languages. Function literals and the related concept of a *closure* are discussed in "Function Literals and Closures" on page 169.

In Java, the foreach method would probably take an interface, and you would pass an instance of a class that implements the interface (e.g., the way Comparable is typically used).

In Scala, the List[A].foreach method expects an argument of type (A) => Unit, which is a function taking an instance of type A—where A represents the type of the elements of the list (Observer, in this case)—and returning Unit (like void in Java).

We chose to use a var with immutable Lists for the observers in this example. We could have used a val with a mutable type, like ListBuffer. That choice would make a little more sense for a real application, but we wanted to avoid the distraction of explaining new library classes.

Once again, we learned a lot of Scala from a small example. Now let's put our Subject trait to use. Here is ObservableButton, which subclasses Button and mixes in Subject:

```
// code-examples/Traits/ui/observable-button.scala

package ui
import observer._

class ObservableButton(name: String) extends Button(name) with Subject {
  override def click() = {
    super.click()
    notifyObservers
  }
}
```

We start by importing everything in the observer package, using the _ wildcard. Actually, we have only defined the Subject trait in the package.

The new class uses the with keyword to add the Subject trait to the class. Observable Button overrides the click method. Using the super keyword (see "Overriding Abstract and Concrete Methods" on page 112), it first invokes the "superclass" method, Button.click, and then it notifies the observers. Since the new click method overrides Button's concrete implementation, the override keyword is required.

The with keyword is analogous to Java's implements keyword for interfaces. You can specify as many traits as you want, each with its own with keyword.

A class can extend a trait, and a trait can extend a class. In fact, our Widget class earlier could have been declared to be a trait.

If you declare a class that uses one or more traits and it *doesn't* extend another class, you must use the extends keyword for the first trait listed.

If you don't use **extends** for the first trait, e.g., you write the following:

```
// ERROR:
class ObservableButton(name: String) with Button(name) with Subject {...}
```

You'll get an error like this:

```
... error: ';' expected but 'with' found.
       class ObservableButton(name: String) with Button(name) with Subject {...}
                                              ^
```

The error should really say, "**with** found, but **extends** expected."

To demonstrate this code, let's start with a class for observing button clicks that simply counts the number of clicks:

```
// code-examples/Traits/ui/button-count-observer.scala

package ui
import observer._

class ButtonCountObserver {
  var count = 0
  def receiveUpdate(subject: Any) = count += 1
}
```

Finally, let's write a test that exercises all these classes. We will use the Specs library (discussed in "Specs" on page 363) to write a *Behavior-Driven Development* ([BDD]) "specification" that exercises the combined **Button** and **Subject** types:

```
// code-examples/Traits/ui/button-observer-spec.scala

package ui
import org.specs._
import observer._

object ButtonObserverSpec extends Specification {
  "A Button Observer" should {
    "observe button clicks" in {
      val observableButton = new ObservableButton("Okay")
      val buttonObserver = new ButtonCountObserver
      observableButton.addObserver(buttonObserver)

      for (i <- 1 to 3) observableButton.click()
      buttonObserver.count mustEqual 3
    }
  }
}
```

If you downloaded the code examples from the O'Reilly site, you can follow the directions in its *README* files for building and running the examples in this chapter. The output of the **specs** "target" of the build should include the following text:

```
Specification "ButtonCountObserverSpec"
  A Button Observer should
  + observe button clicks
```

```
Total for specification "ButtonCountObserverSpec":
Finished in 0 second, 10 ms
1 example, 1 expectation, 0 failure, 0 error
```

Notice that the strings `A Button Observer should` and `observe button clicks` correspond to strings in the example. The output of a *Specs* run provides a nice summary of the requirements for the items being tested, assuming good choices were made for the strings.

The body of the test creates an "Okay" `ObservableButton` and a `ButtonCountObserver`, which gives the observer to the button. The button is clicked three times, using the `for` loop. The last line requires the observer's `count` to equal 3. If you are accustomed to using an *XUnit*-style TDD tool, like `JUnit` (see [JUnit]) or `ScalaTest` (see [ScalaTest-Tool] and "ScalaTest" on page 361), then the last line is equivalent to the following `JUnit` assertion:

```
assertEquals(3, buttonObserver.count)
```

 The Specs library (see "Specs" on page 363) and the ScalaTest library (see "ScalaTest" on page 361) both support *Behavior-Driven Development* ([BDD]), a style of *Test-Driven Development* ([TDD]) that emphasizes the "specification" role of tests.

Suppose we need only one `ObservableButton` instance? We actually don't have to declare a class that subclasses `Button` with `Subject`. We can incorporate the trait when we create the instance.

The next example shows a revised Specs file that instantiates a `Button` with `Subject` mixed in as part of the declaration:

```
// code-examples/Traits/ui/button-observer-anon-spec.scala

package ui
import org.specs._
import observer._

object ButtonObserverAnonSpec extends Specification {
  "A Button Observer" should {
    "observe button clicks" in {
      val observableButton = new Button("Okay") with Subject {
        override def click() = {
          super.click()
          notifyObservers
        }
      }

      val buttonObserver = new ButtonCountObserver
      observableButton.addObserver(buttonObserver)

      for (i <- 1 to 3) observableButton.click()
      buttonObserver.count mustEqual 3
```

```
      }
    }
  }
```

The revised declaration of observableButton actually creates an anonymous class in which we override the click method, as before. The main difference with creating anonymous classes in Java is that we can incorporate traits in this process. Java does not let you implement a new interface while instantiating a class.

Finally, note that the inheritance hierarchy for an instance can be complex if it mixes in traits that extend other traits, etc. We'll discuss the details of the hierarchy in "Linearization of an Object's Hierarchy" on page 159.

Stackable Traits

There are a couple of refinements we can do to improve the reusability of our work and to make it easier to use more than one trait at a time, i.e., to "stack" them.

First, let's introduce a new trait, Clickable, an abstraction for any widget that responds to clicks:

```
// code-examples/Traits/ui2/clickable.scala

package ui2

trait Clickable {
  def click()
}
```

 We're starting with a new package, ui2, to make it easier to keep older and newer versions of the examples distinct in the downloadable code.

The Clickable trait looks just like a Java interface; it is completely abstract. It defines a single, abstract method, click. The method is abstract because it has no body. If Clickable were a class, we would have to add the abstract keyword in front of the class keyword. This is not necessary for traits.

Here is the refactored button, which uses the trait:

```
// code-examples/Traits/ui2/button.scala

package ui2

import ui.Widget

class Button(val label: String) extends Widget with Clickable {
  def click() = {
    // Logic to give the appearance of clicking a button...
```

```
    }
}
```

This code is like Java code that implements a `Clickable` interface.

When we previously defined `ObservableButton` (in "Traits As Mixins" on page 76), we overrode `Button.click` to notify the observers. We had to duplicate that logic in `ButtonObserverAnonSpec` when we declared `observableButton` as a `Button` instance that mixed in the `Subject` trait directly. Let's eliminate this duplication.

When we refactor the code this way, we realize that we don't really care about observing buttons; we care about observing clicks. Here is a trait that focuses solely on observing `Clickable`:

```
// code-examples/Traits/ui2/observable-clicks.scala

package ui2
import observer._

trait ObservableClicks extends Clickable with Subject {
  abstract override def click() = {
    super.click()
    notifyObservers
  }
}
```

The `ObservableClicks` trait extends `Clickable` and mixes in `Subject`. It then overrides the `click` method with an implementation that looks almost the same as the overridden method shown in "Traits As Mixins" on page 76. The important difference is the `abstract` keyword.

Look closely at this method. It calls `super.click()`, but what is `super` in this case? At this point, it could only appear to be `Clickable`, which *declares* but does not *define* the `click` method, or it could be `Subject`, which doesn't have a `click` method. So, `super` can't be bound, at least not yet.

In fact, `super` will be bound when this trait is mixed into an instance that defines a concrete `click` method, such as `Button`. Therefore, we need an `abstract` keyword on `ObservableClicks.click` to tell the compiler (and the reader) that `click` is not yet fully implemented, even though `ObservableClicks.click` has a body.

 Except for declaring abstract classes, the `abstract` keyword is only required on a method in a trait when the method has a body, but it calls the `super` method that doesn't have a concrete implementation in parents of the trait.

Let's use this trait with `Button` and its concrete `click` method in a *Specs* test:

```
// code-examples/Traits/ui2/button-clickable-observer-spec.scala

package ui2
```

```
import org.specs._
import observer._
import ui.ButtonCountObserver

object ButtonClickableObserverSpec extends Specification {
  "A Button Observer" should {
    "observe button clicks" in {
      val observableButton = new Button("Okay") with ObservableClicks
      val buttonClickCountObserver = new ButtonCountObserver
      observableButton.addObserver(buttonClickCountObserver)

      for (i <- 1 to 3) observableButton.click()
      buttonClickCountObserver.count mustEqual 3
    }
  }
}
```

Compare this code to `ButtonObserverAnonSpec`. We instantiate a `Button` with the `ObservableClicks` trait mixed in, but now there is no override of `click` required. Hence, this client of `Button` doesn't have to worry about properly overriding `click`. The hard work is already done by `ObservableClicks`. The desired behavior is *composed declaratively* when needed.

Let's finish our example by adding a second trait. The JavaBeans specification (see [JavaBeansSpec]) has the idea of "vetoable" events, where listeners for changes to a JavaBean can veto the change. Let's implement something similar with a trait that vetoes more than a set number of clicks:

```
// code-examples/Traits/ui2/vetoable-clicks.scala

package ui2
import observer._

trait VetoableClicks extends Clickable {
  val maxAllowed = 1  // default
  private var count = 0

  abstract override def click() = {
    if (count < maxAllowed) {
      count += 1
      super.click()
    }
  }
}
```

Once again, we override the `click` method. As before, the override must be declared `abstract`. The maximum allowed number of clicks defaults to 1. You might wonder what we mean by "defaults" here. Isn't the field declared to be a `val`? There is no constructor defined to initialize it to another value. We'll revisit these questions in "Overriding Members of Classes and Traits" on page 111.

This trait also declares a `count` variable to keep track of the number of clicks seen. It is declared `private`, so it is invisible outside the trait (see "Visibility

Rules" on page 96). The overridden `click` method increments `count`. It only calls the `super.click()` method if the count is less than or equal to the `maxAllowed` count.

Here is a Specs object that demonstrates `ObservableClicks` and `VetoableClicks` working together. Note that a separate `with` keyword is required for each trait, as opposed to using one keyword and separating the names with commas, as Java does for `implements` clauses:

```
// code-examples/Traits/ui2/button-clickable-observer-vetoable-spec.scala

package ui2
import org.specs._
import observer._
import ui.ButtonCountObserver

object ButtonClickableObserverVetoableSpec extends Specification {
  "A Button Observer with Vetoable Clicks" should {
    "observe only the first button click" in {
      val observableButton =
          new Button("Okay") with ObservableClicks with VetoableClicks
      val buttonClickCountObserver = new ButtonCountObserver
      observableButton.addObserver(buttonClickCountObserver)

      for (i <- 1 to 3) observableButton.click()
      buttonClickCountObserver.count mustEqual 1
    }
  }
}
```

The expected observer count is 1. The `observableButton` is declared as follows:

```
new Button("Okay") with ObservableClicks with VetoableClicks
```

We can infer that the `click` override in `VetoableClicks` is called *before* the `click` override in `ObservableClicks`. Loosely speaking, since our anonymous class doesn't define `click` itself, the method lookup proceeds *right to left*, as declared. It's actually more complicated than that, as we'll see later in "Linearization of an Object's Hierarchy" on page 159.

In the meantime, what happens if we use the traits in the reverse order?

```
// code-examples/Traits/ui2/button-vetoable-clickable-observer-spec.scala

package ui2
import org.specs._
import observer._
import ui.ButtonCountObserver

object ButtonVetoableClickableObserverSpec extends Specification {
  "A Vetoable Button with Click Observer" should {
    "observe all the button clicks, even when some are vetoed" in {
      val observableButton =
          new Button("Okay") with VetoableClicks with ObservableClicks
      val buttonClickCountObserver = new ButtonCountObserver
      observableButton.addObserver(buttonClickCountObserver)
```

```
      for (i <- 1 to 3) observableButton.click()
      buttonClickCountObserver.count mustEqual 3
    }
  }
}
```

Now the expected observer count is 3. `ObservableClicks` now has precedence over `VetoableClicks`, so the count of clicks is incremented, even when some clicks are subsequently vetoed!

So, the order of declaration matters, which is important to remember for preventing unexpected behavior when traits impact each other. Perhaps another lesson to note is that splitting objects into too many fine-grained traits can obscure the order of execution in your code!

Breaking up your application into small, focused traits is a powerful way to create reusable, scalable abstractions and "components." Complex behaviors can be built up through *declarative composition* of traits. We will explore this idea in greater detail in "Scalable Abstractions" on page 313.

Constructing Traits

Traits don't support auxiliary constructors, nor do they accept an argument list for the primary constructor, the body of a trait. Traits can extend classes or other traits. However, they can't pass arguments to the parent class constructor (even literal values), so traits can only extend classes that have a no-argument primary or auxiliary constructor.

However, like classes, the body of a trait is executed every time an instance is created that uses the trait, as demonstrated by the following script:

```
// code-examples/Traits/trait-construction-script.scala

trait T1 {
  println( "  in T1: x = " + x )
  val x=1
  println( "  in T1: x = " + x )
}
trait T2 {
  println( "  in T2: y = " + y )
  val y="T2"
  println( "  in T2: y = " + y )
}

class Base12 {
  println( "  in Base12: b = " + b )
  val b="Base12"
  println( "  in Base12: b = " + b )
}
class C12 extends Base12 with T1 with T2 {
  println( "  in C12: c = " + c )
  val c="C12"
```

```
      println( "  in C12: c = " + c )
    }
    println( "Creating C12:" )
    new C12
    println( "After Creating C12" )
```

Running this script with the scala command yields the following output:

```
Creating C12:
  in Base12: b = null
  in Base12: b = Base12
  in T1: x = 0
  in T1: x = 1
  in T2: y = null
  in T2: y = T2
  in C12: c = null
  in C12: c = C12
After Creating C12
```

Notice the order of invocation of the class and trait constructors. Since the declaration of C12 is extends Base12 with T1 with T2, the order of construction for this simple class hierarchy is left to right, starting with the base class Base12, followed by the traits T1 and T2, and ending with the C12 constructor body. (For constructing arbitrarily complex hierarchies, see "Linearization of an Object's Hierarchy" on page 159.)

So, while you can't pass construction parameters to traits, you can initialize fields with default values or leave them abstract. We actually saw this before in our Subject trait, where the Subject.observers field was initialized to an empty list.

If a concrete field in a trait does not have a suitable default value, there is no "fail-safe" way to initialize the value. All the alternative approaches require some ad hoc steps by users of the trait, which is error-prone because they might do it wrong or forget to do it all. Perhaps the field should be left abstract, so that classes or other traits that use this trait are forced to define the value appropriately. We'll discuss overriding abstract and concrete members in detail in Chapter 6.

Another solution is to move that field to a separate class, where the construction process can guarantee that the correct initialization data is supplied by the user. It might be that the whole trait should actually be a class instead, so you can define a constructor for it that initializes the field.

Class or Trait?

When considering whether a "concept" should be a trait or a class, keep in mind that traits as mixins make the most sense for "adjunct" behavior. If you find that a particular trait is used most often as a parent of other classes, so that the child classes *behave as* the parent trait, then consider defining the trait as a class instead, to make this logical relationship more clear. (We said *behaves as*, rather than *is a*, because the former is the more precise definition of inheritance, based on the *Liskov Substitution Principle*—see [Martin2003], for example.)

Avoid concrete fields in traits that can't be initialized to suitable default values. Use abstract fields instead, or convert the trait to a class with a constructor. Of course, stateless traits don't have any issues with initialization.

It's a general principle of good object-oriented design that an instance should always be in a known valid state, starting from the moment the construction process finishes.

Recap and What's Next

In this chapter, we learned how to use traits to encapsulate and share cross-cutting concerns between classes. We covered when and how to use traits, how to "stack" multiple traits, and the rules for initializing values within traits.

In the next chapter, we explore how the fundamentals of object-oriented programming work in Scala. Even if you're an old hand at object-oriented programming, you'll want to read the next several chapters to understand the particulars of Scala's approach to OOP.

CHAPTER 5

Basic Object-Oriented Programming in Scala

Scala is an object-oriented language like Java, Python, Ruby, Smalltalk, and others. If you're coming from the Java world, you'll notice some notable improvements over the limitations of Java's object model.

We assume you have some prior experience with object-oriented programming (OOP), so we will not discuss the basic principles here, although some common terms and concepts are discussed in the Glossary on page 393. See [Meyer1997] for a detailed introduction to OOP; see [Martin2003] for a recent treatment of OOP principles in the context of "agile software development"; see [GOF1995] to learn about *design patterns*; and see [WirfsBrock2003] for a discussion of object-oriented design concepts.

Class and Object Basics

Let's review the terminology of OOP in Scala.

 We saw previously that Scala has the concept of a declared `object`, which we'll dig into in "Classes and Objects: Where Are the Statics?" on page 148. We'll use the term *instance* to refer to a class instance generically, meaning either an `object` or an instance of a `class`, to avoid the potential for confusion between these two concepts.

Classes are declared with the keyword `class`. We will see later that additional keywords can also be used, like `final` to prevent creation of *derived* classes and `abstract` to indicate that the class can't be instantiated, usually because it contains or inherits member declarations without providing concrete definitions for them.

An instance can refer to itself using the `this` keyword, just as in Java and similar languages.

Following Scala's convention, we use the term *method* for a function that is tied to an instance. Some other object-oriented languages use the term "member function." Method definitions start with the def keyword.

Like Java, but unlike Ruby and Python, Scala allows *overloaded methods*. Two or more methods can have the same name as long as their full *signatures* are unique. The *signature* includes the type name, the list of parameters with types, and the method's return value.

There is an exception to this rule due to *type erasure*, which is a feature of the JVM only, but is used by Scala on both the JVM and .NET platforms, to minimize incompatibilities. Suppose two methods are identical except that one takes a parameter of type List[String] while the other takes a parameter of type List[Int], as follows:

```
// code-examples/BasicOOP/type-erasure-wont-compile.scala
// WON'T COMPILE

object Foo {
  def bar(list: List[String]) = list.toString
  def bar(list: List[Int]) = list.size.toString
}
```

You'll get a compilation error on the second method because the two methods will have an identical signature after type erasure.

The scala interpreter will let you type in both methods. It simply drops the first version. However, if you try to load the previous example using the :load file command, you'll get the same error scalac raises.

We'll discuss type erasure in more detail in Chapter 12.

Also by convention, we use the term *field* for a variable that is tied to an instance. The term *attribute* is often used in other languages (like Ruby). Note that the state of an instance is the union of all the values currently represented by the instance's fields.

As we discussed in "Variable Declarations" on page 24, read-only ("value") fields are declared using the val keyword, and read-write fields are declared using the var keyword.

Scala also allows types to be declared in classes, as we saw in "Abstract Types And Parameterized Types" on page 47.

We use the term *member* to refer to a field, method, or type in a generic way. Note that field and method members (but not type members) share the same *namespace*, unlike Java. We'll discuss this more in "When Accessor Methods and Fields Are Indistinguishable: The Uniform Access Principle" on page 123.

Finally, new instances of *reference types* are created from a class using the new keyword, as in languages like Java and C#. Note that you can drop the parentheses when using a *default* constructor (i.e., one that takes no arguments). In some cases, literal values can be used instead, e.g., `val name = "Programming Scala"` is equivalent to `val name = new String("Programming Scala")`.

Instances of *value types* (`Int`, `Double`, etc.), which correspond to the primitives in languages like Java, are always created using literal values, e.g., `1`, `3.14`. In fact, there are no public constructors for these types, so an expression like `val i = new Int(1)` won't compile.

We'll discuss the difference between reference and value types in "The Scala Type Hierarchy" on page 155.

Parent Classes

Scala supports single inheritance, not multiple inheritance. A child (or derived) class can have one and only one parent (or base) class. The sole exception is the root of the Scala class hierarchy, `Any`, which has no parent.

We've seen several examples of parent and child classes. Here are snippets of one of the first we saw, in "Abstract Types And Parameterized Types" on page 47:

```
// code-examples/TypeLessDoMore/abstract-types-script.scala

import java.io._

abstract class BulkReader {
  // ...
}

class StringBulkReader(val source: String) extends BulkReader {
  // ...
}

class FileBulkReader(val source: File) extends BulkReader {
  // ...
}
```

As in Java, the keyword `extends` indicates the parent class, in this case `BulkReader`. In Scala, `extends` is also used when a class inherits a trait as its parent (even when it mixes in other traits using the `with` keyword). Also, `extends` is used when one trait is the child of another trait or class. Yes, traits can inherit classes.

If you don't `extend` a parent class, the default parent is `AnyRef`, a direct child class of `Any`. (We discuss the difference between `Any` and `AnyRef` when we discuss the Scala type hierarchy in "The Scala Type Hierarchy" on page 155.)

Constructors in Scala

Scala distinguishes between a *primary constructor* and zero or more *auxiliary constructors*. In Scala, the primary constructor is the entire body of the class. Any parameters that the constructor requires are listed after the class name. We've seen many examples of this already, as in the `ButtonWithCallbacks` example we used in Chapter 4:

```scala
// code-examples/Traits/ui/button-callbacks.scala

package ui

class ButtonWithCallbacks(val label: String,
    val clickedCallbacks: List[() => Unit]) extends Widget {

  require(clickedCallbacks != null, "Callback list can't be null!")

  def this(label: String, clickedCallback: () => Unit) =
    this(label, List(clickedCallback))

  def this(label: String) = {
    this(label, Nil)
    println("Warning: button has no click callbacks!")
  }

  def click() = {
    // ... logic to give the appearance of clicking a physical button ...
    clickedCallbacks.foreach(f => f())
  }
}
```

The `ButtonWithCallbacks` class represents a button on a graphical user interface. It has a label and a list of callback functions that are invoked if the button is clicked. Each callback function takes no arguments and returns `Unit`. The `click` method iterates through the list of callbacks and invokes each one.

`ButtonWithCallbacks` defines three constructors. The primary constructor, which is the body of the entire class, has a parameter list that takes a label string and a list of callback functions. Because each parameter is declared as a `val`, the compiler generates a private field corresponding to each parameter (a different internal name is used), along with a public reader method that has the same name as the parameter. "Private" and "public" have the same meaning here as in most object-oriented languages. We'll discuss the various visibility rules and the keywords that control them in "Visibility Rules" on page 96.

If a parameter has the `var` keyword, a public writer method is also generated with the parameter's name as a prefix, followed by _=. For example, if `label` were declared as a `var`, the writer method would be named `label_=` and it would take a single argument of type `String`.

There are times when you don't want the accessor methods to be generated automatically. In other words, you want the field to be *private*. Add the `private` keyword before the `val` or `var` keyword, and the accessor methods won't be generated. (See "Visibility Rules" on page 96 for more details.)

For you Java programmers, Scala doesn't follow the JavaBeans [Java-BeansSpec] convention that field reader and writer methods begin with get and set, respectively, followed by the field name with the first character capitalized. We'll see why when we discuss the *Uniform Access Principle* in "When Accessor Methods and Fields Are Indistinguishable: The Uniform Access Principle" on page 123. However, you can get JavaBeans-style *getters* and *setters* when you need them using the scala.reflect.BeanProperty annotation, as we'll discuss in "JavaBean Properties" on page 374.

When an instance of the class is created, each field corresponding to a parameter in the parameter list will be initialized with the parameter automatically. No constructor logic is required to initialize these fields, in contrast to most other object-oriented languages.

The first statement in the ButtonWithCallbacks class (i.e., the constructor) body is a test to ensure that a non-null list has been passed to the constructor. (It does allow an empty Nil list, however.) It uses the convenient require function that is imported automatically into the current scope (as we'll discuss in "The Predef Object" on page 145). If the list is null, require will throw an exception. The require function and its companion assume are very useful for *Design by Contract* programming, as discussed in "Better Design with Design By Contract" on page 340.

Here is part of a full specification for ButtonWithCallbacks that demonstrates the require statement in use:

```
// code-examples/Traits/ui/button-callbacks-spec.scala
package ui
import org.specs._

object ButtonWithCallbacksSpec extends Specification {
  "A ButtonWithCallbacks" should {
    // ...
    "not be constructable with a null callback list" in {
      val nullList:List[() => Unit] = null
      val errorMessage =
        "requirement failed: Callback list can't be null!"
      (new ButtonWithCallbacks("button1", nullList)) must throwA(
        new IllegalArgumentException(errorMessage))
    }
  }
}
```

Scala even makes it difficult to pass null as the second parameter to the constructor; it won't type check when you compile it. However, you can assign null to a value, as shown. If we didn't have the must throwA(...) clause, we would see the following exception thrown:

```
java.lang.IllegalArgumentException: requirement failed: Callback list can't be null!
        at scala.Predef$.require(Predef.scala:112)
        at ui.ButtonWithCallbacks.<init>(button-callbacks.scala:7)
    ...
```

`ButtonWithCallbacks` defines two auxiliary constructors for the user's convenience. The first auxiliary constructor accepts a label and a single callback. It calls the primary constructor, passing the label and a new `List` to wrap the single callback.

The second auxiliary constructor accepts just a label. It calls the primary constructor with `Nil` (which represents an empty `List` object). The constructor then prints a warning message that there are no callbacks, since lists are immutable and there is no way to replace the callback list `val` with a new one.

To avoid infinite recursion, Scala requires each auxiliary constructor to invoke another constructor defined before it (see [ScalaSpec2009]). The constructor invoked may be either another auxiliary constructor or the primary constructor, and it must be the first statement in the auxiliary constructor's body. Additional processing can occur after this call, such as the warning message printed in our example.

 Because all auxiliary constructors eventually invoke the primary constructor, logic checks and other initializations done in the body will be performed consistently for all instances created.

There are a few advantages of Scala's constraints on constructors:

Elimination of duplication
Because auxiliary constructors invoke the primary constructor, potential duplication of construction logic is largely eliminated.

Code size reduction
As shown in the examples, when one or more of the primary constructor parameters is declared as a `val` or a `var`, Scala automatically generates a field, the appropriate accessor methods (unless they are declared **private**), and the initialization logic for when instances are created.

There is also at least one disadvantage of Scala's constraints on constructors:

Less flexibility
Sometimes it's just not convenient to have one constructor body that all constructors are forced to use. However, we find these circumstances to be rare. In such cases, it may simply be that the class has too many responsibilities and it should be refactored into smaller classes.

Calling Parent Class Constructors

The primary constructor in a derived class must invoke one of the parent class constructors, either the primary constructor or an auxiliary constructor. In the following example, a class derived from `ButtonWithCallbacks`, called `RadioButtonWithCallbacks`, invokes the primary `ButtonWithCallbacks` constructor. "Radio" buttons can be either on or off:

```
// code-examples/BasicOOP/ui/radio-button-callbacks.scala

package ui

/**
 * Button with two states, on or off, like an old-style,
 * channel-selection button on a radio.
 */
class RadioButtonWithCallbacks(
  var on: Boolean, label: String, clickedCallbacks: List[() => Unit])
      extends ButtonWithCallbacks(label, clickedCallbacks) {

  def this(on: Boolean, label: String, clickedCallback: () => Unit) =
      this(on, label, List(clickedCallback))

  def this(on: Boolean, label: String) = this(on, label, Nil)
}
```

The primary constructor for RadioButtonWithCallbacks takes three parameters: an **on** state (**true** or **false**), a label, and a list of callbacks. It passes the label and list of callbacks to its parent class, ButtonWithCallbacks. The **on** parameter is declared as a **var**, so it is mutable. on is also the one constructor parameter unique to a radio button, so it is kept as an attribute of RadioButtonWithCallbacks.

For consistency with its parent class, RadioButtonWithCallbacks also declares two auxiliary constructors. Note that they must invoke a preceding constructor in RadioButton WithCallbacks, as before. They can't invoke a ButtonWithCallbacks constructor directly. Declaring all these constructors in each class could get tedious after a while, but we explored techniques in Chapter 4 that can eliminate repetition.

 While **super** is used to invoke overridden methods, as in Java, it cannot be used to invoke a super class constructor.

Nested Classes

Scala lets you nest class declarations, like many object-oriented languages. Suppose we want all Widgets to have a map of properties. These properties could be size, color, whether or not the widget is visible, etc. We might use a simple map to hold the properties, but let's assume that we also want to control access to the properties, and to perform other operations when they change.

Here is one way we might expand our original Widget example from "Traits As Mixins" on page 76 to add this feature:

```
// code-examples/BasicOOP/ui/widget.scala

package ui
```

```
abstract class Widget {
  class Properties {
    import scala.collection.immutable.HashMap

    private var values: Map[String, Any] = new HashMap

    def size = values.size

    def get(key: String) = values.get(key)

    def update(key: String, value: Any) = {
      // Do some preprocessing, e.g., filtering.
      values = values.update(key, value)
      // Do some postprocessing.
    }
  }

  val properties = new Properties
}
```

We added a **Properties** class that has a private, mutable reference to an immutable **HashMap**. We also added three public methods that retrieve the size (i.e., the number of properties defined), retrieve a single element in the map, and update the map with a new element, respectively. We might need to do additional work in the **update** method, and we've indicated as much with comments.

 You can see from the previous example that Scala allows classes to be declared inside one another, or "nested." A nested class make sense when you have enough related functionality to lump together in a class, but the functionality is only ever going to be used by its "outer" class.

So far, we've covered how to declare classes, how to instantiate them, and some of the basics of inheritance. In the next section, we'll discuss visibility rules within classes and objects.

Visibility Rules

 For convenience, we'll use the word "type" in this section to refer to classes and traits generically, as opposed to referring to member **type** declarations. We'll include those when we use the term "member" generically, unless otherwise indicated.

Most object-oriented languages have constructs to constrain the visibility (or scope) of type and type-member declarations. These constructs support the object-oriented form of encapsulation, where only the essential public abstraction of a class or trait is exposed and implementation information is hidden from view.

You'll want to use public visibility for anything that users of your classes and objects should see and use. Keep in mind that the set of publicly visible members form the abstraction exposed by the type, along with the type's name itself.

The conventional wisdom in object-oriented design is that fields should be private or protected. If access is required, it should happen through methods, but not everything should be accessible by default. The virtue of the *Uniform Access Principle* (see "When Accessor Methods and Fields Are Indistinguishable: The Uniform Access Principle" on page 123) is that we can give the user the semantics of public field access via either a method or direct access to a field, whichever is appropriate for the task.

> The art of good object-oriented design includes defining minimal, clear, and cohesive public abstractions.

There are two kinds of "users" of a type: derived types, and code that works with instances of the type. Derived types usually need more access to the members of their parent types than users of instances do.

Scala's visibility rules are similar to Java's, but tend to be both more consistently applied and more flexible. For example, in Java, if an inner class has a `private` member, the enclosing class can see it. In Scala, the enclosing class can't see a `private` member, but Scala provides another way to declare it visible to the enclosing class.

As in Java and C#, the keywords that modify visibility, such as `private` and `protected`, appear at the beginning of declarations. You'll find them before the `class` or `trait` keywords for types, before the `val` or `var` for fields, and before the `def` for methods.

> You can also use an access modifier keyword on the primary constructor of a class. Put it after the type name and type parameters, if any, and before the argument list, as in this example: `class Restricted[+A] private (name: String) {...}`

Table 5-1 summarizes the visibility scopes.

Table 5-1. Visibility scopes

Name	Keyword	Description
public	*none*	Public members and types are visible everywhere, across all boundaries.
protected	protected	Protected members are visible to the defining type, to derived types, and to nested types. Protected types are visible only within the same package and subpackages.

Name	Keyword	Description
private	`private`	Private members are visible only within the defining type and nested types. Private types are visible only within the same package.
scoped protected	`protected[scope]`	Visibility is limited to `scope`, which can be a package, type, or `this` (meaning the same instance, when applied to members, or the enclosing package, when applied to types). See the text below for details.
scoped private	`private[scope]`	Synonymous with scoped protected visibility, except under inheritance (discussed below).

Let's explore these visibility options in more detail. To keep things simple, we'll use fields for member examples. Method and type declarations behave the same way.

 Unfortunately, you can't apply any of the visibility modifiers to packages. Therefore, a package is always public, even when it contains no publicly visible types.

Public Visibility

Any declaration without a visibility keyword is "public," meaning it is visible everywhere. There is no **public** keyword in Scala. This is in contrast to Java, which defaults to public visibility only within the enclosing package (i.e., "package private"). Other object-oriented languages, like Ruby, also default to public visibility:

```scala
// code-examples/BasicOOP/scoping/public.scala

package scopeA {
  class PublicClass1 {
    val publicField = 1

    class Nested {
      val nestedField = 1
    }

    val nested = new Nested
  }

  class PublicClass2 extends PublicClass1 {
    val field2  = publicField + 1
    val nField2 = new Nested().nestedField
  }
}

package scopeB {
  class PublicClass1B extends scopeA.PublicClass1

  class UsingClass(val publicClass: scopeA.PublicClass1) {
    def method = "UsingClass:" +
      " field: " + publicClass.publicField +
```

```
          " nested field: " + publicClass.nested.nestedField
    }
  }
```

You can compile this file with scalac. It should compile without error.

Everything is public in these packages and classes. Note that scopeB.UsingClass can access scopeA.PublicClass1 and its members, including the instance of Nested and its public field.

Protected Visibility

Protected visibility is for the benefit of implementers of derived types, who need a little more access to the details of their parent types. Any member declared with the protected keyword is visible only to the defining type, including other instances of the same type and any derived types. When applied to a type, protected limits visibility to the enclosing package.

Java, in contrast, makes protected members visible throughout the enclosing package. Scala handles this case with scoped private and protected access:

```
// code-examples/BasicOOP/scoping/protected-wont-compile.scala
// WON'T COMPILE

package scopeA {
  class ProtectedClass1(protected val protectedField1: Int) {
    protected val protectedField2 = 1

    def equalFields(other: ProtectedClass1) =
      (protectedField1 == other.protectedField1) &&
      (protectedField1 == other.protectedField1) &&
      (nested == other.nested)

    class Nested {
      protected val nestedField = 1
    }

    protected val nested = new Nested
  }

  class ProtectedClass2 extends ProtectedClass1(1) {
    val field1 = protectedField1
    val field2 = protectedField2
    val nField = new Nested().nestedField  // ERROR
  }

  class ProtectedClass3 {
    val protectedClass1 = new ProtectedClass1(1)
    val protectedField1 = protectedClass1.protectedField1 // ERROR
    val protectedField2 = protectedClass1.protectedField2 // ERROR
    val protectedNField = protectedClass1.nested.nestedField // ERROR
  }
```

```
    protected class ProtectedClass4

    class ProtectedClass5 extends ProtectedClass4
    protected class ProtectedClass6 extends ProtectedClass4
  }

  package scopeB {
    class ProtectedClass4B extends scopeA.ProtectedClass4 // ERROR
  }
```

When you compile this file with **scalac**, you get the following output. (The file names before the N: line numbers have been removed from the output to better fit the space.)

```
16: error: value nestedField cannot be accessed in ProtectedClass2.this.Nested
        val nField = new Nested().nestedField
                                  ^
20: error: value protectedField1 cannot be accessed in scopeA.ProtectedClass1
        val protectedField1 = protectedClass1.protectedField1
                                              ^
21: error: value protectedField2 cannot be accessed in scopeA.ProtectedClass1
        val protectedField2 = protectedClass1.protectedField2
                                              ^
22: error: value nested cannot be accessed in scopeA.ProtectedClass1
        val protectedNField = protectedClass1.nested.nestedField
                                              ^
32: error: class ProtectedClass4 cannot be accessed in package scopeA
      class ProtectedClass4B extends scopeA.ProtectedClass4
                                            ^
5 errors found
```

The // ERROR comments in the listing mark the lines that fail to parse.

ProtectedClass2 can access protected members of ProtectedClass1, since it derives from it. However, it can't access the protected nestedField in protectedClass1.nested. Also, ProtectedClass3 can't access protected members of the ProtectedClass1 instance it uses.

Finally, because ProtectedClass4 is declared **protected**, it is not visible in the scopeB package.

Private Visibility

Private visibility completely hides implementation details, even from the implementers of derived classes. Any member declared with the **private** keyword is visible only to the defining type, including other instances of the same type. When applied to a type, **private** limits visibility to the enclosing package:

```
// code-examples/BasicOOP/scoping/private-wont-compile.scala
// WON'T COMPILE

package scopeA {
  class PrivateClass1(private val privateField1: Int) {
    private val privateField2 = 1
```

```
    def equalFields(other: PrivateClass1) =
      (privateField1 == other.privateField1) &&
      (privateField2 == other.privateField2) &&
      (nested == other.nested)

    class Nested {
      private val nestedField = 1
    }

    private val nested = new Nested
  }

  class PrivateClass2 extends PrivateClass1(1) {
    val field1 = privateField1  // ERROR
    val field2 = privateField2  // ERROR
    val nField = new Nested().nestedField // ERROR
  }

  class PrivateClass3 {
    val privateClass1 = new PrivateClass1(1)
    val privateField1 = privateClass1.privateField1 // ERROR
    val privateField2 = privateClass1.privateField2 // ERROR
    val privateNField = privateClass1.nested.nestedField // ERROR
  }

  private class PrivateClass4

  class PrivateClass5 extends PrivateClass4  // ERROR
  protected class PrivateClass6 extends PrivateClass4 // ERROR
  private class PrivateClass7 extends PrivateClass4
}

package scopeB {
  class PrivateClass4B extends scopeA.PrivateClass4  // ERROR
}
```

Compiling this file yields the following output:

```
14: error: not found: value privateField1
      val field1 = privateField1
                   ^
15: error: not found: value privateField2
      val field2 = privateField2
                   ^
16: error: value nestedField cannot be accessed in PrivateClass2.this.Nested
      val nField = new Nested().nestedField
                               ^
20: error: value privateField1 cannot be accessed in scopeA.PrivateClass1
      val privateField1 = privateClass1.privateField1
                                       ^
21: error: value privateField2 cannot be accessed in scopeA.PrivateClass1
      val privateField2 = privateClass1.privateField2
                                       ^
22: error: value nested cannot be accessed in scopeA.PrivateClass1
      val privateNField = privateClass1.nested.nestedField
                                       ^
```

```
27: error: private class PrivateClass4 escapes its defining scope as part
of type scopeA.PrivateClass4
    class PrivateClass5 extends PrivateClass4
                                ^
28: error: private class PrivateClass4 escapes its defining scope as part
of type scopeA.PrivateClass4
    protected class PrivateClass6 extends PrivateClass4
                                          ^
33: error: class PrivateClass4 cannot be accessed in package scopeA
    class PrivateClass4B extends scopeA.PrivateClass4
                                        ^

9 errors found
```

Now, `PrivateClass2` can't access private members of its parent class `PrivateClass1`. They are completely invisible to the subclass, as indicated by the error messages. Nor can it access a private field in a `Nested` class.

Just as for the case of `protected` access, `PrivateClass3` can't access private members of the `PrivateClass1` instance it is using. Note, however, that the `equalFields` method can access private members of the `other` instance.

The declarations of `PrivateClass5` and `PrivateClass6` fail because, if allowed, they would enable `PrivateClass4` to "escape its defining scope." However, the declaration of `PrivateClass7` succeeds because it is also declared to be private. Curiously, our previous example was able to declare a public class that subclassed a protected class without a similar error.

Finally, just as for `protected` type declarations, the `private` types can't be subclassed outside the same package.

Scoped Private and Protected Visibility

Scala allows you to fine-tune the scope of visibility with the scoped **private** and **protected** visibility declarations. Note that using **private** or **protected** in a scoped declaration is interchangeable, as they behave identically, except under inheritance when applied to members.

 While either choice behaves the same in most scenarios, it is more common to see **private[X]** rather than **protected[X]** used in code. In the core libraries included with Scala, the ratio is roughly five to one.

Let's begin by considering the only differences in behavior between scoped private and scoped protected—how they behave under inheritance when members have these scopes:

```
// code-examples/BasicOOP/scoping/scope-inheritance-wont-compile.scala
// WON'T COMPILE

package scopeA {
```

```
class Class1 {
  private[scopeA]   val scopeA_privateField = 1
  protected[scopeA] val scopeA_protectedField = 2
  private[Class1]   val class1_privateField = 3
  protected[Class1] val class1_protectedField = 4
  private[this]     val this_privateField = 5
  protected[this]   val this_protectedField = 6
}

class Class2 extends Class1 {
  val field1 = scopeA_privateField
  val field2 = scopeA_protectedField
  val field3 = class1_privateField        // ERROR
  val field4 = class1_protectedField
  val field5 = this_privateField          // ERROR
  val field6 = this_protectedField
}
}

package scopeB {
  class Class2B extends scopeA.Class1 {
    val field1 = scopeA_privateField      // ERROR
    val field2 = scopeA_protectedField
    val field3 = class1_privateField      // ERROR
    val field4 = class1_protectedField
    val field5 = this_privateField        // ERROR
    val field6 = this_protectedField
  }
}
```

Compiling this file yields the following output:

```
17: error: not found: value class1_privateField
    val field3 = class1_privateField    // ERROR
                 ^
19: error: not found: value this_privateField
    val field5 = this_privateField      // ERROR
                 ^
26: error: not found: value scopeA_privateField
    val field1 = scopeA_privateField    // ERROR
                 ^
28: error: not found: value class1_privateField
    val field3 = class1_privateField    // ERROR
                 ^
30: error: not found: value this_privateField
    val field5 = this_privateField      // ERROR
                 ^
5 errors found
```

The first two errors, inside Class2, show us that a derived class inside the same package can't reference a member that is scoped private to the parent class or this, but it can reference a private member scoped to the package (or type) that encloses both Class1 and Class2.

In contrast, for a derived class outside the same package, it has no access to any of the scoped private members of Class1.

However, all the scoped protected members are visible in both derived classes.

We'll use scoped private declarations for the rest of our examples and discussion, since use of scoped private is a little more common in the Scala library than scoped protected, when the previous inheritance scenarios aren't a factor.

First, let's start with the most restrictive visibility, private[this], as it affects type members:

```scala
// code-examples/BasicOOP/scoping/private-this-wont-compile.scala
// WON'T COMPILE

package scopeA {
  class PrivateClass1(private[this] val privateField1: Int) {
    private[this] val privateField2 = 1

    def equalFields(other: PrivateClass1) =
      (privateField1 == other.privateField1) && // ERROR
      (privateField2 == other.privateField2) &&
      (nested == other.nested)

    class Nested {
      private[this] val nestedField = 1
    }

    private[this] val nested = new Nested
  }

  class PrivateClass2 extends PrivateClass1(1) {
    val field1 = privateField1  // ERROR
    val field2 = privateField2  // ERROR
    val nField = new Nested().nestedField  // ERROR
  }

  class PrivateClass3 {
    val privateClass1 = new PrivateClass1(1)
    val privateField1 = privateClass1.privateField1  // ERROR
    val privateField2 = privateClass1.privateField2  // ERROR
    val privateNField = privateClass1.nested.nestedField // ERROR
  }
}
```

Compiling this file yields the following output:

```
5: error: value privateField1 is not a member of scopeA.PrivateClass1
        (privateField1 == other.privateField1) &&
                                ^
14: error: not found: value privateField1
       val field1 = privateField1
                    ^
15: error: not found: value privateField2
       val field2 = privateField2
                    ^
```

```
16: error: value nestedField is not a member of PrivateClass2.this.Nested
        val nField = new Nested().nestedField
                                  ^
20: error: value privateField1 is not a member of scopeA.PrivateClass1
        val privateField1 = privateClass1.privateField1
                                          ^
21: error: value privateField2 is not a member of scopeA.PrivateClass1
        val privateField2 = privateClass1.privateField2
                                          ^
22: error: value nested is not a member of scopeA.PrivateClass1
        val privateNField = privateClass1.nested.nestedField
                                          ^
7 errors found
```

 Lines 6–8 also won't parse. Since they are part of the expression that started on line 5, the compiler stopped after the first error.

The private[this] members are only visible to the same instance. An instance of the same class can't see private[this] members of another instance, so the equalFields method won't parse.

Otherwise, the visibility of class members is the same as **private** without a scope specifier.

When declaring a type with private[this], use of this effectively binds to the enclosing package, as shown here:

```scala
// code-examples/BasicOOP/scoping/private-this-pkg-wont-compile.scala
// WON'T COMPILE

package scopeA {
  private[this] class PrivateClass1

  package scopeA2 {
    private[this] class PrivateClass2
  }

  class PrivateClass3 extends PrivateClass1  // ERROR
  protected class PrivateClass4 extends PrivateClass1 // ERROR
  private class PrivateClass5 extends PrivateClass1
  private[this] class PrivateClass6 extends PrivateClass1

  private[this] class PrivateClass7 extends scopeA2.PrivateClass2 // ERROR
}

package scopeB {
  class PrivateClass1B extends scopeA.PrivateClass1 // ERROR
}
```

Compiling this file yields the following output:

```
8: error: private class PrivateClass1 escapes its defining scope as part
of type scopeA.PrivateClass1
    class PrivateClass3 extends PrivateClass1
                                ^
9: error: private class PrivateClass1 escapes its defining scope as part
of type scopeA.PrivateClass1
    protected class PrivateClass4 extends PrivateClass1
                                          ^
13: error: type PrivateClass2 is not a member of package scopeA.scopeA2
    private[this] class PrivateClass7 extends scopeA2.PrivateClass2
                                                      ^
17: error: type PrivateClass1 is not a member of package scopeA
    class PrivateClass1B extends scopeA.PrivateClass1
                                       ^
four errors found
```

In the same package, attempting to declare a **public** or **protected** subclass fails. Only **private** and **private[this]** subclasses are allowed. Also, **PrivateClass2** is scoped to **scopeA2**, so you can't declare it outside **scopeA2**. Similarly, an attempt to declare a class in unrelated **scopeB** using **PrivateClass1** also fails.

Hence, when applied to types, **private[this]** is equivalent to Java's **package private** visibility.

Next, let's examine type-level visibility, **private[T]**, where **T** is a type:

```
// code-examples/BasicOOP/scoping/private-type-wont-compile.scala
// WON'T COMPILE

package scopeA {
  class PrivateClass1(private[PrivateClass1] val privateField1: Int) {
    private[PrivateClass1] val privateField2 = 1

    def equalFields(other: PrivateClass1) =
      (privateField1 == other.privateField1) &&
      (privateField2 == other.privateField2) &&
      (nested     == other.nested)

    class Nested {
      private[Nested] val nestedField = 1
    }

    private[PrivateClass1] val nested = new Nested
    val nestedNested = nested.nestedField   // ERROR
  }

  class PrivateClass2 extends PrivateClass1(1) {
    val field1 = privateField1 // ERROR
    val field2 = privateField2 // ERROR
    val nField = new Nested().nestedField  // ERROR
  }

  class PrivateClass3 {
    val privateClass1 = new PrivateClass1(1)
    val privateField1 = privateClass1.privateField1  // ERROR
```

```
      val privateField2 = privateClass1.privateField2  // ERROR
      val privateNField = privateClass1.nested.nestedField // ERROR
  }
}
```

Compiling this file yields the following output:

```
12: error: value nestedField cannot be accessed in PrivateClass1.this.Nested
        val nestedNested = nested.nestedField
                                  ^
15: error: not found: value privateField1
        val field1 = privateField1
                     ^
16: error: not found: value privateField2
        val field2 = privateField2
                     ^
17: error: value nestedField cannot be accessed in PrivateClass2.this.Nested
        val nField = new Nested().nestedField
                                  ^
21: error: value privateField1 cannot be accessed in scopeA.PrivateClass1
        val privateField1 = privateClass1.privateField1
                                          ^
22: error: value privateField2 cannot be accessed in scopeA.PrivateClass1
        val privateField2 = privateClass1.privateField2
                                          ^
23: error: value nested cannot be accessed in scopeA.PrivateClass1
        val privateNField = privateClass1.nested.nestedField
                                          ^
7 errors found
```

A private[PrivateClass1] member is visible to other instances, so the equalFields
method now parses. Hence, private[T] is not as restrictive as private[this]. Note
that PrivateClass1 can't see Nested.nestedField because that field is declared
private[Nested].

 When members of T are declared private[T] the behavior is equivalent
to private. It is not equivalent to private[this], which is more
restrictive.

What if we change the scope of Nested.nestedField to be private[PrivateClass1]? Let's
see how private[T] affects nested types:

```
// code-examples/BasicOOP/scoping/private-type-nested-wont-compile.scala
// WON'T COMPILE

package scopeA {
  class PrivateClass1 {
    class Nested {
      private[PrivateClass1] val nestedField = 1
    }

    private[PrivateClass1] val nested = new Nested
    val nestedNested = nested.nestedField
```

```
    }

    class PrivateClass2 extends PrivateClass1 {
      val nField = new Nested().nestedField    // ERROR
    }

    class PrivateClass3 {
      val privateClass1 = new PrivateClass1
      val privateNField = privateClass1.nested.nestedField // ERROR
    }
  }
```

Compiling this file yields the following output:

```
10: error: value nestedField cannot be accessed in PrivateClass2.this.Nested
        def nField = new Nested().nestedField
                                  ^
14: error: value nested cannot be accessed in scopeA.PrivateClass1
        val privateNField = privateClass1.nested.nestedField
                                          ^

two errors found
```

Now `nestedField` is visible to `PrivateClass1`, but it is still invisible outside of `Private`
`Class1`. This is how `private` works in Java.

Let's examine scoping using a package name:

```
// code-examples/BasicOOP/scoping/private-pkg-type-wont-compile.scala
// WON'T COMPILE

package scopeA {
  private[scopeA] class PrivateClass1

  package scopeA2 {
    private [scopeA2] class PrivateClass2
    private [scopeA]  class PrivateClass3
  }

  class PrivateClass4 extends PrivateClass1
  protected class PrivateClass5 extends PrivateClass1
  private class PrivateClass6 extends PrivateClass1
  private[this] class PrivateClass7 extends PrivateClass1

  private[this] class PrivateClass8 extends scopeA2.PrivateClass2 // ERROR
  private[this] class PrivateClass9 extends scopeA2.PrivateClass3
}

package scopeB {
  class PrivateClass1B extends scopeA.PrivateClass1 // ERROR
}
```

Compiling this file yields the following output:

```
14: error: class PrivateClass2 cannot be accessed in package scopeA.scopeA2
      private[this] class PrivateClass8 extends scopeA2.PrivateClass2
                                                        ^
19: error: class PrivateClass1 cannot be accessed in package scopeA
```

```
  class PrivateClass1B extends scopeA.PrivateClass1
                                      ^
two errors found
```

Note that PrivateClass2 can't be subclassed outside of scopeA2, but PrivateClass3 can be subclassed in scopeA, because it is declared private[scopeA].

Finally, let's look at the effect of package-level scoping of type members:

```
// code-examples/BasicOOP/scoping/private-pkg-wont-compile.scala
// WON'T COMPILE

package scopeA {
  class PrivateClass1 {
    private[scopeA] val privateField = 1

    class Nested {
      private[scopeA] val nestedField = 1
    }

    private[scopeA] val nested = new Nested
  }

  class PrivateClass2 extends PrivateClass1 {
    val field  = privateField
    val nField = new Nested().nestedField
  }

  class PrivateClass3 {
    val privateClass1 = new PrivateClass1
    val privateField  = privateClass1.privateField
    val privateNField = privateClass1.nested.nestedField
  }

  package scopeA2 {
    class PrivateClass4 {
      private[scopeA2] val field1 = 1
      private[scopeA]  val field2 = 2
    }
  }

  class PrivateClass5 {
    val privateClass4 = new scopeA2.PrivateClass4
    val field1 = privateClass4.field1  // ERROR
    val field2 = privateClass4.field2
  }
}

package scopeB {
  class PrivateClass1B extends scopeA.PrivateClass1 {
    val field1 = privateField   // ERROR
    val privateClass1 = new scopeA.PrivateClass1
    val field2 = privateClass1.privateField  // ERROR
  }
}
```

Compiling this file yields the following output:

```
28: error: value field1 cannot be accessed in scopeA.scopeA2.PrivateClass4
        val field1 = privateClass4.field1
                                   ^
35: error: not found: value privateField
        val field1 = privateField
                     ^
37: error: value privateField cannot be accessed in scopeA.PrivateClass1
        val field2 = privateClass1.privateField
                                   ^

three errors found
```

The only errors are when we attempt to access members scoped to scopeA from the unrelated package scopeB and when we attempt to access a member from a nested package scopeA2 that is scoped to that package.

When a type or member is declared private[P], where P is the enclosing package, then it is equivalent to Java's package private visibility.

Final Thoughts on Visibility

Scala visibility declarations are very flexible, and they behave consistently. They provide fine-grained control over visibility at all possible scopes, from the instance level (private[this]) up to package-level visibility (private[P], for a package P). For example, they make it easier to create "components" with types exposed outside of the component's top-level package, while hiding implementation types and type members within the "component's" packages.

Finally, we have observed a potential "gotcha" with hidden members of traits.

Be careful when choosing the names of members of traits. If two traits have a member of the same name and the traits are used in the same instance, a name collision will occur even if both members are private.

Fortunately, the compiler catches this problem.

Recap and What's Next

We introduced the basics of Scala's object model, including constructors, inheritance, nesting of classes, and rules for visibility.

In the next chapter we'll explore Scala's more advanced OOP features, including overriding, companion objects, case classes, and rules for equality between objects.

CHAPTER 6

Advanced Object-Oriented Programming In Scala

We've got the basics of OOP in Scala under our belt, but there's plenty more to learn.

Overriding Members of Classes and Traits

Classes and traits can declare *abstract* members: *fields*, *methods*, and *types*. These members must be defined by a derived class or trait before an instance can be created. Most object-oriented languages support abstract methods, and some also support abstract fields and types.

 When overriding a concrete member, Scala requires the `override` keyword. It is optional when a subtype defines ("overrides") an abstract member. Conversely, don't use `override` unless you are actually overriding a member.

Requiring the `override` keyword has several benefits:

- It catches misspelled members that were intended to be overrides. The compiler will throw an error that the member doesn't override anything.

- It catches a potentially subtle bug that can occur if a new member is added to a base class where the member's name collides with an older derived class member that is unknown to the base class developer. That is, the derived-class member was never intended to override a base-class member. Because the derived class member won't have the `override` keyword, the compiler will throw an error when the new base-class member is introduced.

- Having to add the keyword reminds you to consider what members should or should not be overridden.

Java has an optional @Override annotation for methods. It helps catch errors of the first type (misspellings), but it can't help with errors of the second type, since using the annotation is optional.

Attempting to Override final Declarations

However, if a declaration includes the final keyword, then overriding the declaration is prohibited. In the following example, the fixedMethod is declared final in the parent class. Attempting to compile the example will result in a compilation error:

```
// code-examples/AdvOOP/overrides/final-member-wont-compile.scala
// WON'T COMPILE.

class NotFixed {
  final def fixedMethod = "fixed"
}

class Changeable2 extends NotFixed {
  override def fixedMethod = "not fixed"    // ERROR
}
```

This constraint applies to classes and traits as well as members. In this example, the class Fixed is declared final, so an attempt to derive a new type from it will also fail to compile:

```
// code-examples/AdvOOP/overrides/final-class-wont-compile.scala
// WON'T COMPILE.

final class Fixed {
  def doSomething = "Fixed did something!"
}

class Changeable1 extends Fixed      // ERROR
```

 Some of the types in the Scala library are final, including JDK classes like String and all the "value" types derived from AnyVal (see "The Scala Type Hierarchy" on page 155).

For declarations that aren't final, let's examine the rules and behaviors for overriding, starting with methods.

Overriding Abstract and Concrete Methods

Let's extend our familiar Widget base class with an abstract method draw, to support "rendering" the widget to a display, web page, etc. We'll also override a concrete method familiar to any Java programmer, toString(), using an ad hoc format. As before, we will use a new package, ui3.

Drawing is actually a *cross-cutting concern*. The state of a `Widget` is one thing; how it is rendered on different platforms, thick clients, web pages, mobile devices, etc., is a separate issue. So, drawing is a very good candidate for a trait, especially if you want your GUI abstractions to be portable. However, to keep things simple, we will handle drawing in the `Widget` hierarchy itself.

Here is the revised `Widget` class, with `draw` and `toString` methods:

```
// code-examples/AdvOOP/ui3/widget.scala

package ui3

abstract class Widget {
  def draw(): Unit
  override def toString() = "(widget)"
}
```

The `draw` method is abstract because it has no body; that is, the method isn't followed by an equals sign (=), nor any text after it. Therefore, `Widget` has to be declared `abstract` (it was optional before). Each concrete subclass of `Widget` will have to implement `draw` or rely on a parent class that implements it. We don't need to return anything from `draw`, so its return value is `Unit`.

The `toString()` method is straightforward. Since `AnyRef` defines `toString`, the `override` keyword is required for `Widget.toString`.

Here is the revised `Button` class, with `draw` and `toString` methods:

```
// code-examples/AdvOOP/ui3/button.scala

package ui3

class Button(val label: String) extends Widget with Clickable {

  def click() = {
    // Logic to give the appearance of clicking a button...
  }

  def draw() = {
    // Logic to draw the button on the display, web page, etc.
  }

  override def toString() =
    "(button: label=" + label + ", " + super.toString() + ")"
}
```

`Button` implements the abstract method `draw`. No `override` keyword is required. `Button` also overrides `toString`, so the `override` keyword is required. Note that `super.toString` is called.

The super keyword is analogous to this, but it binds to the parent type, which is the aggregation of the parent class and any mixed-in traits. The search for super.toString will find the "closest" parent type toString, as determined by the linearization process (see "Linearization of an Object's Hierarchy" on page 159). In this case, since Clickable doesn't define toString, Widget.toString will be called.

Overriding a concrete method should be done rarely, because it is error-prone. Should you invoke the parent method? If so, when? Do you call it before doing anything else, or afterward? While the writer of the parent method might document the overriding constraints for the method, it's difficult to ensure that the writer of a derived class will honor those constraints. A much more robust approach is the *Template Method Pattern* (see [GOF1995]).

Overriding Abstract and Concrete Fields

Most object-oriented languages allow you to override mutable fields (var). Fewer OO languages allow you to define abstract fields or override concrete immutable fields (val). For example, it's common for a base class constructor to initialize a mutable field and for a derived class constructor to change its value.

We'll discuss overriding fields in traits and classes separately, as traits have some particular issues.

Overriding Abstract and Concrete Fields in Traits

Recall our VetoableClicks trait in "Stackable Traits" on page 82. It defines a val named maxAllowed and initializes it to 1. We would like the ability to override the value in a class that mixes in this trait.

Unfortunately, in Scala version 2.7.X, it is not possible to override a val defined in a *trait*. However it is possible to override a val defined in a parent *class*. Version 2.8 of Scala does support overriding a val in a trait.

Because the override behavior for a val in a trait is changing, you should avoid relying on the ability to override it, if you are currently using Scala version 2.7.X. Use another approach instead.

Unfortunately, the version 2.7 compiler accepts code that attempts to override a trait-defined val, but the override does not actually happen, as illustrated by this example:

```
// code-examples/AdvOOP/overrides/trait-val-script.scala
// DANGER! Silent failure to override a trait's "name" (V2.7.5 only).
// Works as expected in V2.8.0.
```

```
trait T1 {
  val name = "T1"
}

class Base

class ClassWithT1 extends Base with T1 {
  override val name = "ClassWithT1"
}

val c = new ClassWithT1()
println(c.name)

class ClassExtendsT1 extends T1 {
  override val name = "ClassExtendsT1"
}

val c2 = new ClassExtendsT1()
println(c2.name)
```

If you run this script with scala version 2.7.5, the output is the following:

```
T1
T1
```

Reading the script, we would have expected the two T1 strings to be ClassWithT1 and ClassExtendsT1, respectively.

However, if you run this script with scala version 2.8.0, you get this output:

```
ClassWithT1
ClassExtendsT1
```

 Attempts to override a trait-defined val will be accepted by the compiler, but have no effect in Scala version 2.7.X.

There are three workarounds you can use with Scala version 2.7. The first is to use some advanced options for scala and scalac. The -Xfuture option will enable the override behavior supported in version 2.8. The -Xcheckinit option will analyze your code and report whether the behavior change will break it. The option -Xexperimental, which enables many experimental changes, will also warn you that the val override behavior is different.

The second workaround is to make the val abstract in the trait. This forces an instance using the trait to assign a value. Declaring a val in a trait abstract is a perfectly useful design approach for both versions of Scala. In fact, this will be the best design choice, when there is no appropriate default value to assign to the val in the trait:

```
// code-examples/AdvOOP/overrides/trait-abs-val-script.scala

trait AbstractT1 {
  val name: String
```

```
}

class Base

class ClassWithAbstractT1 extends Base with AbstractT1 {
  val name = "ClassWithAbstractT1"
}

val c = new ClassWithAbstractT1()
println(c.name)

class ClassExtendsAbstractT1 extends AbstractT1 {
  val name = "ClassExtendsAbstractT1"
}

val c2 = new ClassExtendsAbstractT1()
println(c2.name)
```

This script produces the output that we would expect:

```
ClassWithAbstractT1
ClassExtendsAbstractT1
```

So, an abstract **val** works fine, *unless* the field is used in the trait body in a way that will fail until the field is properly initialized. Unfortunately, the proper initialization won't occur until after the trait's body has executed. Consider the following example:

```
// code-examples/AdvOOP/overrides/trait-invalid-init-val-script.scala
// ERROR: "value" read before initialized.

trait AbstractT2 {
  println("In AbstractT2:")
  val value: Int
  val inverse = 1.0/value      // ???
  println("AbstractT2: value = "+value+", inverse = "+inverse)
}

val c2b = new AbstractT2 {
  println("In c2b:")
  val value = 10
}
println("c2b.value = "+c2b.value+", inverse = "+c2b.inverse)
```

While it appears that we are creating an instance of the trait with **new AbstractT2 ...**, we are actually using an anonymous class that implicitly extends the trait. This script shows what happens when **inverse** is calculated:

```
In AbstractT2:
AbstractT2: value = 0, inverse = Infinity
In c2b:
c2b.value = 10, inverse = Infinity
```

As you might expect, the **inverse** is calculated too early. Note that a divide by zero exception isn't thrown; the compiler recognizes the value is infinite, but it hasn't actually "tried" the division yet!

The behavior of this script is actually quite subtle. As an exercise, try selectively removing (or commenting out) the different println statements, one at a time. Observe what happens to the results. Sometimes inverse is initialized properly! (Hint: remove the println("In c2b:") statement. Then try putting it back, but after the val value = 10 line.)

What this experiment really shows is that side effects (i.e., from the println statements) can be unexpected and subtle, especially during initialization. It's best to avoid them.

Scala provides two solutions to this problem: *lazy values*, which we discuss in "Lazy Vals" on page 190, and *pre-initialized fields*, which is demonstrated in the following refinement to the previous example:

```
// code-examples/AdvOOP/overrides/trait-pre-init-val-script.scala

trait AbstractT2 {
  println("In AbstractT2:")
  val value: Int
  val inverse = 1.0/value
  println("AbstractT2: value = "+value+", inverse = "+inverse)
}

val c2c = new {
  // Only initializations are allowed in pre-init. blocks.
  // println("In c2c:")
  val value = 10
} with AbstractT2

println("c2c.value = "+c2c.value+", inverse = "+c2c.inverse)
```

We instantiate an anonymous inner class, initializing the value field in the block, before the with AbstractT2 clause. This guarantees that value is initialized before the body of AbstractT2 is executed, as shown when you run the script:

```
In AbstractT2:
AbstractT2: value = 10, inverse = 0.1
c2c.value = 10, inverse = 0.1
```

Also, if you selectively remove any of the println statements, you get the same expected and now predictable results.

Now let's consider the second workaround we described earlier, changing the declaration to var. This solution is more suitable if a good default value exists and you don't want to require instances that use the trait to always set the value. In this case, change the val to a var, either a public var or a private var hidden behind reader and writer methods. Either way, we can simply reassign the value in a derived trait or class.

Returning to our VetoableClicks example, here is the modified VetoableClicks trait that uses a public var for maxAllowed:

```
// code-examples/AdvOOP/ui3/vetoable-clicks.scala

package ui3
import observer._

trait VetoableClicks extends Clickable {
  var maxAllowed = 1        // default
  private var count = 0
  abstract override def click() = {
    count += 1
    if (count <= maxAllowed)
      super.click()
  }
}
```

Here is a new specs object, `ButtonClickableObserverVetoableSpec2`, that demonstrates changing the value of `maxAllowed`:

```
// code-examples/AdvOOP/ui3/button-clickable-observer-vetoable2-spec.scala
package ui3

import org.specs._
import observer._
import ui.ButtonCountObserver

object ButtonClickableObserverVetoableSpec2 extends Specification {
  "A Button Observer with Vetoable Clicks" should {
    "observe only the first 'maxAllowed' clicks" in {
      val observableButton =
        new Button("Okay") with ObservableClicks with VetoableClicks {
          maxAllowed = 2
        }
      observableButton.maxAllowed mustEqual 2
      val buttonClickCountObserver = new ButtonCountObserver
      observableButton.addObserver(buttonClickCountObserver)
      for (i <- 1 to 3) observableButton.click()
      buttonClickCountObserver.count mustEqual 2
    }
  }
}
```

No `override var` is required. We just assign a new value. Since the body of the trait is executed before the body of the class using it, reassigning the field value happens *after* the initial assignment in the trait's body. However, as we saw before, that reassignment could happen too late if the field is used in the trait's body in some calculation that will become invalid by a reassignment later! You can avoid this problem if you make the field private and define a public writer method that redoes any dependent calculations.

Another disadvantage of using a `var` declaration is that `maxAllowed` was not intended to be writable. As we will see in Chapter 8, read-only values have important benefits. We would prefer for `maxAllowed` to be read-only, at least after the construction process completes.

We can see that the simple act of changing the `val` to a `var` causes potential problems for the maintainer of `VetoableClicks`. Control over that field is now lost. The maintainer must carefully consider whether or not the value will change and if a change will invalidate the state of the instance. This issue is especially pernicious in multithreaded systems (see "The Problems of Shared, Synchronized State" on page 193).

> Avoid `var` fields when possible (in classes as well as traits). Consider public `var` fields especially risky.

Overriding Abstract and Concrete Fields in Classes

In contrast to traits, overriding a `val` declared in a class works as expected. Here is an example with both a `val` override and a `var` reassignment in a derived class:

```
// code-examples/AdvOOP/overrides/class-field-script.scala

class C1 {
  val name = "C1"
  var count = 0
}

class ClassWithC1 extends C1 {
  override val name = "ClassWithC1"
  count = 1
}

val c = new ClassWithC1()
println(c.name)
println(c.count)
```

The `override` keyword is required for the *concrete* `val` field `name`, but not for the `var` field `count`. This is because we are changing the initialization of a constant (`val`), which is a "special" operation.

If you run this script, the output is the following:

```
ClassWithC1
1
```

Both fields are overridden in the derived class, as expected. Here is the same example modified so that both the `val` and the `var` are abstract in the base class:

```
// code-examples/AdvOOP/overrides/class-abs-field-script.scala

abstract class AbstractC1 {
  val name: String
  var count: Int
}

class ClassWithAbstractC1 extends AbstractC1 {
  val name = "ClassWithAbstractC1"
```

```
    var count = 1
}

val c = new ClassWithAbstractC1()
println(c.name)
println(c.count)
```

The **override** keyword is not required for **name** in **ClassWithAbstractC1**, since the original declaration is abstract. The output of this script is the following:

```
ClassWithAbstractC1
1
```

It's important to emphasize that **name** and **count** are *abstract* fields, not concrete fields with default values. A similar-looking declaration of **name** in a Java class, **String name;**, would declare a concrete field with the default value (**null** in this case). Java doesn't support abstract fields or types (as we'll discuss next), only methods.

Overriding Abstract Types

We introduced abstract type declarations in "Abstract Types And Parameterized Types" on page 47. Recall the **BulkReader** example from that section:

```
// code-examples/TypeLessDoMore/abstract-types-script.scala

import java.io._

abstract class BulkReader {
  type In
  val source: In
  def read: String
}

class StringBulkReader(val source: String) extends BulkReader {
  type In = String
  def read = source
}

class FileBulkReader(val source: File) extends BulkReader {
  type In = File
  def read = {
    val in = new BufferedInputStream(new FileInputStream(source))
    val numBytes = in.available()
    val bytes = new Array[Byte](numBytes)
    in.read(bytes, 0, numBytes)
    new String(bytes)
  }
}

println( new StringBulkReader("Hello Scala!").read )
println( new FileBulkReader(new File("abstract-types-script.scala")).read )
```

Abstract types are an alternative to parameterized types, which we'll explore in "Understanding Parameterized Types" on page 249. Like parameterized types, they provide an abstraction mechanism at the type level.

The example shows how to declare an abstract type and how to define a concrete value in derived classes. BulkReader declares type In without initializing it. The concrete derived class StringBulkReader provides a concrete value using type In = String.

Unlike fields and methods, it is not possible to override a concrete type definition. However, the abstract declaration can constrain the allowed concrete type values. We'll learn how in Chapter 12.

Finally, you probably noticed that this example also demonstrates defining an abstract field, using a constructor parameter, and an abstract method.

For another example, let's revisit our Subject trait from "Traits As Mixins" on page 76. The definition of the Observer type is a *structural type* with a method named receiveUpdate. Observers must have this "structure." Let's generalize the implementation now, using an abstract type:

```
// code-examples/AdvOOP/observer/observer2.scala

package observer

trait AbstractSubject {
  type Observer

  private var observers = List[Observer]()
  def addObserver(observer:Observer) = observers ::= observer
  def notifyObservers = observers foreach (notify(_))

  def notify(observer: Observer): Unit
}

trait SubjectForReceiveUpdateObservers extends AbstractSubject {
  type Observer = { def receiveUpdate(subject: Any) }

  def notify(observer: Observer): Unit = observer.receiveUpdate(this)
}

trait SubjectForFunctionalObservers extends AbstractSubject {
  type Observer = (AbstractSubject) => Unit

  def notify(observer: Observer): Unit = observer(this)
}
```

Now, AbstractSubject declares type Observer as abstract (implicitly, because there is no definition). Since the original structural type is gone, we don't know exactly how to notify an observer. So, we also added an abstract method notify, which a concrete class or trait will define as appropriate.

The `SubjectForReceiveUpdateObservers` derived trait defines `Observer` with the same structural type we used in the original example, and `notify` simply calls `receiveUpdate`, as before.

The `SubjectForFunctionalObservers` derived trait defines `Observer` to be a function taking an instance of `AbstractSubject` and returning `Unit`. All `notify` has to do is call the observer function, passing the subject as the sole argument. Note that this implementation is similar to the approach we used in our original button implementation, `ButtonWithCallbacks`, where the "callbacks" were user-supplied functions. (See "Introducing Traits" on page 75 and a revisited version in "Constructors in Scala" on page 91.)

Here is a specification that exercises these two variations, observing button clicks as before:

```scala
// code-examples/AdvOOP/observer/button-observer2-spec.scala

package ui
import org.specs._
import observer._

object ButtonObserver2Spec extends Specification {
  "An Observer watching a SubjectForReceiveUpdateObservers button" should {
    "observe button clicks" in {
      val observableButton =
        new Button(name) with SubjectForReceiveUpdateObservers {
          override def click() = {
            super.click()
            notifyObservers
          }
        }
      val buttonObserver = new ButtonCountObserver
      observableButton.addObserver(buttonObserver)
      for (i <- 1 to 3) observableButton.click()
      buttonObserver.count mustEqual 3
    }
  }
  "An Observer watching a SubjectForFunctionalObservers button" should {
    "observe button clicks" in {
      val observableButton =
        new Button(name) with SubjectForFunctionalObservers {
          override def click() = {
            super.click()
            notifyObservers
          }
        }
      var count = 0
      observableButton.addObserver((button) => count += 1)
      for (i <- 1 to 3) observableButton.click()
      count mustEqual 3
    }
  }
}
```

First we exercise `SubjectForReceiveUpdateObservers`, which looks very similar to our earlier examples. Next we exercise `SubjectForFunctionalObservers`. In this case, we don't need another "observer" instance at all. We just maintain a `count` variable and pass a *function literal* to `addObserver` to increment the count (and ignore the button).

The main virtue of `SubjectForFunctionalObservers` is its minimalism. It requires no special instances, no traits defining abstractions, etc. For many cases, it is an ideal approach.

`AbstractSubject` is more reusable than the original definition of `Subject`, because it imposes fewer constraints on potential observers.

 `AbstractSubject` illustrates that an abstraction with fewer concrete details is usually more reusable.

But wait, there's more! We'll revisit the use of abstract types and the Observer Pattern in "Scalable Abstractions" on page 313.

When Accessor Methods and Fields Are Indistinguishable: The Uniform Access Principle

Suppose a user of `ButtonCountObserver` from "Traits As Mixins" on page 76 accesses the `count` member:

```
// code-examples/Traits/ui/button-count-observer-script.scala

val bco = new ui.ButtonCountObserver
val oldCount = bco.count
bco.count = 5
val newCount = bco.count
println(newCount + " == 5 and " + oldCount + " == 0?")
```

When the `count` field is read or written, as in this example, are methods called or is the field accessed directly? As originally declared in `ButtonCountObserver`, the field is accessed directly. However, the user doesn't really care. In fact, the following two definitions are functionally equivalent, from the perspective of the user:

```
class ButtonCountObserver {
  var count = 0  // public field access (original definition)
  // ...
}

class ButtonCountObserver {
  private var cnt = 0 // private field
  def count = cnt       // reader method
  def count_=(newCount: Int) = cnt = newCount  // writer method
  // ...
}
```

This equivalence is an example of the *Uniform Access Principle*. Clients read and write field values as if they are publicly accessible, even though in some cases they are actually calling methods. The maintainer of `ButtonCountObserver` has the freedom to change the implementation without forcing users to make code changes.

The reader method in the second version does not have parentheses. Recall that consistency in the use of parentheses is required if a method definition omits parentheses. This is only possible if the method takes no arguments. For the Uniform Access Principle to work, we want to define field reader methods without parentheses. (Contrast that with Ruby, where method parentheses are always optional as long as the parse is unambiguous.)

The writer method has the format `count_=(...)`. As a bit of syntactic sugar, the compiler allows invocations of methods with this format to be written in either of the following ways:

```
obj.field_=(newValue)
// or
obj.field = newValue
```

We named the private variable `cnt` in the alternative definition. Scala keeps field and method names in the *same* namespace, which means we can't name the field `count` if a method is named `count`. Many languages, like Java, don't have this restriction because they keep field and method names in separate namespaces. However, these languages can't support the Uniform Access Principle as a result, unless they build in ad hoc support in their grammars or compilers.

Since member `object` definitions behave similar to fields from the caller's perspective, they are also in the same namespace as methods and fields. Hence, the following class would not compile:

```
// code-examples/AdvOOP/overrides/member-namespace-wont-compile.scala
// WON'T COMPILE

class IllegalMemberNameUse {
  def member(i: Int) = 2 * i
  val member = 2          // ERROR
  object member {         // ERROR
    def apply() = 2
  }
}
```

There is one other benefit of this namespace "unification." If a parent class declares a parameterless method, then a subclass can override that method with a `val`. If the parent's method is concrete, then the **override** keyword is required:

```
// code-examples/AdvOOP/overrides/method-field-class-script.scala

class Parent {
  def name = "Parent"
}
```

```scala
class Child extends Parent {
  override val name = "Child"
}

println(new Child().name)    // => "Child"
```

If the parent's method is abstract, then the **override** keyword is optional:

```scala
// code-examples/AdvOOP/overrides/abs-method-field-class-script.scala

abstract class AbstractParent {
  def name: String
}

class ConcreteChild extends AbstractParent {
  val name = "Child"
}

println(new ConcreteChild().name)    // => "Child"
```

This also works for traits. If the trait's method is concrete, we have the following:

```scala
// code-examples/AdvOOP/overrides/method-field-trait-script.scala

trait NameTrait {
  def name = "NameTrait"
}

class ConcreteNameClass extends NameTrait {
  override val name = "ConcreteNameClass"
}

println(new ConcreteNameClass().name)    // => "ConcreteNameClass"
```

If the trait's method is abstract, we have the following:

```scala
// code-examples/AdvOOP/overrides/abs-method-field-trait-script.scala

trait AbstractNameTrait {
  def name: String
}

class ConcreteNameClass extends AbstractNameTrait {
  val name = "ConcreteNameClass"
}

println(new ConcreteNameClass().name)    // => "ConcreteNameClass"
```

Why is this feature useful? It allows derived classes and traits to use a simple field access when that is sufficient, or a method call when more processing is required, such as lazy initialization. The same argument holds for the Uniform Access Principle, in general.

Overriding a **def** with a **val** in a subclass can also be handy when interoperating with Java code. Turn a getter into a **val** by placing it in the constructor. You'll see this in action in the following example, in which our Scala class **Person** implements a hypothetical **PersonInterface** from some legacy Java code:

```
class Person(val getName: String) extends PersonInterface
```

If you only have a few accessors in the Java code you're integrating with, this technique makes quick work of them.

What about overriding a parameterless method with a `var`, or overriding a `val` or `var` with a method? These are not permitted because they can't match the behaviors of the things they are overriding.

If you attempt to use a `var` to override a parameterless method, you get an error that the writer method, `override name_=`, is not overriding anything. This would also be inconsistent with a philosophical goal of functional programming, that a method that takes no parameters should always return the same result. To do otherwise would require side effects in the implementation, which functional programming tries to avoid, for reasons we will examine in Chapter 8. Because a `var` is changeable, the no-parameter "method" defined in the parent type would no longer return the same result consistently.

If you could override a `val` with a method, there would be no way for Scala to guarantee that the method would always return the same value, consistent with `val` semantics. That issue doesn't exist with a `var`, of course, but you would have to override the `var` with two methods, a reader and a writer. The Scala compiler doesn't support that substitution.

Companion Objects

Recall that fields and methods defined in `objects` serve the role that class "static" fields and methods serve in languages like Java. When `object`-based fields and methods are closely associated with a particular `class`, they are normally defined in a *companion object*.

We mentioned companion objects briefly in Chapter 1, and we discussed the `Pair` example from the Scala library in Chapter 2. Let's fill in the remaining details now.

First, recall that if a `class` (or a `type` referring to a class) and an `object` are declared in the same file, in the same package, and with the same name, they are called a *companion class* (or *companion type*) and a *companion object*, respectively.

There is no namespace collision when the name is reused in this way, because Scala stores the class name in the type namespace, while it stores the object name in the term namespace (see [ScalaSpec2009]).

The two most interesting methods frequently defined in a companion object are `apply` and `unapply`.

Apply

Scala provides some syntactic sugar in the form of the `apply` method. When an instance of a class is followed by parentheses with a list of zero or more parameters, the compiler invokes the `apply` method for that instance. This is true for an `object` with a defined `apply` method (such as a companion object), as well as an instance of a `class` that defines an `apply` method.

In the case of an `object`, `apply` is conventionally used as a *factory* method, returning a new instance. This is what `Pair.apply` does in the Scala library. Here is `Pair` from the standard library:

```
type Pair[+A, +B] = Tuple2[A, B]
object Pair {
  def apply[A, B](x: A, y: B) = Tuple2(x, y)
  def unapply[A, B](x: Tuple2[A, B]): Option[Tuple2[A, B]] = Some(x)
}
```

So, you can create a new `Pair` as follows:

```
val p = Pair(1, "one")
```

It looks like we are somehow creating a `Pair` instance without a `new`. Rather than calling a `Pair` constructor directly, we are actually calling `Pair.apply` (i.e., the companion object `Pair`), which then calls `Tuple2.apply` on the `Tuple2` companion object!

> If there are several alternative constructors for a class and it also has a companion object, consider defining fewer constructors on the class and defining several overloaded `apply` methods on the companion object to handle the variations.

However, `apply` is not limited to instantiating the companion class. It could instead return an instance of a subclass of the companion class. Here is an example where we define a companion object `Widget` that uses regular expressions to parse a string representing a `Widget` subclass. When a match occurs, the subclass is instantiated and the new instance is returned:

```
// code-examples/AdvOOP/objects/widget.scala

package objects

abstract class Widget {
  def draw(): Unit
  override def toString() = "(widget)"
}

object Widget {
  val ButtonExtractorRE = """\(button: label=([^,]+),\s+\(Widget\)\)""".r
  val TextFieldExtractorRE = """\(textfield: text=([^,]+),\s+\(Widget\)\)""".r

  def apply(specification: String): Option[Widget] = specification match {
```

```
    case ButtonExtractorRE(label)    => new Some(new Button(label))
    case TextFieldExtractorRE(text) => new Some(new TextField(text))
    case _ => None
  }
}
```

`Widget.apply` receives a string "specification" that defines which class to instantiate. The string might come from a configuration file with widgets to create at startup, for example. The string format is the same format used by `toString()`. Regular expressions are defined for each type. (*Parser combinators* are an alternative. They are discussed in "External DSLs with Parser Combinators" on page 230.)

The `match` expression applies each regular expression to the string. A case expression like:

```
case ButtonExtractorRE(label) => new Some(new Button(label))
```

means that the string is matched against the `ButtonExtractorRE` regular expression. If successful, it extracts the substring in the first capture group in the regular expression and assigns it to the variable `label`. Finally, a new `Button` with this label is created, wrapped in a `Some`. We'll learn how this extraction process works in the next section, "Unapply" on page 129.

A similar case handles `TextField` creation. (`TextField` is not shown. See the online code examples.) Finally, if `apply` can't match the string, it returns `None`.

Here is a `specs` object that exercises `Widget.apply`:

```
// code-examples/AdvOOP/objects/widget-apply-spec.scala

package objects
import org.specs._

object WidgetApplySpec extends Specification {
  "Widget.apply with a valid widget specification string" should {
    "return a widget instance with the correct fields set" in {
      Widget("(button: label=click me, (Widget))") match {
        case Some(w) => w match {
          case b:Button => b.label mustEqual "click me"
          case x => fail(x.toString())
        }
        case None => fail("None returned.")
      }
      Widget("(textfield: text=This is text, (Widget))") match {
        case Some(w) => w match {
          case tf:TextField => tf.text mustEqual "This is text"
          case x => fail(x.toString())
        }
        case None => fail("None returned.")
      }
    }
  }
  "Widget.apply with an invalid specification string" should {
    "return None" in {
```

```
        Widget("(button: , (Widget)") mustEqual None
      }
    }
  }
```

The first match statement implicitly invokes `Widget.apply` with the string `"(button: label=click me, (Widget))"`. If a button wrapped in a `Some` is not returned with the label `"click me"`, this test will fail. Next, a similar test for a `TextField` widget is done. The final test uses an invalid string and confirms that `None` is returned.

A drawback of this particular implementation is that we have hardcoded a dependency on each derived class of `Widget` in `Widget` itself, which breaks the *Open-Closed Principle* (see [Meyer1997] and [Martin2003]). A better implementation would use a factory design pattern from [GOF1995]. Nevertheless, the example illustrates how an `apply` method can be used as a real factory.

There is no requirement for `apply` in an `object` to be used as a factory. Neither is there any restriction on the argument list or what `apply` returns. However, because it is so common to use `apply` in an `object` as a factory, use caution when using `apply` for other purposes, as it could confuse users. However, there are good counterexamples, such as the use of `apply` in Domain-Specific Languages (see Chapter 11).

The factory convention is less commonly used for `apply` defined in classes. For example, in the Scala standard library, `Array.apply(i: int)` returns the element at index `i` in the array. Many of the other collections use `apply` in a similar way. So, users can write code like the following:

```
val a = Array(1,2,3,4)
println(a(2))  // => 3
```

Finally, as a reminder, although `apply` is handled specially by the compiler, it is otherwise no different from any other method. You can overload it, you can invoke it directly, etc.

Unapply

The name `unapply` suggests that it does the "opposite" operation of `apply`. Indeed, it is used to extract the constituent parts of an instance. Pattern matching uses this feature extensively. Hence, `unapply` is often defined in companion objects and is used to extract the field values from instances of the corresponding companion types. For this reason, `unapply` methods are called *extractors*.

Here is an expanded `button.scala` with a `Button` object that defines an `unapply` extractor method:

```
// code-examples/AdvOOP/objects/button.scala

package objects
import ui3.Clickable

class Button(val label: String) extends Widget with Clickable {
```

```
  def click() = {
    // Logic to give the appearance of clicking a button...
  }

  def draw() = {
    // Logic to draw the button on the display, web page, etc.
  }

  override def toString() = "(button: label="+label+", "+super.toString()+")"
}

object Button {
  def unapply(button: Button) = Some(button.label)
}
```

Button.unapply takes a single Button argument and returns a Some wrapping the label value. This demonstrates the protocol for unapply methods. They return a Some wrapping the extracted fields. (We'll see how to handle more than one field in a moment.)

Here is a specs object that exercises Button.unapply:

```
// code-examples/AdvOOP/objects/button-unapply-spec.scala

package objects
import org.specs._

object ButtonUnapplySpec extends Specification {
  "Button.unapply" should {
    "match a Button object" in {
      val b = new Button("click me")
      b match {
        case Button(label) =>
        case _ => fail()
      }
    }
    "match a RadioButton object" in {
      val b = new RadioButton(false, "click me")
      b match {
        case Button(label) =>
        case _ => fail()
      }
    }
    "not match a non-Button object" in {
      val tf = new TextField("hello world!")
      tf match {
        case Button(label) => fail()
        case _ =>
      }
    }
    "extract the Button's label" in {
      val b = new Button("click me")
      b match {
        case Button(label) => label mustEqual "click me"
        case _ => fail()
      }
```

```
      }
      "extract the RadioButton's label" in {
        val rb = new RadioButton(false, "click me, too")
        rb match {
          case Button(label) => label mustEqual "click me, too"
          case _ => fail()
        }
      }
    }
  }
}
```

The first three examples (in clauses) confirm that `Button.unapply` is only called for actual `Button` instances or instances of derived classes, like `RadioButton`.

Since `unapply` takes a `Button` argument (in this case), the Scala runtime type checks the instance being matched. It then looks for a companion object with an `unapply` method and invokes that method, passing the instance. The default case clause `case _` is invoked for the instances that don't type check as compatible. The pattern matching process is fully type-safe.

The remaining examples (in clauses) confirm that the correct values for the `label` are extracted. The Scala runtime automatically extracts the item in the `Some`.

What about extracting multiple fields? For a fixed set of known fields, a `Some` wrapping a `Tuple` is returned, as shown in this updated version of `RadioButton`:

```
// code-examples/AdvOOP/objects/radio-button.scala

package objects

/**
 * Button with two states, on or off, like an old-style,
 * channel-selection botton on a radio.
 */
class RadioButton(val on: Boolean, label: String) extends Button(label)

object RadioButton {
  def unapply(button: RadioButton) = Some((button.on, button.label))
                // equivalent to: = Some(Pair(button.on, button.label))
}
```

A `Some` wrapping a `Pair(button.on, button.label)` is returned. As we discuss in "The Predef Object" on page 145, `Pair` is a *type* defined to be equal to `Tuple2`. Here is the corresponding `specs` object that tests it:

```
// code-examples/AdvOOP/objects/radio-button-unapply-spec.scala

package objects
import org.specs._

object RadioButtonUnapplySpec extends Specification {
  "RadioButton.unapply" should {
    "should match a RadioButton object" in {
      val b = new RadioButton(true, "click me")
      b match {
```

```
                    case RadioButton(on, label) =>
                    case _ => fail()
                }
            }
            "not match a Button (parent class) object" in {
                val b = new Button("click me")
                b match {
                    case RadioButton(on, label) => fail()
                    case _ =>
                }
            }
            "not match a non-RadioButton object" in {
                val tf = new TextField("hello world!")
                tf match {
                    case RadioButton(on, label) => fail()
                    case _ =>
                }
            }
            "extract the RadioButton's on/off state and label" in {
                val b = new RadioButton(true, "click me")
                b match {
                    case RadioButton(on, label) => {
                        label mustEqual "click me"
                        on    mustEqual true
                    }
                    case _ => fail()
                }
            }
        }
    }
}
```

Apply and UnapplySeq for Collections

What if you want to build a collection from a variable argument list passed to `apply`?
What if you want to extract the first few elements from a collection and you don't care
about the rest of it?

In this case, you define `apply` and `unapplySeq` ("unapply sequence") methods. Here are
those methods from Scala's own `List` class:

```
def apply[A](xs: A*): List[A] = xs.toList

def unapplySeq[A](x: List[A]): Some[List[A]] = Some(x)
```

The [A] type parameterization on these methods allows the `List object`, which is not
parameterized, to construct a new `List[A]`. (See "Understanding Parameterized
Types" on page 249 for more details.) Most of the time, the type parameter will be
inferred based on the context.

The parameter list `xs: A*` is a variable argument list. Callers of `apply` can pass as many
`A` instances as they want, including none. Internally, variable argument lists are stored
in an `Array[A]`, which inherits the `toList` method from `Iterable` that we used here.

This is a handy idiom for API writers. Accepting variable arguments to a function can be convenient for users, and converting the arguments to a List is often ideal for internal management.

Here is an example script that uses List.apply implicitly:

```
// code-examples/AdvOOP/objects/list-apply-example-script.scala

val list1 = List()
val list2 = List(1, 2.2, "three", 'four)
val list3 = List("1", "2.2", "three", "four")
println("1: "+list1)
println("2: "+list2)
println("3: "+list3)
```

The 'four is a *symbol*, essentially an interned string. Symbols are more commonly used in Ruby, for example, where the same symbol would be written as :four. Symbols are useful for representing identities consistently.

This script yields the following output:

```
1: List()
2: List(1, 2.2, three, 'four)
3: List(1, 2.2, three, four)
```

The unapplySeq method is trivial; it returns the input list wrapped in a Some. However, this is sufficient for pattern matching, as shown in this example:

```
// code-examples/AdvOOP/objects/list-unapply-example-script.scala

val list = List(1, 2.2, "three", 'four)
list match {
  case List(x, y, _*) => println("x = "+x+", y = "+y)
  case _ => throw new Exception("No match! "+list)
}
```

The List(x, y, _*) syntax means we will only match on a list with at least two elements, and the first two elements will be assigned to x and y. We don't care about the rest of the list. The _* matches zero or more remaining elements.

The output is the following:

```
x = 1, y = 2.2
```

We'll have much more to say about List and pattern matching in "Lists in Functional Programming" on page 173.

Companion Objects and Java Static Methods

There is one more thing to know about companion objects. Whenever you define a main method to use as the entry point for an application, Scala requires you to put it in an object. However, at the time of this writing, main methods cannot be defined in a companion object. Because of implementation details in the generated code, the JVM won't find the main method. This issue may be resolved in a future release. For now, you must define any main method in a *singleton* object (i.e., a "non-companion" object; see [ScalaTips]). Consider the following example of a simple **Person** class and companion object that attempts to define main:

```
// code-examples/AdvOOP/objects/person.scala

package objects

class Person(val name: String, val age: Int) {
  override def toString = "name: " + name + ", age: " + age
}

object Person {
  def apply(name: String, age: Int) = new Person(name, age)
  def unapply(person: Person) = Some((person.name, person.age))

  def main(args: Array[String]) = {
    // Test the constructor...
    val person = new Person("Buck Trends", 18)
    assert(person.name == "Buck Trends")
    assert(person.age  == 21)
  }
}

object PersonTest {
  def main(args: Array[String]) = Person.main(args)
}
```

This code compiles fine, but if you attempt to invoke `Person.main`, using `scala -cp ... objects.Person`, you get the following error:

```
java.lang.NoSuchMethodException: objects.Person.main([Ljava.lang.String;)
```

The `objects/Person.class` file exists. If you decompile it with `javap -classpath ... objects.Person` (refer to "The scalap, javap, and jad Command-Line Tools" on page 350), you can see that it doesn't contain a main method. If you decompile `objects/Person$.class`, the file for the companion object's byte code, it has a main method, but notice that it isn't declared **static**. So, attempting to invoke `scala -cp ... objects.Person$` also fails to find the "static" main:

```
java.lang.NoSuchMethodException: objects.Person$.main is not static
```

The separate *singleton* object **PersonTest** defined in this example has to be used. Decompiling it with `javap -classpath ... objects.PersonTest` shows that it has a **static** main method. If you invoke it using `scala -cp ... objects.PersonTest`, the `PersonTest.main` method is invoked, which in turn invokes `Person.main`. You get an assertion error from the second call to **assert**, which is intentional:

```
java.lang.AssertionError: assertion failed
    at scala.Predef$.assert(Predef.scala:87)
    at objects.Person$.test(person.scala:15)
```

```
    at objects.PersonTest$.main(person.scala:20)
    at objects.PersonTest.main(person.scala)
    ...
```

In fact, this is a general issue with methods defined in companion objects that need to be visible to Java code as static methods. They aren't static in the byte code. You have to put these methods in singleton objects instead. Consider the following Java class that attempts to create a user with `Person.apply`:

```
// code-examples/AdvOOP/objects/PersonUserWontCompile.java
// WON'T COMPILE

package objects;

public class PersonUserWontCompile {
  public static void main(String[] args) {
    Person buck = Person.apply("Buck Trends", 100);  // ERROR
    System.out.println(buck);
  }
}
```

If we compile it (after compiling `Person.scala`), we get the following error:

```
$ javac -classpath ... objects/PersonUserWontCompile.java
objects/PersonUserWontCompile.java:5: cannot find symbol
symbol  : method apply(java.lang.String,int)
location: class objects.Person
        Person buck = Person.apply("Buck Trends", 100);
                            ^
1 error
```

However, we can use the following singleton object:

```
// code-examples/AdvOOP/objects/person-factory.scala

package objects

object PersonFactory {
  def make(name: String, age: Int) = new Person(name, age)
}
```

Now the following Java class will compile:

```
// code-examples/AdvOOP/objects/PersonUser.java

package objects;

public class PersonUser {
  public static void main(String[] args) {
    // The following line won't compile.
    // Person buck = Person.apply("Buck Trends", 100);
    Person buck = PersonFactory.make("Buck Trends", 100);
    System.out.println(buck);
  }
}
```

Do not define `main` or any other method in a *companion* object that needs to be visible to Java code as a **static** method. Define it in a *singleton* object, instead.

If you have no other choice but to call a method in a companion object from Java, you can explicitly create an instance of the object with **new**, since the object is a "regular" Java class in the byte code, and call the method on the instance.

Case Classes

In "Matching on Case Classes" on page 67, we briefly introduced you to *case classes*. Case classes have several useful features, but also some drawbacks.

Let's rewrite the Shape example we used in "A Taste of Concurrency" on page 16 to use case classes. Here is the original implementation:

```
// code-examples/IntroducingScala/shapes.scala

package shapes {
  class Point(val x: Double, val y: Double) {
    override def toString() = "Point(" + x + "," + y + ")"
  }

  abstract class Shape() {
    def draw(): Unit
  }

  class Circle(val center: Point, val radius: Double) extends Shape {
    def draw() = println("Circle.draw: " + this)
    override def toString() = "Circle(" + center + "," + radius + ")"
  }

  class Rectangle(val lowerLeft: Point, val height: Double, val width: Double)
      extends Shape {
    def draw() = println("Rectangle.draw: " + this)
    override def toString() =
      "Rectangle(" + lowerLeft + "," + height + "," + width + ")"
  }

  class Triangle(val point1: Point, val point2: Point, val point3: Point)
      extends Shape() {
    def draw() = println("Triangle.draw: " + this)
    override def toString() =
      "Triangle(" + point1 + "," + point2 + "," + point3 + ")"
  }
}
```

Here is the example rewritten using the **case** keyword:

```
// code-examples/AdvOOP/shapes/shapes-case.scala

package shapes {
```

```
case class Point(x: Double, y: Double)

abstract class Shape() {
  def draw(): Unit
}

case class Circle(center: Point, radius: Double) extends Shape() {
  def draw() = println("Circle.draw: " + this)
}

case class Rectangle(lowerLeft: Point, height: Double, width: Double)
    extends Shape() {
  def draw() = println("Rectangle.draw: " + this)
}

case class Triangle(point1: Point, point2: Point, point3: Point)
    extends Shape() {
  def draw() = println("Triangle.draw: " + this)
}
}
```

Adding the **case** keyword causes the compiler to add a number of useful features automatically. The keyword suggests an association with **case** expressions in pattern matching. Indeed, they are particularly well suited for that application, as we will see.

First, the compiler automatically converts the constructor arguments into immutable fields (**vals**). The **val** keyword is optional. If you want mutable fields, use the **var** keyword. So, our constructor argument lists are now shorter.

Second, the compiler automatically implements **equals**, **hashCode**, and **toString** methods to the class, which use the fields specified as constructor arguments. So, we no longer need our own **toString** methods. In fact, the generated **toString** methods produce the same outputs as the ones we implemented ourselves. Also, the body of **Point** is gone because there are no methods that we need to define!

The following script uses these methods that are now in the shapes:

```
// code-examples/AdvOOP/shapes/shapes-usage-example1-script.scala

import shapes._

val shapesList = List(
  Circle(Point(0.0, 0.0), 1.0),
  Circle(Point(5.0, 2.0), 3.0),
  Rectangle(Point(0.0, 0.0), 2, 5),
  Rectangle(Point(-2.0, -1.0), 4, 3),
  Triangle(Point(0.0, 0.0), Point(1.0, 0.0), Point(0.0, 1.0)))

val shape1 = shapesList.head  // grab the first one.
println("shape1: "+shape1+". hash = "+shape1.hashCode)
for (shape2 <- shapesList) {
  println("shape2: "+shape2+". 1 == 2 ? "+(shape1 == shape2))
}
```

This script outputs the following:

```
shape1: Circle(Point(0.0,0.0),1.0). hash = 2061963534
shape2: Circle(Point(0.0,0.0),1.0). 1 == 2 ? true
shape2: Circle(Point(5.0,2.0),3.0). 1 == 2 ? false
shape2: Rectangle(Point(0.0,0.0),2.0,5.0). 1 == 2 ? false
shape2: Rectangle(Point(-2.0,-1.0),4.0,3.0). 1 == 2 ? false
shape2: Triangle(Point(0.0,0.0),Point(1.0,0.0),Point(0.0,1.0)). 1 == 2 ? false
```

As we'll see in "Equality of Objects" on page 142, the == method actually invokes the equals method.

Even outside of case expressions, automatic generation of these three methods is very convenient for simple, "structural" classes, i.e., classes that contain relatively simple fields and behaviors.

Third, when the case keyword is used, the compiler automatically creates a *companion object* with an apply factory method that takes the same arguments as the *primary* constructor. The previous example used the appropriate apply methods to create the Points, the different Shapes, and also the List itself. That's why we don't need new; we're actually calling apply(x,y) in the Point companion object, for example.

 You can have *secondary* constructors in case classes, but there will be no overloaded apply method generated that has the same argument list. You'll have to use new to create instances with those constructors.

The companion object also gets an unapply extractor method, which extracts all the fields of an instance in an elegant fashion. The following script demonstrates the extractors in pattern matching case statements:

```scala
// code-examples/AdvOOP/shapes/shapes-usage-example2-script.scala

import shapes._

val shapesList = List(
  Circle(Point(0.0, 0.0), 1.0),
  Circle(Point(5.0, 2.0), 3.0),
  Rectangle(Point(0.0, 0.0), 2, 5),
  Rectangle(Point(-2.0, -1.0), 4, 3),
  Triangle(Point(0.0, 0.0), Point(1.0, 0.0), Point(0.0, 1.0)))

def matchOn(shape: Shape) = shape match {
  case Circle(center, radius) =>
    println("Circle: center = "+center+", radius = "+radius)
  case Rectangle(ll, h, w) =>
    println("Rectangle: lower-left = "+ll+", height = "+h+", width = "+w)
  case Triangle(p1, p2, p3) =>
    println("Triangle: point1 = "+p1+", point2 = "+p2+", point3 = "+p3)
  case _ =>
    println("Unknown shape!"+shape)
}
```

```
shapesList.foreach { shape => matchOn(shape) }
```

This script outputs the following:

```
Circle: center = Point(0.0,0.0), radius = 1.0
Circle: center = Point(5.0,2.0), radius = 3.0
Rectangle: lower-left = Point(0.0,0.0), height = 2.0, width = 5.0
Rectangle: lower-left = Point(-2.0,-1.0), height = 4.0, width = 3.0
Triangle: point1 = Point(0.0,0.0), point2 = Point(1.0,0.0), point3 = Point(0.0,1.0)
```

Syntactic Sugar for Binary Operations

By the way, remember in "Matching on Sequences" on page 65 when we discussed matching on lists? We wrote this **case** expression:

```
def processList(l: List[Any]): Unit = l match {
  case head :: tail => ...
  ...
}
```

It turns out that the following expressions are identical:

```
case head :: tail => ...
case ::(head, tail) => ...
```

We are using the companion object for the case class named ::, which is used for non-empty lists. When used in **case** expressions, the compiler supports this special infix operator notation for invocations of unapply.

It works not only for unapply methods with two arguments, but also with one or more arguments. We could rewrite our matchOn method this way:

```
def matchOn(shape: Shape) = shape match {
  case center Circle radius => ...
  case ll Rectangle (h, w) => ...
  case p1 Triangle (p2, p3) => ...
  case _ => ...
}
```

For an unapply that takes one argument, you would have to insert an empty set of parentheses to avoid a parsing ambiguity:

```
case arg Foo () => ...
```

From the point of view of clarity, this syntax is elegant for some cases when there are two arguments. For lists, **head :: tail** matches the expressions for building up lists, so there is a beautiful symmetry when the extraction process uses the same syntax. However, the merits of this syntax are less clear for other examples, especially when there are N != 2 arguments.

The copy Method in Scala Version 2.8

In Scala version 2.8, another instance method is automatically generated, called copy. This method is useful when you want to make a new instance of a case class that is identical to another instance with a few fields changed. Consider the following example script:

```
// code-examples/AdvOOP/shapes/shapes-usage-example3-v28-script.scala
// Scala version 2.8 only.

import shapes._

val circle1 = Circle(Point(0.0, 0.0), 2.0)
val circle2 = circle1 copy (radius = 4.0)

println(circle1)
println(circle2)
```

The second circle is created by copying the first and specifying a new radius. The copy method implementation that is generated by the compiler exploits the new named and default parameters in Scala version 2.8, which we discussed in "Method Default and Named Arguments (Scala Version 2.8)" on page 26. The generated implementation of Circle.copy looks roughly like the following:

```
case class Circle(center: Point, radius: Double) extends Shape() {
  ...
  def copy(center: Point = this.center, radius: Double = this.radius) =
    new Circle(center, radius)
}
```

So, default values are provided for all the arguments to the method (only two in this case). When using the copy method, the user specifies by name only the fields that are changing. The values for the rest of the fields are used without having to reference them explicitly.

Case Class Inheritance

Did you notice that the new Shapes code in "Case Classes" on page 136 did not put the case keyword on the abstract Shape class? This is allowed by the compiler, but there are reasons for not having one case class inherit another. First, it can complicate field initialization. Suppose we make Shape a case class. Suppose we want to add a string field to all shapes representing an id that the user wants to set. It makes sense to define this field in Shape. Let's make these two changes to Shape:

```
abstract case class Shape(id: String) {
  def draw(): Unit
}
```

Now the derived shapes need to pass the id to the Shape constructor. For example, Circle would become the following:

```
case class Circle(id: String, center: Point, radius: Double) extends Shape(id){
  def draw(): Unit
}
```

However, if you compile this code, you'll get errors like the following:

```
... error: error overriding value id in class Shape of type String;
 value id needs `override' modifier
    case class Circle(id: String, center: Point, radius: Double) extends Shape(id){
                      ^
```

Remember that both definitions of id, the one in Shape and the one in Circle, are considered val field definitions! The error message tells us the answer; use the override keyword, as we discussed in "Overriding Members of Classes and Traits" on page 111. So, the complete set of required modifications are as follows:

```
// code-examples/AdvOOP/shapes/shapes-case-id.scala

package shapesid {
  case class Point(x: Double, y: Double)

  abstract case class Shape(id: String) {
    def draw(): Unit
  }

  case class Circle(override val id: String, center: Point, radius: Double)
      extends Shape(id) {
    def draw() = println("Circle.draw: " + this)
  }

  case class Rectangle(override val id: String, lowerLeft: Point,
      height: Double, width: Double) extends Shape(id) {
    def draw() = println("Rectangle.draw: " + this)
  }

  case class Triangle(override val id: String, point1: Point,
      point2: Point, point3: Point) extends Shape(id) {
    def draw() = println("Triangle.draw: " + this)
  }
}
```

Note that we also have to add the val keywords. This works, but it is somewhat ugly.

A more ominous problem involves the generated equals methods. Under inheritance, the equals methods don't obey all the standard rules for robust object equality. We'll discuss those rules in "Equality of Objects" on page 142. For now, consider the following example:

```
// code-examples/AdvOOP/shapes/shapes-case-equals-ambiguity-script.scala

import shapesid._

case class FancyCircle(name: String, override val id: String,
    override val center: Point, override val radius: Double)
      extends Circle(id, center, radius) {
  override def draw() = println("FancyCircle.draw: " + this)
```

```
}
    val fc = FancyCircle("me", "circle", Point(0.0,0.0), 10.0)
    val c  = Circle("circle", Point(0.0,0.0), 10.0)
    format("FancyCircle == Circle? %b\n", (fc == c))
    format("Circle == FancyCircle? %b\n", (c  == fc))
```

If you run this script, you get the following output:

```
FancyCircle == Circle? false
Circle == FancyCircle? true
```

So, `Circle.equals` evaluates to `true` when given a `FancyCircle` with the same values for the `Circle` fields. The reverse case isn't true. While you might argue that, as far as `Circle` is concerned, they really *are* equal, most people would argue that this is a risky, "relaxed" interpretation of equality. It's true that a future version of Scala could generate `equals` methods for `case` classes that do exact type-equality checking.

So, the conveniences provided by case classes sometimes lead to problems. It is best to avoid inheritance of one case class by another. Note that it's fine for a case class to inherit from a non-case class or trait. It's also fine for a non-case class or trait to inherit from a case class.

Because of these issues, it is possible that case class inheritance will be deprecated and removed in future versions of Scala.

    Avoid inheriting a case class from another case class.

Equality of Objects

Implementing a reliable equality test for instances is difficult to do correctly. *Effective Java* ([Bloch2008]) and the Scaladoc page for `AnyRef.equals` describe the requirements for a good equality test. A very good description of the techniques for writing correct `equals` and `hashCode` methods can be found in [Odersky2009], which uses Java syntax, but is adapted from Chapter 28 of *Programming in Scala* ([Odersky2008]). Consult these references when you need to implement your own `equals` and `hashCode` methods. Recall that these methods are created automatically for `case` classes.

Here we focus on the different equality methods available in Scala and their meanings. There are some slight inconsistencies between the Scala specification (see [ScalaS-pec2009]) and the Scaladoc pages for the equality-related methods for `Any` and `AnyRef`, but the general behavior is clear.

    Some of the equality methods have the same names as equality methods
in other languages, but the semantics are sometimes different!

The equals Method

The equals method tests for *value* equality. That is, obj1 equals obj2 is true if both obj1 and obj2 have the same value. They do not need to refer to the same instance.

Hence, equals behaves like the equals method in Java and the eql? method in Ruby.

The == and != Methods

While == is an operator in many languages, it is a method in Scala, defined as final in Any. It tests for *value* equality, like equals. That is, obj1 == obj2 is true if both obj1 and obj2 have the same value. In fact, == delegates to equals. Here is part of the Scaladoc entry for Any.==:

```
o == arg0 is the same as o.equals(arg0).
```

Here is the corresponding part of the Scaladoc entry for AnyRef.==:

```
o == arg0 is the same as if (o eq null) arg0 eq null else o.equals(arg0).
```

As you would expect, != is the negation, i.e., it is equivalent to !(obj1 == obj2).

Since == and != are declared final in Any, you can't override them, but you don't need to, since they delegate to equals.

 In Java, C++, and C#, the == operator tests for *reference*, not *value* equality. In contrast, Ruby's == operator tests for *value* equality. Whatever language you're used to, make sure to remember that in Scala, == is testing for value equality.

The ne and eq Methods

The eq method tests for *reference* equality. That is, obj1 eq obj2 is true if both obj1 and obj2 point to the same location in memory. These methods are only defined for AnyRef.

Hence, eq behaves like the == operator in Java, C++, and C#, but not == in Ruby.

The ne method is the negation of eq, i.e., it is equivalent to !(obj1 eq obj2).

Array Equality and the sameElements Method

Comparing the contents of two Arrays doesn't have an obvious result in Scala:

```
scala> Array(1, 2) == Array(1, 2)
res0: Boolean = false
```

That's a surprise! Thankfully, there's a simple solution in the form of the sameElements method:

```
scala> Array(1, 2).sameElements(Array(1, 2))
res1: Boolean = true
```

Much better. Remember to use `sameElements` when you want to test if two `Arrays` contain the same elements.

While this may seem like an inconsistency, encouraging an explicit test of the equality of two mutable data structures is a conservative approach on the part of the language designers. In the long run, it should save you from unexpected results in your conditionals.

Recap and What's Next

We explored the fine points of overriding members in derived classes. We learned about object equality, case classes, and companion classes and objects.

In the next chapter, we'll learn about the Scala type hierarchy—in particular, the `Predef` object that includes many useful definitions. We'll also learn about Scala's alternative to Java's `static` class members and the *linearization* rules for method lookup.

The Scala Object System

The Predef Object

For your convenience, whenever you compile code, the Scala compiler automatically imports the definitions in the `java.lang` package (`javac` does this, too). On the .NET platform, it imports the `system` package. The compiler also imports the definitions in the analogous Scala package, `scala`. Hence, common Java or .NET types can be used without explicitly importing them or fully qualifying them with the `java.lang.` prefix, in the Java case. Similarly, a number of common, Scala-specific types are made available without qualification, such as `List`. Where there are Java and Scala type names that overlap, like `String`, the Scala version is imported last, so it "wins."

The compiler also automatically imports the `Predef` object, which defines or imports several useful types, objects, and functions.

 You can learn a lot of Scala by viewing the source for `Predef`. It is available by clicking the "source" link in the `Predef` Scaladoc page, or you can download the full source code for Scala at *http://www.scala-lang .org/*.

Table 7-1 shows a partial list of the items imported or defined by `Predef` on the Java platform.

Table 7-1. Items imported or defined by Predef

Types	Character, Class, Error, Function, Integer, Map, Pair, Runnable, Set, String, Throwable, Triple.
Exceptions	Exception, ArrayIndexOutOfBoundsException, ClassCastException, IllegalArgumentException, IndexOutOfBoundsException, NoSuchElementException, NullPointerException, NumberFormatException, RuntimeException, StringIndexOutOfBoundsException, UnsupportedOperationException.
Values	Map, Set.

Objects	Pair, Triple.
Classes	Ensuring, ArrowAssoc.
Methods	Factory methods to create *tuples*; overloaded versions of exit, error, assert, assume, and require; *implicit* type conversion methods; I/O methods like readLine, println, and format; and a method currentThread, which calls java.lang.Thread.currentThread.

Predef declares the types and exceptions listed in the table using the type keyword. They are definitions that equal the corresponding scala.<Type> or java.lang.<Type> classes, so they behave like "aliases" or imports for the corresponding classes. For example, String is declared as follows:

```
type String = java.lang.String
```

In this case, the declaration has the same net effect as an import java.lang.String statement would have.

But didn't we just say that definitions in java.lang are imported automatically, like String? The reason there is a type definition is to enable support for a uniform string type across all runtime environments. The definition is only redundant on the JVM.

The type Pair is an "alias" for Tuple2:

```
type Pair[+A, +B] = Tuple2[A, B]
```

There are two type parameters, A and B, one for each item in the pair. Recall from "Abstract Types And Parameterized Types" on page 47 that we explained the meaning of the + in front of each type parameter.

Briefly, a Pair[A2,B2], for some A2 and B2, is a *subclass* of Pair[A1,B1], for some A1 and B1, if A2 is a subtype of A1 and B2 is a subtype of B1. In "Understanding Parameterized Types" on page 249, we'll discuss + and other type qualifiers in more detail.

The Pair class also has a *companion object* Pair with an apply factory method, as discussed in "Companion Objects" on page 126. Hence, we can create Pair instances as in this example:

```
val p = Pair(1, "one")
```

Pair.apply is called with the two arguments. The types A and B, shown in the definition of Pair, are inferred. A new Tuple2 instance is returned.

Map and Set appear in both the types and values lists. In the values list, they are assigned the *companion objects* scala.collection.immutable.Map and scala.collection.immutable.Set, respectively. Hence, Map and Set in Predef are *values*, not object definitions, because they refer to objects defined elsewhere, whereas Pair and Triple are defined in Predef itself. The types Map and Set are assigned the corresponding immutable classes.

The `ArrowAssoc` class defines two methods: ->, and the Unicode equivalent →. The utility of these methods was demonstrated previously in "Option, Some, and None: Avoiding nulls" on page 41, where we created a map of U.S. state capitals:

```scala
val stateCapitals = Map(
  "Alabama" -> "Montgomery",
  "Alaska"  -> "Juneau",
  // ...
  "Wyoming" -> "Cheyenne")
// ...
```

The definition of the `ArrowAssoc` class and the `Map` and `Set` values in `Predef` make the convenient `Map` initialization syntax possible. First, when Scala sees `Map(...)` it calls the `apply` method on the `Map` companion object, just as we discussed for `Pair`.

`Map.apply` expects zero or more `Pairs` (e.g., `(a1, b2)`, `(a2, b2)`, `...`), where each tuple holds a name and value. In the example, the tuple types are all inferred to be of type `Pair[String,String]`. The declaration of `Map.apply` is as follows:

```scala
object Map {
  ...
  def apply[A, B](elems : (A, B)*) : Map[A, B] = ...
}
```

Recall that there can be no type parameters on the `Map` companion object because there can be only one instance. However, `apply` can have type parameters.

The apply method takes a *variable-length argument list*. Internally, x will be a subtype of `Array[X]`. So, for `Map.apply`, `elems` is of type `Array[(A,B)]` or `Array[Tuple2[A,B]]`, if you prefer.

So, now that we know what `Map.apply` expects, how do we get from a -> b to (a, b)?

`Predef` also defines an *implicit* type conversion method called `any2ArrowAssoc`. The compiler knows that `String` does not define a -> method, so it looks for an *implicit* conversion *in scope* to a type that defines such a method, such as `ArrowAssoc`. The `any2ArrowAssoc` method performs that conversion. It has the following implementation:

```scala
implicit def any2ArrowAssoc[A](x: A): ArrowAssoc[A] = new ArrowAssoc(x)
```

It is applied to each item to the left of an arrow ->, e.g., the `"Alabama"` string. These strings are wrapped in `ArrowAssoc` instances, upon which the -> method is then invoked. This method has the following implementation:

```scala
class ArrowAssoc[A](x: A) {
  ...
  def -> [B](y: B): Tuple2[A, B] = Tuple2(x, y)
}
```

When it is invoked, it is passed the string on the righthand side of the ->. The method returns a tuple with the value, `("Alabama", "Montgomery")`, for example. In this way, each `key -> value` is converted into a tuple and the resulting comma-separated list of tuples is passed to the `Map.apply` factory method.

The description may sound complicated at first, but the beauty of Scala is that this map initialization syntax is not an ad hoc language feature, such as a special-purpose operator -> defined in the language grammar. Instead, this syntax is defined with normal definitions of types and methods, combined with a few general-purpose parsing conventions, such as support for *implicits*. Furthermore, it is all *type-safe*. You can use the same techniques to write your own convenient "operators" for mini *Domain-Specific Languages* (see Chapter 11).

Implicit type conversions are discussed in more detail in "Implicit Conversions" on page 186.

Next, recall from Chapter 1 that we were able to replace calls to Console.println(...) with println(...). This "bare" println method is defined in Predef, then imported automatically by the compiler. The definition calls the corresponding method in Console. Similarly, all the other I/O methods defined by Predef, e.g., readLine and format, call the corresponding Console methods.

Finally, the assert, assume, and require methods are each overloaded with various argument list options. They are used for runtime testing of boolean conditions. If a condition is false, an exception is thrown. The Ensuring class serves a similar purpose. You can use these features for *Design by Contract* programming, as discussed in "Better Design with Design By Contract" on page 340.

For the full list of features defined by Predef, see the corresponding Scaladoc entry in [ScalaAPI2008].

Four Ways to Create a Two-Item Tuple

We now know four ways to create a two-item tuple (*twople?*):

1. ("Hello", 3.14)
2. Pair("Hello", 3.14)
3. Tuple2("Hello", 3.14)
4. "Hello" → 3.14

Classes and Objects: Where Are the Statics?

Many object-oriented languages allow classes to have class-level constants, fields, and methods, called "static" members in Java, C#, and C++. These constants, fields, and methods are not associated with any *instances* of the class.

An example of a class-level field is a shared logging instance used by all instances of a class for logging messages. An example of a class-level constant is the default logging "threshold" level.

An example of a class-level method is a "finder" method that locates all instances of the class in some repository that match some user-specified criteria. Another example is a *factory* method, as used in one of the factory-related design patterns (see [GOF1995]).

To remain consistent with the goal that "everything is an object" in Scala, class-level fields and methods are not supported. Instead, Scala supports declarations of classes that are *singletons*, using the `object` keyword instead of the `class` keyword. The `objects` provide an object-oriented approach to "static" data and methods. Hence, Scala does not even have a `static` keyword.

`Objects` are instantiated automatically and lazily by the runtime system (see Section 5.4 of [ScalaSpec2009]). Just as for classes and traits, the body of the `object` is the constructor, but since the system instantiates the object, there is no way for the user to specify a parameter list for the constructor, so they aren't supported. Any data defined in the object has to be initialized with default values. For the same reasons, auxiliary constructors can't be used and are not supported.

We've already seen some examples of objects, such as the `specs` objects used previously for tests, and the `Pair` type and its *companion object*, which we explored in "The Predef Object" on page 145:

```
type Pair[+A, +B] = Tuple2[A, B]
object Pair {
  def apply[A, B](x: A, y: B) = Tuple2(x, y)
  def unapply[A, B](x: Tuple2[A, B]): Option[Tuple2[A, B]] = Some(x)
}
```

To reference an object field or method, you use the syntax `object_name.field` or `object_name.method(...)`, respectively. For example, `Pair.apply(...)`. Note that this is the same syntax that is commonly used in languages with static fields and methods.

When an object named `MyObject` is compiled to a class file, the class file name will be `MyObject$.class`.

In Java and C#, the convention for defining constants is to use `final static` fields. (C# also has a `constant` keyword for simple fields, like `ints` and `strings`.) In Scala, the convention is to use `val` fields in objects.

Finally, recall from "Nested Classes" on page 95 that class definitions can be nested within other class definitions. This property generalizes for objects. You can define nested objects, traits, and classes inside other objects, traits, and classes.

Package Objects

Scala version 2.8 introduces a new scoping construct called *package objects*. They are used to define types, variables, and methods that are visible at the level of the corresponding package. To understand their usefulness, let's see an example from Scala version 2.8 itself. The collection library is being reorganized to refine the package structure and to use it more consistently (among other changes). The Scala team faced a dilemma. They wanted to move types to new packages, but avoid breaking backward compatibility. The `package object` construct provided a solution, along with other benefits.

For example, the immutable `List` is defined in the `scala` package in version 2.7, but it is moved to the `scala.collection.immutable` package in version 2.8. Despite the change, `List` is made visible in the `scala` package using `package object scala`, found in the *src/library/scala/package.scala* file in the version 2.8 source code distribution. Note the file name. It's not required, but it's a useful convention for package objects. Here is the full package object definition (at the time of this writing; it could change before the 2.8.0 final version is released):

```
package object scala {
  type Iterable[+A] = scala.collection.Iterable[A]
  val Iterable = scala.collection.Iterable

  @deprecated("use Iterable instead") type Collection[+A] = Iterable[A]
  @deprecated("use Iterable instead") val Collection = Iterable

  type Seq[+A] = scala.collection.Sequence[A]
  val Seq = scala.collection.Sequence

  type RandomAccessSeq[+A] = scala.collection.Vector[A]
  val RandomAccessSeq = scala.collection.Vector

  type Iterator[+A] = scala.collection.Iterator[A]
  val Iterator = scala.collection.Iterator

  type BufferedIterator[+A] = scala.collection.BufferedIterator[A]

  type List[+A] = scala.collection.immutable.List[A]
  val List = scala.collection.immutable.List

  val Nil = scala.collection.immutable.Nil

  type ::[A] = scala.collection.immutable.::[A]
  val :: = scala.collection.immutable.::

  type Stream[+A] = scala.collection.immutable.Stream[A]
  val Stream = scala.collection.immutable.Stream

  type StringBuilder = scala.collection.mutable.StringBuilder
  val StringBuilder = scala.collection.mutable.StringBuilder
}
```

Note that pairs of declarations like `type List[+]` = ... and `val List` = ... are effectively "aliases" for the companion class and object, respectively. Because the contents of the `scala` package are automatically imported by the compiler, you can still reference all the definitions in this object in any scope without an explicit import statement for fully qualified names.

Other than the way the members in package objects are scoped, they behave just like other object declarations. While this example contains only `val`s and `type`s, you can also define methods, and you can subclass another class or trait and mix in other traits.

Another benefit of package objects is that it provides a more succinct implementation of what was an awkward idiom before. Without package objects, you would have to put definitions in an ad hoc object inside the desired package, then import from the object. For example, here is how `List` would have to be handled without a package object:

```
package scala {
  object toplevel {
    ...
    type List[+A] = scala.collection.immutable.List[A]
    val List = scala.collection.immutable.List
    ...
  }
}

...
import scala.toplevel._
...
```

Finally, another benefit of package objects is the way they provide a clear separation between the abstractions exposed by a package and the implementations that should be hidden inside it. In a larger application, a package object could be used to expose all the public types, values, and operations (methods) for a "component," while everything else in the package and nested packages could be treated as internal implementation details.

Sealed Class Hierarchies

Recall from "Case Classes" on page 136 that we demonstrated pattern matching with our `Shapes` hierarchy, which use case classes. We had a default `case _ => ...` expression. It's usually wise to have one. Otherwise, if someone defines a new subtype of `Shape` and passes it to this `match` statement, a runtime `scala.MatchError` will be thrown, because the new shape won't match the shapes covered in the match statement. However, it's not always possible to define reasonable behavior for the default case.

There is an alternative solution if you know that the case class hierarchy is unlikely to change and you can define the whole hierarchy in *one file*. In this situation, you can add the `sealed` keyword to the declaration of the common base class. When sealed, the compiler knows all the possible classes that could appear in the `match` expression, because all of them must be defined in the same source file. So, if you cover all those classes in the `case` expressions (either explicitly or through shared parent classes), then you can safely eliminate the default `case` expression.

Here is an example using the HTTP 1.1 methods (see [HTTP1.1]), which are not likely to change very often, so we declare a "sealed" set of case classes for them:

```scala
// code-examples/ObjectSystem/sealed/http-script.scala

sealed abstract class HttpMethod()
case class Connect(body: String) extends HttpMethod
case class Delete (body: String) extends HttpMethod
case class Get    (body: String) extends HttpMethod
case class Head   (body: String) extends HttpMethod
case class Options(body: String) extends HttpMethod
case class Post   (body: String) extends HttpMethod
case class Put    (body: String) extends HttpMethod
case class Trace  (body: String) extends HttpMethod

def handle (method: HttpMethod) = method match {
  case Connect (body) => println("connect: " + body)
  case Delete  (body) => println("delete: "  + body)
  case Get     (body) => println("get: "      + body)
  case Head    (body) => println("head: "     + body)
  case Options (body) => println("options: " + body)
  case Post    (body) => println("post: "     + body)
  case Put     (body) => println("put: "      + body)
  case Trace   (body) => println("trace: "    + body)
}

val methods = List(
  Connect("connect body..."),
  Delete ("delete body..."),
  Get    ("get body..."),
  Head   ("head body..."),
  Options("options body..."),
  Post   ("post body..."),
  Put    ("put body..."),
  Trace  ("trace body..."))

methods.foreach { method => handle(method) }
```

This script outputs the following:

```
connect: connect body...
delete: delete body...
get: get body...
head: head body...
options: options body...
post: post body...
put: put body...
trace: trace body...
```

No default case is necessary, since we cover all the possibilities. Conversely, if you omit one of the classes and you don't provide a default case or a case for a shared parent class, the compiler warns you that the "match is not exhaustive." For example, if you comment out the case for Put, you get this warning:

```
warning: match is not exhaustive!
missing combination            Put

def handle (method: HttpMethod) = method match {
...
```

You also get a MatchError exception if a Put instance is passed to the match.

Using sealed has one drawback. Every time you add or remove a class from the hierarchy, you have to modify the file, since the entire hierarchy has to be declared in the same file. This breaks the *Open-Closed Principle* (see [Meyer1997] and [Martin2003]), which is a solution to the practical problem that it can be costly to modify existing code, retest it (and other code that uses it), and redeploy it. It's much less "costly" if you can extend the system by adding new derived types in *separate* source files. This is why we picked the HTTP method hierarchy for the example. The list of methods is very stable.

Avoid sealed case class hierarchies if the hierarchy changes frequently (for an appropriate definition of "frequently").

Finally, you may have noticed some duplication in the example. All the concrete classes have a body field. Why didn't we put that field in the parent HttpMethod class? Because we decided to use case classes for the concrete classes, we'll run into the same problem with case class inheritance that we discussed in "Case Class Inheritance" on page 140, where we added a shared id field in the Shape hierarchy. We need the body argument for each HTTP method's constructor, yet it will be made a field of each method type automatically. So, we would have to use the override val technique we demonstrated previously.

We could remove the case keywords and implement the methods and companion objects that we need. However, in this case, the duplication is minimal and tolerable.

What if we want to use case classes, yet also reference the body field in HttpMethod? Fortunately, we know that Scala will generate a body reader method in every concrete subclass (as long as we use the name body consistently!). So, we can declare that method abstract in HttpMethod, then use it as we see fit. The following example demonstrates this technique:

```
// code-examples/ObjectSystem/sealed/http-body-script.scala

sealed abstract class HttpMethod() {
    def body: String
    def bodyLength = body.length
```

```
    }

    case class Connect(body: String) extends HttpMethod
    case class Delete (body: String) extends HttpMethod
    case class Get     (body: String) extends HttpMethod
    case class Head    (body: String) extends HttpMethod
    case class Options(body: String) extends HttpMethod
    case class Post    (body: String) extends HttpMethod
    case class Put     (body: String) extends HttpMethod
    case class Trace   (body: String) extends HttpMethod

    def handle (method: HttpMethod) = method match {
      case Connect (body) => println("connect: " + body)
      case Delete  (body) => println("delete: "  + body)
      case Get     (body) => println("get: "     + body)
      case Head    (body) => println("head: "    + body)
      case Options (body) => println("options: " + body)
      case Post    (body) => println("post: "    + body)
      case Put     (body) => println("put: "     + body)
      case Trace   (body) => println("trace: "   + body)
    }

    val methods = List(
      Connect("connect body..."),
      Delete ("delete body..."),
      Get     ("get body..."),
      Head    ("head body..."),
      Options("options body..."),
      Post    ("post body..."),
      Put     ("put body..."),
      Trace   ("trace body..."))

    methods.foreach { method =>
      handle(method)
      println("body length? " + method.bodyLength)
    }
```

We declared body abstract in HttpMethod. We added a simple bodyLength method that calls body. The loop at the end of the script calls bodyLength. Running this script produces the following output:

```
connect: connect body...
body length? 15
delete: delete body...
body length? 14
get: get body...
body length? 11
head: head body...
body length? 12
options: options body...
body length? 15
post: post body...
body length? 12
put: put body...
body length? 11
```

```
trace: trace body...
body length? 13
```

As always, every feature has pluses and minuses. Case classes and sealed class hierarchies have very useful properties, but they aren't suitable for all situations.

The Scala Type Hierarchy

We have mentioned a number of types in Scala's type hierarchy already. Let's look at the general structure of the hierarchy, as illustrated in Figure 7-1.

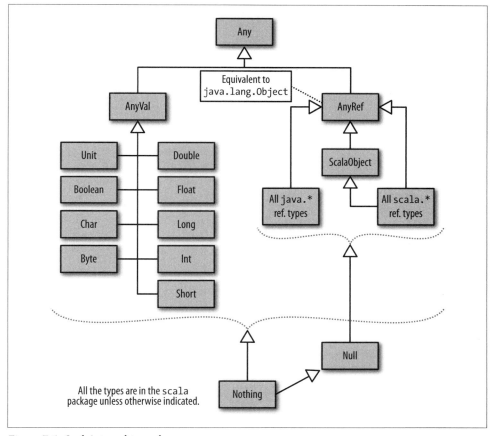

Figure 7-1. Scala's type hierarchy

Tables 7-2 and 7-3 discuss the types shown in Figure 7-1, as well as some other important types that aren't shown. Some details are omitted for clarity. When the underlying "runtime" is discussed, the points made apply equally to the JVM and the .NET CLR, except where noted.

Table 7-2. Any, AnyVal, and AnyRef

Name	Parent	Description
Any	*none*	The root of the hierarchy. Defines a few *final* methods like ==, !=, isInstanceOf[T] (for type checking), and asInstanceOf[T] (for type casting), as well as default versions of equals, hashCode, and toString, which are designed to be overridden by subclasses.
AnyVal	Any	The parent of all *value* types, which correspond to the *primitive* types on the runtime platform, plus Unit. All the AnyVal instances are immutable *value instances*, and all the AnyVal types are abstract final. Hence, none of them can be instantiated with new. Rather, new instances are created with *literal* values (e.g., 3.14 for a Double) or by calling methods on instances that return new values.
AnyRef	Any	The parent of all *reference* types, including all java.* and scala.* types. It is equivalent to java.lang.Object for the JVM and object (System.Object) for the .NET runtime. Instances of reference types are created with new.

The *value types* are children of AnyVal.

Table 7-3. Direct subtypes of AnyVal, the value types

Name	Runtime primitive type
Boolean	Boolean (true and false).
Byte	Byte.
Char	Char.
Short	Short.
Int	Int.
Long	Long.
Float	Float.
Double	Double.
Unit	Serves the same role as void in most imperative languages. Used primarily as a function return value. There is only one instance of Unit, named (). Think of it as a tuple with zero items.

All other types, the *reference types*, are children of AnyRef. Table 7-4 lists some of the more commonly used reference types. Note that there are some significant differences between the version 2.7.X and 2.8 collections.

Table 7-4. Direct and indirect subtypes of AnyRef, the reference types

Name	Parent	Description
Collection[+T]	Iterable[T]	Trait for collections of known size.
Either[+T1, +T2]	AnyRef	Used most often as a return type when a method could return an instance of one of two unrelated types. For example, an exception or a "successful" result. The Either can be pattern matched for its Left or Right subtypes. (It is analogous to Option, with Some and None.) For the

Name	Parent	Description
		exception-handling idiom, it is conventional to use Left for the exception.
FunctionN[-T$_1$, -T$_2$, ..., -T$_N$, +R]	AnyRef	Trait representing a function that takes N arguments, each of which can have its own type, and returns a value of type R. (Traits are defined for N = 0 to 22.) The *variance annotations* (+ and -) in front of the types will be explained in "Variance Under Inheritance" on page 251.
Iterable[+T]	AnyRef	Trait with methods for operating on collections of instances. Users implement the abstract elements method to return an Iterable instance.
List[+T]	Seq[T]	sealed abstract class for ordered collections with functional-style list semantics. It is the most widely used collection in Scala, so it is defined in the scala package, rather than one of the collection packages. (In Scala version 2.8, it is actually defined in scala.collec tion.immutable and "aliased" in package object scala). It has two subclasses, case object Nil, which extends List[Noth ing] and represents an empty list, and case final class :: [T], which represents a non-empty list, characterized by a head element and a tail list, which would be Nil for a one-element list.
Nothing	*All other types*	Nothing is the subtype of *all* other types. It has no instances. It is used primarily for defining other types in a type-safe way, such as the special List subtype Nil. See also "Nothing and Null" on page 267.
Null	*All reference types*	Null has one instance, null, corresponding to the runtime's concept of null.
Option[T]	Product	Wraps an optional item. It is a sealed abstract type and the only allowed instances are an instance of its derived case class Some[T], wrapping an instance of T, or its derived case object None, which extends Option[Nothing].
Predef	AnyRef	An object that defines and imports many commonly used types and methods. See "The Predef Object" on page 145 for details.
Product	AnyRef	Trait with methods for determining arity and getting the nth item in a "Cartesian product." Subtraits are defined for Product, called ProductN, for dimension N from 1 through 22.
ScalaObject	AnyRef	*Mixin* trait added to all Scala reference type instances.
Seq[+T]	Collection[T]	Trait for ordered collections.
TupleN	ProductN	Separate case classes for arity N = 1 through 22. Tuples support the *literal* syntax (x1, x2, ..., xN).

Besides List, some of the other library collections include Map, Set, Queue, and Stack. These other collections come in two varieties: mutable and immutable. The immutable collections are in the package scala.collection.immutable, while the mutable collections are in scala.collection.mutable. Only an immutable version of List is provided; for a mutable list, use a ListBuffer, which can return a List via the toList method. For Scala version 2.8, the collections implementations reuse code from scala.collection.generic. Users of the collections would normally not use any types defined in this package. We'll explore some of these collections in greater detail in "Functional Data Structures" on page 172.

Consistent with its emphasis on *functional programming* (see Chapter 8), Scala encourages you to use the immutable collections, since List is automatically imported and Predef defines types Map and Set that refer to the immutable versions of these collections. All other collections have to be imported explicitly.

Predef defines a number of implicit conversion methods for the value types (excluding Unit). There are implicit conversions to the corresponding scala.runtime.RichX types. For example, the byteWrapper method converts a Byte to a scala.runtime.RichByte. There are implicit conversions between the "numeric" types—Byte, Short, Int, Long, and Float—to the other types that are "wider" than the original. For example, Byte to Int, Int to Long, Int to Double, etc. Finally, there are conversions to the corresponding Java wrapper types, e.g., Int to java.lang.Integer. We discuss implicit conversions in more detail in "Implicit Conversions" on page 186.

There are several examples of Option elsewhere, e.g., "Option, Some, and None: Avoiding nulls" on page 41. Here is a script that illustrates using an Either return value to handle a thrown exception or successful result (adapted from *http://dcsobral.blogspot .com/2009/06/catching-exceptions.html*):

```
// code-examples/ObjectSystem/typehierarchy/either-script.scala

def exceptionToLeft[T](f: => T): Either[java.lang.Throwable, T] = try {
  Right(f)
} catch {
  case ex => Left(ex)
}

def throwsOnOddInt(i: Int) = i % 2 match {
  case 0 => i
  case 1 => throw new RuntimeException(i + " is odd!")
}

for(i <- 0 to 3)
  exceptionToLeft(throwsOnOddInt(i)) match {
    case Left(ex) => println("Oops, got exception " + ex.toString)
    case Right(x) => println(x)
  }
```

The exceptionToLeft method evaluates f. It catches a Throwable and returns it as the Left value or returns the normal result as the Right value. The for loop uses this method to invoke throwsOnOddInt. It pattern matches on the result and prints an appropriate message. The output of the script is the following:

```
0
Oops, got exception java.lang.RuntimeException: 1 is odd!
2
Oops, got exception java.lang.RuntimeException: 3 is odd!
```

A `FunctionN` trait, where `N` is 0 to 22, is instantiated for an anonymous function with `N` arguments. So, consider the following anonymous function:

```
(t1: T1, ..., tN: TN) => new R(...)
```

It is syntactic sugar for the following creation of an anonymous class:

```
new FunctionN {
  def apply(t1: T1, ..., tN: TN): R = new R(...)

  // other methods
}
```

We'll revisit `FunctionN` in "Variance Under Inheritance" on page 251 and "Function Types" on page 277.

Linearization of an Object's Hierarchy

Because of single inheritance, the inheritance hierarchy would be linear, if we ignored mixed-in traits. When traits are considered, each of which may be derived from other traits and classes, the inheritance hierarchy forms a directed, acyclic graph (see [ScalaSpec2009]). The term *linearization* refers to the algorithm used to "flatten" this graph for the purposes of resolving method lookup priorities, constructor invocation order, binding of `super`, etc.

Informally, we saw in "Stackable Traits" on page 82 that when an instance has more than one trait, they bind right to left, as declared. Consider the following example of linearization:

```
// code-examples/ObjectSystem/linearization/linearization1-script.scala

class C1 {
  def m = List("C1")
}

trait T1 extends C1 {
  override def m = { "T1" :: super.m }
}

trait T2 extends C1 {
  override def m = { "T2" :: super.m }
}

trait T3 extends C1 {
  override def m = { "T3" :: super.m }
}

class C2 extends T1 with T2 with T3 {
  override def m = { "C2" :: super.m }
}

val c2 = new C2
println(c2.m)
```

Running this script yields the following output:

```
List(C2, T3, T2, T1, C1)
```

This list of strings built up by the m methods reflects the *linearization* of the inheritance hierarchy, with a few missing pieces we'll discuss shortly. We'll also see why C1 is at the end of the list. First, let's see what the invocation sequence of the constructors looks like:

```scala
// code-examples/ObjectSystem/linearization/linearization2-script.scala

var clist = List[String]()

class C1 {
  clist ::= "C1"
}

trait T1 extends C1 {
  clist ::= "T1"
}

trait T2 extends C1 {
  clist ::= "T2"
}

trait T3 extends C1 {
  clist ::= "T3"
}

class C2 extends T1 with T2 with T3 {
  clist ::= "C2"
}

val c2 = new C2
println(clist.reverse)
```

Running this script yields the following output:

```
List(C1, T1, T2, T3, C2)
```

So, the construction sequence is the reverse. (We had to reverse the list on the last line, because the way it was constructed put the elements in the reverse order.) This invocation order makes sense. For proper construction to occur, the parent types need to be constructed before the derived types, since a derived type often uses fields and methods in the parent types during its construction process.

The output of the first linearization script is actually missing three types at the end. The full linearization for reference types actually ends with ScalaObject, AnyRef, and Any. So the linearization for C2 is actually:

```
List(C2, T3, T2, T1, C1, ScalaObject, AnyRef, Any)
```

Scala inserts the ScalaObject trait as the last mixin, just before AnyRef and Any that are the penultimate and ultimate parent classes of any reference type. Of course, these three types do not show up in the output of the scripts, because we used an ad hoc m method to figure out the behavior by building up an output string.

The "value types," subclasses of AnyVal, are all declared abstract final. The compiler manages instantiation of them. Since we can't subclass them, their linearizations are simple and straightforward.

The linearization defines the order in which method lookup occurs. Let's examine it more closely.

All our classes and traits define the method m. The one in C2 is called first, since the instance is of that type. C2.m calls super.m, which resolves to T3.m. The search appears to be *breadth-first*, rather than *depth-first*. If it were depth-first, it would invoke C1.m after T3.m. Afterward, T3.m, T2.m, then T1.m, and finally C1.m are invoked. C1 is the parent of the three traits. From which of the traits did we traverse to C1? Actually, it is breadth-first, with "delayed" evaluation, as we will see. Let's modify our first example and see how we got to C1:

```scala
// code-examples/ObjectSystem/linearization/linearization3-script.scala

class C1 {
  def m(previous: String) = List("C1("+previous+")")
}

trait T1 extends C1 {
  override def m(p: String) = { "T1" :: super.m("T1") }
}

trait T2 extends C1 {
  override def m(p: String) = { "T2" :: super.m("T2") }
}

trait T3 extends C1 {
  override def m(p: String) = { "T3" :: super.m("T3") }
}

class C2 extends T1 with T2 with T3 {
  override def m(p: String) = { "C2" :: super.m("C2") }
}

val c2 = new C2
println(c2.m(""))
```

Now we pass the name of the caller of super.m as a parameter, then C1 prints out who called it. Running this script yields the following output:

```
List(C2, T3, T2, T1, C1(T1))
```

It's the last one, T1. We might have expected T3 from a "naïve" application of breadth-first traversal.

Here is the actual algorithm for calculating the linearization. A more formal definition is given in [ScalaSpec2009].

Linearization Algorithm for Reference Types

1. Put the actual type of the instance as the first element.

2. Starting with the *rightmost* parent type and working *left*, compute the linearization of each type, appending its linearization to the cumulative linearization. (Ignore ScalaObject, AnyRef, and Any for now.)

3. Working from *left to right*, remove any type if it appears again to the *right* of the current position.

4. Append ScalaObject, AnyRef, and Any.

This explains how we got to C1 from T1 in the previous example. T3 and T2 also have it in their linearizations, but they come before T1, so the C1 terms they contributed were deleted.

Let's work through the algorithm using a slightly more involved example:

```scala
// code-examples/ObjectSystem/linearization/linearization4-script.scala

class C1 {
  def m = List("C1")
}

trait T1 extends C1 {
  override def m = { "T1" :: super.m }
}

trait T2 extends C1 {
  override def m = { "T2" :: super.m }
}

trait T3 extends C1 {
  override def m = { "T3" :: super.m }
}

class C2A extends T2 {
  override def m = { "C2A" :: super.m }
}

class C2 extends C2A with T1 with T2 with T3 {
  override def m = { "C2" :: super.m }
}

def calcLinearization(obj: C1, name: String) = {
  val lin = obj.m ::: List("ScalaObject", "AnyRef", "Any")
  println(name + ":  " + lin)
}

calcLinearization(new C2, "C2 ")
println("")
calcLinearization(new T3 {}, "T3 ")
calcLinearization(new T2 {}, "T2 ")
```

```
calcLinearization(new T1 {}, "T1 ")
calcLinearization(new C2A, "C2A")
calcLinearization(new C1, "C1 ")
```

The output is the following:

```
C2 :  List(C2, T3, T1, C2A, T2, C1, ScalaObject, AnyRef, Any)

T3 :  List(T3, C1, ScalaObject, AnyRef, Any)
T2 :  List(T2, C1, ScalaObject, AnyRef, Any)
T1 :  List(T1, C1, ScalaObject, AnyRef, Any)
C2A:  List(C2A, T2, C1, ScalaObject, AnyRef, Any)
C1 :  List(C1, ScalaObject, AnyRef, Any)
```

To help us along, we calculated the linearizations for the other types, and we also appended `ScalaObject`, `AnyRef`, and `Any` to remind ourselves that they should also be there. We also removed the logic to pass the caller's name to `m`. That caller of `C1` will *always* be the element to its immediate left.

So, let's work through the algorithm for `C2` and confirm our results. We'll suppress the `ScalaObject`, `AnyRef`, and `Any` for clarity, until the end. See Table 7-5.

Table 7-5. Hand calculation of C2 linearization: C2 extends C2A with T1 with T2 with T3 {...}

#	Linearization	Description
1	C2	Add the type of the instance.
2	C2, T3, C1	Add the linearization for T3 (farthest on the right).
3	C2, T3, C1, T2, C1	Add the linearization for T2.
4	C2, T3, C1, T2, C1, T1, C1	Add the linearization for T1.
5	C2, T3, C1, T2, C1, T1, C1, C2A, T2, C1	Add the linearization for C2A.
6	C2, T3, T2, T1, C2A, T2, C1	Remove duplicates of C1; all but the *last* C1.
7	C2, T3, T1, C2A, T2, C1	Remove duplicate T2; all but the *last* T2.
8	C2, T3, T1, C2A, T2, C1, ScalaObject, AnyRef, Any	Finish!

What the algorithm does is push any shared types to the right until they come after *all* the types that derive from them.

Try modifying the last script with different hierarchies and see if you can reproduce the results using the algorithm.

 Overly complex type hierarchies can result in method lookup "surprises." If you have to work through this algorithm to figure out what's going on, try to simplify your code.

Recap and What's Next

We have finished our survey of Scala's object model. If you come from an object-oriented language background, you now know enough about Scala to replace your existing object-oriented language with object-oriented Scala.

However, there is much more to come. Scala supports *functional programming*, which offers powerful mechanisms for addressing a number of design problems, such as concurrency. We'll see that functional programming appears to contradict object-oriented programming, at least on the surface. That said, a guiding principle behind Scala is that these two paradigms complement each other more than they conflict. Combined, they give you more options for building robust, scalable software. Scala lets you choose the techniques that work best for your needs.

CHAPTER 8

Functional Programming in Scala

Every decade or two, a major computing idea goes mainstream. These ideas may have lurked in the background of academic computer science research, or possibly in some lesser-known field of industry. The transition to mainstream acceptance comes in response to a perceived problem for which the idea is well suited. Object-oriented programming, which was invented in the 1960s, went mainstream in the 1980s, arguably in response to the emergence of graphical user interfaces, for which the OOP paradigm is a natural fit.

Functional programming appears to be experiencing a similar breakout. Long the topic of computer science research and even older than object-oriented programming, functional programming offers effective techniques for concurrent programming, which is growing in importance.

Because functional programming is less widely understood than object-oriented programming, we won't assume that you have prior experience with it. We'll start this chapter with plenty of background information. As you'll see, functional programming is not only a very effective way to approach concurrent programming, which we'll explore in depth in Chapter 9, but functional programming can also improve your objects.

Of course, we can't provide an exhaustive introduction to functional programming. To learn more about it, [O'Sullivan2009] has a more detailed introduction in the context of the Haskell language. [Abelson1996], [VanRoy2004], and [Turbak2008] offer thorough introductions to general programming approaches, including functional programming. Finally, [Okasaki1998] and [Rabhi1999] discuss functional data structures and algorithms in detail.

What Is Functional Programming?

Don't all programming languages have functions of some sort? Whether they are called methods, procedures, or GOTOs, programmers are always dealing in functions.

Functional programming is based on the behavior of functions in the mathematical sense, with all the implications that starting point implies.

Functions in Mathematics

In mathematics, functions have no *side effects*. Consider the classic function `sin(x)`:

```
y = sin(x)
```

No matter how much work `sin(x)` does, all the results are returned and assigned to `y`. No global state of any kind is modified internally by `sin(x)`. Hence, we say that such a function is free of *side effects*, or *pure*.

This property simplifies enormously the challenge of analyzing, testing, and debugging a function. You can do these things without having to know anything about the context in which the function is invoked, except for any other functions it might call. However, you can analyze them in the same way, working bottom up to verify the whole "stack."

This obliviousness to the surrounding context is known as *Referential Transparency*. You can call such a function anywhere and be confident that it will always behave the same way. If no global state is modified, concurrent invocation of the function is straightforward and reliable.

In functional programming, you can compose functions from other functions. For example, `tan(x) = sin(x)/cos(x)`. An implication of composability is that functions can be treated as values. In other words, functions are *first-class*, just like data. You can assign functions to variables. You can pass functions to other functions. You can return functions as values from functions. In the functional paradigm, functions become a primitive type, a building block that's just as essential to the work of programming as integers or strings.

When a function takes other functions as arguments or returns a function, it is called a *higher-order function*. In mathematics, two examples of higher-order functions from calculus are derivation and integration.

Variables that Aren't

The word "variable" takes on a new meaning in functional programming. If you come from a procedural or object-oriented programming background, you are accustomed to variables that are *mutable*. In functional programming, variables are *immutable*.

This is another consequence of the mathematical orientation. In the expression `y = sin(x)`, once you pick `x`, then `y` is fixed. As another example, if you increment the integer 3 by 1, you don't "modify the 3 object," you create a new value to represent 4.

To be more precise, it is the values that are immutable. Functional programming languages prevent you from assigning a new value to a variable that already has a value.

Immutability is difficult when you're not used to it. If you can't change a variable, then you can't have loop counters, for example. We're accustomed to objects that change their state when we call methods on them. Learning to think in immutable terms takes some effort.

However, immutability has enormous benefits for concurrency. Almost all the difficulty of multithreaded programming lies in synchronizing access to shared, mutable state. If you remove mutability, then the problems essentially go away. It is the combination of referentially transparent functions and immutable values that make functional programming compelling as a better way to write concurrent software.

These qualities benefit programs in other ways. Almost all the constructs we have invented in 60-odd years of computer programming have been attempts to manage complexity. Higher-order functions and referential transparency provide very flexible building blocks for composing programs.

Immutability greatly reduces regression bugs, many of which are caused by *unintended* state changes in one part of a program due to *intended* changes in another part. There are other contributors to such *non-local* effects, but mutability is one of the most important.

It's common in object-oriented designs to encapsulate access to data structures in objects. If these structures are mutable, we can't simply share them with clients. We have to add special accessor methods to control access, so clients can't modify them outside our control. These additions increase code size, which increases the testing and maintenance burden, and they increase the effort required by clients to understand the ad hoc features of our APIs.

In contrast, when we have immutable data structures, many of these problems simply go away. We can provide access to collections without fear of data loss or corruption. Of course, the general principles of minimal coupling still apply; should clients care if a Set or List is used, as long as foreach is available?

Immutable data also implies that lots of copies will be made, which can be expensive. Functional data structures optimize for this problem (see [Okasaki1998]) and many of the built-in Scala types are efficient at creating new copies from existing copies.

It's time to dive into the practicalities of functional programming in Scala. We'll discuss other aspects and benefits of the approach as we proceed.

Functional Programming in Scala

As a hybrid object-functional language, Scala does not require functions to be pure, nor does it require variables to be immutable. It does, however, encourage you to write your code this way whenever possible. You have the freedom to use procedural or object-oriented techniques when and where they seem most appropriate.

Though functional languages are all about eliminating side effects, a language that *never* allowed for side effects would be useless. Input and output (IO) are inherently about side effects, and IO is essential to all programming tasks. For this reason, all functional languages provide mechanisms for performing side effects in a controlled way.

Scala doesn't restrict what you can do, but we encourage you to use immutable values and pure functions and methods whenever possible. When mutability and side effects are necessary, pursue them in a "principled" way, isolated in well-defined modules and focused on individual tasks.

If you're new to functional programming, keep in mind that it's easy to fall back to old habits. We encourage you to master the functional side of Scala and to learn to use it effectively.

 A function that returns Unit implies that the function has pure side effects, meaning that if it does any useful work, that work must be all side effects, since the function doesn't return anything.

We've seen many examples of higher-order functions and composability in Scala. For example, List.map takes a function to transform each element of the list to something else:

```
// code-examples/FP/basics/list-map-example-script.scala

List(1, 2, 3, 4, 5) map { _ * 2 }
```

Recall that _ * 2 is a *function literal* that is shorthand for i => i * 2. For each argument to the function, you can use _ if the argument is used only once. We also used the infix operator notation to invoke map. Here's an example that "reduces" the same list by multiplying all the elements together:

```
// code-examples/FP/basics/list-reduceLeft-example-script.scala

List(1, 2, 3, 4, 5) reduceLeft { _ * _ }
```

The first _ represents the argument that is accumulating the value of the reduction, and the second _ represents the current element of the list.

Both examples successfully "looped" through the list without the use of a mutable counter to track iterations. Most containers in the Scala library provide functionally pure iteration methods. In other cases, recursion is the preferred way to traverse a data structure or perform an algorithm. We'll return to this topic in "Recursion" on page 170.

Function Literals and Closures

Let's expand our previous `map` example a bit:

```
// code-examples/FP/basics/list-map-closure-example-script.scala

var factor = 3
val multiplier = (i:Int) => i * factor

val l1 = List(1, 2, 3, 4, 5) map multiplier

factor = 5
val l2 = List(1, 2, 3, 4, 5) map multiplier

println(l1)
println(l2)
```

We defined a variable, `factor`, to use as the multiplication factor, and we pulled out the previous anonymous function into a value called `multiplier` that now uses `factor`. Then we map over a list of integers, as we did before. After the first call to `map`, we change `factor` and map again. Here is the output:

```
List(3, 6, 9, 12, 15)
List(5, 10, 15, 20, 25)
```

Even though `multiplier` was an immutable function value, its behavior changed when `factor` changed.

There are two *free variables* in `multiplier`: `i` and `factor`. One of them, `i`, is a *formal parameter* to the function. Hence, it is *bound* to a new value each time `multiplier` is called.

However, `factor` is not a formal parameter, but a reference to a variable in the enclosing scope. Hence, the compiler creates a *closure* that encompasses (or "closes over") `multiplier` and the external context of the unbound variables `multiplier` references, thereby binding those variables as well.

This is why the behavior of `multiplier` changed after changing `factor`. It references `factor` and reads its current value each time. If a function has no external references, then it is trivially closed over itself. No external context is required.

Purity Inside Versus Outside

If we called `sin(x)` thousands of times with the same value of `x`, it would be wasteful if it calculated the same value every single time. Even in "pure" functional libraries, it is common to perform internal optimizations like caching previously computed values (sometimes called *memoization*). Caching introduces side effects, as the state of the cache is modified.

However, this lack of purity should be opaque to the user (except perhaps in terms of the performance impact). If you are designing functional libraries, ensure that they preserve the purity of their abstractions, including the behavior of referential transparency and its implications for concurrency.

You can see examples of functional libraries with mutable internals in the Scala library. The methods in List often use mutable local variables for efficient traversal. The local variables are thread-safe, as are the traversals, since Lists themselves are immutable.

Recursion

Recursion plays a larger role in pure functional programming than in imperative programming, in part because of the restriction that variables are immutable. For example, you can't have loop counters, which would change on each pass through a loop. One way to implement looping in a purely functional way is with recursion.

Calculating factorials provides a good example. Here is an imperative loop implementation:

```
// code-examples/FP/recursion/factorial-loop-script.scala

def factorial_loop(i: BigInt): BigInt = {
  var result = BigInt(1)
  for (j <- 2 to i.intValue)
    result *= j
  result
}

for (i <- 1 to 10)
  format("%s: %s\n", i, factorial_loop(i))
```

Both the loop counter j and the result are mutable variables. (For simplicity, we're ignoring input numbers that are less than or equal to zero.) The output of the script is the following:

```
1: 1
2: 2
3: 6
4: 24
5: 120
6: 720
7: 5040
8: 40320
9: 362880
10: 3628800
```

Here's a first pass at a recursive implementation:

```
// code-examples/FP/recursion/factorial-recur1-script.scala

def factorial(i: BigInt): BigInt = i match {
  case _ if i == 1 => i
  case _ => i * factorial(i - 1)
}
```

```
for (i <- 1 to 10)
  format("%s: %s\n", i, factorial(i))
```

The output is the same, but now there are no mutable variables. Recursion not only helps us avoid mutable variables, it is also the most natural way to express some functions, particularly mathematical functions. The recursive definition in our second `factorial` is structurally similar to a definition for factorials that you might see in a mathematics book.

However, there are two potential problems with recursion: the performance overhead of repeated function invocations and the risk of stack overflow.

Performance problems in a recursive scenario can sometimes be addressed with *memoization*, but care should be taken that the space requirements of caching don't outweigh the performance benefits.

Stack overflow can be avoided by converting the recursive invocation into a loop of some kind. In fact, the Scala compiler can do this conversion for you for some kinds of recursive invocations, which we describe next.

Tail Calls and Tail-Call Optimization

A particular kind of recursion is called *tail-call* recursion, which occurs when a function calls itself as its final operation. Tail-call recursion is very important because it is the easiest kind of recursion to optimize by conversion into a loop. Loops eliminate the potential of a stack overflow, and they improve performance by eliminating the recursive function call overhead. While tail recursion optimizations are not yet supported natively on the JVM, `scalac` can do them.

However, our factorial example is not a tail recursion, because `factorial` calls itself and *then* does a multiplication with the results. There is a way to implement `factorial` in a tail recursive way. We actually saw an implementation in "Nesting Method Definitions" on page 28. However, that example didn't use some constructs we've learned about since, such as `for` comprehensions and pattern matching. So, here's a new implementation of `factorial`, calculated with tail-call recursion:

```
// code-examples/FP/recursion/factorial-recur2-script.scala

def factorial(i: BigInt): BigInt = {
  def fact(i: BigInt, accumulator: BigInt): BigInt = i match {
    case _ if i == 1 => accumulator
    case _ => fact(i - 1, i * accumulator)
  }
  fact(i, 1)
}

for (i <- 1 to 10)
  format("%s: %s\n", i, factorial(i))
```

This script produces the same output as before. Now, `factorial` does all the work with a nested method, `fact`, that is tail recursive because it passes an `accumulator` argument to hold the computation in progress. This argument is computed with a multiplication *before* the recursive call to `fact`, which is now the very last thing that is done. In our previous implementation, this multiplication was done *after* the call to `fact`. When we call `fact(1)`, we simply return the accumulated value.

If you call our original non-tail recursive implementation of `factorial` with a large number—say 10,000—you'll cause a stack overflow on a typical desktop computer. The tail-recursive implementation works successfully, returning a very large number.

This idiom of nesting a tail-recursive function that uses an accumulator is a very useful technique for converting many recursive algorithms into tail recursions that can be optimized into loops by `scalac`.

 The tail-call optimization won't be applied when a method that calls itself might be overridden in a derived type. The method must be private or final, defined in an `object`, or nested in another method (like `fact` earlier). The new `@tailrec` annotation in version 2.8 will trigger an error if the compiler can't optimize the annotated method. (See "Annotations" on page 289.)

Trampoline for Tail Calls

A *trampoline* is a loop that works through a list of functions, calling each one in turn. The metaphor of bouncing the functions off a trampoline is the source of the name.

Consider a kind of recursion where a function A doesn't call itself recursively, but instead it calls another function B, which calls A, which calls B, etc. This kind of back-and-forth recursion can also be converted into a loop using a trampoline. Note that trampolines impose a performance overhead, but they are ideal for pure functional recursions (versus an imperative equivalent) that would otherwise exhaust the stack.

Support for this optimization is planned for Scala version 2.8, although it has not yet been implemented at the time of this writing.

Functional Data Structures

There are several data structures that are common in functional programming, most of which are containers, like collections. Languages like Erlang rely on very few types, while other functional languages provide a richer type system.

The common data structures support the same subset of higher-order functions for read-only traversal and access to the elements in the data structures. These features make them suitable as "protocols" for minimizing the coupling between components, while supporting data exchange.

In fact, these data structures and their operations are so useful that many languages support them, including those that are not considered functional languages, like Java and Ruby. Java doesn't support higher-order functions directly. Instead, function values have to be wrapped in objects. Ruby uses `procs` and `lambdas` as function values.

Lists in Functional Programming

Lists are the most common data structure in functional programming. They are the core of the first functional programming language, Lisp.

In the interest of immutability, a new list is created when you add an element to a list. It is conventional to prepend the new element to the list, as we've seen before:

```
// code-examples/FP/datastructs/list-script.scala

val list1 = List("Programming", "Scala")
val list2 = "People" :: "should" :: "read" :: list1
println(list2)
```

Because the `::` operator binds to the right, the definition of `list2` is equivalent to both of the following variations:

```
val list2 = ("People" :: ("should" :: ("read" :: list1)))
val list2 = list1.::("read").::("should").::("People")
```

In terms of performance, prepending is O(1). We'll see why when we dive into Scala's implementation of `List` in "A Closer Look at Lists" on page 261, after we have learned more about *parameterized types* in Scala.

Unlike some of the other collections, Scala only defines an immutable `List`. However, it also defines some mutable list types, such as `ListBuffer` and `LinkedList`

Maps in Functional Programming

Perhaps the second most common data structure is the map, referred to as a *hash* or *dictionary* in other languages, and not to be confused with the `map` function we saw earlier. Maps are used to hold pairs of keys and values.

In the interest of minimalism, maps could be implemented with lists. Every even element in the list (counting from zero) could be a key, followed by the value in the next odd position. In practice, maps are usually implemented in other ways for efficiency.

Scala supports the special initialization syntax we saw previously:

```
val stateCapitals = Map(
  "Alabama" -> "Montgomery",
  "Alaska"  -> "Juneau",
  // ...
  "Wyoming" -> "Cheyenne")
```

The `scala.collection.Map[A,+B]` trait only defines methods for reading the `Map`. There are derived traits for immutable and mutable maps, `scala.collection.immuta ble.Map[A,+B]` and `scala.collection.mutable.Map[A,B]`, respectively. They define + and - operators for adding and removing elements, and ++ and -- operators for adding and removing elements defined in `Iterators` of `Pairs`, where each `Pair` is a key-value pair.

 You might have noticed that the + does not appear in front of the `B` type parameters for `scala.collection.mutable.Map`. You'll see why in "Variance of Mutable Types" on page 255.

Sets in Functional Programming

Sets are like lists, but they require each element to be unique. Sets could also be implemented using lists, as long as the equivalent of the list "cons" operator (::) first checks that the element doesn't already exist in the storage list. This property means that element insertion would be O(N) if a storage list were used, and the order of the elements in the set wouldn't necessarily match the order of "insertion" operations. In practice, sets are usually implemented with more efficient data structures.

Just as for `Map`, the `scala.collection.Set[A]` trait only defines methods for reading the `Set`. There are derived traits for immutable and mutable sets, `scala.collec tion.immutable.Set[A]` and `scala.collection.mutable.Set[A]`, respectively. They define + and - operators for adding and removing elements, and ++ and -- operators for adding and removing elements defined in `Iterators` (which could be other sets, lists, etc.).

Other Data Structures in Functional Programming

Other familiar data structures, like `Tuples` and `Arrays`, will appear in functional languages. Typically, they're used to provide some convenient feature not supported by a more common functional type. In most cases they could be replaced with lists.

Traversing, Mapping, Filtering, Folding, and Reducing

The functional collections we just discussed—lists, maps, sets, as well as tuples and arrays—all support several common operations based on read-only traversal. In fact, this uniformity can be exploited if any "container" type also supports these operations. For example, an `Option` contains zero or one elements, if it is a `None` or `Some`, respectively.

Traversal

The standard traversal method for Scala containers is **foreach**, which is defined by the **Iterable** traits that the containers mix in. It is O(N) in the number of elements. Here is an example of its use for lists and maps:

```
// code-examples/FP/datastructs/foreach-script.scala

List(1, 2, 3, 4, 5) foreach { i => println("Int: " + i) }

val stateCapitals = Map(
  "Alabama" -> "Montgomery",
  "Alaska"  -> "Juneau",
  "Wyoming" -> "Cheyenne")

stateCapitals foreach { kv => println(kv._1 + ": " + kv._2) }
```

The signature of **foreach** is the following:

```
trait Iterable[+A] {
  ...
  def foreach(f : (A) => Unit) : Unit = ...
  ...
}
```

foreach is a higher-order function that takes a function argument: the operation to perform on each element. Note that for a map, **A** is actually a tuple, as shown in the example. Also, **foreach** returns **Unit**. **foreach** is not intended to create new collections; we'll see examples of operations that create collections shortly.

Once you have **foreach**, you can implement all the other traversal operations we'll discuss next, and more. A look at **Iterable** will show that it supports methods for filtering collections, finding elements that match specified criteria, calculating the number of elements, and so forth.

The methods we'll discuss next are hallmarks of functional programming: mapping, filtering, folding, and reducing.

Mapping

We've encountered the **map** method before. It returns a new collection of the same size as the original collection. It is also a member of **Iterable**, and its signature is:

```
trait Iterable[+A] {
  ...
  def map[B](f : (A) => B) : Iterable[B] = ...
  ...
}
```

The passed-in function (f) can transform an original element of type A to a new type B. Here is an example:

```
// code-examples/FP/datastructs/map-script.scala

val stateCapitals = Map(
  "Alabama" -> "Montgomery",
  "Alaska"  -> "Juneau",
  "Wyoming" -> "Cheyenne")

val lengths = stateCapitals map { kv => (kv._1, kv._2.length) }
println(lengths)
```

This script produces the output ArrayBuffer((Alabama,10), (Alaska,6), (Wyoming, 8)). That is, we convert the Pair[String,String] elements to an ArrayBuffer of Pair[String,Int] elements. Where did the ArrayBuffer come from? It turns out that Iterable.map creates and returns an ArrayBuffer as the new Iterable collection.

This brings up a general conflict between immutable types and object-oriented type hierarchies. If a base type creates a new instance on modification, how does it know what kind of type to create?

You could solve this problem two ways. First, you could have each type in the hierarchy override methods like map to return an instance of their own type. This approach is error-prone, though, as it would be easy to forget to override all such methods when a new type is added.

Even if you always remember to override each method, you have the dilemma of how to implement the override. Do you call the **super** method to reuse the algorithm, then iterate through the returned instance to create a new instance of the correct type? That would be inefficient. You could copy and paste the algorithm into each override, but that creates issues of code bloat, maintainability, and skew.

There's an alternative approach: don't even try. How is the new instance that is returned actually used? Do we really care if it has the "wrong" type? Keep in mind that all we usually care about are the low-level abstractions like lists, maps, and sets. In the case of functional data structures, the derived types we might implement using object-oriented inheritance are most often implementation optimizations. The Scala type hierarchy for containers does have a few levels of abstractions at the bottom, e.g., Collection extends Iterable extends AnyRef, but above Collection are Seq (parent of List), Map, Set, etc.

That said, if you really need a Map, you can create one easily enough:

```
// code-examples/FP/datastructs/map2-script.scala

val stateCapitals = Map(
  "Alabama" -> "Montgomery",
  "Alaska"  -> "Juneau",
  "Wyoming" -> "Cheyenne")

val map2 = stateCapitals map { kv => (kv._1, kv._2.length) }
```

```
// val lengths = Map(map2)  // ERROR: won't work
val lengths = Map[String,Int]() ++ map2

println(lengths)
```

The commented-out line suggests that it would be nice if you could simply pass the new Iterable to Map.apply, but this doesn't work. Here is the signature of Map.apply:

```
object Map {
  ...
  def apply[A, B](elems : (A, B)*) : Map[A, B] = ...
  ...
}
```

It expects a variable argument list, not an Iterable. However, we can create an empty map of the right type and then add the new Iterable to it, using the ++ method, which returns a new Map.

So, we can get the Map we want when we must have one. While it would be nice if methods like map returned the same collection type, we saw that there is no easy way to do this. Instead, we accept that map and similar methods return an abstraction like Iterable and then rely on the specific subtypes to take Iterables as input arguments for populating the collection.

A related Map operation is flatMap, which can be used to "flatten" a hierarchical data structure, remove "empty" elements, etc. Hence, unlike map, it may not return a new collection of the same size as the original collection:

```
// code-examples/FP/datastructs/flatmap-script.scala

val graph = List(
  "a", List("b1", "b2", "b3"), List("c1", List("c21", Nil, "c22"), Nil, "e")
)

def flatten(list: List[_]): List[_] = list flatMap {
  case head :: tail => head :: flatten(tail)
  case Nil => Nil
  case x => List(x)
}

println(flatten(graph))
```

This script reduces the hierarchical graph to List(a, b1, b2, b3, c1, c21, c22, e). Notice that the Nil elements have been removed. We used List[_] because we won't know what the type parameters are for any embedded lists when we're traversing the outer list, due to *type erasure*.

Here is the signature for flatMap, along with map, for comparison:

```
trait Iterable[+A] {
  ...
  def map[B]    (f : (A) => B) : Iterable[B] = ...
  def flatMap[B](f : (A) => Iterable[B]) : Iterable[B]
```

```
      ...
  }
```

Each pass must return an Iterable[B], not a B. After going through the collection, flatMap will "flatten" all those Iterables into one collection. Note that flatMap won't flatten elements beyond one level. If our function literal leaves nested lists intact, they won't be flattened for us.

Filtering

It is common to traverse a collection and extract a new collection from it with elements that match certain criteria:

```scala
// code-examples/FP/datastructs/filter-script.scala

val stateCapitals = Map(
  "Alabama" -> "Montgomery",
  "Alaska"  -> "Juneau",
  "Wyoming" -> "Cheyenne")

val map2 = stateCapitals filter { kv => kv._1 startsWith "A" }

println( map2 )
```

There are several different kinds of methods defined in Iterable for filtering or otherwise returning part of the original collection (comments adapted from the Scaladocs):

```scala
trait Iterable[+A] {
  ...
  // Returns this iterable without its n first elements. If this iterable
  // has less than n elements, the empty iterable is returned.
  def drop (n : Int) : Collection[A] = ...

  // Returns the longest suffix of this iterable whose first element does
  // not satisfy the predicate p.
  def dropWhile (p : (A) => Boolean) : Collection[A] = ...

  // Apply a predicate p to all elements of this iterable object and
  // return true, iff there is at least one element for which p yields true.
  def exists (p : (A) => Boolean) : Boolean = ...

  // Returns all the elements of this iterable that satisfy the predicate p.
  // The order of the elements is preserved.
  def filter (p : (A) => Boolean) : Iterable[A] = ...

  // Find and return the first element of the iterable object satisfying a
  // predicate, if any.
  def find (p : (A) => Boolean) : Option[A] = ...

  // Returns index of the first element satisying a predicate, or -1.
  def findIndexOf (p : (A) => Boolean) : Int = ...

  // Apply a predicate p to all elements of this iterable object and return
  // true, iff the predicate yields true for all elements.
```

```scala
    def forall (p : (A) => Boolean) : Boolean = ...

    // Returns the index of the first occurence of the specified object in
    // this iterable object.
    def indexOf [B >: A](elem : B) : Int = ...

    // Partitions this iterable in two iterables according to a predicate.
    def partition (p : (A) => Boolean) : (Iterable[A], Iterable[A]) = ...

    // Checks if the other iterable object contains the same elements.
    def sameElements [B >: A](that : Iterable[B]) : Boolean = ...

    // Returns an iterable consisting only over the first n elements of this
    // iterable, or else the whole iterable, if it has less than n elements.
    def take (n : Int) : Collection[A] = ...

    // Returns the longest prefix of this iterable whose elements satisfy the
    // predicate p.
    def takeWhile (p : (A) => Boolean) : Iterable[A] = ...
}
```

Types like `Map` and `Set` have additional methods.

Folding and Reducing

We'll discuss folding and reducing in the same section, as they're similar. Both are operations for "shrinking" a collection down to a smaller collection or a single value.

Folding starts with an initial "seed" value and processes each element in the context of that value. In contrast, reducing doesn't start with a user-supplied initial value. Rather, it uses the first element as the initial value:

```scala
// code-examples/FP/datastructs/foldreduce-script.scala

List(1,2,3,4,5,6) reduceLeft(_ + _)

List(1,2,3,4,5,6).foldLeft(10)(_ * _)
```

This script reduces the list of integers by adding them together, returning 21. It then folds the same list using multiplication with a seed of 10, returning 7,200.

Reducing can't work on an empty collection, since there would be nothing to return. In this case, an exception is thrown. Folding on an empty collection will simply return the seed value.

Folding also offers more options for the final result. Here is a "fold" operation that is really a map operation:

```scala
// code-examples/FP/datastructs/foldleft-map-script.scala

List(1, 2, 3, 4, 5, 6).foldLeft(List[String]()) {
  (list, x) => ("<" + x + ">") :: list
}.reverse
```

It returns List(<1>, <2>, <3>, <4>, <5>, <6>). Note that we had to call **reverse** on the result to get back a list in the same order as the input list.

Here are the signatures for the various fold and reduce operations in `Iterable`:

```
trait Iterable[+A] {
  ...
  // Combines the elements of this iterable object together using the
  // binary function op, from left to right, and starting with the value z.
  def foldLeft [B](z : B)(op : (B, A) => B) : B

  // Combines the elements of this list together using the binary function
  // op, from right to left, and starting with the value z.
  def foldRight [B](z : B)(op : (A, B) => B) : B

  // Similar to foldLeft but can be used as an operator with the order of
  // list and zero arguments reversed. That is, z /: xs is the same as
  // xs foldLeft z
  def /: [B](z : B)(op : (B, A) => B) : B

  // An alias for foldRight. That is, xs :\ z is the same as xs foldRight z
  def :\ [B](z : B)(op : (A, B) => B) : B

  // Combines the elements of this iterable object together using the
  // binary operator op, from left to right
  def reduceLeft [B >: A](op : (B, A) => B) : B

  // Combines the elements of this iterable object together using the
  // binary operator op, from right to left
  def reduceRight [B >: A](op : (A, B) => B) : B
```

Many people consider the operator forms, :\ for `foldRight` and /: for `foldLeft`, to be a little too obscure and hard to remember. Don't forget the importance of communicating with your readers when writing code.

Why are there left and right forms of fold and reduce? For the first examples we showed, adding and multiplying a list of integers, they would return the same result. Consider a `foldRight` version of our last example that used fold to map the integers to strings:

```
// code-examples/FP/datastructs/foldright-map-script.scala

List(1, 2, 3, 4, 5, 6).foldRight(List[String]()) {
  (x, list) => ("<" + x + ">") :: list
}
```

This script produces List(<1>, <2>, <3>, <4>, <5>, <6>), without having to call **reverse**, as we did before. Note also that the arguments to the function literal are reversed compared to the arguments for `foldLeft`, as required by the definition of `foldRight`.

Both `foldLeft` and `reduceLeft` process the elements from left to right. Here is the `foldLeft` sequence for List(1,2,3,4,5,6).foldLeft(10)(_ * _):

```
((((((10 * 1) * 2) * 3) * 4) * 5) * 6)
((((((10) * 2) * 3) * 4) * 5) * 6)
```

```
(((((20) * 3) * 4) * 5) * 6)
((((60) * 4) * 5) * 6)
(((240) * 5) * 6)
((1200) * 6)
(7200)
```

Here is the `foldRight` sequence:

```
(1 * (2 * (3 * (4 * (5 * (6 * 10))))))
(1 * (2 * (3 * (4 * (5 * (60))))))
(1 * (2 * (3 * (4 * (300)))))
(1 * (2 * (3 * (1200))))
(1 * (2 * (3600)))
(1 * (7200))
(7200)
```

It turns out that `foldLeft` and `reduceLeft` have one very important advantage over their "right-handed" brethren: they are tail-call recursive, and as such they can benefit from tail-call optimization.

If you stare at the previous breakdowns for multiplying the integers, you can probably see why they are tail-call recursive. Recall that a tail call must be the last operation in an iteration. For each line in the `foldRight` sequence, the outermost multiplication can't be done until the innermost multiplications all complete, so the operation isn't tail recursive.

In the following script, the first line prints 1784293664, while the second line causes a stack overflow:

```
// code-examples/FP/datastructs/reduceleftright-script.scala

println((1 to 1000000) reduceLeft(_ + _))
println((1 to 1000000) reduceRight(_ + _))
```

So why have both kinds of recursion? If you're not worried about overflow, a right recursion might be the most natural fit for the operation you are doing. Recall that when we used `foldLeft` to map integers to strings, we had to reverse the result. That was easy enough to do in that case, but in general, the result of a left recursion might not always be easy to convert to the right form.

Functional Options

You'll find the functional operations we've explored throughout the Scala library, and not exclusively on collection classes. The always handy `Option` container supports `filter`, `map`, `flatMap`, and other functionally oriented methods that are applied only if the `Option` isn't empty (that is, if it's a `Some` and not a `None`).

Let's see this in practice:

```
// code-examples/FP/datastructs/option-script.scala

val someNumber = Some(5)
val noneNumber = None
```

```
for (option <- List(noneNumber, someNumber)) {
  option.map(n => println(n * 5))
}
```

In this example, we attempt to multiply the contents of two `Options` by five. Normally, trying to multiply a `null` value would result in an error. But because the implementation of `map` on `Option` only applies the passed-in function when it's non-empty, we don't have to worry about testing for the presence of a value or handling an exception when we map over the `None`.

Functional operations on `Options` save us from extra conditional expressions or pattern matching. Pattern matching, though, is a powerful tool within the context of functional programming, as we'll explore in the next section.

Pattern Matching

We've seen many examples of pattern matching throughout this book. We got our first taste in "A Taste of Concurrency" on page 16, where we used pattern matching in our Actor that drew geometric shapes. We discussed pattern matching in depth in "Pattern Matching" on page 63.

Pattern matching is a fundamental tool in functional programming. It's just as important as polymorphism is in object-oriented programming, although the goals of the two techniques are very different.

Pattern matching is an elegant way to decompose objects into their constituent parts for processing. On the face of it, pattern matching for this purpose seems to violate the goal of encapsulation that objects provide. Immutability, though, largely rectifies this conflict. The risk that the parts of an object might be changed outside of the control of the enclosing object is avoided.

For example, if we have a `Person` class that contains a list of addresses, we don't mind exposing that list to clients if the list is immutable. They can't unexpectedly change the list.

However, exposing constituent parts potentially couples clients to the *types* of those parts. We can't change how the parts are implemented without breaking the clients. A way to minimize this risk is to expose the lowest-level abstractions possible. When clients access a person's addresses, do they really need to know that they are stored in a `List`, or is it sufficient to know that they are stored in an `Iterable` or `Seq`? If so, then we can change the implementation of the addresses as long as they still support those abstractions. Of course, we've known for a long time in object-oriented programming that you should only couple to abstractions, not concrete details (for example, see [Martin2003]).

Functional pattern matching and object-oriented polymorphism are powerful complements to each other. We saw this in the Actor example in "A Taste of Concurrency" on page 16, where we matched on the Shape abstraction, but called the polymorphic draw operation.

Partial Functions

You've seen *partially applied* functions, or partial functions, throughout this book. When you've seen an underscore passed to a method, you've probably seen partial application at work.

Partial functions are expressions in which not all of the arguments defined in a function are supplied as parameters to the function. In Scala, partial functions are used to bundle up a function, including its parameters and return type, and assign that function to a variable or pass it as an argument to another function.

This is a bit confusing until we see it in practice:

```
// code-examples/FP/partial/partial-script.scala

def concatUpper(s1: String, s2: String): String = (s1 + " " + s2).toUpperCase

val c = concatUpper _
println(c("short", "pants"))

val c2 = concatUpper("short", _: String)
println(c2("pants"))
```

Calling concatUpper with an underscore (_) turns the method into a function value. In the first part of the example, we've assigned a partially applied version of concatUpper to the value c. We then *apply* it, implicitly calling the apply method on c by passing parameters to it directly. The returned value is then printed.

In the second part, we've specified the first parameter to concatUpper but not the second, although we have specified the type of the second parameter. We've assigned this variant to a second value, c2. To produce the same output as we saw before, we need only pass in a single value when we apply c2. We've applied part of the function in the assignment to c2, and we "fill in the blanks" when we call c2 on the next line.

We've seen partially applied functions without the underscore syntax as well:

```
List("short", "pants").map(println)
```

In this example, println is the partially applied function. It's applied when invoked by mapping over each element in the list. Because the map operation expects a function as an argument, we don't need to write map(println _). The trailing underscore that turns println into a function value is implied, in this context.

Another way of thinking of partial functions is as functions that will inform you when you supply them with parameters that are out of their domain. Every partial function is, as you might guess, of the type `PartialFunction`. This trait defines a method `orElse` that takes another `PartialFunction`. Should the first partial function not apply, the second will be invoked.

Again, this is easier understood in practice:

```
// code-examples/FP/partial/orelse-script.scala

val truthier: PartialFunction[Boolean, String] = { case true => "truthful" }
val fallback: PartialFunction[Boolean, String] = { case x => "sketchy" }
val tester = truthier orElse fallback

println(tester(1 == 1))
println(tester(2 + 2 == 5))
```

In this example, `tester` is a partial function composed of two other partial functions, `truthier` and `fallback`. In the first `println` statement, `truthier` is executed because the partial function's internal case matches. In the second, `fallback` is executed because the value of the expression is outside of the domain of `truthier`.

The `case` statements we've seen through our exploration of Scala are expanded internally to partially applied functions. The functions provide the abstract method `isDefinedAt`, a feature of the `PartialFunction` trait used to specify the boundaries of a partial function's domain:

```
// code-examples/FP/partial/isdefinedat-script.scala

val pantsTest: PartialFunction[String, String] = {
  case "pants" => "yes, we have pants!"
}

println(pantsTest.isDefinedAt("pants"))
println(pantsTest.isDefinedAt("skort"))
```

Here, our partial function is a test for the string `"pants"`. When we inquire as to whether the string `"pants"` is defined for this function, the result is `true`. But for the string `"skort"`, the result is `false`. Were we defining our own partial function, we could provide an implementation of `isDefinedAt` that performs any arbitrary test for the boundaries of our function.

Currying

Just as you encountered partially applied functions before we defined them, you've also seen *curried* functions. Named after mathematician Haskell Curry (from whom the Haskell language also get its name), currying transforms a function that takes multiple parameters into a chain of functions, each taking a single parameter.

In Scala, curried functions are defined with multiple parameter lists, as follows:

```
def cat(s1: String)(s2: String) = s1 + s2
```

Of course, we could define more than two parameters on a curried function, if we like.

We can also use the following syntax to define a curried function:

```
def cat(s1: String) = (s2: String) => s1 + s2
```

While the previous syntax is more readable, in our estimation, using this syntax eliminates the requirement of a trailing underscore when treating the curried function as a partially applied function.

Calling our curried string concatenation function looks like this in the Scala REPL:

```
scala> cat("foo")("bar")
res1: java.lang.String = foobar
```

We can also convert methods that take multiple parameters into a curried form with the `Function.curried` method:

```
scala> def cat(s1: String, s2: String) = s1 + s2
cat: (String,String)java.lang.String

scala> val curryCat = Function.curried(cat _)
curryCat: (String) => (String) => java.lang.String = <function>

scala> cat("foo", "bar") == curryCat("foo")("bar")
res2: Boolean = true
```

In this example, we transform a function that takes two arguments, **cat**, into its curried equivalent that takes multiple parameter lists. If **cat** had taken three parameters, its curried equivalent would take three lists of arguments, and so on. The two forms are functionally equivalent, as demonstrated by the equality test, but **curryCat** can now be used as the basis of a partially applied function as well:

```
scala> val partialCurryCat = curryCat("foo")(_)
partialCurryCat: (String) => java.lang.String = <function>

scala> partialCurryCat("bar")
res3: java.lang.String = foobar
```

In practice, the primary use for currying is to specialize functions for particular types of data. You can start with an extremely general case, and use the curried form of a function to narrow down to particular cases.

As a simple example of this approach, the following code provides specialized forms of a base function that handles multiplication:

```
def multiplier(i: Int)(factor: Int) = i * factor
val byFive = multiplier(5) _
val byTen = multiplier(10) _
```

We start with **multiplier**, which takes two parameters: an integer, and another integer to multiply the first one by. We then curry two special cases of **multiplier** into function values. Note the trailing underscores, which indicate to the compiler that the preceding expression is to be curried. In particular, the wildcard underscores indicate that the remaining arguments (in this example, one argument) are unspecified.

In the Scala console, we get predictable output when calling our curried functions:

```
scala> byFive(2)
res4: Int = 10

scala> byTen(2)
res5: Int = 20
```

We'll revisit the **curry** method in "Function Types" on page 277.

As you can see, currying and partially applied functions are closely related concepts. You may see them referred to almost interchangeably, but what's important is their application (no pun intended).

Implicits

There are times when you have an instance of one type and you need to use it in a context where a different, but perhaps a similar type is required. For the "one-off" case, you might create an instance of the required type using the state of the instance you already have. However, for the general case, if there are many such occurrences in the code, you would rather have an automated conversion mechanism.

A similar problem occurs when you call one or more functions repeatedly and have to pass the same value to all the invocations. You might like a way of specifying a default value for that parameter, so it is not necessary to specify it explicitly all the time.

The Scala keyword **implicit** can be used to support both needs.

Implicit Conversions

Consider the following code fragment:

```
val name: String = "scala"
println(name.capitalize.reverse)
```

It prints the following:

```
alacS
```

We saw in "The Predef Object" on page 145 that **Predef** defines the **String** type to be **java.lang.String**, yet the methods **capitalize** and **reverse** aren't defined on **java.lang.String**. How did this code work?

The Scala library defines a "wrapper" class called **scala.runtime.RichString** that has these methods, and the compiler converted the **name** string to it implicitly using a special method defined in **Predef** called **stringWrapper**:

```
implicit def stringWrapper(x: String) = new runtime.RichString(x)
```

The **implicit** keyword tells the compiler it can use this method for an "implicit" conversion from a **String** to a **RichString**, whenever the latter is required. The compiler detected an attempt to call a **capitalize** method, and it determined that **RichString** has such a method. Then it looked within the current scope for an `implicit` method that converts `String` to `RichString`, finding `stringWrapper`.

As we'll see in "Views and View Bounds" on page 263, these conversion methods are sometimes called *views*, in the sense that our `stringWrapper` conversion provides a view from `String` to `RichString`.

`Predef` defines many other implicit conversion methods, most of which follow the naming convention `old2New`, where `old` is the type of object available and `New` is the desired type. However, there is no restriction on the names of conversion methods. There are also a number of other `Rich` wrapper classes defined in the `scala.runtime` package.

Here is a summary of the lookup rules used by the compiler to find and apply conversion methods. For more details, see [ScalaSpec2009]:

1. No conversion will be attempted if the object and method combination type check successfully.
2. Only methods with the `implicit` keyword are considered.
3. Only implicit methods in the current scope are considered, as well as implicit methods defined in the *companion object* of the *target* type.
4. Implicit methods aren't chained to get from the available type, through intermediate types, to the `target` type. Only a method that takes a single available type instance and returns a target type instance will be considered.
5. No conversion is attempted if more than one possible conversion method could be applied. There must be one and only one possibility.

What if you can't define a conversion method in a companion object, to satisfy the third rule, perhaps because you can't modify or create the companion object? In this case, define the method somewhere else and import it. Normally, you will define an `object` with just the conversion method(s) needed. Here is an example:

```
// code-examples/FP/implicits/implicit-conversion-script.scala
import scala.runtime.RichString

class FancyString(val str: String)

object FancyString2RichString {
    implicit def fancyString2RichString(fs: FancyString) =
        new RichString(fs.str)
}

import FancyString2RichString._

val fs = new FancyString("scala")
println(fs.capitalize.reverse)
```

We can't modify `RichString` or `Predef` to add an implicit conversion method for our custom `FancyString` class. Instead, we define an `object` named `FancyString2Rich String` and define the conversion method in it. We then import the contents of this object and the converter gets invoked implicitly in the last line. The output of this script is the following:

```
alacS
```

This pattern for effectively adding new methods to classes has been called *Pimp My Library* (see [Odersky2006]).

Implicit Function Parameters

We saw in Chapter 2 that Scala version 2.8 adds support for default argument values, like you find in other languages like Ruby and C++. There are two other ways to achieve the same effect in all versions of Scala. The first is to use function currying, as we have seen. The second way is to define *implicit* values, using the `implicit` keyword.

Let's examine how implicit values work:

```scala
// code-examples/FP/implicits/implicit-parameter-script.scala
import scala.runtime.RichString

def multiplier(i: Int)(implicit factor: Int) {
  println(i * factor)
}

implicit val factor = 2

multiplier(2)
multiplier(2)(3)
```

Our multiplier takes two lists of parameters. The latter includes an integer value, `factor`, marked `implicit`. This keyword informs the compiler to seek the value for `factor` from the surrounding scope, if available, or to use whatever parameter has been explicitly supplied to the function.

We've defined our own `factor` value in scope, and that value is used in the first call to `multiplier`. In the second call, we're explicitly passing in a value for `factor` and it overrides the value in the surrounding scope.

Essentially, implicit function parameters behave as parameters with a default value, with the key difference being that the value comes from the surrounding scope. Had our `factor` value resided in a class or object, we would have had to import it into the local scope. If the compiler can't determine the value to use for an implicit parameter, an error of "no implicit argument matching parameter" will occur.

Final Thoughts on Implicits

Implicits can be perilously close to "magic." When used excessively, they obfuscate the code's behavior for the reader. Also, be careful about the implementation of a conversion method, especially if the return type is not explicitly declared. If a future change to the method also changes the return type in some subtle way, the conversion may suddenly fail to work. In general, implicits can cause mysterious behavior that is hard to debug!

When deciding how to implement "default" values for method arguments, a major advantage of using default argument values (in Scala version 2.8) is that the method maintainer decides what to use as the default value. The implementation is more straightforward and you avoid the "magic" of implicit methods. However, a disadvantage of using default argument values is that it might be desirable to use a different "default" value based on the context in which the method is being called. Scala version 2.8 provides some flexibility, as you can use an expression for an argument, not just a constant value. However, that flexibility might not be enough, in which case implicits are a very flexible and powerful alternative.

 Use implicits sparingly and cautiously. Also, consider adding an explicit return type to "non-trivial" conversion methods.

Call by Name, Call by Value

Typically, parameters to functions are *by-value* parameters; that is, the value of the parameter is determined before it is passed to the function. In most circumstances, this is the behavior we want and expect.

But what if we need to write a function that accepts as a parameter an expression that we don't want evaluated until it's called within our function? For this circumstance, Scala offers *by-name* parameters.

A by-name parameter is specified by omitting the parentheses that normally accompany a function parameter, as follows:

```
def myCallByNameFunction(callByNameParameter: => ReturnType)
```

Without this syntactic shortcut, this method definition would look like the following:

```
def myCallByNameFunction(callByNameParameter: () => ReturnType)
```

And what's more, we would have to include those unsightly, empty parentheses in every call to that method. Use of by-name parameters removes that requirement.

We can use by-name parameters to implement powerful looping constructs, among other things. Let's go crazy and implement our own `while` loop, throwing currying into the mix:

```
// code-examples/FP/overrides/call-by-name-script.scala

def whileAwesome(conditional: => Boolean)(f: => Unit) {
  if (conditional) {
    f
    whileAwesome(conditional)(f)
  }
}

var count = 0

whileAwesome(count < 5) {
  println("still awesome")
  count += 1
}
```

What would happen if we removed the arrow between `conditional:` and `Boolean`? The expression `count < 5` would be evaluated to `true` before being passed into our custom `while` loop, and the message "still awesome" would be printed to the console indefinitely. By delaying evaluation until `conditional` is called inside our function with a by-name parameter, we get the behavior we expect.

Lazy Vals

In "Overriding Abstract and Concrete Fields in Traits" on page 114, we showed several scenarios where the order of initialization for fields in override scenarios can be problematic. We discussed one solution, *pre-initialized fields*. Now we discuss the other solution we mentioned previously, `lazy vals`.

Here is that example rewritten with a `lazy val`:

```
// code-examples/FP/overrides/trait-lazy-init-val-script.scala

trait AbstractT2 {
  println("In AbstractT2:")
  val value: Int
  lazy val inverse = { println("initializing inverse:"); 1.0/value }
  //println("AbstractT2: value = "+value+", inverse = "+inverse)
}

val c2d = new AbstractT2 {
  println("In c2d:")
  val value = 10
}

println("Using c2d:")
println("c2d.value = "+c2d.value+", inverse = "+c2d.inverse)
```

The is the output of the script:

```
In AbstractT2:
In c2d:
Using c2d:
```

```
initializing inverse:
c2d.value = 10, inverse = 0.1
```

As before, we are using an anonymous inner class that implicitly extends the trait. The body of the class, which initializes `value`, is evaluated *after* the trait's body. However, note that `inverse` is declared `lazy`, which means that the righthand side will be evaluated only when `inverse` is actually *used*. In this case, that happens in the last `println` statement. Only then is `inverse` initialized, using `value`, which is properly initialized at this point.

Try uncommenting the `println` statement at the end of the `AbstractT2` body. What happens now?

```
In AbstractT2:
initializing inverse:
AbstractT2: value = 0, inverse = Infinity
In c2d:
Using c2d:
c2d.value = 10, inverse = Infinity
```

This `println` forces `inverse` to be evaluated inside the body of `AbstractT2`, before `value` is initialized by the class body, thereby reproducing the problem we had before.

This example raises an important point; if other `val`s use the `lazy val` in the same class or trait body, they should be declared `lazy`, too. Also, watch out for function calls in the body that use the `lazy val`.

 If a `val` is `lazy`, make sure all uses of the `val` are also `lazy`!

So, how is a `lazy val` different from a method call? In a method call, the body is executed *every* time the method is invoked. For a `lazy val`, the initialization "body" is evaluated only once, when the variable is used for the first time. This one-time evaluation makes little sense for a mutable field. Therefore, the `lazy` keyword is not allowed on `var`s. (They can't really make use of it anyway.)

You can also use `lazy val`s to avoid costly initializations that you may not actually need and to defer initializations that slow down application startup. They work well in constructors, where it's clear to other programmers that all the one-time heavy lifting for initializing an instance is done in one place.

Another use for laziness is to manage potentially infinite data structures where only a manageable subset of the data will actually be used. In fact, mathematic notation is inherently lazy. When we write the Fibonacci sequence, for example, we might write it as an infinite sequence, something like this:

```
Fib = 1, 1, 2, 3, 5, 8, ...
```

Some pure functional languages are lazy by default, so they mimic this behavior as closely as possible. This can work without exhausting resources if the user never tries to use more than a finite subset of these values. Scala is not lazy by default, but it does offer support for working with infinite data structures. We'll address this topic in "Infinite Data Structures and Laziness" on page 285.

Recap: Functional Component Abstractions

When object-oriented programming went mainstream in the late '80s and early '90s, there was great hope that it would usher in an era of reusable software components. It didn't really work out that way, except in some rare cases, like the windowing APIs of various platforms.

Why did this not happen? There are certainly many reasons, but a likely source is the fact that simple source or binary interoperability protocols never materialized that would glue these components together. The richness of object APIs was the very factor that undermined componentization.

Component models that have succeeded are all based on very simple foundations. Integrated circuits (ICs) in electronics plug into buses with 2^n signaling wires that are boolean, either on or off. From that very simple protocol, the most explosive growth of any industry in human history was born.

HTTP is another good example. With a handful of message types and a very simple standard for message content, it set the stage for the Internet revolution. RESTful web services built on top of HTTP are also proving successful as components, but they are just complex enough that care is required to ensure that they work successfully.

So, is there hope for a binary or source-level component model? It probably won't be object-oriented, as we've seen. Rather, it could be more functional.

Components should interoperate by exchanging a few immutable data structures, e.g., lists and maps, that carry both data and "commands." Such a component model would have the simplicity necessary for success and the richness required to perform real work. Notice how that sounds a lot like HTTP and REST.

In fact, the Actor model has many of these qualities, as we'll explore in the next chapter.

CHAPTER 9

Robust, Scalable Concurrency with Actors

The Problems of Shared, Synchronized State

Concurrency isn't easy. Getting a program to do more than one thing at a time has traditionally meant hassling with mutexes, race conditions, lock contention, and the rest of the unpleasant baggage that comes along with multithreading. Event-based concurrency models alleviate some of these concerns, but can turn large programs into a rat's nest of callback functions. No wonder, then, that concurrent programming is a task most programmers dread, or avoid altogether by retreating to multiple independent processes that share data externally (for example, through a database or message queue).

A large part of the difficulty of concurrent programming comes down to state: how do you know what your multithreaded program is doing, and when? What value does a particular variable hold when you have 2 threads running, or 5, or 50? How can you guarantee that your program's many tendrils aren't clobbering one another in a race to take action? A thread-based concurrency paradigm poses more questions than it answers.

Thankfully, Scala offers a reasonable, flexible approach to concurrency that we'll explore in this chapter.

Actors

Though you may have heard of Scala and Actors in the same breath, Actors aren't a concept unique to Scala. Actors, originally intended for use in Artificial Intelligence research, were first put forth in 1973 (see [Hewitt1973] and [Agha1987]). Since then, variations on the idea of Actors have appeared in a number of programming languages, most notably in Erlang and Io. As an abstraction, Actors are general enough that they can be implemented as a library (as in Scala), or as the fundamental unit of a computational system.

Actors in Abstract

Fundamentally, an Actor is an object that receives messages and takes action on those messages. The order in which messages arrive is unimportant to an Actor, though some Actor implementations (such as Scala's) queue messages in order. An Actor might handle a message internally, or it might send a message to another Actor, or it might create another Actor to take action based on the message. Actors are a very high-level abstraction.

Unlike traditional object systems (which, you might be thinking to yourself, have many of the same properties we've described), Actors don't enforce a sequence or ordering to their actions. This inherent eschewing of sequentiality, coupled with independence from shared global state, allow Actors to do their work in parallel. As we'll see later on, the judicious use of immutable data fits the Actor model ideally, and further aids in safe, comprehensible concurrent programming.

Enough theory. Let's see Actors in action.

Actors in Scala

At their most basic, Actors in Scala are objects that inherit from `scala.actors.Actor`:

```
// code-examples/Concurrency/simple-actor-script.scala

import scala.actors.Actor

class Redford extends Actor {
  def act() {
    println("A lot of what acting is, is paying attention.")
  }
}

val robert = new Redford
robert.start
```

As we can see, an Actor defined in this way must be both instantiated and started, similar to how threads are handled in Java. It must also implement the abstract method `act`, which returns `Unit`. Once we've started this simple Actor, the following sage advice for thespians is printed to the console:

```
A lot of what acting is, is paying attention.
```

The `scala.actors` package contains a factory method for creating Actors that avoids much of the setup in the above example. We can import this method and other convenience methods from `scala.actors.Actors._`. Here is a factory-made Actor:

```
// code-examples/Concurrency/factory-actor-script.scala

import scala.actors.Actor
import scala.actors.Actor._

val paulNewman = actor {
  println("To be an actor, you have to be a child.")
}
```

While a subclass that extends the Actor class must define act in order to be concrete, a factory-produced Actor has no such limitation. In this shorter example, the body of the method passed to actor is effectively promoted to the act method from our first example. Predictably, this Actor also prints a message when run. Illuminating, but we still haven't shown the essential piece of the Actors puzzle: sending messages.

Sending Messages to Actors

Actors can receive any sort of object as a message, from strings of text to numeric types to whatever classes you've cooked up in your programs. For this reason, Actors and pattern matching go hand in hand. An Actor should only act on messages of familiar types; a pattern match on the class and/or contents of a message is good defensive programming and increases the readability of Actor code:

```
// code-examples/Concurrency/pattern-match-actor-script.scala

import scala.actors.Actor
import scala.actors.Actor._

val fussyActor = actor {
  loop {
    receive {
      case s: String => println("I got a String: " + s)
      case i: Int => println("I got an Int: " + i.toString)
      case _ => println("I have no idea what I just got.")
    }
  }
}

fussyActor ! "hi there"
fussyActor ! 23
fussyActor ! 3.33
```

This example prints the following when run:

```
I got a String: hi there
I got an Int: 23
I have no idea what I just got.
```

The body of fussyActor is a receive method wrapped in a loop. loop is essentially a nice shortcut for while(true); it does whatever is inside its block repeatedly. receive blocks until it gets a message of a type that will satisfy one of its internal pattern matching cases.

The final lines of this example demonstrate use of the ! (exclamation point, or *bang*) method to send messages to our Actor. If you've ever seen Actors in Erlang, you'll find this syntax familiar. The Actor is always on the lefthand side of the bang, and the message being sent to said Actor is always on the right. If you need a mnemonic for this granule of syntactic sugar, imagine that you're an irate director shouting commands at your Actors.

The Mailbox

Every Actor has a *mailbox* in which messages sent to that Actor are queued. Let's see an example where we inspect the size of an Actor's mailbox:

```
// code-examples/Concurrency/actor-mailbox-script.scala

import scala.actors.Actor
import scala.actors.Actor._

val countActor = actor {
  loop {
    react {
      case "how many?" => {
        println("I've got " + mailboxSize.toString + " messages in my mailbox.")
      }
    }
  }
}

countActor ! 1
countActor ! 2
countActor ! 3
countActor ! "how many?"
countActor ! "how many?"
countActor ! 4
countActor ! "how many?"
```

This example produces the following output:

```
I've got 3 messages in my mailbox.
I've got 3 messages in my mailbox.
I've got 4 messages in my mailbox.
```

Note that the first and second lines of output are identical. Because our Actor was set up solely to process messages of the string "how many?", those messages didn't remain in its mailbox. Only the messages of types we didn't know about—in this case, Int—remained unprocessed.

 If you see an Actor's mailbox size ballooning unexpectedly, you're probably sending messages of a type that the Actor doesn't know about. Include a catchall case (_) when pattern matching messages to find out what's harassing your Actors.

Actors in Depth

Now that we've got a basic sense of what Actors are and how they're used in Scala, let's put them to work. Specifically, let's put them to work cutting hair. The *sleeping barber problem* (see [SleepingBarberProblem]) is one of a popular set of computer science hypotheticals designed to demonstrate issues of concurrency and synchronization.

The problem is this: a hypothetical barber shop has just one barber with one barber chair, and three chairs in which customers may wait for a haircut. Without customers around, the barber sleeps. When a customer arrives, the barber wakes up to cut his hair. If the barber is busy cutting hair when a customer arrives, the customer sits down in an available chair. If a chair isn't available, the customer leaves.

The sleeping barber problem is usually solved with semaphores and mutexes, but we've got better tools at our disposal. Straight away, we see several things to model as Actors: the barber is clearly one, as are the customers. The barbershop itself could be modeled as an Actor, too; there need not be a real-world parallel to verbal communication in an Actor system, even though we're sending messages.

Let's start with the sleeping barber's customers, as they have the simplest responsibilities:

```
// code-examples/Concurrency/sleepingbarber/customer.scala

package sleepingbarber

import scala.actors.Actor
import scala.actors.Actor._

case object Haircut

class Customer(val id: Int) extends Actor {
  var shorn = false

  def act() = {
    loop {
      react {
        case Haircut => {
          shorn = true
          println("[c] customer " + id + " got a haircut")
        }
      }
    }
  }
}
```

For the most part, this should look pretty familiar: we declare the package in which this code lives, we import code from the `scala.actors` package, and we define a class that extends `Actor`. There are a few details worth noting, however.

First of all, there's our declaration of `case object Haircut`. A common pattern when working with Actors in Scala is to use a `case object` to represent a message without internal data. If we wanted to include, say, the time at which the haircut was completed, we'd use a case class instead. We declare Haircut here because it's a message type that will be sent solely to customers.

Note as well that we're storing one bit of mutable state in each Customer: whether or not they've gotten a haircut. In their internal loop, each Customer waits for a Haircut message and, upon receipt of one, we set the shorn boolean to true. Customer uses the asynchronous react method to respond to incoming messages. If we needed to return the result of processing the message, we would use receive, but we don't, and in the process we save some memory and thread use under the hood.

Let's move on to the barber himself. Because there's only one barber, we could have used the actor factory method technique mentioned earlier to create him. For testing purposes, we've instead defined our own Barber class:

```scala
// code-examples/Concurrency/sleepingbarber/barber.scala

package sleepingbarber

import scala.actors.Actor
import scala.actors.Actor._
import scala.util.Random

class Barber extends Actor {
  private val random = new Random()

  def helpCustomer(customer: Customer) {
    if (self.mailboxSize >= 3) {
      println("[b] not enough seats, turning customer " + customer.id + " away")
    } else {
      println("[b] cutting hair of customer " + customer.id)
      Thread.sleep(100 + random.nextInt(400))
      customer ! Haircut
    }
  }

  def act() {
    loop {
      react {
        case customer: Customer => helpCustomer(customer)
      }
    }
  }
}
```

The core of the Barber class looks very much like the Customer. We loop around react, waiting for a particular type of object. To keep that loop tight and readable, we call a method, helpCustomer, when a new Customer is sent to the barber. Within that method we employ a check on the mailbox size to serve as our "chairs" that customers may occupy; we could have the Barber or Shop classes maintain an internal Queue, but why bother when each Actor's mailbox already is one?

If three or more customers are in the queue, we simply ignore that message; it's then discarded from the barber's mailbox. Otherwise, we simulate a semi-random delay (always at least 100 milliseconds) for the time it takes to cut a customer's hair, then send off a `Haircut` message to that customer. (Were we not trying to simulate a real-world scenario, we would of course remove the call to `Thread.sleep()` and allow our barber to run full tilt.)

Next up, we have a simple class to represent the barbershop itself:

```scala
// code-examples/Concurrency/sleepingbarber/shop.scala

package sleepingbarber

import scala.actors.Actor
import scala.actors.Actor._

class Shop extends Actor {
  val barber = new Barber()
  barber.start

  def act() {
    println("[s] the shop is open")

    loop {
      react {
        case customer: Customer => barber ! customer
      }
    }
  }
}
```

By now, this should all look very familiar. Each `Shop` creates and starts a new `Barber`, prints a message telling the world that the shop is open, and sits in a loop waiting for customers. When a `Customer` comes in, he's sent to the barber. We now see an unexpected benefit of Actors: they allow us to describe concurrent business logic in easily understood terms. "Send the customer to the barber" makes perfect sense, much more so than "Notify the barber, unlock the mutex around the customer seats, increment the number of free seats," and so forth. Actors get us closer to our domain.

Finally, we have a driver for our simulation:

```scala
// code-examples/Concurrency/sleepingbarber/barbershop-simulator.scala

package sleepingbarber

import scala.actors.Actor._
import scala.collection.{immutable, mutable}
import scala.util.Random

object BarbershopSimulator {
  private val random = new Random()
  private val customers = new mutable.ArrayBuffer[Customer]()
  private val shop = new Shop()
```

```
def generateCustomers {
  for (i <- 1 to 20) {
    val customer = new Customer(i)
    customer.start()
    customers += customer
  }

  println("[!] generated " + customers.size + " customers")
}

// customers arrive at random intervals
def trickleCustomers {
  for (customer <- customers) {
    shop ! customer
    Thread.sleep(random.nextInt(450))
  }
}

def tallyCuts {
  // wait for any remaining concurrent actions to complete
  Thread.sleep(2000)

  val shornCount = customers.filter(c => c.shorn).size
  println("[!] " + shornCount + " customers got haircuts today")
}

def main(args: Array[String]) {
  println("[!] starting barbershop simulation")
  shop.start()

  generateCustomers
  trickleCustomers
  tallyCuts

  System.exit(0)
}
```

After "opening the shop," we generate a number of `Customer` objects, assigning a numeric ID to each and storing the lot in an `ArrayBuffer`. Next, we "trickle" the customers in by sending them as messages to the shop and sleeping for a semi-random amount of time between loops. At the end of our simulated day, we tally up the number of customers who got haircuts by filtering out the customers whose internal `shorn` boolean was set to `true` and asking for the size of the resulting sequence.

Compile and run the code within the `sleepingbarber` directory as follows:

```
fsc *.scala
scala -classpath . sleepingbarber.BarbershopSimulator
```

Throughout our code, we've prefixed console messages with abbreviations for the classes from which the messages were printed. When we look at an example run of our simulator, it's easy to see where each message came from:

```
[!] starting barbershop simulation
[s] the shop is open
[!] generated 20 customers
[b] cutting hair of customer 1
[b] cutting hair of customer 2
[c] customer 1 got a haircut
[c] customer 2 got a haircut
[b] cutting hair of customer 3
[c] customer 3 got a haircut
[b] cutting hair of customer 4
[b] cutting hair of customer 5
[c] customer 4 got a haircut
[b] cutting hair of customer 6
[c] customer 5 got a haircut
[b] cutting hair of customer 7
[c] customer 6 got a haircut
[b] not enough seats, turning customer 8 away
[b] cutting hair of customer 9
[c] customer 7 got a haircut
[b] not enough seats, turning customer 10 away
[c] customer 9 got a haircut
[b] cutting hair of customer 11
[b] cutting hair of customer 12
[c] customer 11 got a haircut
[b] cutting hair of customer 13
[c] customer 12 got a haircut
[b] cutting hair of customer 14
[c] customer 13 got a haircut
[b] not enough seats, turning customer 15 away
[b] not enough seats, turning customer 16 away
[b] not enough seats, turning customer 17 away
[b] cutting hair of customer 18
[c] customer 14 got a haircut
[b] cutting hair of customer 19
[c] customer 18 got a haircut
[b] cutting hair of customer 20
[c] customer 19 got a haircut
[c] customer 20 got a haircut
[!] 15 customers got haircuts today
```

You'll find that each run's output is, predictably, slightly different. Every time the barber takes a bit longer to cut hair than it does for several customers to enter, the "chairs" (the barber's mailbox queue) fill up, and new customers simply leave.

Of course, we have to include the standard caveats that come with simple examples. For one, it's possible that our example may not be suitably random, particularly if random values are retrieved within a millisecond of one another. This is a byproduct of the way the JVM generates random numbers, and a good reminder to be careful about randomness in concurrent programs. You'd also want to replace the sleep inside tallyCuts with a clearer signal that the various actors in the system are done doing their work, perhaps by making the BarbershopSimulation an Actor and sending it messages that indicate completion.

Try modifying the code to introduce more customers, additional message types, different delays, or to remove the randomness altogether. If you're an experienced multithreaded programmer, you might try writing your own sleeping barber implementation just to compare and contrast. We're willing to bet that an implementation in Scala with Actors will be terser and easier to maintain.

Effective Actors

To get the most out of Actors, there are few things to remember. First, note that there are several methods you can use to get different types of behavior out of your Actors. Table 9-1 should help clarify when to use each method.

Table 9-1. Actor methods

Method	Returns	Description
act	Unit	Abstract, top-level method for an Actor. Typically contains one of the following methods inside it.
receive	Result of processing message	Blocks until a message of matched type is received.
receiveWithin	Result of processing message	Like receive, but unblocks after specified number of milliseconds.
react	Nothing	Requires less overhead (threads) than receive.
reactWithin	Nothing	Like react, but unblocks after specified number of milliseconds.

Typically, you'll want to use **react** wherever possible. If you need the results of processing a message (that is, you need a synchronous response from sending a message to an Actor), use the **receiveWithin** variant to reduce your chances of blocking indefinitely on an Actor that's gotten wedged.

Another strategy to keep your Actor-based code asynchronous is the use of *futures*. A future is a placeholder object for a value that hasn't yet been returned from an asynchronous process. You can send a message to an Actor with the !! method; a variant of this method allows you to pass along a partial function that is applied to the future value. As you can see from the following example, retrieving a value from a Future is as straightforward as invoking its **apply** method. Note that retrieving a value from a Future is a blocking operation:

```
// code-examples/Concurrency/future-script.scala
import scala.actors.Futures._

val eventually = future(5 * 42)
println(eventually())
```

Each Actor in your system should have clear responsibilities. Don't use Actors for general-purpose, highly stateful tasks. Instead, think like a director: what are the distinct roles in the "script" of your application, and what's the least amount of

---

information each Actor needs to do its job? Give each Actor just a couple of responsibilities, and use messages (usually in the form of a `case class` or `case object`) to delegate those responsibilities to other Actors.

Don't be hesitant to copy data when writing Actor-centric code. The more immutable your design, the less likely you are to end up with unexpected state. The more you communicate via messages, the less you have to worry about synchronization. All those messages and immutable variables might appear to be overly costly. But, with today's plentiful hardware, trading memory overhead for clarity and predictability seems more than fair for most applications.

Lastly, know when Actors aren't appropriate. Just because Actors are a great way to handle concurrency in Scala doesn't mean that they're the *only* way, as we'll see soon. Traditional threading and locking may better suit write-heavy critical paths for which a messaging approach would incur too much overhead. In our experience, you can use a purely Actor-based design to prototype a concurrent solution, then use profiling tools to suss out parts of your application that might benefit from a different approach.

Traditional Concurrency in Scala: Threading and Events

While Actors are a great way to handle concurrent operations, they're not the only way to do so in Scala. As Scala is interoperable with Java, the concurrency concepts that you may be familiar with on the JVM still apply.

One-Off Threads

For starters, Scala provides a handy way to run a block of code in a new thread:

```
// code-examples/Concurrency/threads/by-block-script.scala

new Thread { println("this will run in a new thread") }
```

A similar construct is available in the `scala.concurrent` package, as a method on the `ops` object to run a block asynchronously with `spawn`:

```
// code-examples/Concurrency/threads/spawn.scala

import scala.concurrent.ops._

object SpawnExample {
  def main(args: Array[String]) {
    println("this will run synchronously")

    spawn {
      println("this will run asychronously")
    }
  }
}
```

Using java.util.concurrent

If you're familiar with the venerable `java.util.concurrent` package, you'll find it just as easy to use from Scala (or hard to use, depending on your point of view). Let's use `Executors` to create a pool of threads. We'll use the thread pool to run a simple class, implementing Java's `Runnable` interface for thread-friendly classes, that identifies which thread it's running on:

```
// code-examples/Concurrency/threads/util-concurrent-script.scala

import java.util.concurrent._

class ThreadIdentifier extends Runnable {
  def run {
    println("hello from Thread " + currentThread.getId)
  }
}

val pool = Executors.newFixedThreadPool(5)

for (i <- 1 to 10) {
  pool.execute(new ThreadIdentifier)
}
```

As is standard in Java concurrency, the `run` method is where a threaded class starts. Every time our `pool` executes a new `ThreadIdentifier`, its `run` method is invoked. A look at the output tells us that we're running on the five threads in the pool, with IDs ranging from 9 to 13:

```
hello from Thread 9
hello from Thread 10
hello from Thread 11
hello from Thread 12
hello from Thread 13
hello from Thread 9
hello from Thread 11
hello from Thread 10
hello from Thread 10
hello from Thread 13
```

This is, of course, just scratching the surface of what is available in `java.util.concurrent`. You'll find that your existing knowledge of Java's approach to multithreading still applies in Scala. What's more, you'll be able to accomplish the same tasks using less code, which should contribute to maintainability and productivity.

Events

Threading and Actors aren't the only way to do concurrency. Event-based concurrency, a particular approach to asynchronous or *non-blocking I/O* (NIO), has become a favored way to write servers that need to scale to thousands of simultaneous clients. Eschewing the traditional one-to-one relationship of threads to clients, this model of concurrency exposes events that occur when particular conditions are met (for example, when data is received from a client over a network socket). Typically, the programmer will associate a callback method with each event that's relevant to her program.

While the `java.nio` package provides a variety of useful primitives for non-blocking I/O (buffers, channels, etc.), it's still a fair bit of work to cobble together an event-based concurrent program from those simple parts. Enter Apache MINA, built atop Java NIO and described on its home page as "a network application framework which helps users develop high performance and high scalability network applications easily" (see [MINA]).

While MINA may be easier to use than Java's built-in NIO libraries, we've gotten used to some conveniences of Scala that just aren't available in MINA. The open source Naggati library (see [Naggati]) adds a Scala-friendly layer atop MINA that, according to its author, "makes it easy to build protocol filters [using a] sequential style." Essentially, Naggati is a DSL for parsing network protocols, with MINA's powerful NIO abilities under the hood.

Let's use Naggati to write the foundations of an SMTP email server. To keep things simple, we're only dealing with two SMTP commands: HELO and QUIT. The former command identifies a client, and the latter ends the client's session.

We'll keep ourselves honest with a test suite, facilitated by the Specs Behavior-Driven Development library (see "Specs" on page 363):

```
// .../smtpd/src/test/scala/com/programmingscala/smtpd/SmtpDecoderSpec.scala

package com.programmingscala.smtpd

import java.nio.ByteOrder
import net.lag.naggati._
import org.apache.mina.core.buffer.IoBuffer
import org.apache.mina.core.filterchain.IoFilter
import org.apache.mina.core.session.{DummySession, IoSession}
import org.apache.mina.filter.codec._
import org.specs._
import scala.collection.{immutable, mutable}

object SmtpDecoderSpec extends Specification {
  private var fakeSession: IoSession = null
  private var fakeDecoderOutput: ProtocolDecoderOutput = null
  private var written = new mutable.ListBuffer[Request]

  def quickDecode(s: String): Unit = {
    Codec.decoder.decode(fakeSession, IoBuffer.wrap(s.getBytes), fakeDecoderOutput)
  }

  "SmtpRequestDecoder" should {
    doBefore {
      written.clear()
      fakeSession = new DummySession
```

```
        fakeDecoderOutput = new ProtocolDecoderOutput {
          override def flush(nextFilter: IoFilter.NextFilter, s: IoSession) = {}
          override def write(obj: AnyRef) = written += obj.asInstanceOf[Request]
        }
      }

    "parse HELO" in {
      quickDecode("HELO client.example.org\n")
      written.size mustEqual 1
      written(0).command mustEqual "HELO"
      written(0).data mustEqual "client.example.org"
    }

    "parse QUIT" in {
      quickDecode("QUIT\n")
      written.size mustEqual 1
      written(0).command mustEqual "QUIT"
      written(0).data mustEqual null
    }
  }
}
```

After setting up an environment for each test run, our suite exercises the two SMTP commands we're interested in. The doBefore block runs before each test, guaranteeing that mock session and output buffers are in a clean state. In each test we're passing a string of hypothetical client input to our as-yet-unimplemented Codec, then verifying that the resulting Request (a case class) contains the correct command and data fields. As the QUIT command doesn't require any additional information from the client, we simply check that data is null.

With our tests in place, let's implement a basic codec (an encoder and decoder) for SMTP:

```
// .../smtpd/src/main/scala/com/programmingscala/smtpd/Codec.scala

package com.programmingscala.smtpd

import org.apache.mina.core.buffer.IoBuffer
import org.apache.mina.core.session.{IdleStatus, IoSession}
import org.apache.mina.filter.codec._
import net.lag.naggati._
import net.lag.naggati.Steps._

case class Request(command: String, data: String)
case class Response(data: IoBuffer)

object Codec {
  val encoder = new ProtocolEncoder {
    def encode(session: IoSession, message: AnyRef, out: ProtocolEncoderOutput) = {
      val buffer = message.asInstanceOf[Response].data
      out.write(buffer)
    }

    def dispose(session: IoSession): Unit = {
```

```
      // no-op, required by ProtocolEncoder trait
    }
  }

  val decoder = new Decoder(readLine(true, "ISO-8859-1") { line =>
    line.split(' ').first match {
      case "HELO" => state.out.write(Request("HELO", line.split(' ')(1))); End
      case "QUIT" => state.out.write(Request("QUIT", null)); End
      case _ => throw new ProtocolError("Malformed request line: " + line)
    }
  })
}
```

We first define a `Request case class` in which to store request data as it arrives. Then we specify the `encoder` portion of our codec, which exists simply to write data out. A `dispose` method is defined (but not fleshed out) to fulfill the contract of the `ProtocolEncoder` trait.

The decoder is what we're really interested in. `readRequest` reads a line, picks out the first word in that line, and pattern matches on it to find SMTP commands. In the case of a `HELO` command, we also grab the subsequent string on that line. The results are placed in a `Request` object and written out to `state`. As you might imagine, `state` stores our progress throughout the parsing process.

Though trivial, the above example demonstrates just how easy it is to parse protocols with Naggati. Now that we've got a working codec, let's combine Naggati and MINA with Actors to wire up a server.

First, a few lines of setup grunt work to get things going for our SMTP server:

```scala
// .../smtpd/src/main/scala/com/programmingscala/smtpd/Main.scala

package com.programmingscala.smtpd

import net.lag.naggati.IoHandlerActorAdapter
import org.apache.mina.filter.codec.ProtocolCodecFilter
import org.apache.mina.transport.socket.SocketAcceptor
import org.apache.mina.transport.socket.nio.{NioProcessor, NioSocketAcceptor}
import java.net.InetSocketAddress
import java.util.concurrent.{Executors, ExecutorService}
import scala.actors.Actor._

object Main {
  val listenAddress = "0.0.0.0"
  val listenPort = 2525

  def setMaxThreads = {
    val maxThreads = (Runtime.getRuntime.availableProcessors * 2)
    System.setProperty("actors.maxPoolSize", maxThreads.toString)
  }

  def initializeAcceptor = {
    var acceptorExecutor = Executors.newCachedThreadPool()
    var acceptor =
```

```
        new NioSocketAcceptor(acceptorExecutor, new NioProcessor(acceptorExecutor))
      acceptor.setBacklog(1000)
      acceptor.setReuseAddress(true)
      acceptor.getSessionConfig.setTcpNoDelay(true)
      acceptor.getFilterChain.addLast("codec",
            new ProtocolCodecFilter(smtpd.Codec.encoder, smtpd.Codec.decoder))
      acceptor.setHandler(
            new IoHandlerActorAdapter(session => new SmtpHandler(session)))
      acceptor.bind(new InetSocketAddress(listenAddress, listenPort))
    }

    def main(args: Array[String]) {
      setMaxThreads
      initializeAcceptor
      println("smtpd: up and listening on " + listenAddress + ":" + listenPort)
    }
  }
```

To ensure that we're getting the most out of the Actor instances in our server, we set
the `actors.maxPoolSize` system property to twice the number of available processors
on our machine. We then initialize an `NioSocketAcceptor`, a key piece of MINA machinery that accepts new connections from clients. The final three lines of this configuration are critical, as they put our codec to work, tell the acceptor to handle requests
with a special object, and start the server listening for new connections on port 2525
(real SMTP servers run on the privileged port 25).

The aforementioned special object is an Actor wrapped in an `IoHandlerActorAdapter`,
a bridging layer between Scala Actors and MINA that's provided by Naggati. This is
the piece of our server that talks back to the client. Now that we know what the client
is saying, thanks to the decoder, we actually know what to say back!

```
// .../smtpd/src/main/scala/com/programmingscala/smtpd/SmtpHandler.scala

package com.programmingscala.smtpd

import net.lag.naggati.{IoHandlerActorAdapter, MinaMessage, ProtocolError}
import org.apache.mina.core.buffer.IoBuffer
import org.apache.mina.core.session.{IdleStatus, IoSession}
import java.io.IOException
import scala.actors.Actor
import scala.actors.Actor._
import scala.collection.{immutable, mutable}

class SmtpHandler(val session: IoSession) extends Actor {
  start

  def act = {
    loop {
      react {
        case MinaMessage.MessageReceived(msg) =>
            handle(msg.asInstanceOf[smtpd.Request])
        case MinaMessage.SessionClosed => exit()
        case MinaMessage.SessionIdle(status) => session.close
        case MinaMessage.SessionOpened => reply("220 localhost Tapir SMTPd 0.1\n")
```

```
      case MinaMessage.ExceptionCaught(cause) => {
        cause.getCause match {
          case e: ProtocolError => reply("502 Error: " + e.getMessage + "\n")
          case i: IOException   => reply("502 Error: " + i.getMessage + "\n")
          case _                => reply("502 Error unknown\n")
        }
        session.close
      }
    }
  }
}

private def handle(request: smtpd.Request) = {
  request.command match {
    case "HELO" => reply("250 Hi there " + request.data + "\n")
    case "QUIT" => reply("221 Peace out girl scout\n"); session.close
  }
}

private def reply(s: String) = {
  session.write(new smtpd.Response(IoBuffer.wrap(s.getBytes)))
}

}
```

Straight away, we see the same pattern that we saw in the Actors examples earlier in this chapter: looping around a **react** block that pattern matches on a limited set of cases. In SmtpHandler, all of those cases are *events* provided by MINA. For example, MINA will send us `MinaMessage.SessionOpened` when a client connects and `MinaMessage.SessionClosed` when a client disconnects.

The case we're most interested in is `MinaMessage.MessageReceived`. We're handed a familiar `Request` object with each newly received valid message, and we can pattern match on the `command` field to take appropriate action. When the client says HELO, we can reply with an acknowledgement. When the client says QUIT, we say goodbye and disconnect him.

Now that we've got all the pieces in place, let's have a conversation with our server:

```
[al3x@jaya ~]$ telnet localhost 2525
Trying ::1...
Connected to localhost.
Escape character is '^]'.
220 localhost Tapir SMTPd 0.1
HELO jaya.local
250 Hi there jaya.local
QUIT
221 Peace out girl scout
Connection closed by foreign host.
```

A brief conversation, to be sure, but our server works! Now, what happens if we throw something unexpected at it?

```
[al3x@jaya ~]$ telnet localhost 2525
Trying ::1...
Connected to localhost.
Escape character is '^]'.
220 localhost Tapir SMTPd 0.1
HELO jaya.local
250 Hi there jaya.local
BAD COMMAND
502 Error: Malformed request line: BAD COMMAND
Connection closed by foreign host.
```

Nicely handled. Good thing we took the time to dig out those exceptions when we received a `MinaMessage.ExceptionCaught` in our `SmtpHandler` Actor.

Of course, what we've built just handles the beginning and end of a complete SMTP conversation. As an exercise, try filling out the rest of the commands. Or, to skip ahead to something very much akin to what we've built here, check out the open source Mailslot project on GitHub (see [Mailslot]).

Recap and What's Next

We learned how to build scalable, robust concurrent applications using Scala's Actor library that avoid the problems of traditional approaches based on synchronized access to shared, mutable state. We also demonstrated that Java's powerful built-in threading model is easily accessible from Scala. Finally, we learned how to combine Actors with the powerful MINA NIO framework and Naggati to develop event-driven, asynchronous network servers from the ground up in just a few lines of code.

The next chapter examines Scala's built-in support for working with XML.

CHAPTER 10

Herding XML in Scala

XML has long since become the *lingua franca* of machine-to-machine communication on the Internet. The format's combination of human readability, standardization, and tool support has made working with XML an inevitability for programmers. Yet, writing code that deals in XML is an unpleasant chore in most programming languages. Scala improves this situation.

As with the Actor functionality we learned about in Chapter 9, Scala's XML support is implemented partly as a library, with some built-in syntax support. It feels to the programmer like an entirely natural part of the language. Convenient operators add a spoonful of syntactic sugar to the task of diving deep into complex document structures, and pattern matching further sweetens the deal. Outputting XML is just as pleasant.

Unusual in programming languages and particularly handy, Scala allows inline XML. Most anywhere you might put a string, you can put XML. This feature makes templating and configuration a breeze, and lets us test our use of XML without so much as opening a file.

Let's explore working with XML in Scala. First, we'll look at reading and navigating an XML document. Finally, we'll produce XML output programmatically and demonstrate uses for inline XML.

Reading XML

We'll start with the basics: how to turn a string full of XML into a data structure we can work with:

```
// code-examples/XML/reading/from-string-script.scala

import scala.xml._

val someXMLInAString = """
<sammich>
  <bread>wheat</bread>
```

```
  <meat>salami</meat>
  <condiments>
    <condiment expired="true">mayo</condiment>
    <condiment expired="false">mustard</condiment>
  </condiments>
</sammich>
"""

val someXML = XML.loadString(someXMLInAString)
assert(someXML.isInstanceOf[scala.xml.Elem])
```

All fine and well. We've transformed the string into a **NodeSeq**, Scala's type for storing a sequence of XML nodes. Were our XML document in a file on disk, we could have used the **loadFile** method from the same package.

Since we're supplying the XML ourselves, we can skip the **XML.loadString** step and just assign a chunk of markup to a **val** or **var**:

```
// code-examples/XML/reading/inline-script.scala

import scala.xml._

val someXML =
<sammich>
  <bread>wheat</bread>
  <meat>salami</meat>
  <condiments>
    <condiment expired="true">mayo</condiment>
    <condiment expired="false">mustard</condiment>
  </condiments>
</sammich>

assert(someXML.isInstanceOf[scala.xml.Elem])
```

Exploring XML

If we paste the previous example into the interpreter, we can explore our sandwich using some handy tools provided by **NodeSeq**:

```
scala> someXML \ "bread"
res2: scala.xml.NodeSeq = <bread>wheat</bread>
```

That backslash—what the documentation calls a *projection function*—says, "Find me elements named **bread**." We'll always get a **NodeSeq** back when using a projection function. If we're only interested in what's between the tags, we can use the **text** method:

```
scala> (someXML \ "bread").text
res3: String = wheat
```

 It's valid syntax to say someXML \ "bread" text, without parentheses or the dot before the call to text. You'll still get the same result, but it's harder to read. Parentheses make your intent clear.

We've only inspected the outermost layer of our sandwich. Let's try to get a `NodeSeq` of the condiments:

```
scala> someXML \ "condiment"
res4: scala.xml.NodeSeq =
```

What went wrong? The \ function doesn't descend into child elements of an XML structure. To do that, we use its sister function, \\ (two backslashes):

```
scala> someXML \\ "condiment"
res5: scala.xml.NodeSeq = <condiment expired="true">mayo</condiment>
    <condiment expired="false">mustard</condiment>
```

Much better. (We split the single output line into two lines so it would fit on the page.) We dove into the structure and pulled out the two `<condiment>` elements. Looks like one of the condiments has gone bad, though. We can find out if any of the condiments has expired by extracting its `expired` attribute. All it takes is an @ before the attribute name:

```
scala> (someXML \\ "condiment")(0) \ "@expired"
res6: scala.xml.NodeSeq = true
```

We used the (0) to pick the first of the two condiments that were returned by (`someXML \\ "condiment"`).

Looping and Matching XML

The previous bit of code extracted the *value* of the `expired` attribute (`true`, in this case), but it didn't tell us which condiment is expired. If we were handed an arbitrary XML sandwich, how would we identify the expired condiments? We can loop through the XML:

```
// code-examples/XML/reading/for-loop-script.scala

for (condiment <- (someXML \\ "condiment")) {
  if ((condiment \ "@expired").text == "true")
    println("the " + condiment.text + " has expired!")
}
```

Because `NodeSeq` inherits the same familiar attributes that most Scala collection types carry, tools like `for` loops apply directly. In the example just shown, we extract the `<condiment>` nodes, loop over each of them, and test whether or not their `expired` attribute equals the string `"true"`. We have to specify that we want the `text` of a given `condiment`; otherwise, we'd get a string representation of the entire line of XML.

We can also use pattern matching on XML structures. Cases in pattern matches can be written in terms of XML literals; expressions between curly braces ({}) escape back to standard Scala pattern matching syntax. To match all XML nodes in the escaped portion of a pattern match, use an underscore (wildcard) followed by an asterisk (_*). To bind what you've matched on to a variable, prefix the match with the variable name and an @ sign.

Let's put all that together into one example. We'll include the original XML document again so you can follow along as we pattern match on XML:

```scala
// code-examples/XML/reading/pattern-matching-script.scala

import scala.xml._

val someXML =
<sammich>
  <bread>wheat</bread>
  <meat>salami</meat>
  <condiments>
    <condiment expired="true">mayo</condiment>
    <condiment expired="false">mustard</condiment>
  </condiments>
</sammich>

someXML match {
  case <sammich>{ingredients @ _*}</sammich> => {
    for (cond @ <condiments>{_*}</condiments> <- ingredients)
      println("condiments: " + cond.text)
  }
}
```

Here, we bind the contents of our `<sammich>` structure (that is, what's inside the opening and closing tag) to a variable called `ingredients`. Then, as we iterate through the ingredients in a `for` loop, we assign the elements that are between the `<condiments>` tags to a temporary variable, `cond`. Each `cond` is printed.

The same tools that let us easily manipulate complex data structures in Scala are readily available for XML processing. As a readable alternative to XSLT, Scala's XML library makes reading and parsing XML a breeze. It also gives us equally powerful tools for writing XML, which we'll explore in the next section.

Writing XML

While some languages construct XML through complex object serialization mechanisms, Scala's support for XML literals makes writing XML far simpler. Essentially, when you want XML, just write XML. To interpolate variables and expressions, escape out to Scala with curly braces, as we did in the pattern matching examples earlier:

```scala
scala> var name = "Bob"
name: java.lang.String = Bob

scala> val bobXML =
     | <person>
     |   <name>{name}</name>
     | </person>
bobXML: scala.xml.Elem =
<person>
  <name>Bob</name>
</person>
```

As we can see, the name variable was substituted when we constructed the XML document assigned to bobXML. That evaluation only occurs once; were name subsequently redefined, the <name> element of bobXML would still contain the string "Bob".

A Real-World Example

For a more complete example, let's say we're designing that favorite latter-day "hello world," a blogging system. We'll start with a class to represent an Atom-friendly blog post:

```
// code-examples/XML/writing/post.scala

import java.text.SimpleDateFormat
import java.util.Date

class Post(val title: String, val body: String, val updated: Date) {
  lazy val dashedDate = {
    val dashed = new SimpleDateFormat("yy-MM-dd")
    dashed.format(updated)
  }

  lazy val atomDate = {
    val rfc3339 = new SimpleDateFormat("yyyy-MM-dd'T'h:m:ss'-05:00'")
    rfc3339.format(updated)
  }

  lazy val slug = title.toLowerCase.replaceAll("\\W", "-")
  lazy val atomId  = "tag:example.com," + dashedDate + ":/" + slug
}
```

Beyond the obvious title and body attributes, we've defined several lazily loaded values in our Post class. These attributes will come in handy when we transmute our posts into an Atom feed, the standard way to syndicate blogs between computers on the Web. Atom documents are a flavor of XML, and a perfect application for demonstrating the process of outputting XML with Scala.

We'll define an AtomFeed class that takes a sequence of Post objects as its sole argument:

```
// code-examples/XML/writing/atom-feed.scala

import scala.xml.XML

class AtomFeed(posts: Seq[Post]) {
  val feed =
  <feed xmlns="http://www.w3.org/2005/Atom">
    <title>My Blog</title>
    <subtitle>A fancy subtitle.</subtitle>
    <link href="http://example.com/"/>
    <link href="http://example.com/atom.xml" rel="self"/>
    <updated>{posts(0).atomDate}</updated>
    <author>
      <name>John Doe</name>
      <uri>http://example.com/about.html</uri>
```

```
      </author>
      <id>http://example.com/</id>
      {for (post <- posts) yield
      <entry>
        <title>{post.title}</title>
        <link href={"http://example.com/" + post.slug + ".html"} rel="alternate"/>
        <id>{post.atomId}</id>
        <updated>{post.atomDate}</updated>
        <content type="html">{post.body}</content>
        <author>
          <name>John Doe</name>
          <uri>http://example.com/about.html</uri>
        </author>
      </entry>
      }
    </feed>

    def write = XML.saveFull("/tmp/atom-example.xml", feed, "UTF-8", true, null)
  }
```

We're making heavy use of the ability to escape out to Scala expressions in this example. Whenever we need a piece of dynamic information—for example, the date of the first post in the sequence, formatted for the Atom standard—we simply escape out and write Scala as we normally would. In the latter half of the `<feed>` element, we use a `for` comprehension to `yield` successive blocks of dynamically formatted XML.

The `write` method of `AtomFeed` demonstrates the use of the `saveFull` method, provided by the `scala.xml` library. `saveFull` writes an XML document to disk, optionally in different encoding schemes and with different document type declarations. Alternately, the `save` method within the same package will make use of any `java.io.Writer` variant, should you need buffering, piping, etc.

Writing XML with Scala is straightforward: construct the document you need with inline XML, use interpolation where dynamic content is to be substituted, and make use of the handy convenience methods to write your completed documents to disk or to other output streams.

Recap and What's Next

XML has become ubiquitous in software applications, yet few languages make working with XML a simple task. We learned how Scala accelerates XML development by making it easy to read and write XML.

In the next chapter, we'll learn how Scala provides rich support for creating your own Domain-Specific Languages (DSLs).

CHAPTER 11

Domain-Specific Languages in Scala

A *Domain-Specific Language* is a programming language that mimics the terms, idioms, and expressions used among experts in the targeted domain. Code written in a DSL reads like structured prose for the domain. Ideally, a domain expert with little experience in programming can read, understand, and validate this code. Sometimes, a domain expert might be able to write DSL code, even if he isn't a professional programmer.

DSLs are a large topic. We'll only touch the surface of DSLs and Scala's impressive support for them. For more information on DSLs in general, see [Fowler2009], [Ford2009], and [Deursen]. The basic build tool we used for the book's examples, sake, uses a DSL similar to the venerable make and its Ruby cousin rake. (See the README in the code download archive for details.) For other examples of Scala "internal" and "external" DSLs, see [Ghosh2008a] and [Ghosh2008b]. For some advanced work on DSLs using Scala, [Hofer2008] explores polymorphic substitution of alternative implementations for DSL abstractions, which is useful for analysis, optimization, composition, etc.

Well-crafted DSLs offer several benefits:

Encapsulation
A DSL hides implementation details and exposes only those abstractions relevant to the domain.

Efficiency
Because implementation details are encapsulated, a DSL optimizes the effort required to write or modify code for application features.

Communication
A DSL helps developers understand the domain and domain experts to verify that the implementation meets the requirements.

Quality
A DSL minimizes the "impedance mismatch" between feature requirements, as expressed by domain experts, and the implementing source code, thereby minimizing potential bugs.

However, DSLs also have several drawbacks:

Difficulties of creating good DSLs
> Good DSLs are harder to design than traditional APIs. The latter tend to follow language idioms for API design, where uniformity is important. Even then, elegant, effective, and easy-to-use APIs are difficult to design. In contrast, each DSL should reflect the unique language idioms of its domain. The DSL designer has much greater latitude, which also means it is much harder to determine the "best" design choices.

Long-term maintenance
> DSLs can require more maintenance over the long term to factor in domain changes. Also, new developers will require more time to learn how to use and maintain a DSL.

However, when a DSL is appropriate for an application—e.g., when it would be used frequently to implement and change functionality—a well-designed DSL can be a powerful tool for building flexible and robust applications.

From the implementation point of view, DSLs are often classified as *internal* and *external*.

An *internal* (sometimes called *embedded*) DSL is an idiomatic way of writing code in a general-purpose programming language, like Scala. No special-purpose parser is necessary for internal DSLs. Instead, they are parsed just like any other code written in the language. In contrast, an *external* DSL is a custom language with its own custom grammar and parser.

Internal DSLs are easier to create because they don't require a special-purpose parser. On the other hand, the constraints of the underlying language limit the options for expressing domain concepts. External DSLs remove this constraint. You can design the language any way you want, as long as you can write a reliable parser for it. The downside of external DSLs is the requirement to write and use a custom parser.

DSLs have been around a long time. For example, internal DSLs written in Lisp are as old as Lisp itself. Interest in DSLs has surged recently, driven in part by the Ruby community, because they are very easy to implement in Ruby. As we'll see, Scala provides excellent support for the creation of internal and external DSLs.

Internal DSLs

Let's create an internal DSL for a payroll application that computes an employee's paycheck every pay period, which will be two weeks long. The paycheck will include the employee's *net* salary, which is the *gross* salary minus the *deductions* for taxes, insurance premiums (at least in some countries), retirement fund contributions, etc.

To better understand the contrasts between code that makes use of DSLs and code that does not, let's try both techniques on the same problem. Here's how the paycheck might be calculated for two employees, without the help of a DSL:

```
// code-examples/DSLs/payroll/api/payroll-api-script.scala

import payroll.api._
import payroll.api.DeductionsCalculator._
import payroll._
import payroll.Type2Money._

val buck = Employee(Name("Buck", "Trends"), Money(80000))
val jane = Employee(Name("Jane", "Doe"), Money(90000))

List(buck, jane).foreach { employee =>
  // Assume annual is based on 52 weeks.
  val biweeklyGross = employee.annualGrossSalary / 26.

  val deductions = federalIncomeTax(employee, biweeklyGross) +
          stateIncomeTax(employee, biweeklyGross) +
          insurancePremiums(employee, biweeklyGross) +
          retirementFundContributions(employee, biweeklyGross)

  val check = Paycheck(biweeklyGross, biweeklyGross - deductions, deductions)

  format("%s %s: %s\n", employee.name.first, employee.name.last, check)
}
```

For each employee, the script calculates the gross pay for the pay period, the deductions, and the resulting net. These values are placed into a **Paycheck**, which is printed out. Before we describe the types we are using, notice a few things about the **foreach** loop that does the work.

First, it is noisy. For example, it mentions **employee** and **biweeklyGross** incessantly. A DSL will help us minimize that "noise" and focus on what's really going on.

Second, notice that the code is imperative. It says "divide this, add that," and so forth. We'll see that our DSLs look similar, but they are more declarative, hiding the work from the user.

Here is the simple **Paycheck** class used in the script:

```
// code-examples/DSLs/payroll/paycheck.scala

package payroll

/** We're ignoring invalid (?) cases like a negative net
 *  when deductions exceed the gross.
 */
case class Paycheck(gross: Money, net: Money, deductions: Money) {

  def plusGross (m: Money)      = Paycheck(gross + m, net + m, deductions)
  def plusDeductions (m: Money) = Paycheck(gross,     net - m, deductions + m)
}
```

The Employee type uses a Name type:

```
// code-examples/DSLs/payroll/employee.scala

package payroll

case class Name(first: String, last: String)

case class Employee(name: Name, annualGrossSalary: Money)
```

The Money type handles arithmetic, rounding to four decimal places, etc. It ignores currency, except for the toString method. Proper financial arithmetic is notoriously difficult to do correctly for real-world transactions. This implementation is not perfectly accurate, but it's close enough for our purposes. [MoneyInJava] provides useful information on doing real money calculations:

```
// code-examples/DSLs/payroll/money.scala

package payroll
import java.math.{BigDecimal => JBigDecimal,
    MathContext => JMathContext, RoundingMode => JRoundingMode}

/** Most arithmetic is done using JBigDecimals for tighter control.
 */
class Money(val amount: BigDecimal) {

  def + (m: Money)  =
      Money(amount.bigDecimal.add(m.amount.bigDecimal))
  def - (m: Money)  =
      Money(amount.bigDecimal.subtract(m.amount.bigDecimal))
  def * (m: Money)  =
      Money(amount.bigDecimal.multiply(m.amount.bigDecimal))
  def / (m: Money)  =
      Money(amount.bigDecimal.divide(m.amount.bigDecimal,
          Money.scale, Money.jroundingMode))

  def <  (m: Money)  = amount <  m.amount
  def <= (m: Money)  = amount <= m.amount
  def >  (m: Money)  = amount >  m.amount
  def >= (m: Money)  = amount >= m.amount

  override def equals (o: Any) = o match {
    case m: Money => amount equals m.amount
    case _ => false
  }

  override def hashCode = amount.hashCode * 31

  // Hack: Must explicitly call the correct conversion: double2Double
  override def toString =
      String.format("$%.2f", double2Double(amount.doubleValue))
}

object Money {
  def apply(amount: BigDecimal)  = new Money(amount)
```

```
    def apply(amount: JBigDecimal) = new Money(scaled(new BigDecimal(amount)))
    def apply(amount: Double)      = new Money(scaled(BigDecimal(amount)))
    def apply(amount: Long)        = new Money(scaled(BigDecimal(amount)))
    def apply(amount: Int)         = new Money(scaled(BigDecimal(amount)))

    def unapply(m: Money) = Some(m.amount)

    protected def scaled(d: BigDecimal) = d.setScale(scale, roundingMode)

    val scale = 4
    val jroundingMode = JRoundingMode.HALF_UP
    val roundingMode  = BigDecimal.RoundingMode.ROUND_HALF_UP
    val context = new JMathContext(scale, jroundingMode)
}

object Type2Money {
    implicit def bigDecimal2Money(b: BigDecimal)   = Money(b)
    implicit def jBigDecimal2Money(b: JBigDecimal) = Money(b)
    implicit def double2Money(d: Double)           = Money(d)
    implicit def long2Money(l: Long)               = Money(l)
    implicit def int2Money(i: Int)                 = Money(i)
}
```

Note that we use `scala.BigDecimal`, which wraps `java.math.BigDecimal`, as the storage type for financial figures.

Deductions are calculated using four helper methods in `payroll.api.Deductions Calculator`:

```
// code-examples/DSLs/payroll/api/deductions-calc.scala

package payroll.api
import payroll.Type2Money._

object DeductionsCalculator {
    def federalIncomeTax(empl: Employee, gross: Money) = gross * .25

    def stateIncomeTax(empl: Employee, gross: Money) = gross * .05

    def insurancePremiums(empl: Employee, gross: Money) = Money(500)

    def retirementFundContributions(empl: Employee, gross: Money) = gross * .10
}
```

Each method might use the employee information and the gross salary for the pay period. In this case, we use very simple algorithms based on just the gross salary, except for insurance premiums, which we treat as a fixed value.

Running the script for the payroll API produces the following output:

```
(665) $ scala -cp ... payroll-api-script.scala
Buck Trends: Paycheck($3076.92,$1346.15,$1730.77)
Jane Doe: Paycheck($3461.54,$1576.92,$1884.62)
```

A Payroll Internal DSL

The previous code works well enough, but suppose we wanted to show it to the Accounting Department to confirm that we're calculating paychecks correctly. Most likely, they would get lost in the Scala idioms. Suppose further that we need the ability to customize this algorithm frequently—for example, because it needs to be customized for different employee types (salaried, hourly, etc.), or to modify the deduction calculations. Ideally, we would like to enable the accountants to do these customizations themselves, without our help.

We might achieve these goals if we can express the logic in a DSL that is sufficiently intuitive to an accountant. Can we morph our API example into such a DSL?

Returning to the script for the payroll API, what if we hide most of the explicit references to context information, like the employee, gross salary, and deduction values? Consider the following text:

```
Rules to calculate an employee's paycheck:
  employee's gross salary for 2 weeks
  minus deductions for
    federalIncomeTax, which      is  25%  of gross
    stateIncomeTax, which        is  5%   of gross
    insurancePremiums, which     are 500. in gross's currency
    retirementFundContributions are 10%  of gross
```

This reads like normal English, not code. We have included some "bubble" words (see [Ford2009]) that aid readability but don't necessarily correspond to anything essential, such as to, an, is, for, of, and which. We'll eliminate some of these unnecessary words and keep others in our Scala DSL.

Compared to the version in the payroll API script, there's a lot less clutter obscuring the essentials of the algorithm. This is because we have minimized explicit references to the contextual information. We only mention employee twice. We mention gross five times, but hopefully in "intuitive" ways.

There are many possible internal Scala DSLs we could construct that resemble this ad hoc DSL. Here is one of them, again in a script, which produces the same output as before:

```scala
// code-examples/DSLs/payroll/dsl/payroll-dsl-script.scala

import payroll._
import payroll.dsl._
import payroll.dsl.rules_

val payrollCalculator = rules { employee =>
  employee salary_for 2.weeks minus_deductions_for { gross =>
    federalIncomeTax              is  (25.  percent_of gross)
    stateIncomeTax                is  (5.   percent_of gross)
    insurancePremiums             are (500. in gross.currency)
    retirementFundContributions are (10.  percent_of gross)
  }
```

```
    }
    val buck = Employee(Name("Buck", "Trends"), Money(80000))
    val jane = Employee(Name("Jane", "Doe"), Money(90000))

    List(buck, jane).foreach { employee =>
      val check = payrollCalculator(employee)
      format("%s %s: %s\n", employee.name.first, employee.name.last, check)
    }
```

We'll go through the implementation step by step, but first, let's summarize the features of Scala that allow us to implement this DSL.

Infix Operator Notation

Consider this line in the definition of `payrollCalculator`:

```
    employee salary_for 2.weeks minus_deductions_for { gross =>
```

This infix notation is equivalent to the following less-readable form:

```
    employee.salary_for(2.weeks).minus_deductions_for { gross =>
```

You can see why we wrote `2.weeks` earlier, because the result of this expression is passed to `salary_for`. Without the period, the infix expression would be parsed as `employee.salary_for(2).weeks...`. There is no `weeks` method on `Int`, of course. We'll revisit this expression in a moment.

Method chaining like this is often implemented where each method returns `this` so you can continue calling methods on the same instance. Note that returning `this` allows those method calls to occur in any order. If you need to impose a specific ordering, then return an instance of a different type. For example, if `minus_deductions_for` must be called after `salary_for`, then `salary_for` should return a new instance.

Because chaining is so easy, we could have created separate methods for `salary`, `for`, `minus`, and `deductions`, allowing us to write the following expression:

```
    employee salary for 2.weeks minus deductions for { gross =>
```

Note that calls to `for` are preceded by different calls with very different meanings. So, if the same instance is used throughout, it would have to track the "flow" internally. Chaining different instances would eliminate this problem. However, since no computations are actually needed between these words, we chose the simpler design where words are joined together, separated by _.

Implicit Conversions and User-Defined Types

Returning to `2.weeks`, since `Int` doesn't have a `weeks` method, we use an implicit conversion to a `Duration` instance that wraps an `Int` specifying an amount:

```
// code-examples/DSLs/payroll/dsl/duration.scala

package payroll.dsl

case class Duration(val amount: Int) {
  /** @return the number of work days in "amount" weeks. */
  def weeks = amount * 5

  /** @return the number of work days in "amount" years. */
  def years = amount * 260
}
```

The weeks method multiples that amount by 5 to return the corresponding amount of work days. Hence, we designed the payroll calculator to work with days as the unit of time. This decision is completely hidden behind the DSL. Should we later add support for work hours, it would be easy to refactor the design to use hours instead.

Duration is one of the ad hoc types that we designed to encapsulate the implicit context, to implement helper methods for the DSL, etc. We'll discuss the implicit conversion method we need in a moment.

Apply Methods

A number of the implementation objects use apply to invoke behavior. The rules object encapsulates the process of building the rules for payroll calculation. Its apply method takes a function literal, Employee => Paycheck.

Payroll Rules DSL Implementation

Now let's explore the implementation, starting with the rules object and working our way down:

```
// code-examples/DSLs/payroll/dsl/payroll.scala

package payroll.dsl
import payroll._

object rules {

  def apply(rules: Employee => Paycheck) = new PayrollBuilderRules(rules)

  implicit def int2Duration(i: Int) = Duration(i)

  implicit def employee2GrossPayBuilder(e: Employee) =
      new GrossPayBuilder(e)

  implicit def grossPayBuilder2DeductionsBuilder(b: GrossPayBuilder)
      = new DeductionsBuilder(b)

  implicit def double2DeductionsBuilderDeductionHelper(d: Double) =
      new DeductionsBuilderDeductionHelper(d)
}
```

```
import rules._
...
```

The function literal argument for **rules.apply** is used to construct a **PayrollBuilder Rules** that will process the specified rules. It is used at the very beginning of the DSL.

```
val payrollCalculator = rules { employee => ...
```

The **rules** object also defines implicit conversions. The first one is used by the **2.weeks** expression. It converts **2** into a **Duration** instance, which we discussed previously. The other conversions are used later in the DSL to enable transparent conversion of **Doubles**, **Employees**, etc. into wrapper instances that we will describe shortly.

Note that the **rules** object is imported so these conversions are visible in the rest of the current file. It will also need to be imported in files that use the DSL.

The **PayrollBuilderRules** is our first wrapper instance. It evaluates the function literal for the whole rule set, wrapped in a **try/catch** block:

```
// code-examples/DSLs/payroll/dsl/payroll.scala
...
class PayrollException(message: String, cause: Throwable)
    extends RuntimeException(message, cause)

protected[dsl] class PayrollBuilderRules(rules: Employee => Paycheck) {
  def apply(employee: Employee) = {
    try {
      rules(employee)
    } catch {
      case th: Throwable => new PayrollException(
        "Failed to process payroll for employee: " + employee, th)
    }
  }
}
...
```

Note that we protect access to **PayrollBuilderRules**, because we don't want clients using it directly. However, we left the exception public for use in **catch** clauses. (You can decide whether or not you like wrapping a thrown exception in a "domain-specific" exception, as shown.)

Note that we have to pass the employee as a "context" instance in the function literal. We said that it is desirable to make the context as implicit as possible. A common theme in our implementation classes, like **PayrollBuilderRules**, is to hold context information in wrapper instances and to minimize their visibility in the DSL. An alternative approach would be to store context in singleton objects so other instances can get to them. This approach raises thread safety issues, unfortunately.

To see what we mean concerning the context, consider the part of our script that uses the payroll DSL, where the deductions are specified:

```
... { gross =>
  federalIncomeTax           is (25.  percent_of gross)
```

```
    stateIncomeTax              is  (5.  percent_of gross)
    insurancePremiums           are (500. in gross.currency)
    retirementFundContributions are (10. percent_of gross)
}
```

Consider the insurance premiums, for which a flat `Money(500)` is deducted. Why didn't we just write `insurancePremiums are 500.`, instead? It turns out we have to "sneak" the `gross` instance into the expression somehow. The name `gross` implies that it is a `Money` representing the employee's salary for the pay period. *Tricksey DSLses!!* It is actually another helper instance, `DeductionsBuilder`, which holds the whole paycheck, including the gross pay, and the employee instance. The name `gross` is used merely because it reads well in the places where it is used.

This block is calculating the deductions and deducting them from the gross pay to determine the net pay. The `gross` instance handles this process. There is no "communication" between the four lines of the function literal. Furthermore, `federalIncome Tax`, `insurancePremiums`, etc. are objects with no connection to `DeductionsBuilder` (as we'll see shortly). It would be great if they could be members of `DeductionsBuilder` or perhaps some other wrapper instance enclosing this scope. Then each line would be a method call on one or the other wrapper. Unfortunately, this doesn't work. Hence, each line must specify the `gross` instance to maintain continuity. We jump through various hoops to support the syntax, yet allow `gross` to be available, as needed.

So, we contrived the convention that "raw" numbers, like the insurance deduction, have to be qualified by the particular currency used for the gross pay. We'll see how the expression `500. in gross.currency` works in a moment. It is something of a hack, but it reads well and it solves our design problem.

Here is a possible alternative design that would have avoided the problem:

```
... { builder =>
  builder federalIncomeTax            (25.  percent_of gross)
  builder stateIncomeTax              (5.   percent_of gross)
  builder insurancePremiums           500.
  builder retirementFundContributions (10.  percent_of gross)
}
```

Now the fact that a `builder` is being used is more explicit, and `federalIncomeTax`, `insurancePremiums`, etc. are methods on the builder. We opted for a more readable style, with the penalty of a harder implementation. You'll sometimes hear the phrase *fluent interface* used to refer to DSLs that emphasize readability.

Here is `GrossPayBuilder`:

```
// code-examples/DSLs/payroll/dsl/payroll.scala
...
import payroll.Type2Money._

protected[dsl] class GrossPayBuilder(val employee: Employee) {

  var gross: Money = 0
```

```
def salary_for(days: Int) = {
  gross += dailyGrossSalary(employee.annualGrossSalary) * days
  this
}

// Assume 260 working days: 52 weeks (including vacation) * 5 days/week.
def weeklyGrossSalary(annual: Money) = annual / 52.0
def dailyGrossSalary(annual: Money)  = annual / 260.0
}
...
```

Recall that rules defines an implicit conversion from Employee to this type. It is invoked by the expression employee salary_for, so the GrossPayBuilder.salary_for method can be called. GrossPayBuilder initializes the gross and appends new values to it whenever salary_for is called, which assumes we're adding gross pay in increments of days. Finally, salary_for returns this to support chaining.

Deduction calculation is the most complex part. When minus_deductions_for is used in the DSL, it triggers the implicit conversion defined in rules from the GrossPay Builder to a DeductionsBuilder:

```
// code-examples/DSLs/payroll/dsl/payroll.scala
...
protected[dsl] class DeductionsBuilder(gpb: GrossPayBuilder) {

  val employee = gpb.employee
  var paycheck: Paycheck = new Paycheck(gpb.gross, gpb.gross, 0)

  def currency = this

  def minus_deductions_for(deductionRules: DeductionsBuilder => Unit) = {
    deductionRules(this)
    paycheck
  }

  def addDeductions(amount: Money) = paycheck = paycheck plusDeductions amount

  def addDeductionsPercentageOfGross(percentage: Double) = {
    val amount = paycheck.gross * (percentage/100.)
    addDeductions(amount)
  }
}
...
```

DeductionsBuilder saves the employee from the passed-in GrossPayBuilder, which it doesn't save as a field. It also initializes the paycheck using the calculated gross pay.

Note that the currency method simply returns this. We don't need to do anything with the actual currency when this method is invoked. Instead, it is used to support a design idiom that we'll discuss shortly.

The minus_deductions_for does the important work. It invokes the function literal with the individual rules and then returns the completed Paycheck instance, which is ultimately what rules.apply returns.

Our remaining two methods are used to calculate individual deductions. They are called from `DeductionsBuilderDeductionHelper`, which we show now:

```
// code-examples/DSLs/payroll/dsl/payroll.scala
...
class DeductionCalculator {
  def is(builder: DeductionsBuilder) = apply(builder)
  def are(builder: DeductionsBuilder) = apply(builder)

  def apply(builder: DeductionsBuilder) = {}
}

object federalIncomeTax extends DeductionCalculator
object stateIncomeTax extends DeductionCalculator
object insurancePremiums extends DeductionCalculator
object retirementFundContributions extends DeductionCalculator

protected[dsl] class DeductionsBuilderDeductionHelper(val factor: Double) {
  def in (builder: DeductionsBuilder) = {
    builder addDeductions Money(factor)
    builder
  }
  def percent_of (builder: DeductionsBuilder) = {
    builder addDeductionsPercentageOfGross factor
    builder
  }
}
```

Now we see that `federalIncomeTax`, etc. are singleton objects. Note the "synonym" methods `is` and `are`. We used `are` for the objects with plural names, like `insurancePremiums`, and `is` for the singular objects, like `federalIncomeTax`. In fact, since both methods delegate to `apply`, they are effectively bubble words that the user could omit. That is, the following two DSL lines are equivalent:

```
federalIncomeTax is (25. percent_of gross)
federalIncomeTax    (25. percent_of gross)
```

The `apply` method takes `DeductionsBuilder` and does nothing with it! In fact, by the time `apply` is called, the deduction has already been calculated and factored into the paycheck. By implication, the presence of expressions like `federalIncomeTax is` are effectively syntactic sugar (at least as this DSL is currently implemented). They are a fancy form of comments, but at least they have the virtue of type checking the "kinds" of deductions that are allowed. Of course, as the implementation evolves, these instances might do real work.

To see why `DeductionCalculator.apply` is empty, let's discuss `DeductionsBuilderDeductionHelper`. Recall that the `rules` object has an implicit conversion method to convert a `Double` to a `DeductionsBuilderDeductionHelper`. Once we have a helper instance, we can call either the `in` method or the `percent_of` method. Every line in the deductions function literal exploits this instance.

For example, (25. percent_of gross) is roughly equivalent to the following steps:

1. Call to rules.double2DeductionsBuilderDeductionHelper(25.) to create a new DeductionsBuilderDeductionHelper(25.)
2. Call to the helper's percent_of(gross) method, where gross is a DeductionsBuilder
3. gross.addDeductionsPercentageOfGross(factor)

In other words, we used DeductionsBuilderDeductionHelper to convert an expression of the form Double method DeductionsBuilder into an expression of the form DeductionsBuilder method2 Double. DeductionsBuilder accumulates each deduction into the paycheck we're building.

The expression 500. in gross.currency works almost identically. Deductions Builder.currency is effectively another bubble word; it simply returns this, but gives a readable idiom for the DSL. The in method simply converts the Double to a Money and passes it to DeductionsBuilder.addDeductions.

So DeductionCalculator.apply does nothing, because all the work is already done by the time apply is called.

Internal DSLs: Final Thoughts

So which is better, the original API implementation or the DSL implementation? The DSL implementation is complex. Like any language, testing its robustness can be a challenge. Users will try many combinations of expressions. They will probably not understand the compiler error messages that refer to the internals we've hidden behind the DSL.

Designing a quality DSL is difficult. With an API, you can follow the Scala library conventions for types, method names, etc. However, with a DSL, you're trying to imitate the language of a new domain. It's hard to get it right.

It's worth the effort, though. A well-designed DSL minimizes the translation effort between requirements and code, thereby improving communications with stakeholders about requirements. DSLs also facilitate rapid feature change and hide distracting implementation details. As always, there is a cost/benefit analysis you should make when deciding whether to use a DSL.

Assuming you've made the "go" decision, a common problem in DSL design is the *finishing problem* (see [Ford2009]). How do you know when you've finished building up the state of an instance and it's ready to use?

We solved this problem in two ways. First, we nested the calculation steps in a function literal. As soon as rules(employee) was invoked, the paycheck was built to completion. Also, all the steps were evaluated "eagerly." We didn't need to put in all the rules, then run them at the end. Our only ordering requirement was the need to calculate the gross pay first, since the deductions are based on it. We enforced the correct order of invocation using instances of different types.

There are cases in which you can't evaluate the build steps eagerly. For example, a DSL that builds up a SQL query string can't run a query after each step of the build process. In this case, evaluation has to wait until the query string is completely built.

By contrast, if your DSL steps are stateless, chained method invocation works just fine. In this case, it doesn't matter when you stop calling chained methods. If you chain methods that build up state, you'll have to add some sort of **done** method and trust the users to always use it at the end.

External DSLs with Parser Combinators

When you write a parser for an external DSL, you can use a parser generator tool like Antlr (see [Antlr]). However, the Scala library includes a powerful parser combinator library that can be used for parsing most external DSLs that have a context-free grammar. An attractive feature of this library is the way it defines an internal DSL that makes parser definitions look very similar to familiar grammar notations, like EBNF (Extended Backus-Naur Form—see [BNF]).

About Parser Combinators

Parser combinators are building blocks for parsers. Parsers that handle specific kinds of input—floating-point numbers, integers, etc.—can be combined together to form other parser combinators for larger expressions. A combinator framework makes it easy to combine parsers to handle sequential and alternative cases, repetition, optional terms, etc.

We'll learn more about parsing techniques and terminology as we proceed. A complete exposition of parsing techniques is beyond our scope, but our example should get you started. You can find additional examples of parsers written using Scala's parser combinator library in [Spiewak2009b], [Ghosh2008a], and [Odersky2008].

A Payroll External DSL

For our parser combinator example, we'll reuse the example we just discussed for internal DSLs. We'll modify the grammar slightly, since our external DSL does not have to be valid Scala syntax. Other changes will make parser construction easier. Here's an example written in the external DSL:

```
paycheck for employee "Buck Trends" is salary for 2 weeks minus deductions for {
  federal income tax              is  25. percent of gross,
  state income tax                is  5.  percent of gross,
  insurance premiums              are 500. in gross currency,
  retirement fund contributions are 10. percent of gross
}
```

Compare this example to the internal DSL we defined in "A Payroll Internal DSL" on page 222:

```
... = rules { employee =>
  employee salary_for 2.weeks minus_deductions_for { gross =>
    federalIncomeTax           is  (25.  percent_of gross)
    stateIncomeTax             is  (5.   percent_of gross)
    insurancePremiums          are (500. in gross.currency)
    retirementFundContributions are (10.  percent_of gross)
  }
}
...
```

In our new DSL, we insert a specific employee in the script. We wouldn't expect a user to copy and paste this script for every employee. A natural extension that we won't pursue would allow the user to loop over all salaried employees in a database, for example.

Some of the differences are "gratuitous"; we could have used the same syntax we used previously. These changes include removing underscores between words in some expressions and expanding camel-case words into space-separated words. That is, we turned some single words into multi-word expressions. We made these changes because they will be easy to implement using parser combinators, but using the same multi-word expressions would have added a lot of complexity to the internal DSL's implementation.

We no longer need "local variables" like **employee** and **gross**. Those words still appear in the DSL, but our parser will keep track of the corresponding instances internally.

The remaining changes are punctuation. It is still convenient to surround the list of deductions with curly braces. We now use a comma to separate the individual deductions, as that will make the parser's job easier. We can also drop the parentheses we used earlier.

To see how closely the internal DSL for Scala's parser combinator library resembles the context-free grammar, let's start with the grammar itself, written in a variation of EBNF. We'll omit commas to separate sequences, for clarity:

```
paycheck = empl gross deduct;

empl = "paycheck" "for" "employee" employeeName;

gross = "is" "salary" "for" duration;

deduct = "minus" "deductions" "for" "{" deductItems "}";

employeeName = "\"" name " " name "\"";

name = ...

duration = decimalNumber weeksDays;

weeksDays = "week" | "weeks" | "day" | "days";
```

```
deductItems = ε | deductItem { "," deductItem };

deductItem = deductKind deductAmount;

deductKind = tax | insurance | retirement;

tax = fedState "income" "tax";

fedState = "federal" | "state";

insurance = "insurance" "premiums";

retirement = "retirement" "fund" "contributions";

deductAmount = percentage | amount;

percentage = toBe doubleNumber "percent" "of" "gross";

amount = toBe doubleNumber "in" "gross" "currency";

toBe = "is" | "are";

decimalNumber = ...

doubleNumber = ...
```

We can see that most of the *terminals* (the literal strings paycheck, for, employee, the characters { and }, etc.) will be bubble words, as defined in the previous section. We'll ignore these after parsing. The ε is used to indicate an empty production for deductItems, although there will rarely be no deductions!

We didn't spell out the details for decimal numbers, double numbers, and allowed letters in the employee names. We simply elided those definitions. We'll handle the details later.

Each line in the grammar defines a *production rule*. The end of the definition is marked with a semicolon. A *nonterminal* appears on the lefthand side of the equals sign. The righthand side consists of terminals (e.g., the literal strings and characters we just mentioned) that require no further parsing, other nonterminals (including possibly a recursive reference to the lefthand side nonterminal), and operators that express relationships between the items. Notice that the grammar forms have a hierarchical decomposition, although not a directed acyclic graph, as generally speaking these grammars can have cycles.

We have a context-free grammar because every production rule has a single nonterminal on the lefthand side of the equals sign, i.e., without any additional context information required to specify the production's applicability and meaning.

Production rules like toBe = "is" | "are" mean the is production (a terminal in this case) *or* the are production will match. This is an example of an *alternative composition*.

When productions are separated by white space on the righthand side of another production, e.g., `prod1 prod2`, both productions are required to appear sequentially for a match. (Most EBNF formats actually require a comma to separate these items.) Hence, these expressions are more like "and" expressions, but *sequential composition* is so common that no & operator is used, the analog of | for alternative composition.

The production rule with `"{" deductItem { "," deductItem } "}"` demonstrates how to specify optional (zero or more) repetitions. This expression matches a literal { character, followed by a `deductItem` (another production), followed by zero or more expressions consisting of a literal comma `,` and another `deductItem`, and finally ending with a literal } character. Sometimes an asterisk is used to indicate repetition zero or more times, e.g., `prod *`. For repetition at least once, `prod +` is sometimes used.

Finally, if we had optional items in our grammar, we would enclose them in square brackets, `[...]`. There are other kinds of composition operators possible (and supported in the Scala library), a few of which we'll discuss. See the [ScalaAPI2008] entry for `Parsers` for more details.

A Scala Implementation of the External DSL Grammar

Here is the parser written using Scala's parser combinators. At this point, we won't do anything to actually calculate an employee's paycheck, so we'll append `V1` to the class name:

```
// code-examples/DSLs/payroll/pcdsl/payroll-parser-comb-v1.scala

package payroll.pcdsl
import scala.util.parsing.combinator._
import org.specs._
import payroll._
import payroll.Type2Money._

class PayrollParserCombinatorsV1 extends JavaTokenParsers {

  def paycheck = empl ~ gross ~ deduct

  def empl = "paycheck" ~> "for" ~> "employee" ~> employeeName

  def gross = "is" ~> "salary" ~> "for" ~> duration

  def deduct = "minus" ~> "deductions" ~> "for" ~> "{" ~> deductItems  <~ "}"

  // stringLiteral provided by JavaTokenParsers
  def employeeName = stringLiteral

  // decimalNumber provided by JavaTokenParsers
  def duration = decimalNumber ~ weeksDays

  def weeksDays = "weeks" | "week" | "days" | "day"

  def deductItems = repsep(deductItem, "," )
```

```scala
    def deductItem = deductKind ~> deductAmount

    def deductKind = tax | insurance | retirement

    def tax = fedState <~ "income" <~ "tax"

    def fedState = "federal" | "state"

    def insurance = "insurance" ~> "premiums"

    def retirement = "retirement" ~> "fund" ~> "contributions"

    def deductAmount = percentage | amount

    def percentage = toBe ~> doubleNumber <~ "percent" <~ "of" <~ "gross"

    def amount = toBe ~> doubleNumber <~ "in" <~ "gross" <~ "currency"

    def toBe = "is" | "are"

    // floatingPointNumber provided by JavaTokenParsers
    def doubleNumber = floatingPointNumber
}
```

The body of `PayrollParserCombinatorsV1` looks very similar to the grammar we defined for the DSL. Each production rule becomes a method. The terminating semicolon is dropped, but since the production is a method, it would be valid Scala to leave it in.

Where we had whitespace between each production on the righthand side, we now use a combinator operator, either ~, ~>, or <~. The combinator for sequential composition is ~, used when we want to retain for further processing the results produced by both productions on the left and right sides of the ~. For example, when processing the `paycheck` production, we want to keep all three results from `empl`, `gross`, and `deduct`. Hence we use two ~ operators:

```scala
    def paycheck = empl ~ gross ~ deduct
```

We use another sequential composition combinator ~> when we no longer need the result of the production to the *left*. For example, when processing the `empl` production, we only want to keep the parse result for the last production, `employeeName`:

```scala
    def empl = "paycheck" ~> "for" ~> "employee" ~> employeeName
```

Similarly, we use <~ when we no longer need the result for the production to the *right*. For example, when processing the `tax` production, we only want to keep the result of the first production, `fedState`:

```scala
    def tax = fedState <~ "income" <~ "tax"
```

Our heavy use of the <~ sequential combinator in the various productions related to deductions indicates that we aren't keeping track of the source of each deduction, just the amount of the deduction. A real paycheck application would print this information, of course. Our aim is for simplicity. As an exercise, consider how `PayrollParser`

`CombinatorsV1` and the subsequent refinements below would change if we tracked this information. Would you necessarily keep the parsed strings or track the information some other way?

The "or" case is expressed with the | method, just as in the grammar:

```
def weeksDays = "weeks" | "week" | "days" | "day"
```

The **rep** method can be used for zero or more repetitions. We actually use a similar method, **repsep**, which lets us specify a separator, in our case a comma (,):

```
def deduct = ... ~> "{" ~> repsep(deductItem, "," ) <~ "}"
```

Note that **deduct** combines several features we have just described.

Like repetition, there is an **opt** method for optional terms, which we aren't using.

`PayrollParserCombinatorsV1` inherits from `JavaTokenParsers`, which inherits from `RegexParsers`, which inherits from the root parser trait `Parsers`. It's well known that parsing non-trivial grammars with just regular expressions tends to break down pretty quickly. However, using regular expressions to parse individual terms inside a parsing framework can be very effective. In our example, we exploit the productions in `JavaTokenParsers` to parse quoted strings (for the employee's name), decimal literals, and floating-point literals.

Let's try it out! Here is a specification that exercises the parser for two cases, without and with deductions:

```
// code-examples/DSLs/payroll/pcdsl/payroll-parser-comb-v1-spec.scala

package payroll.pcdsl
import scala.util.parsing.combinator._
import org.specs._
import payroll._
import payroll.Type2Money._

object PayrollParserCombinatorsV1Spec
  extends Specification("PayrollParserCombinatorsV1") {

  "PayrollParserCombinatorsV1" should {
    "parse rules when there are no deductions" in {
      val input = """paycheck for employee "Buck Trends"
                    is salary for 2 weeks minus deductions for {}"""
      val p = new PayrollParserCombinatorsV1
      p.parseAll(p.paycheck, input) match {
        case p.Success(r,_) => r.toString mustEqual
                  """(("Buck Trends"~(2~weeks))~List())"""
        case x => fail(x.toString)
      }
    }
  }

  "calculate the gross, net, and deductions for the pay period" in {
    val input =
        """paycheck for employee "Buck Trends"
          is salary for 2 weeks minus deductions for {
```

```
                  federal income tax               is  25.  percent of gross,
                  state income tax                 is   5.  percent of gross,
                  insurance premiums               are 500. in gross currency,
                  retirement fund contributions are 10.  percent of gross
              }"""
    val p = new PayrollParserCombinatorsV1
    p.parseAll(p.paycheck, input) match {
      case p.Success(r,_) => r.toString mustEqual
          """(("Buck Trends"~(2~weeks))~List(25., 5., 500., 10.))"""
      case x => fail(x.toString)
    }
  }
 }
}
```

This part of the specification shows us how to instantiate and use the parser:

```
val p = new PayrollParserCombinatorsV1

p.parseAll(p.paycheck, input) match {
  case p.Success(r,_) => r.toString mustEqual "..."
  case x => fail(x.toString)
}
```

The `parseAll` method is defined in a parent class. We invoke the top-level production method, `paycheck`, and pass its return value as the first argument to `parseAll` and pass the string to parse as the second argument.

If the parsing process is successful, the result of the parse is returned as an instance of type `p.Success[+T]`, a case class declared in the `Parsers` trait. Why is there a `p.` prefix? It indicates that `p.Success` is a *path-dependent type*, which we will discuss in "Path-Dependent Types" on page 272. For now, just know that even though `Success` is defined in the `Parsers` trait, the actual type of the instance is dependent on the `Payroll ParserCombinatorsV1` instance we created. In other words, if we had another parser, say `p2` of type `MyOtherParser`, then `p2.Success[String]` would be different from `p.Success[String]` and one could not be substituted for the other.

The `Success` instance contains two fields. The first is the result of the parse, an instance of type `T` (assigned to `r` in the `case` clause). The second is the remaining input string to parse, which will be empty after a successful parse (we will have parsed the whole string at this point). This string is assigned to `_`.

If the parse fails, the returned instance is either a `p.Failure` or `p.Error`, which our example handles with a generic `case` clause. Both are derived from `p.NoSuccess`, which contains fields for an error message and the unconsumed input at the point of failure. A `p.Failure` in a parser will trigger backtracking so that a retry with a different parser can be invoked by the parser framework, if possible. An `Error` result does not trigger backtracking and is used to signal more serious problems.

For completeness, both `p.Success` and `p.NoSuccess` derive from `p.ParseResult`.

We have two big unanswered questions: what do the production methods actually return, and what is the type of the result instance returned in the p.Success?

The production methods themselves return parsers. Most of them in our example return p.Parser[String] (again, a path-dependent type). However, because the deduct method handles repetition (it invokes the repsep method), it actually returns a p.Parser[List[String]]. When this parser is used, it will return a List[String], with one string corresponding to each match in the repetition.

So, our call to p.parseAll(p.paycheck, input) earlier parses the input string using the parser returned by p.paycheck. That brings us to the second question: what is the result of a successful parse?

To see what's returned, compile the *PayrollParserCombinatorsV1* file listed at the beginning of this section and invoke the scala interpreter with the -cp option to include the directory where the class files were written (it will be *build* if you used the build process for the code example distribution).

Once in the interpreter, enter the following expressions after the scala> prompt. (You can also find this input the *payroll-parser-comb-script.scala* file in the code example distribution.)

```
scala> import scala.util.parsing.combinator._
import scala.util.parsing.combinator._

scala> import payroll.pcdsl._
import payroll.pcdsl._

scala> val p = new PayrollParserCombinatorsV1
p: payroll.pcdsl.PayrollParserCombinatorsV1 = \
    payroll.pcdsl.PayrollParserCombinatorsV1@79e84310

scala> p.empl
res0: p.Parser[String] = Parser (~>)

scala> p.weeksDays
res2: p.Parser[String] = Parser (|)

scala> p.doubleNumber
res3: p.Parser[String] = Parser ()

scala> p.deduct
res1: p.Parser[List[String]] = Parser (<~)

scala> p.paycheck
res4: p.Parser[p.~[p.~[String,p.~[String,String]],List[String]]] = Parser (~)

scala> p.parseAll(p.weeksDays, "weeks")
res5: p.ParseResult[String] = [1.6] parsed: weeks

scala> val input = """paycheck for employee "Buck Trends"
    | is salary for 2 weeks minus deductions for {}"""
input: java.lang.String =
```

```
paycheck for employee "Buck Trends"
        is salary for 2 weeks minus deductions for {}

scala> p.parseAll(p.paycheck, input)
res6: p.ParseResult[p.~[p.~[String,p.~[String,String]],List[String]]] = \
    [2.53] parsed: (("Buck Trends"~(2~weeks))~List())

scala>
```

We import the necessary types and create a `PayrollParserCombinatorsV1` instance. Then we call several of the production methods to see what kind of `Parser` each returns. The first three—`empl`, `weeksDays`, and `doubleNumber`—return `p.Parser[String]`.

Note what's written on the righthand side in the output for the first three parsers: `empl`, `weeksDays`, and `doubleNumber`. We see `Parser` (`~>`), `Parser` (`|`), and `Parser` (), respectively. The parsers returned reflect the definitions of the production rules, where `empl` ends with a combinator of the form `prod1 ~> prod2`, `weeksDays` returns a combinator of the form `prod1 | prod2`, and `doubleNumber` returns a parser for a single production.

Because `deduct` consists of combinators that handle repetition, the parser returned by `deduct` is of type `p.Parser[List[String]]`, as we stated previously. The righthand side of the output is `Parser` (`<~`), because the definition of `deduct` ends with `prod1 <~ prod2`.

Things get more interesting when we look at the top-level production, `paycheck`. What is `p.Parser[p.~[p.~[String,p.~[String,String]],List[String]]]` = `Parser` (`~`) supposed to mean? Well, the righthand side should be easy to understand now; the definition of `paycheck` ends in `prod1 ~ prod2`. What is the type parameter for `p.Parser` on the lefthand side of the equals sign?

The `Parsers` trait also defines a case class named `~` that represents a pair of sequential rules:

```
case class ~[+a, +b](_1: a, _2: b) {
  override def toString = "("+ _1 +"~"+ _2 +")"
}
```

The actual path-dependent type in our example is `p.~[+a,+b]`. Hence, the type parameter T in `p.Parser[T]` is `p.~[p.~[String,p.~[String,String]],List[String]]`, which is a hierarchical tree of types.

Let's break it down, working our way inside out. Note that there are three `p.~`. We'll start with the innermost type, `p.~[String,String]`, and map the type declaration to the output we saw in the `scala` session `"Buck Trends"~(2~weeks~List())`.

The `p.~[String,String]` corresponds to the parser that handles expressions like `2 weeks`. Hence, the instance created when we parsed our example string was the instance `p.~("2", "weeks")`. Calling the `p.~.toString` method produces the output (`2~weeks`).

Working out one level, we have `p.~[String,p.~[String,String]]`. This combination parses `paycheck for employee "Buck Trends" is salary for 2 weeks`. Recall that we discard paycheck for employee and is salary for, keeping only the Buck Trends and 2 weeks. So we create an instance p.~("Buck Trends", p.~("2", "weeks")). Calling toString again results in the string ("Buck Trends"~(2~weeks)).

Finally, at the outermost level, you can see we have the following: p.~[p.~[String,p.~[String,String]],List[String]]. We've already discussed everything up to the last List[String], which comes from the deduct production:

```
def deduct = "minus" ~> "deductions" ~> "for" ~>
             "{" ~> repsep(deductItem, "," ) <~ "}"
```

We discard everything except for the list of zero or more deductItems. There are none in our example, so we get an empty list for which toString returns List(). Therefore, calling p.~.toString on our outermost type, the one that parameterizes p.Parser, returns the string "Buck Trends"~(2~weeks~List()). We're done!

Well, not quite. We're still not calculating an actual paycheck for ol' Buck. Let's complete our implementation.

Generating Paychecks with the External DSL

As we parse the DSL, we want to look up the employee by name, fetch his or her gross salary for the specified pay period, and then calculate the deductions as we go. When the parser returned by paycheck finishes, we want to return a Pair with the Employee instance and the completed Paycheck.

We will reuse "domain" classes like Employee, Money, Paycheck, etc. from earlier in the chapter. To do the calculations on demand, we will create a second iteration of PayrollParserCombinatorsV1 that we'll call PayrollParserCombinators. We'll modify the parsers returned by some of the production methods to return new kinds of parsers. We'll also do administrative work like storing running context data, as needed. Our implementation won't be thread-safe. You'll want to ensure that only one thread uses a given PayrollParserCombinators. We could make it more robust, but doing so isn't the goal of this exercise.

Here is our final PayrollParserCombinators:

```
// code-examples/DSLs/payroll/pcdsl/payroll-parser-comb.scala

package payroll.pcdsl
import scala.util.parsing.combinator._
import org.specs._
import payroll._
import payroll.Type2Money._

class UnknownEmployee(name: Name) extends RuntimeException(name.toString)

class PayrollParserCombinators(val employees: Map[Name, Employee])
  extends JavaTokenParsers {

  var currentEmployee: Employee = null
```

```scala
  var grossAmount: Money = Money(0)

  /** @return Parser[(Employee, Paycheck)] */
  def paycheck = empl ~ gross ~ deduct ^^ {
    case e ~ g ~ d => (e, Paycheck(g, g-d, d))
  }

  /** @return Parser[Employee] */
  def empl = "paycheck" ~> "for" ~> "employee" ~> employeeName ^^ { name =>
    val names = name.substring(1, name.length-1).split(" ") // remove ""
    val n = Name(names(0), names(1));
    if (! employees.contains(n))
      throw new UnknownEmployee(n)
    currentEmployee = employees(n)
    currentEmployee
  }

  /** @return Parser[Money] */
  def gross = "is" ~> "salary" ~> "for" ~> duration ^^ { dur =>
    grossAmount = salaryForDays(dur)
    grossAmount
  }

  def deduct = "minus" ~> "deductions" ~> "for" ~> "{" ~> deductItems  <~ "}"

  /**
   * "stringLiteral" provided by JavaTokenParsers
   * @return Parser[String]
   */
  def employeeName = stringLiteral

  /**
   * "decimalNumber" provided by JavaTokenParsers
   * @return Parser[Int]
   */
  def duration = decimalNumber ~ weeksDays ^^ {
    case n ~ factor => n.toInt * factor
  }

  def weeksDays = weeks | days

  def weeks = "weeks?".r ^^ { _ => 5 }

  def days = "days?".r ^^ { _ => 1 }

  /** @return Parser[Money] */
  def deductItems = repsep(deductItem, ",") ^^ { items =>
    items.foldLeft(Money(0)) {_ + _}
  }

  /** @return Parser[Money] */
  def deductItem = deductKind ~> deductAmount

  def deductKind = tax | insurance | retirement
```

```
    def tax = fedState <~ "income" <~ "tax"

    def fedState = "federal" | "state"

    def insurance = "insurance" ~> "premiums"

    def retirement = "retirement" ~> "fund" ~> "contributions"

    def deductAmount = percentage | amount

    /** @return Parser[Money] */
    def percentage = toBe ~> doubleNumber <~ "percent" <~ "of" <~ "gross"  ^^ {
      percentage => grossAmount * (percentage / 100.)
    }

    def amount = toBe ~> doubleNumber <~ "in" <~ "gross" <~ "currency" ^^ {
      Money(_)
    }

    def toBe = "is" | "are"

    def doubleNumber = floatingPointNumber ^^ { _.toDouble }

    // Support method. Assume 260 (52 * 5) paid work days/year
    def salaryForDays(days: Int) =
        (currentEmployee.annualGrossSalary / 260.0) * days
  }
```

For simplicity, we'll use a map of "known" employees, keyed by Name instances, that we save as a field in PayrollParserCombinators. A real implementation would probably use a data store of some kind.

There are two other fields: currentEmployee, which remembers which employee we are processing, and grossAmount, which remembers the gross amount of pay for the employee for the pay period. Both fields have a slight *design smell*. They are mutable. They are set only once per parse, but not when they are declared, only when we parse the input that allows us to calculate them. You might have also noticed that if the same PayrollParserCombinators instance is used more than once, we don't reset these fields to their default values. No doubt it would be possible to write scripts in the DSL that exploit this bug.

These weaknesses are not inherent to parser combinators. They reflect simplifications we used for our purposes. As an exercise, you might try improving the implementation to eliminate these weaknesses.

We have added Javadoc-style @return annotations for most of the productions to make it clear what they are now returning. In some cases, the productions are unchanged, as the original parser instances are fine as is. Most of the changes reflect our desire to calculate the paycheck as we go.

Consider the new paycheck production:

```
/** @return Parser[(Employee, Paycheck)] */
def paycheck = empl ~ gross ~ deduct ^^ {
  case e ~ g ~ d => (e, Paycheck(g, g-d, d))
}
```

Now, we return a `Pair` with the `Employee` and the computed `Paycheck`. The `empl` ~ `gross` ~ `deduct` combination would still return `Parser[String]` (we'll drop the path-dependent prefix for now). We have added a new combinator `^^`, e.g., `prod1 ^^ func1`, where `func1` is a function. If `prod1` succeeds, then the result of applying `func1` to the result of `prod1` is returned. That is, we return `func1(prod1)`.

For `paycheck`, we give it a function literal that does a pattern match to extract the three results from `empl`, `gross`, and `deduct`, respectively. We create a 2-tuple (`Pair`) with e, the `Employee`, and a `Paycheck` calculated from the gross salary for the pay period (in g) and the sum of all the deductions (in d).

It's important to keep clear that the anonymous function passed as an argument to `^^` returns a tuple (`Employee, Paycheck`), but the production `paycheck` method itself returns a `Parser[(Employee, Paycheck)]`. This pattern has been true from the beginning, actually, where `Strings` were always involved in our first version. It will remain true for all the production rules in `PayrollParserCombinators`.

The `empl` production assumes the employee's first name and last name are given. (Obviously, this would be inadequate in a real application.)

```
/** @return Parser[Employee] */
def empl = "paycheck" ~> "for" ~> "employee" ~> employeeName ^^ { name =>
    val names = name.substring(1, name.length-1).split(" ") // remove ""
    val n = Name(names(0), names(1));
    if (! employees.contains(n))
      throw new UnknownEmployee(n)
    currentEmployee = employees(n)
    currentEmployee
}
```

To construct the name, the embedded double quotes have to be removed, which is why we start by extracting the substring that tosses the first and last characters. The name is used to look up the `Employee` instance in the map, saving the value in the `currentEmployee` field. In general, there is not a lot of "graceful" error handling in `PayrollParserCombinators`. However, the `empl` method handles the case where no employee is found with the specified name, throwing an `UnknownEmployee` exception when this occurs.

The rest of the productions work similarly. Sometimes, a parser converts an input string to an `Int` (e.g., `duration`) or a `Money` (e.g., `gross`). An interesting case is `deduct`. It folds the list of deductions into a single deduction amount, using addition. The `foldLeft` method takes two argument lists. The first has a single argument that specifies the initial value, in this case, zero `Money`. The second argument list has a single function literal argument that takes two arguments: the accumulated value of the folding operation, and an item from the list. In this case, we return the sum of the arguments. So, `foldLeft` iterates over the `items` collection, adding them together. See "Traversing, Mapping, Filtering, Folding, and Reducing" on page 174 for more information on `foldLeft` and related operations.

The `weeks` and `days` productions remind us that we are using parser combinators based on regular-expressions. (We're also using `stringLiteral`, `decimalNumber`, and `floatingPointNumber` provided by `JavaTokenParsers`.) Note that `weeks` and `days` ignore the parsed string. They just return a multiplication factor used to determine total days in the pay period in the `duration` production rule.

There are other combinator methods for applying functions to parser results in different ways. See the `Parsers` Scaladoc page for details.

The following (somewhat incomplete) specification shows the calculation of paychecks when there are no deductions and when there are several deductions:

```scala
// code-examples/DSLs/payroll/pcdsl/payroll-parser-comb-spec.scala

package payroll.pcdsl
import scala.util.parsing.combinator._
import org.specs._
import payroll._
import payroll.Type2Money._

// Doesn't test "sad path" scenarios...
object PayrollParserCombinatorsSpec
    extends Specification("PayrollParserCombinators") {

  val salary = Money(100000.1)  // for a full year
  val gross = salary / 26.      // for two weeks
  val buck = Employee(Name("Buck", "Trends"), salary)
  val employees = Map(buck.name -> buck)

  implicit def money2double(m: Money) = m.amount.doubleValue

  "PayrollParserCombinators" should {
    "calculate the gross == net when there are no deductions" in {
      val input = """paycheck for employee "Buck Trends"
                    is salary for 2 weeks minus deductions for {}"""
      val p = new PayrollParserCombinators(employees)
      p.parseAll(p.paycheck, input) match {
        case p.Success(Pair(employee, paycheck),_) =>
          employee mustEqual buck
          paycheck.gross must beCloseTo(gross, Money(.001))
          paycheck.net must beCloseTo(gross, Money(.001))
          // zero deductions?
          paycheck.deductions must beCloseTo(Money(0.), Money(.001))
        case x => fail(x.toString)
      }
    }

    "calculate the gross, net, and deductions for the pay period" in {
      val input =
```

```
        """paycheck for employee "Buck Trends"
            is salary for 2 weeks minus deductions for {
                federal income tax            is  25.  percent of gross,
                state income tax              is  5.   percent of gross,
                insurance premiums            are 500. in gross currency,
                retirement fund contributions are 10.  percent of gross
            }"""

    val p = new PayrollParserCombinators(employees)
    p.parseAll(p.paycheck, input) match {
      case p.Success(Pair(employee, paycheck),_) =>
        employee mustEqual buck
        val deductions = (gross * .4) + Money(500)
        val net = gross - deductions
        paycheck.gross must beCloseTo(gross, Money(.001))
        paycheck.net must beCloseTo(net, Money(.001))
        paycheck.deductions must beCloseTo(deductions, Money(.001))
      case x => fail(x.toString)
    }
  }
 }
 }
}
```

If you work out what the results should be from the input strings, you'll see that the implementation correctly calculates the paycheck.

Besides the many small details that differ between this implementation of the external DSL and the previous implementation of the internal DSL, there is one big conceptual difference from the two implementations. Here we are computing the paycheck as we parse code written in the external DSL. In the internal DSL case, we generated a paycheck calculator when we parsed the DSL. Afterward, we used that calculator to compute paychecks for one employee at a time. We could have generated a paycheck calculator like we did before, but we chose a simpler approach to focus on the construction of the parser itself. Also, as we discussed earlier, we weren't as careful about thread safety and other issues in the implementation.

Internal Versus External DSLs: Final Thoughts

Scala provides rich support for creating your own internal and external DSLs. However, a non-trivial DSL can be a challenge to implement and debug. For the examples in this chapter, the parser combinators implementation was easier to design and write than the implementation for the internal DSL. However, we found that debugging the internal DSL was easier.

You must also consider how robust the parser must be when handling invalid input. Depending on the level of sophistication of the users of the DSL, you may need to provide very good feedback when errors occur, especially when your users are non-programmers. The parser combinator library in Scala version 2.8 will provide improved support for error recovery and reporting, compared to the version 2.7.X library.

The version 2.8 library will also provide support for writing *packrat parsers* that can implement unambiguous *parsing expression grammars* (PEGs). The 2.8 implementation of packrat parsers also supports *memoization*, which helps improve performance, among other benefits. If you need a fast parser, a packrat parser will take you further before you need to consider more specialized tools, like parser generators.

Recap and What's Next

It's tempting to create DSLs with abandon. DSLs in Scala can be quite fun to work with, but don't underestimate the effort required to create robust DSLs that meet your clients usability needs, nor long-term maintenance and support issues.

If you choose to write a DSL, you have rich options in Scala. The syntax is flexible yet powerful enough that an internal DSL may be sufficient. A internal DSL is an excellent starting point, especially if other programmers will be the primary writers of code in the DSL.

If you expect your non-programming stakeholders to read or even write code written in the DSL, it might be worth the extra effort to create an external DSL that eliminates as many of the programming-language idioms as possible. Consider whether the code written in the DSL will need to be processed for other purposes, like generating documentation, spreadsheets, etc. Since you will have to write a parser for the DSL anyway, it might be straightforward to write others to handle these different purposes.

In the next chapter, we'll explore the richness of Scala's type system. We've learned many of its features already. Now, we'll explore the type system in full detail.

CHAPTER 12

The Scala Type System

Scala is a statically typed language. Its type system is one of the most sophisticated in any programming language, in part because it combines comprehensive ideas from functional programming and object-oriented programming. The type system tries to be logically comprehensive, complete, and consistent. It exceeds limitations in Java's type system while containing innovations that appear in Scala for the first time.

However, the type system can be intimidating at first, especially if you come from a dynamically typed language like Ruby or Python. Fortunately, type inference hides most of the complexities away. Most of the time, you don't need to know the particulars, so we encourage you not to worry that you must master the type system in order to use Scala effectively. You might choose to skim this chapter if you're new to Scala, so you'll know where to look when type-related questions arise later.

Still, the more you know about the type system, the more you will be able to exploit its features in your programs. This is especially true for library writers, who will want to understand when to use parameterized types versus abstract types, which type parameters should be covariant, contravariant, or invariant under subtyping, and so forth. Also, some understanding of the type system will help you understand and debug the occasional compilation failure related to typing. Finally, this understanding will help you make sense of the type information shown in the sources and Scaladocs for Scala libraries.

If you didn't understand some of the terms we used in the preceding paragraphs, don't worry. We'll explain them and why they are useful. We're not going to discuss Scala's type system in exhaustive detail. Rather, we want you to come away with a pragmatic understanding of the type system. You should develop an awareness of the features available, what purposes they serve, and how to read and understand type declarations.

We'll also highlight similarities with Java's type system, since it may be a familiar point of reference for you. Understanding the differences is also useful for interoperability with Java libraries. To focus the discussion, we won't cover the .NET type system, except to point out some notable differences that .NET programmers will want to know.

Reflecting on Types

Scala supports the same reflection capabilities that Java and .NET support. The syntax is different in some cases.

First, you can use the same methods you might use in Java or .NET code. The following script shows some of the reflection methods available on the JVM, through `java.lang.Object` and `java.lang.Class`:

```scala
// code-examples/TypeSystem/reflection/jvm-script.scala

trait T[A] {
  val vT: A
  def mT = vT
}

class C extends T[String] {
  val vT = "T"
  val vC = "C"
  def mC = vC

  class C2
  trait T2
}

val c = new C
val clazz = c.getClass           // method from java.lang.Object
val clazz2 = classOf[C]          // Scala method: classOf[C] ~ C.class
val methods = clazz.getMethods   // method from java.lang.Class<T>
val ctors = clazz.getConstructors  // ...
val fields = clazz.getFields
val annos = clazz.getAnnotations
val name  = clazz.getName
val parentInterfaces = clazz.getInterfaces
val superClass = clazz.getSuperclass
val typeParams = clazz.getTypeParameters
```

Note that these methods are only available on subtypes of `AnyRef`.

The `classOf[T]` method returns the runtime representation for a Scala type. It is analogous to the Java expression `T.class`. Using `classOf[T]` is convenient when you have a type that you want information about, while `getClass` is convenient for retrieving the same information from an instance of the type.

However, `classOf[T]` and `getClass` return slightly different values, reflecting the effect of *type erasure* on the JVM, in the case of `getClass`:

```scala
scala> classOf[C]
res0: java.lang.Class[C] = class C

scala> c.getClass
res1: java.lang.Class[_] = class C
```

Although .NET does not have type erasure, meaning it supports *reified types*, the .NET version of Scala currently follows the JVM's erasure model in order to avoid incompatibilities that would require a "forked" implementation.

We'll discuss a workaround for erasure, called `Manifest`s, after we discuss *parameterized types* in the next section.

Scala also provides methods for testing whether an object matches a type and also for casting an object to a type.

`x.isInstanceOf[T]` will return `true` if the instance `x` is of type `T`. However, this test is subject to type erasure. For example, `List(3.14159).isInstanceOf[List[String]]` will return `true` because the type parameter of `List` is lost at the byte code level. However, you'll get an "unchecked" warning from the compiler.

`x.asInstanceOf[T]` will cast `x` to `T` or throw a `ClassCastException` if `T` and the type of `x` are not compatible. Once again, type erasure must be considered with parameterized types. The expression `List(3.14159).asInstanceOf[List[String]]` will succeed.

Note that these two operations are methods and not keywords in the language, and their names are deliberately somewhat verbose. Normally, type checks and casts like these should be avoided. For type checks, use pattern matching instead. For casts, consider why a cast is necessary and determine if a refactoring of the design can eliminate the requirement for a cast.

 At the time of this writing, there are some experimental features that might appear in the final version 2.8 release in the `scala.reflect` package. These features are designed to make reflective examination and invocation of code easier than using the corresponding Java methods.

Understanding Parameterized Types

We introduced *parameterized types* and *methods* in Chapter 1, and filled in a few more details in "Abstract Types And Parameterized Types" on page 47. If you come from a Java or C# background, you probably already have some knowledge of parameterized types and methods. Now we explore the details of Scala's sophisticated support for parameterized types.

Scala's parameterized types are similar to Java and C# generics and C++ templates. They provide the same capabilities as Java generics, but with significant differences and extensions, reflecting the sophistication of Scala's type system.

To recap, a declaration like `class List[+A]` means that `List` is parameterized by a single type, represented by `A`. The `+` is called a *variance annotation*. We'll come back to it in "Variance Under Inheritance" on page 251.

Sometimes, a parameterized type like List is called a *type constructor*, because it is used to create specific types. For example, List is the type constructor for List[String] and List[Int], which are different types (although they are actually implemented with the same byte code due to *type erasure*). In fact, it's more accurate to say that all traits and classes are type constructors. Those without type parameters are effectively zero-argument, parameterized types.

 If you write class StringList[String] extends List[String] {...}, Scala will interpret String as the name of the type parameter, not the creation of a type based on actual Strings. You want to write class StringList extends List[String] {...}.

Manifests

There is an experimental feature in Scala (since version 2.7.2), called Manifests, that captures type information that is erased in the byte code. This feature is not documented in the Scaladocs, but you can examine the source for the scala.reflect.Manifest trait. [Ortiz2008] discusses Manifests and provides examples of their use.

A Manifest is declared as an implicit argument to a method or type that wants to capture the erased type information. Unlike most implicit arguments, the user does not need to supply an in-scope Manifest value or method. Instead, the compiler generates one automatically. Here is an example that illustrates some of the strengths and weaknesses of Manifests:

```
// code-examples/TypeSystem/manifests/manifest-script.scala

import scala.reflect.Manifest

object WhichList {
  def apply[B](value: List[B])(implicit m: Manifest[B]) = m.toString match {
    case "int"               => println( "List[Int]" )
    case "double"            => println( "List[Double]" )
    case "java.lang.String"  => println( "List[String]" )
    case _                   => println( "List[???]" )
  }
}

WhichList(List(1, 2, 3))
WhichList(List(1.1, 2.2, 3.3))
WhichList(List("one", "two", "three"))

List(List(1, 2, 3), List(1.1, 2.2, 3.3), List("one", "two", "three")) foreach {
  WhichList(_)
}
```

WhichList tries to determine the type of list passed in. It uses the value of the Manifest's toString method to determine this information. Notice that it works when the list is constructed inside the call to WhichList.apply. It does *not* work when a previously constructed list is passed to WhichList.apply.

The compiler exploits the type information it knows in the first case to construct the implicit Manifest with the correct B. However, when given previously constructed lists, the crucial type information is already lost.

Hence, Manifests can't "resurrect" type information from byte code, but they can be used to capture and exploit type information before it is erased.

Parameterized Methods

Individual methods can also be parameterized. Good examples are the apply methods in companion objects for parameterized classes. Recall that companion objects are singleton objects associated with a companion class. There is only one instance of a singleton object, as its name implies, so type parameters would be meaningless.

Let's consider object List, the companion object for class List[+A]. Here is the definition of the apply method in object List:

```
def apply[A](xs: A*): List[A] = xs.toList
```

The apply methods takes a variable length list of arguments of type A, which will be inferred from the arguments, and returns a list created from the arguments. Here is an example:

```
val languages = List("Scala", "Java", "Ruby", "C#", "C++", "Python", ...)
val positiveInts = List(1, 2, 3, 4, 5, 6, 7, ...)
```

We'll look at other parameterized methods shortly.

Variance Under Inheritance

An important difference between Java and Scala generics is how *variance* under inheritance works. For example, if a method has an argument of type List[AnyRef], can you pass a List[String] value? In other words, should a List[String] be considered a *subtype* of List[AnyRef]? If so, this kind of variance is called *covariance*, because the supertype-subtype relationship of the container (the parameterized type) "goes in the same direction" as the relationship between the type parameters. In other contexts, you might want *contravariant* or *invariant* behavior, which we'll describe shortly.

In Scala, the variance behavior is defined at the *declaration site* using *variance annotations*: +, -, or nothing. In other words, the type designer decides how the type should vary under inheritance.

Let's examine the three kinds of variance, summarized in Table 12-1, and understand how to use them effectively. We'll assume that T^{sup} is a *supertype* of T and T_{sub} is a *subtype* of T.

Table 12-1. Type variance annotations and their meanings

Annotation	Java equivalent	Description
+	? extends T	*Covariant* subclassing. E.g., List[T_{sub}] is a subtype of List[T].
-	? super T	*Contravariant* subclassing. E.g., X[T^{sup}] is a subtype of X[T].
none	T	*Invariant* subclassing. E.g., Can't substitute Y[T^{sup}] or Y[T_{sub}] for Y[T].

The "Java equivalent" column is a bit misleading; we'll explain why in a moment.

Class List is declared List[+A], which means that List[String] is a subclass of List[AnyRef], so Lists are covariant in the type parameter A. (When a type like List has only one covariant type parameter, you'll often hear the shorthand expression "Lists are covariant" and similarly for types with a single contravariant type parameter.)

The traits FunctionN, for N equals 0 to 22, are used by Scala to implement function values as true objects. Let's pick Function1 as a representative example. It is declared **trait** Function1[-T, +R].

The +R is the return type and has the covariant annotation +. The type for the single argument has the *contravariant* annotation -. For functions with more than one argument, all the argument types have the contravariant annotation. So, for example, using our T, T^{sup}, and T_{sub} types, the following definition would be legal:

```
val f: Function1[T, T] = new Function1[Tsup, Tsub] { ... }
```

Hence, the function traits are covariant in the return type parameter R and contravariant in the argument parameters T_1, T_2, ..., T_N.

So, what does this really mean? Let's look at an example to understand the variance behavior. If you have prior experience with *Design by Contract* (see [DesignByContract]), it might help you to recall how it works, which is very similar. (We will discuss Design by Contract briefly in "Better Design with Design By Contract" on page 340.) This script demonstrates variance under inheritance:

```
// code-examples/TypeSystem/variances/func-script.scala
// WON'T COMPILE

class CSuper              { def msuper = println("CSuper") }
class C        extends CSuper { def m     = println("C") }
class CSub     extends C    { def msub  = println("CSub") }

var f: C => C = (c: C)     => new C       // #1
    f         = (c: CSuper) => new CSub    // #2
    f         = (c: CSuper) => new C       // #3
    f         = (c: C)     => new CSub    // #4
    f         = (c: CSub)   => new CSuper  // #5: ERROR!
```

This script doesn't produce any output. If you run it, it will fail to compile on the last line.

We start by defining a very simple hierarchy of three classes, C and its superclass CSuper and its subtype CSub. Each one defines a method, which we'll exploit shortly.

Next we define a var named f on the line with the #1 comment. It is a function with the signature C => C. More precisely, it is of type Function1(-C,+C). To be clear, the value assigned to f is after the equals sign, (c: C) => new C. We actually ignore the input c value and just create a new C.

Now we assign different anonymous function values to f. We use whitespace to make the similarities and differences stand out when comparing the original declaration of f and the subsequent reassignments. We keep reassigning to f because we are just testing what will and won't compile at this point. Specifically, we want to know what function values we can legally assign to f: (C) => C.

The second assignment on line #2 assigns (x:CSuper) => new CSub as the function value. This also works, because the argument to Function1 is *contravariant*, so we can substitute the *supertype*, while the return type of Function1 is *covariant*, so our function value can return an instance of the *subtype*.

The next two lines also work. On line #3, we use a CSuper for the argument, which works as it did in line #2. We return a C, which also works as expected. Similarly, on line #4, we use C as the argument and CSub as the return type, both of which worked fine in the previous lines.

The last line, #5, does not compile because we are attempting to use a covariant argument in a contravariant position. We're also attempting to use a contravariant return value where only covariant values are allowed.

Why is the behavior correct in these cases? Here's where Design by Contract thinking comes in handy. Let's see how a client might use some of these definitions of f:

```
// code-examples/TypeSystem/variances/func2-script.scala
// WON'T COMPILE

class CSuper            { def msuper = println("CSuper") }
class C        extends CSuper { def m      = println("C") }
class CSub    extends C       { def msub   = println("CSub") }

def useF(f: C => C) = {
  val c1 = new C      // #1
  val c2: C = f(c1)   // #2
  c2.msuper           // #3
  c2.m                // #4
}

useF((c: C)      => new C)          // #5
useF((c: CSuper) => new CSub)       // #6
useF((c: CSub)   => {println(c.msub); new CSuper})   // #7: ERROR!
```

The useF method takes a function C => C as an argument. (We're just passing function literals now, rather than assigning them to f.) It creates a C (line #1) and passes it to the input function to create a new C (line #2). Then it uses the features of C; namely, it calls the msuper and m methods (lines #3 and #4, respectively).

You could say that the useF method specifies a *contract* of behavior. It expects to be passed a function that can take a C and return a C. It will call the passed-in function, passing a C instance to it, and it will expect to receive a C back.

In line #5, we pass useF a function that takes a C and returns a C. The returned C will work with lines #3 and #4, by definition. All is good.

Finally, we come to the point of this example. In line #6, we pass in a function that is "willing" to accept a CSuper and "promises" to return a CSub. That is, this function is type inferred to be Function1[CSuper,CSub]. In effect, it widens the allowed instances by accepting a supertype. Keep in mind that it will never actually be passed a CSuper by useF, only a C. However, since it can accept a wider set of instances, it will work fine if it only gets C instances.

Similarly, by "promising" to return a CSub, this anonymous function narrows the possible values returned to useF. That's OK, too, because useF will accept any C in return, so if it only gets CSubs, it will be happy. Lines #3 and #4 will still work.

Applying the same arguments, we can see why the last line in the script, line #7, fails to compile. Now the anonymous function can only accept a CSub, but useF will pass it a C. The body of the anonymous function would now break, because it calls c.msub, which doesn't exist in C. Similarly, returning a CSuper when a C is expected breaks line #4 in useF, because CSuper doesn't have the m method.

The same arguments are used to explain how contracts can change under inheritance in Design by Contract.

Note that variance annotations only make sense on the type parameters for parameterized types, not parameterized methods, because the annotations affect the behavior of subtyping. Methods aren't subtyped, but the types that contain them might be subtyped.

 The + *variance annotation* means the parameterized type is *covariant* in the type parameter. The - variance annotation means the parameterized type is *contravariant* in the type parameter. No variance annotation means the parameterized type is *invariant* in the type parameter.

Finally, the compiler checks your use of variance annotations for problems like the one we just described in the last lines of the examples. Suppose you attempted to define your own function type this way:

```scala
trait MyFunction2[+T1, +T2, -R] {
  def apply(v1:T1, v2:T2): R = { ... }
  ...
}
```

The compiler would throw the following errors for the apply method:

```
... error: contravariant type R occurs in covariant position in type (T1,T2)R
    def apply(v1:T1, v2:T2):R
        ^
... error: covariant type T1 occurs in contravariant position in type T1 ...
    def apply(v1:T1, v2:T2):R
            ^
... error: covariant type T2 occurs in contravariant position in type T2 ...
    def apply(v1:T1, v2:T2):R
                  ^
```

Variance of Mutable Types

All the parameterized types we've discussed so far have been immutable types. What about the variance behavior of mutable types? The short answer is that only *invariance* is allowed. Consider this example:

```scala
// code-examples/TypeSystem/variances/mutable-type-variance-script.scala
// WON'T COMPILE: Mutable parameterized types can't have variance annotations

class ContainerPlus[+A](var value: A)      // ERROR
class ContainerMinus[-A](var value: A)     // ERROR

println( new ContainerPlus("Hello World!") )
println( new ContainerMinus("Hello World!") )
```

Running this script throws the following errors:

```
... 4: error: covariant type A occurs in contravariant position in type A \
    of parameter of setter value_=
class ContainerPlus[+A](var value: A)      // ERROR
                             ^
... 5: error: contravariant type A occurs in covariant position in type => A \
    of method value
class ContainerMinus[-A](var value: A)     // ERROR
                             ^

two errors found
```

We can make sense of these errors by remembering our discussion of FunctionN type variance under inheritance, where the types of the function arguments are *contravariant* (i.e., -T1) and the return type is *covariant* (i.e., +R).

The problem with a mutable type is that at least one of its fields has the equivalent of read *and* write operations, either through direct access or through accessor methods.

In the first error, we are trying to use a covariant type as an argument to a setter (write) method, but we saw from our discussion of function types that argument types to a method must be contravariant. A covariant type is fine for the getter (read) method.

Similarly, for the second error, we are trying to use a contravariant type as the return value of a read method, which must be covariant. For the write method, the contravariant type is fine.

Hence, the compiler won't let us use a variance annotation on a type that is used for a mutable field. For this reason, all the mutable parameterized types in the Scala library are *invariant* in their type parameters. Some of them have corresponding immutable types that have covariant or contravariant parameters.

Variance In Scala Versus Java

As we said, the variance behavior is defined at the *declaration site* in Scala. In Java, it is defined at the *call site*. The *client* of a type defines the variance behavior desired (see [Naftalin2006]). In other words, when you use a Java generic and specify the type parameter, you also specify the variance behavior (including invariance, which is the default). You can't specify variance behavior at the definition site in Java, although you can use expressions that look similar. Those expressions define *type bounds*, which we'll discuss shortly.

In Java variance specifications, a wildcard ? always appears before the super or extends keyword, as shown earlier in Table 12-1. When we said after the table that the "Java Equivalent" column is a bit misleading, we were referring to the differences between declaration versus call site specifications. There is another way in which the Scala and Java behaviors differ, which we'll cover in "Existential Types" on page 284.

A drawback of call-site variance specifications is that they force the users of Java generics to understand the type system more thoroughly than is necessary for users of Scala parameterized types, who don't need to specify this behavior when using parameterized types. (Scala users also benefit greatly from type inference.)

Let's look at a Java example, a simplified Java version of Scala's Option, Some, and None types:

```java
// code-examples/TypeSystem/variances/Option.java

package variances;

abstract public class Option<T> {
  abstract public boolean isEmpty();

  abstract public T get();

  public T getOrElse(T t) {
    return isEmpty() ? t : get();
  }
}
// code-examples/TypeSystem/variances/Some.java

package variances;

public class Some<T> extends Option<T> {

  public Some(T value) {
    this.value = value;
```

```
      }

    public boolean isEmpty() { return false; }

    private T value;

    public T get() { return value; }

    public String toString() {
      return "Option(" + value + ")";
    }
  }

  // code-examples/TypeSystem/variances/None.java

  package variances;

  public class None<T> extends Option<T> {

    public boolean isEmpty() { return true; }

    public T get() { throw new java.util.NoSuchElementException(); }

    public String toString() {
      return "None";
    }
  }
```

Here is an example that uses this Java Option hierarchy:

```
  // code-examples/TypeSystem/variances/OptionExample.java

  package variances;
  import java.io.*;
  import shapes.*;  // From "Introducing Scala" chapter

  public class OptionExample {
    static String[] shapeNames = {"Rectangle", "Circle", "Triangle", "Unknown"};
    static public void main(String[] args) {

      Option<? extends Shape> shapeOption =
        makeShape(shapeNames[0], new Point(0.,0.), 2., 5.);
      print(shapeNames[0], shapeOption);

      shapeOption = makeShape(shapeNames[1], new Point(0.,0.), 2.);
      print(shapeNames[1], shapeOption);

      shapeOption = makeShape(shapeNames[2],
        new Point(0.,0.), new Point(2.,0.), new Point(0.,2.));
      print(shapeNames[2], shapeOption);

      shapeOption = makeShape(shapeNames[3]);
      print(shapeNames[3], shapeOption);
    }

    static public Option<? extends Shape> makeShape(String shapeName,
```

```
        Object... args) {
    if (shapeName == shapeNames[0])
      return new Some<Rectangle>(new Rectangle((Point) args[0],
        (Double) args[1], (Double) args[2]));
    else if (shapeName == shapeNames[1])
      return new Some<Circle>(new Circle((Point) args[0], (Double) args[1]));
    else if (shapeName == shapeNames[2])
      return new Some<Triangle>(new Triangle((Point) args[0],
        (Point) args[1], (Point) args[2]));
    else
      return new None<Shape>();
  }

  static void print(String name, Option<? extends Shape> shapeOption) {
    System.out.println(name + "? " + shapeOption);
  }
}
```

OptionExample.main uses the Shape hierarchy from Chapter 1, but we have updated it
slightly to exploit features that we've learned since then, such as **case** classes:

```
// code-examples/TypeSystem/shapes/shapes.scala

package shapes {
  case class Point(x: Double, y: Double) {
    override def toString() = "Point(" + x + "," + y + ")"
  }

  abstract class Shape() {
    def draw(): Unit
  }

  case class Circle(center: Point, radius: Double) extends Shape {
    def draw() = println("Circle.draw: " + this)
  }

  case class Rectangle(lowerLeft: Point, height: Double, width: Double)
      extends Shape {
    def draw() = println("Rectangle.draw: " + this)
  }

  case class Triangle(point1: Point, point2: Point, point3: Point)
      extends Shape() {
    def draw() = println("Triangle.draw: " + this)
  }
}
```

Running OptionExample with scala -cp ... variances.OptionExample produces the
following output:

```
Rectangle? Option(Rectangle(Point(0.0,0.0),2.0,5.0))
Circle? Option(Circle(Point(0.0,0.0),2.0))
Triangle? Option(Triangle(Point(0.0,0.0),Point(2.0,0.0),Point(0.0,2.0)))
Unknown? None
```

By the way, we are also demonstrating Scala-Java interoperability, which we'll revisit in "Java Interoperability" on page 369.

OptionExample.main calls the static factory method makeShape, whose arguments are the name of a geometric shape and a variable length list of parameters to pass to the Shape constructors.

Note that makeShape returns Option<? extends Shape>, and when we instantiate a Shape, we return a Some parameterized with the Shape subtype it wraps. If an unknown shape name is passed in, then we return a None<Shape>. We must parameterize a None instance with Shape. Because Scala defines a subtype of *all* types, Nothing, Scala can define None as case object None extends Option[Nothing].

The Java type system provides no way to implement our Java None in a similar way. Having a singleton object None has a number of advantages, including greater efficiency, because we aren't creating lots of little objects, and unambiguous behavior of equals, because we don't need to define the semantics of equality between different type instantiations of our Java None<?> type—for example, None<String> versus None<Shape>.

Finally, note that OptionExample, a client of Option, has to specify type variance, Option<? extends Shape> in several places. In Scala, the client doesn't carry this burden.

Implementation Notes

The implementation of parameterized types and methods is worth noting. The implementations are generated when the defining source file is compiled. For each type parameter, the implementation assumes that Any subtype could be specified (Object is used in Java generics). These aspects have performance implications that we will revisit when we discuss the @specialized annotation in "Annotations" on page 289.

Type Bounds

When defining a parameterized type or method, it may be necessary to specify *bounds* on the type. For example, a parameterized type might assume that a particular type parameter contains certain methods.

Upper Type Bounds

Consider the overloaded apply methods in object scala.Array that create new arrays. There are optimized implementations for each of the AnyVal types. There is another implementation of apply that is parameterized for any type that is a subtype of AnyRef. Here is the implementation in Scala version 2.7.5:

```
object Array {
  ...
  def apply[A <: AnyRef](xs: A*): Array[A] = {
    val array = new Array[A](xs.length)
```

```
        var i = 0
        for (x <- xs.elements) { array(i) = x; i += 1 }
        array
    }
    ...
}
```

The type parameter `A <: AnyRef` means "any type `A` that is a *subtype* of `AnyRef`." Note that a type is always a subtype and a supertype of itself, so `A` could also equal `AnyRef`. So the `<:` operator indicates that the type to the left must be derived from the type to the right, or that they must be the same type. As we said in "Reserved Words" on page 49, this operator is actually a reserved word in the language.

These bounds are called *upper type bounds*, following the de facto convention that diagrams of type hierarchies put subtypes below their supertypes. We followed this convention in the diagram shown in "The Scala Type Hierarchy" on page 155.

Without the bound in this case, i.e., if the signature were `def apply[A](xs: A*): Array[A]`, the declaration would be ambiguous with the other `apply` methods for each of the `AnyVal` types.

 The type signature `A <: B` says that `A` must be a *subtype* of `B`. In Java, this would be expressed as `A extends B` in a type declaration. This is different from *instantiating* a type at a call site, where the syntax `? extends B` is used in Java, indicating the *variance* behavior.

Keep in mind the distinction between type variance and type bounds. For a type like `List`, the *variance* behavior describes how actual types instantiated from it, like `List[AnyRef]` and `List[String]`, are related. In this case, `List[String]` is a subtype of `List[AnyRef]`, since `String` is a subtype of `AnyRef`.

In contrast, lower and upper type bounds limit the allowed types that can be used for a type parameter when instantiating a type from a parameterized type. For example, `def apply[A <: AnyRef]...` says that any type used for `A` must be a subtype of `AnyRef`.

Lower Type Bounds

Similarly, there are circumstances when we might want to express that only **super types** of a particular type are allowed. (Recall that a type is also a supertype of itself.) We call these *lower type bounds*, again because the allowed type would be above the boundary in a typical type hierarchy diagram.

A particularly interesting example is the `::` ("cons") method in class `List[+A]`. Recall that this operator is used to create a new list by prepending an element to a list:

```
class List[+A] {
    ...
    def ::[B >: A](x : B) : List[B] = new scala.::(x, this)
```

```
    ...
}
```

The new list will be of type List[B], specifically a scala.::. The :: *class* (as opposed to the :: *method*) is derived from List. We'll come back to it in a moment.

The :: method can prepend an object of a different type from A, the type of the elements in the original list. The compiler will infer the closest common supertype for A and the parameter x. It will use that supertype as B. Here's an example that prepends a different type of object on a list:

```
// code-examples/TypeSystem/bounds/list-ab-script.scala

val languages = List("Scala", "Java", "Ruby", "C#", "C++", "Python")
val list = 3.14 :: languages
println(list)
```

The script prints the following output:

```
List(3.14, Scala, Java, Ruby, C#, C++, Python)
```

The new list of type List[Any], since Any is the closest common supertype of String and Double. We started with a list of Strings, so A was String. Then we prepended a Double, so the compiler inferred B to be Any, the closest (and only) common supertype.

 The type signature B >: A says that B must be a *supertype* of A. There is no analog in Java; B super A is not supported.

A Closer Look at Lists

Putting these features together, it's worth looking at the implementation of the List class in the Scala library. It illustrates several useful idioms for functional-style, immutable data structures that are fully type-safe, yet flexible. We won't show the entire implementation, and we'll omit the object List, many methods in the List class, and the comments that are used to generate the Scaladocs. We encourage you to look at the complete implementation of List, either by downloading the source distribution from the Scala website (*http://www.scala-lang.org/*) or by browsing to the implementation through the Scaladocs page for List. To avoid confusion with scala.List, we'll use our own package and name, AbbrevList:

```
// code-examples/TypeSystem/bounds/abbrev-list.scala
// Adapted from scala/List.scala in the Scala version 2.7.5 distribution.

package bounds.abbrevlist

sealed abstract class AbbrevList[+A] {

  def isEmpty: Boolean
  def head: A
```

```
    def tail: AbbrevList[A]

    def ::[B >: A] (x: B): AbbrevList[B] = new bounds.abbrevlist.::(x, this)

    final def foreach(f: A => Unit) = {
      var these = this
      while (!these.isEmpty) {
        f(these.head)
        these = these.tail
      }
    }
  }

  // The empty AbbrevList.

  case object AbbrevNil extends AbbrevList[Nothing] {
    override def isEmpty = true

    def head: Nothing =
      throw new NoSuchElementException("head of empty AbbrevList")

    def tail: AbbrevList[Nothing] =
      throw new NoSuchElementException("tail of empty AbbrevList")
  }

  // A non-empty AbbrevList characterized by a head and a tail.

  final case class ::[B](private var hd: B,
      private[abbrevlist] var tl: AbbrevList[B]) extends AbbrevList[B] {

    override def isEmpty: Boolean = false
    def head : B = hd
    def tail : AbbrevList[B] = tl
  }
```

Notice that while `AbbrevList` is immutable, the internal implementation uses mutable variables, e.g., in `forEach`.

There are three types defined, forming a sealed hierarchy. `AbbrevList` (the analog of `List`) is an abstract trait that declares three abstract methods: `isEmpty`, `head`, and `tail`. It defines the "cons" operator (`::`) and a `foreach` method. All the other methods found in `List` could be implemented with these methods, although some methods (like `List.length`) use different implementation options for efficiency.

`AbbrevNil` is the analog of `Nil`. It is a case object that extends `AbbrevList[Nothing]`. It returns `true` from `isEmpty`, and it throws an exception from `head` and `tail`. Because `AbbrevNil` (and `Nil`) have essentially no state and behavior, having an object rather than a class eliminates unnecessary copies, makes `equals` fast and simple, etc.

The `::` class is the analog of `scala.::` derived from `List`. It is declared final. Its arguments are the element to become the `head` of the new list and an existing list, which will be the `tail` of the new list. Note that these values are stored directly as fields. The head and tail methods defined in `AbbrevList` are just reader methods for these fields. There is no other data structure required to represent the list.

This is why prepending a new element to create a new list is an O(1) operation. The `List` class also has a deprecated method + for creating a new list by appending an element to the end of an existing list. That operation is O(N), where N is the length of the list.

As you build up new lists by prepending elements to other lists, a nested hierarchy of :: instances is created. Because the lists are immutable, there are no concerns about corruption if one of the :: is changed in some way.

You can see this nesting if you print out a list, exploiting the `toString` method generated because of the `case` keyword. Here is an example `scala` session:

```
$ scala -cp ...
Welcome to Scala version 2.7.5.final ...
Type in expressions to have them evaluated.
Type :help for more information.

scala> import bounds.abbrevlist._
import bounds.abbrevlist._

scala> 1 :: 2 :: 3 :: AbbrevNil
res1: bounds.abbrevlist.AbbrevList[Int] = ::(1,::(2,::(3,AbbrevNil)))
```

Note the output on the last line, which shows the nesting of (head,tail) elements.

For another example using similar approaches, this time for defining a stack, refer to *http://www.scala-lang.org/node/129.*

Views and View Bounds

We've seen many examples where an `implicit` method was used to convert one type to another—for example, to give the appearance of adding new methods to an existing type, the so-called Pimp My Library pattern. We used this pattern extensively in Chapter 11. You can also use function values that have the `implicit` keyword. We'll see examples of both shortly.

A *view* is an implicit value of function type that converts a type A to B. The function has the type A => B or (=> A) => B (recall that (=> A) is a *by-name parameter*). An in-scope implicit method with the same signature can also be used as a view, e.g., an implicit method imported from an `object`. The term *view* conveys the sense of having a view from one type (A) to another type (B).

A view is applied in two circumstances.

1. When a type A is used in a context where another type B is expected and there is a view in scope that can convert A to B.

2. When a non-existent member m of a type A is referenced, but there is an in-scope view that can convert A to a B that has the m member.

A common example of the second circumstance is the x -> y initialization syntax for Maps, which triggers invocation of Predef.anyToArrowAssoc(x), as we discussed in "The Predef Object" on page 145.

For an example of the first circumstance, Predef also defines many views for converting between AnyVal types and for converting an AnyVal type to its corresponding java.lang type. For example, double2Double converts a scala.Double to a java.lang.Double.

A *view bound* in a type declaration is indicated with the <% keyword, e.g., A <% B. It allows any type to be used for A if it can be converted to B using a view.

A method or class containing such a type parameter is treated as being equivalent to a corresponding method or class with an extra argument list with one element, a view. For example, consider the following method definition with a view bound:

```
def m [A <% B](arglist): R = ...
```

It is effectively the same as this method definition:

```
def m [A](arglist)(implicit viewAB: A => B): R = ...
```

(The implicit parameter viewAB would be given a unique name by the compiler.) Note that we have an additional argument list, as opposed to an additional argument in the existing argument list.

Why does this transformation work? We said that a valid A must have a view in scope that transforms it to a B. The implicit viewAB argument will get invoked inside m to convert all A instances to B instances where needed.

For this to work, there must be a view of the correct type in scope to satisfy the implicit argument. You could also pass a function with the correct signature explicitly as the second argument list when you call m. However, there is one situation where this won't work, which we'll describe after our upcoming example.

For view bounds on types, the implicit view argument list would be added to the primary constructor.

 Traits can't have view bounds for their type parameters, because they can't have constructor argument lists.

To make this more concrete, let's use view bounds to implement a LinkedList class that uses Nodes, where each Node has a payload and a reference to the next Node in the list. First, here is a hierarchy of Nodes:

```
// code-examples/TypeSystem/bounds/node.scala

package bounds

abstract trait Node[+A] {
  def payload: A
  def next: Node[A]
}

case class ::[+A](val payload: A, val next: Node[A]) extends Node[A] {
  override def toString =
    String.format("(%s :: %s)", payload.toString, next.toString)
}

object NilNode extends Node[Nothing] {
  def payload = throw new NoSuchElementException("No payload in NilNode")
  def next    = throw new NoSuchElementException("No next in NilNode")

  override def toString = "*"
}
```

This type hierarchy is modeled after List and AbbrevList earlier. The :: type represents intermediate nodes, and NilNode is analogous to Nil for Lists. We also override toString to give us convenient output, which we'll examine shortly.

The following script defines a LinkedList type that uses Nodes:

```
// code-examples/TypeSystem/bounds/view-bounds-script.scala

import bounds._

implicit def any2Node[A](x: A): Node[A] = bounds.::[A](x, NilNode)

case class LinkedList[A <% Node[A]](val head: Node[A]) {

  def ::[B >: A <% Node[B]](x: Node[B]) =
    LinkedList(bounds.::(x.payload, head))

  override def toString = head.toString
}

val list1 = LinkedList(1)
val list2 = 2 :: list1
val list3 = 3 :: list2
val list4 = "FOUR!" :: list3

println(list1)
println(list2)
println(list3)
println(list4)
```

It starts with a definition of a parameterized implicit method, any2Node, that converts A to Node[A]. It will be used as the implicit view argument when we work with Linked Lists. It creates a "leaf" node using a bounds.:: node with a reference to NilNode as the "next" element in the list.

An alternative would be a function value that converts `Any` to `Node[Any]`:

```
implicit val any2Node = (a: Any) => bounds.::[Any](a, NilNode)
```

Otherwise, the script would run the same, except that some of the temporary lists would be using `Node[Any]` rather than `Node[Int]`.

Look at the declaration of `LinkedList`:

```
case class LinkedList[A <% Node[A]](val head: Node[A]) { ... }
```

It defines a view bound on `A` and takes a single argument, the head `Node` of the list (which may be the head of a chain of `Nodes`). As we see later in the script, even though the constructor expects a `Node[A]` argument, we can pass it an `A` and the implicit view `any2Node` will get invoked. The beauty of this approach is that a client never has to worry about proper construction of `Nodes`. The machinery handles that process automatically.

The class also has a "cons" operator:

```
def ::[B >: A <% Node[B]](x: Node[B]) = ...
```

The type parameter means `` `B is lower bounded by (i.e., is a supertype of) `A`, and `B` also has a view bound of `B <% Node[B]`. As we saw for `List` and `AbbrevList`, the lower bound allows us to prepend items of different types from the original `A` type. This method will have its own implicit view argument, but our parameterized, implicit method, `any2Node`, will be used for this argument, too.

We mentioned previously that if you don't have a view in scope, you could pass a "non-implicit" converter as the second argument list explicitly. This actually won't work in our example, because the constructor and `::` method in `LinkedList` take `Node[A]` arguments, but we call them with `Ints` and `Strings`. We would have to call them with `Node[Int]` and `Node[String]` arguments explicitly. We would also have to invoke `::` in an ugly way—`val list2 = list1.::(2)(converter)`, for example.

Let's clarify the syntax a bit. When you see `B >: A <% Node[B]`, it's tempting to assume that the `<%` should apply to `A` in this expression. It actually applies to `B`. The grammar for type parameters, including view bounds, is the following (see [ScalaSpec2009]):

```
TypeParam       ::= (id | '_') [TypeParamClause] ['>:' Type] ['<:' Type] ['<%' Type]
TypeParamClause ::= '[' VariantTypeParam {',' VariantTypeParam} ']'
VariantTypeParam ::= ['+' | ''] TypeParam
```

So, yes, you can have some very complex, hierarchical types! In our `::` method, the `id` is `B`, the `TypeParamClause` is empty, and we have the `>: A` and `<% Node[B]` expressions on the right. Again, all the bounds expressions apply to the first `id` (`B`) or the underscore (`_`).

The underscore is used for *existential types*, which we'll cover in "Existential Types" on page 284.

Finally, we create a `LinkedList` in the script, prepend some values to create new lists, and then print them out:

```
1 :: *
2 :: 1 :: *
3 :: 2 :: 1 :: *
FOUR! :: 3 :: 2 :: 1 :: *
```

To recap, the view bounds let us work with "payloads" of `Ints` and `Strings` while the implementation handled the necessary conversions to `Nodes`.

View bounds are not used as often as upper and lower bounds, but they provide an elegant mechanism for those times when automatic coercion from one type into another is useful. As always, use implicits with caution; implicit conversions are far from obvious when reading code and debugging mysterious behavior.

Nothing and Null

In "The Scala Type Hierarchy" on page 155, we mentioned that `Null` is a subtype of all `AnyRef` types and `Nothing` is a subtype of all types, including `Null`.

`Null` is declared as a `final trait` (so it can't be subtyped), and it has only one instance, `null`. Since `Null` is a subtype of all `AnyRef` types, you can always assign `null` as an instance of any of those types. Java, in contrast, simply treats `null` as a keyword with special handling by the compiler. However, Java's `null` actually behaves as if it were a subtype of all reference types, just like Scala's `Null`.

On the other hand, since `Null` is not a subtype of `AnyVal`, it is not possible to assign `null` to an `Int`, for example, which is also consistent with the primitive semantics in Java.

`Nothing` is also a `final trait`, but it has no instances. However, it is still useful for defining types. The best example is `Nil`, the empty list, which is a `case object`. It is of type `List[Nothing]`. Because lists are covariant in Scala, as we saw earlier, this makes `Nil` an instance of `List[T]`, for any type T. We also exploited this feature in our `Abbrev List` and `LinkedList` implementations.

Understanding Abstract Types

Besides parameterized types, which are common in statically typed, object-oriented languages, Scala also supports abstract types, which are common in functional languages. We introduced abstract types in "Abstract Types And Parameterized Types" on page 47.

These two features overlap somewhat. Technically, you could implement almost all the idioms that parameterized types support using abstract types and vice versa. However, in practice, each feature is a natural fit for different design problems.

Recall our version of `Observer` that uses abstract types in Chapter 6:

```
// code-examples/AdvOOP/observer/observer2.scala

package observer
```

```scala
trait AbstractSubject {
  type Observer

  private var observers = List[Observer]()
  def addObserver(observer:Observer) = observers ::= observer
  def notifyObservers = observers foreach (notify(_))

  def notify(observer: Observer): Unit
}

trait SubjectForReceiveUpdateObservers extends AbstractSubject {
  type Observer = { def receiveUpdate(subject: Any) }

  def notify(observer: Observer): Unit = observer.receiveUpdate(this)
}

trait SubjectForFunctionalObservers extends AbstractSubject {
  type Observer = (AbstractSubject) => Unit

  def notify(observer: Observer): Unit = observer(this)
}
```

AbstractSubject declares a type Observer with no type bounds. It is defined in the two
derived traits. In SubjectForReceiveUpdateObservers, it is defined to be a *structural
type*. In SubjectForFunctionalObservers, it is defined to be a *function type*. We'll have
more to say about structural and function types later in this chapter.

We can also use type bounds when we declare or refine the declaration of abstract
types. We saw a simple example previously in "Type Projections" on page 279 where
we had a declaration type t <: AnyRef. That is, t had an upper type bound (superclass)
of AnyRef. AnyVal types weren't allowed.

We can also have lower type bounds (subclasses), and we can use most of the *value
types* (see "Value Types" on page 275) in the bounds expressions. Here is an example
illustrating the most common options:

```scala
// code-examples/TypeSystem/abstracttypes/abs-type-examples-script.scala

trait exampleTrait {
  type t1                    // Unconstrained
  type t2 >: t3 <: t1        // t2 must be a supertype of t3 and a subtype of t1
  type t3 <: t1              // t3 must be a subtype of t1
  type t4                    // Unconstrained
  type t5 = List[t4]         // List of t4, whatever t4 will eventually be...

  val v1: t1                 // Can't initialize until t1 defined.
  val v3: t3                 // etc.
  val v2: t2                 // ...
  val v4: t4                 // ...
  val v5: t5                 // ...
}

trait T1 { val name1: String }
```

```
trait T2 extends T1 { val name2: String }
class C(val name1: String, val name2: String) extends T2

object example extends exampleTrait {
  type t1 = T1
  type t2 = T2
  type t3 = C
  type t4 = Int

  val v1 = new T1 { val name1 = "T1"}
  val v3 = new C("C1", "C2")
  val v2 = new T2 { val name1 = "T1"; val name2 = "T2" }
  val v4 = 10
  val v5 = List(1,2,3,4,5)
}
```

The comments explain most of the details. The relationships between t1, t2, and t3
have some interesting points. First, the declaration of t2 says that it must be "between"
t1 and t3. Whatever t1 becomes, it must be a super class of t2 (or equal to it), and t3
must be a subclass of t2 (or equal to it).

Remember from "Type Bounds" on page 259 that we are making a declaration of the
first type after the **type** keyword, t2, not the type in the middle, t3. The rest of
the expression is telling us the bounds of t2.

Consider the next line that declares t3 to be a subtype of t1. If you were to omit the
type bound, the compiler would throw an error, because t3 <: t1 is implied by the
previous declaration of t2. That doesn't mean that you can leave out the declaration of
t3. It has to be there, but it also has to show a consistent type bound with the one
implied in the t2 declaration.

When we revisit the Observer Pattern in "Self-Type Annotations and Abstract Type
Members" on page 317, we'll see another example of type bounds used on abstract
types. We'll see a problem they can cause, along with an elegant solution.

Finally, abstract types don't have variance annotations:

```
// code-examples/TypeSystem/abstracttypes/abs-type-variances-wont-compile.scala
// WON'T COMPILE

trait T1 { val name1: String }
trait T2 extends T1 { val name2: String }
class C(val name1: String, val name2: String) extends T2

trait T {
  type t: +T1    // ERROR, no +/- type variance annotations
  val v
}
```

Remember that the abstract types are *members* of the enclosing type, not type parameters, as for parameterized types. The enclosing type may have an inheritance relationship with other types, but member types behave just like member methods and
variables. They don't affect the inheritance relationships of their enclosing type. Like

other members, abstract types can be declared abstract or concrete. However, they can also be refined in subtypes without being fully defined, unlike variables and methods. Of course, instances can only be created when the abstract types are given concrete definitions.

Parameterized Types Versus Abstract Types

When should you use parameterized types versus abstract types? Parameterized types are the most natural fit for parameterized container types like List and Option. Consider the declaration of Some from the standard library:

```scala
case final class Some[+A](val x : A) { ... }
```

If we tried to convert this to use abstract types, we might start with the following:

```scala
case final class Some(val x : ???) {
  type A
  ...
}
```

What should be the type of the field x? We can't use A because it's not in scope at the point of the constructor argument. We could use Any, but that defeats the value of having appropriately typed declarations.

If a type will have constructor arguments declared using a "placeholder" type that has not yet been defined, then parameterized types are the only good solution (short of using Any or AnyRef).

You can use abstract types as method arguments and return values within a function. However, two problems can arise. First, you can run into problems with path-dependent types (discussed in "Path-Dependent Types" on page 272), where the compiler thinks you are trying to use an incompatible type in a particular context, when in fact they are paths to compatible types. Second, it's awkward to express methods like List.:: ("cons") using abstract types where type changes (expansion in this case) can occur:

```scala
class List[+A] {
  ...
  def ::[B >: A](x : B) : List[B] = new scala.::(x, this)
  ...
}
```

Also, if you want to express variance under inheritance that is tied to the type abstractions, then parameterized types with variance annotations make these behaviors obvious and explicit.

These limitations of abstract types really reflect the tension between object-oriented inheritance and the origin of abstract types in pure functional programming type systems, which don't have inheritance. Parameterized types are more popular in object-oriented languages because they handle inheritance more naturally in most circumstances.

On the other hand, sometimes it's useful to refer to a type abstraction as a member of another type, as opposed to a parameter used to construct new types from a parameterized type. Refining an abstract type declaration through a series of enclosing type refinements can be quite elegant:

```
trait T1 {
  type t
  val v: t
}
trait T2 extends T1 {
  type t <: SomeType1
}
trait T3 extends T2 {
  type t <: SomeType2   // where SomeType2 <: SomeType1
}
class C extends T3 {
  type t = Concrete      // where Concrete <: SomeType2
  val v = new Concrete(...)
}
...
```

This example also shows that abstract types are often used to declare abstract variables of the same type. Less frequently, they are used for method declarations.

When the abstract variables are eventually made concrete, they can either be defined inside the type body, much as they were originally declared, or they can be initialized through constructor arguments. Using constructor arguments lets the user decide on the actual values, while initializing them in the body lets the type designer decide on the appropriate value.

We used constructor arguments in the brief **BulkReader** example we presented in "Abstract Types And Parameterized Types" on page 47:

```
// code-examples/TypeLessDoMore/abstract-types-script.scala

import java.io._

abstract class BulkReader {
  type In
  val source: In
  def read: String
}

class StringBulkReader(val source: String) extends BulkReader {
  type In = String
  def read = source
}

class FileBulkReader(val source: File) extends BulkReader {
  type In = File
  def read = {
    val in = new BufferedInputStream(new FileInputStream(source))
    val numBytes = in.available()
    val bytes = new Array[Byte](numBytes)
```

```
      in.read(bytes, 0, numBytes)
      new String(bytes)
    }
  }

  println( new StringBulkReader("Hello Scala!").read )
  println( new FileBulkReader(new File("abstract-types-script.scala")).read )
```

If you come from an object-oriented background, you will naturally tend to use parameterized types more often than abstract types. The Scala standard library tends to
emphasize parameterized types, too. Still, you should learn the merits of abstract types
and use them when they make sense.

Path-Dependent Types

Languages that let you nest types provide ways to refer to those type *paths*. Scala provides a rich syntax for path-dependent types. Although you will probably use them
rarely, it's useful to understand the basics, as compiler errors often contain type paths.

Consider the following example:

```
// code-examples/TypeSystem/typepaths/type-path-wont-compile.scala
// ERROR: Won't compile

trait Service {
  trait Logger {
    def log(message: String): Unit
  }
  val logger: Logger

  def run = {
    logger.log("Starting " + getClass.getSimpleName + ":")
    doRun
  }

  protected def doRun: Boolean
}

object MyService1 extends Service {
  class MyService1Logger extends Logger {
    def log(message: String) = println("1: "+message)
  }
  override val logger = new MyService1Logger
  def doRun = true  // do some real work...
}

object MyService2 extends Service {
  override val logger = MyService1.logger  // ERROR
  def doRun = true  // do some real work...
}
```

If you compile this file, you get the following error:

```
...:27: error: error overriding value logger in trait Service of type \
    MyService2.Logger;
 value logger has incompatible type MyService1.MyService1Logger
   override val logger = MyService1.logger  // ERROR
            ^
 one error found
```

The error says that the `logger` value in `MyService2` on line 25 has type `MySer`
`vice2.Logger`, even though it's declared to be of type `Logger` in the parent `Service` trait.
Also, we're trying to assign it a value of type `MyService1.MyService1Logger`.

These three types are different in Scala. `Logger` is nested in `Service`, which is the parent
of `MyService1` and `MyService2`. In Scala, that means that the nested `Logger` type is unique
for each of the service types. The actual type is *path-dependent*.

In this case, the easiest solution is to move the declaration of `Logger` outside of
`Service`, thereby removing the path dependency. In other cases, it's possible to qualify
the type so that it resolves to what you want.

There are several kinds of type paths.

C.this

For a class `C`, you can use `C.this` or `this` inside the body to refer to the current instance:

```
class C1 {
  var x = "1"
  def setX1(x:String) = this.x = x
  def setX2(x:String) = C1.this.x = x
}
```

Both `setX1` and `setX2` have the same effect, because `C1.this` is equivalent to `this`.

Inside a type body and outside a method definition, `this` refers to the type itself:

```
trait T1 {
  class C
  val c1 = new C
  val c2 = new this.C
}
```

The values `c1` and `c2` have the same type. The `this` in the expression `this.C` refers to
the trait `T1`.

C.super

You can refer specifically to the parent of a type with `super`:

```
class C2 extends C1
class C3 extends C2 {
  def setX3(x:String) = super.setX1(x)
  def setX4(x:String) = C3.super.setX1(x)
```

```
    def setX5(x:String) = C3.super[C2].setX1(x)
  }
```

`C3.super` is equivalent to `super` in this example. If you want to refer specifically to one of the parents of a type, you can qualify `super` with the type, as shown in `setX5`. This is particularly useful for the case where a type mixes in several traits, each of which overrides the same method. If you need access to one of the methods in a specific trait, you can qualify `super`. However, this qualification can't refer to "grandparent" types.

What if you are calling `super` in a class with several mixins and it extends another type? To which type does `super` bind? Without the qualification, the rules of *linearization* determine the target of `super` (see "Linearization of an Object's Hierarchy" on page 159).

Just as for `this`, you can use `super` to refer to the parent type in a type body outside a method:

```
class C4 {
  class C5
}
class C6 extends C4 {
  val c5a = new C5
  val c5b = new super.C5
}
```

Both `c5a` and `c5b` have the same type.

path.x

You can reach a nested type with a period-delimited path expression:

```
package P1 {
  object O1 {
    object O2 {
      val name = "name"
    }
  }
}
class C7 {
  val name = P1.O1.O2.name
}
```

`C7.name` uses a path to the `name` value in `O2`. The elements of a type path must be *stable*, which roughly means that all elements in the path must be packages, singleton objects, or type declarations that alias the same. The last element in the path can be a class or trait. See [ScalaSpec2009] for the details:

```
object O3 {
  object O4 {
    type t = java.io.File
    class C
    trait T
  }
```

```
    class C2 {
      type t = Int
    }
  }
  class C8 {
    type t1 = O3.O4.t
    type t2 = O3.O4.C
    type t3 = O3.O4.T
//  type t4 = O3.C2.t   // ERROR: C2 is not a "value" in O3
  }
```

Value Types

Because Scala is strongly and statically typed, every value has a type. The term *value types* refers to all the different forms these types take, so it encompasses many forms that are now familiar to us, plus a few new ones we haven't encountered until now.

 We are using the term *value type* here in the same way the term is used by [ScalaSpec2009]. However, elsewhere in the book we also follow the specification's overloaded use of the term to refer to all subtypes of AnyVal.

Type Designators

The conventional type IDs we commonly use are called *type designators*:

```
  class Person          // "Person" is a type designator
  object O { type t }   // "O" and "t" are type designators
  ...
```

They are actually a shorthand syntax for *type projections*, which we cover later.

Tuples

A value of the form $(x_1, \ldots x_N)$ is a tuple value type.

Parameterized Types

When we create a type from a parameterized type, e.g., List[Int] and List[String] from List[A], the types List[Int] and List[String] are value types, because they are associated with declared values, e.g., val names = List[String]().

Annotated Types

When we annotate a type, e.g., @serializable @cloneable class C(val x:String), the actual type includes the annotations.

Compound Types

A declaration of the form T_1 extends T_2 with T_3 { R }, where R is the *refinement* (body), declares a compound type. Any declarations in the refinement are part of the compound type definition. The notion of compound types accounts for the fact that not all types are named, since we can have anonymous types, such as this example scala session:

```
scala> val x = new T1 with T2 {
         type z = String
         val v: z = "Z"
}
x: java.lang.Object with T1 with T2{type z = String; def zv: this.z} = \
     $anon$1@9d9347d
```

Note that path-dependent type this.z in the output.

A particularly interesting case is a declaration of the form val x = new { R }, i.e., without any type IDs. This is equivalent to val x = new AnyRef { R }.

Infix Types

Some parameterized types take two type arguments, e.g., scala.Either[+A,+B]. Scala allows you to declare instances of these types using an infix notation, e.g., a Either b. Consider the following script that uses Either:

```
// code-examples/TypeSystem/valuetypes/infix-types-script.scala

def attempt(operation: => Boolean): Throwable Either Boolean = try {
  Right(operation)
} catch {
  case t: Throwable => Left(t)
}

println(attempt { throw new RuntimeException("Boo!") })
println(attempt { true })
println(attempt { false })
```

The attempt method will evaluate the *call-by-name* parameter operation and return its Boolean result, wrapped in a Right, *or* any Throwable that is caught, wrapped in a Left. The script produces this output:

```
Left(java.lang.RuntimeException: Boo!)
Right(true)
Right(false)
```

Notice the declared return value, Throwable Either Boolean. It is identical to Either[Throwable, Boolean]. Recall from "The Scala Type Hierarchy" on page 155 that when using this exception-handling idiom with Either, it is conventional to use Left for the exception and Right for the normal return value.

Function Types

The functions we have been writing are also typed. $(T_1, T_2, \ldots T_N)$ => R is the type for all functions that take N arguments and return a value of type R.

When there is only one argument, you can drop the parentheses: T => R. A function that takes a *call-by-name* parameter (as discussed in Chapter 8) has the type (=>T) => R. We used a call-by-name argument in our attempt example in the previous section.

Recall that everything in Scala is an object, even functions. The Scala library defines traits for each FunctionN, for N from 0 to 22, inclusive. Here, for example, is the version 2.7.5 source for scala.Function3, omitting most comments and a few other details that don't concern us now:

```
// From Scala version 2.7.5: scala.Function3 (excerpt).
package scala

trait Function3[-T1, -T2, -T3, +R] extends AnyRef {
  def apply(v1:T1, v2:T2, v3:T3): R
  override def toString() = "<function>"

  /** f(x1,x2,x3)  == (f.curry)(x1)(x2)(x3)
   */
  def curry: T1 => T2 => T3 => R = {
    (x1: T1) => (x2: T2) => (x3: T3) => apply(x1,x2,x3)
  }
}
```

As we discussed in "Variance Under Inheritance" on page 251, the FunctionN traits are *contravariant* in the type parameters for the arguments and *covariant* in the return type parameter.

Recall that when you reference any object followed by an argument list, Scala calls the apply method on the object. In this way, any object with an apply method can also be considered a function, providing a nice symmetry with the object-oriented nature of Scala.

When you define a function value, the compiler instantiates the appropriate FunctionN object and uses your definition of the function as the body of apply:

```
// code-examples/TypeSystem/valuetypes/function-types-script.scala

val capitalizer = (s: String) => s.toUpperCase

val capitalizer2 = new Function1[String,String] {
  def apply(s: String) = s.toUpperCase
}

println( List("Programming", "Scala") map capitalizer)
println( List("Programming", "Scala") map capitalizer2)
```

The capitalizer and capitalizer2 function values are effectively the same, where the latter mimics the compiler's output.

We discussed the **curry** method previously in "Currying" on page 184. It returns a new function with N argument lists, each of which has a single argument taken from the original argument list of N arguments. Note that the same **apply** method is invoked:

```
// code-examples/TypeSystem/valuetypes/curried-function-script.scala

val f  = (x: Double, y: Double, z: Double) => x * y / z
val fc = f.curry

val answer1 = f(2., 5., 4.)
val answer2 = fc(2.)(5.)(4.)
println( answer1 + " == " + answer2 + "? " + (answer1 == answer2))

val fc1 = fc(2.)
val fc2 = fc1(5.)
val answer3 = fc2(4.)
println( answer3 + " == " + answer2 + "? " + (answer3 == answer2))
```

This script produces the following output:

```
2.5 == 2.5? true
2.5 == 2.5? true
```

In the first part of the script, we define a **Function3** value **f** that does **Double** arithmetic. We create a new function value **fc** by currying **f**. Then we call both functions with the same arguments and print out the results. As expected, they both produce the same output. (There are no concerns about rounding errors in the comparison here; recall that both functions call the same **apply** method, so they must return the same value.)

In the second part of the script, we exploit the feature of curried functions that we can *partially apply* arguments, creating new functions, until we apply all the arguments. The example also helps us make sense of the declaration of **curry** in **Function3**.

Functions are right-associative, so a type **T1 => T2 => T3 => R** is equivalent to **T1 => (T2 => (T3 => R))**. We see this in the script. In the statement **val fc1 = fc(2.)**, we call **fc** with just the first argument list (corresponding to **T1** equals **Double**). It returns a *new* function of type **T2 => (T3 => R)** or **Double => (Double => Double)**, in our case.

Next, in **val fc2 = fc1(5.)**, we supply the second (**T2**) argument, returning a new function of type **T3 => R**, that is, **Double => Double**. Finally, in **val answer3 = fc2(4.)** we supply the last argument to compute the value of type **R**, that is **Double**.

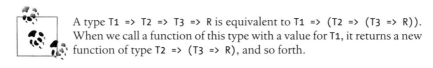

A type **T1 => T2 => T3 => R** is equivalent to **T1 => (T2 => (T3 => R))**. When we call a function of this type with a value for **T1**, it returns a new function of type **T2 => (T3 => R)**, and so forth.

Finally, since functions are instances of traits, you can use the traits as parents of other types. In the Scala library, **Seq[+A]** is a subclass of **PartialFunction[Int,A]**, which is a subclass of **(Int) => A**, i.e., **Function1[Int,A]**.

Type Projections

Type projections are a way to refer to a type declaration nested in another type:

```
// code-examples/TypeSystem/valuetypes/type-projection-script.scala

trait T {
  type t <: AnyRef
}
class C1 extends T {
  type t = String
}
class C2 extends C1

val ic1: C1#t = "C1"
val ic2: C2#t = "C2"
println(ic1)
println(ic2)
```

Both C1#t and C2#t are String. You can also reference the abstract type T#t, but you can't use it in a declaration because it is abstract.

Singleton Types

If you have a value v of a subtype of AnyRef, including null, you can get its *singleton type* using the expression v.type. These expressions can be used as types in declarations. This feature is useful on rare occasions to work around the fact that types are path dependent, which we discussed in "Path-Dependent Types" on page 272. In these cases an object may have a path-dependent type that appears to be incompatible with another path-dependent type, when in fact they are compatible. Using the v.type expression retrieves the singleton type, a "unique" type that eliminates the path dependency. Two values v1 and v2 may have different path-dependent types, but they could have the same singleton type.

This example uses the singleton type for one value in a declaration of another:

```
class C {
  val x = "Cx"
}
val c = new C
val x: c.x.type = c.x
```

Self-Type Annotations

You can use this in a method to refer to the enclosing type, which is useful for referencing a member of the type. Using this is not usually necessary for this purpose, but it's useful occasionally for disambiguating a reference when several values are in scope with the same name. By default, the type of this is the same as the enclosing type, but this is not really essential.

Self-type annotations let you specify additional type expectations for this, and they can be used to create aliases for this. Let's consider the latter case first:

```scala
// code-examples/TypeSystem/selftype/this-alias-script.scala

class C1 { self =>
  def talk(message: String) = println("C1.talk: " + message)
  class C2 {
    class C3 {
      def talk(message: String) = self.talk("C3.talk: " + message)
    }
    val c3 = new C3
  }
  val c2 = new C2
}
val c1 = new C1
c1.talk("Hello")
c1.c2.c3.talk("World")
```

It prints the following:

```
C1.talk: Hello
C1.talk: C3.talk: World
```

We give the outer scope (C1) this the alias self, so we can easily refer to it in C3. We could use self within any method inside the body of C1 or its nested types. Note that the name self is arbitrary, but it is somewhat conventional. In fact, you could say this =>, but it would be completely redundant.

If the self-type annotation has types in the annotation, we get some very different benefits:

```scala
// code-examples/TypeSystem/selftype/selftype-script.scala

trait Persistence {
  def startPersistence: Unit
}

trait Midtier {
  def startMidtier: Unit
}

trait UI {
  def startUI: Unit
}

trait Database extends Persistence {
  def startPersistence = println("Starting Database")
}

trait ComputeCluster extends Midtier {
  def startMidtier = println("Starting ComputeCluster")
}

trait WebUI extends UI {
  def startUI = println("Starting WebUI")
```

```
  }

  trait App {
    self: Persistence with Midtier with UI =>

    def run = {
      startPersistence
      startMidtier
      startUI
    }
  }

  object MyApp extends App with Database with ComputeCluster with WebUI

  MyApp.run
```

This script shows a schematic layout for an **App** (application) infrastructure supporting several tiers/components, persistent storage, midtier, and UI. We'll explore this approach to component design in more detail in Chapter 13.

For now, we just care about the role of self types. Each abstract trait declares a "start" method that does the work of initializing the tier. (We're ignoring issues like success versus failure of startup, etc.) Each abstract tier is implemented by a corresponding concrete trait (not a class, so we can use them as mixins). We have traits for database persistence, some sort of computation cluster to do the heavy lifting for the business logic, and a web-based UI.

The **App** trait wires the tiers together. For example, it does the work of starting the tiers in the run method.

Note the self-type annotation, `self: Persistence with Midtier with UI =>`. It has two practical effects:

1. The body of the trait can assume it is an instance of **Persistence**, **Midtier**, and **UI**, so it can call methods defined in those types, whether or not they are actually defined at this point. We're doing just that in **run**.

2. The concrete type that mixes in this trait must also mix in these three other traits or descendants of them.

In other words, the self type in **App** specifies dependencies on other components. These dependencies are satisfied in **MyApp**, which mixes in the concrete traits for the three tiers.

We could have declared **App** using inheritance instead:

```
  trait App with Persistence with Midtier with UI {

    def run = { ... }
  }
```

This is effectively the same. As we said, the self-type annotation lets the **App** assume it is of type **Persistence**, etc. That's exactly what happens when you mix in a trait, too.

Why, then, are self types useful if they appear to be equivalent to inheritance? There are some theoretical reasons and a few special cases where self-type annotations offer unique benefits. In practice, you could use inheritance for almost all cases. By convention, people use inheritance when they want to imply that a type *behaves as* (inherits from) another type, and they use self-type annotations when they want to express a dependency between a type and other types (see [McIver2009]).

In our case, we don't really think of an App as *being* a UI, database, etc. We think of an App as being composed of those things. Note that in most object-oriented languages, you would express this compositional dependency with member fields, especially if your language doesn't support mixin composition, like Java. For example, you might write App in Java this way:

```
// code-examples/TypeSystem/selftype/JavaApp.java

package selftype;

public abstract class JavaApp {
  public interface Persistence {
    public void startPersistence();
  }

  public interface Midtier {
    public void startMidtier();
  }

  public interface UI {
    public void startUI();
  }

  private Persistence persistence;
  private Midtier midtier;
  private UI ui;

  public JavaApp(Persistence persistence, Midtier midtier, UI ui) {
    this.persistence = persistence;
    this.midtier = midtier;
    this.ui = ui;
  }

  public void run() {
    persistence.startPersistence();
    midtier.startMidtier();
    ui.startUI();
  }
}
```

(We nested the component interfaces inside JavaApp to avoid creating separate files for each one!) You can certainly write applications this way in Scala. However, the self-type approach turns programmatic dependency resolution, i.e., passing dependencies to constructors or setter methods at runtime, into declarative dependency resolution at compile time, which catches errors earlier. Declarative programming, which is a hallmark of functional programming, is generally more robust, succinct, and clear, compared to imperative programming.

We will return to self-type annotations as a component composition model in Chapter 13. See "Self-Type Annotations and Abstract Type Members" on page 317 and "Dependency Injection in Scala: The Cake Pattern" on page 334.

Structural Types

You can think of *structural types* as a type-safe approach to *duck typing*, the popular name for the way method resolution works in dynamically typed languages. In Ruby, for example, when you write starFighter.shootWeapons, the runtime looks for a shootWeapons method on the object referenced by starFighter. That method, if found, might have been defined in the class used to instantiate starFighter or one of its parents or "included" modules. The method might also have been added to the object using the metaprogramming facility of Ruby. Finally, the object might override the catch-all method_missing method and do something reasonable when the object receives the shootWeapons "message."

Scala doesn't support this kind of method resolution, Instead, Scala allows you to specify that an object must adhere to a certain *structure*: that it contains certain types, fields, or methods, without concern for the actual type of the object. We first encountered structural types near the beginning of Chapter 4. Here is the example we saw then, a variation of the Observer Pattern:

```
// code-examples/Traits/observer/observer.scala

package observer

trait Subject {
  type Observer = { def receiveUpdate(subject: Any) }

  private var observers = List[Observer]()
  def addObserver(observer:Observer) = observers ::= observer
  def notifyObservers = observers foreach (_.receiveUpdate(this))
}
```

The declaration type Observer = { def receiveUpdate(subject: Any) } says that any valid observer must have the receiveUpdate method. It doesn't matter what the actual type is for a particular observer.

Structural types have the virtue of minimizing the interface between two things. In this case, the coupling consists of only a single method signature, rather than a type, such as a shared trait. A drawback of a structural type is that we still couple to a particular *name*. If a name is arbitrary, we don't really care about its name so much as its intent. In our example of a single method, we can avoid coupling to the name using a function object instead. In fact, we did this in "Overriding Abstract Types" on page 120.

On the other hand, if the name is a universal convention in some sense, then coupling to it has more merit. For example, foreach is very common name in the Scala library with a particular meaning, so defining a structural type based on foreach might be better for conveying intent to the user, rather than using an anonymous function of some kind.

Existential Types

Existential types are a way of abstracting over types. They let you "acknowledge" that there is a type involved without specifying exactly what it is, usually because you don't know what it is and you don't need that knowledge in the current context.

Existential types are particularly useful for interfacing to Java's type system for three cases:

- The type parameters of generics are "erased" at the byte code level (called *type erasure*). For example, when a List[Int] is created, the Int type is not available in the byte code.
- You might encounter "raw" types, such as pre-Java 5 libraries where collections had no type parameters. (All type parameters are effectively Object.)
- When Java uses wildcards in generics to express variance behavior when the generics are *used*, the actual type is unknown. (We discussed this earlier in "Variance Under Inheritance" on page 251.)

Consider the case of pattern matching on List[A] objects. You might like to write code like the following:

```
// code-examples/TypeSystem/existentials/type-erasure-wont-work.scala
// WARNINGS: Does not work as you might expect.

object ProcessList {
  def apply[B](list: List[B]) = list match {
    case lInt:    List[Int]    => // do something
    case lDouble: List[Double] => // do something
    case lString: List[String] => // do something
    case _                     => // default behavior
  }
}
```

If you compile this with the -unchecked flag on the JVM, you'll get warnings that the type parameters like Int are unchecked, because of type erasure. Hence, we can't distinguish between any of the list types shown.

The Manifests that we discussed previously won't work either, because they can't recover the erased type of B.

We've already learned that the best we can do in pattern matching is to focus on the fact that we have a list and not try to determine the "lost" type parameter for the list instance. For type safety, we have to specify that a list has a parameter, but since we don't know what it is, we use the wildcard _ character for the type parameter, e.g.:

```
case 1: List[_] => // do something "generic" with the list
```

When used in a type context like this, the `List[_]` is actually shorthand for the *existential type*, `List[T] forSome { type T }`. This is the most general case. We're saying the type parameter for the list could be any type. Table 12-2 lists some other examples that demonstrate the use of type bounds.

Table 12-2. Existential type examples

Shorthand	Full	Description
`List[_]`	`List[T] forSome { type T }`	T can be any subtype of Any.
`List[_ <: scala.actors.AbstractActor]`	`List[T] forSome { type T <: scala.actors.AbstractActor }`	T can be any subtype of AbstractActor.
`List[_ >: MyFancyActor <: scala.actors.AbstractActor]`	`List[T] forSome { type T >: MyFancyActor <: scala.actors.AbstractActor }`	T can be any subtype of AbstractActor up to and including the subtype MyFancyActor.

If you think about how Scala syntax for generics is mapped to Java syntax, you might have noticed that an expression like `java.util.List[_ <: scala.actors.AbstractActor]` is structurally similar to the Java variance expression `java.util.List<? extends scala.actors.AbstractActor>`. In fact, they are the same declarations. Although we said that variance behavior in Scala is defined at the declaration site, you can use existential type expressions in Scala to define call-site variance behavior. It is not recommended, for the reasons discussed previously, but you have that option.

You won't see the `forSome` existential type syntax very often in Scala code, because existential types exist primarily to support Java generics while preserving correctness in Scala's type system. Type inference hides the details from us in most contexts. When working with Scala types, the other type constructs we have discussed in this chapter are preferred to existential types.

Infinite Data Structures and Laziness

We described lazy values in Chapter 8. In functional languages that are lazy by default, like Haskell, laziness makes it easy to support *infinite* data structures.

For example, consider the following Scala method `fib` that calculates the Fibonacci number for n in the infinite Fibonacci sequence:

```
def fib(n: Int): Int = n match {
  case 0 | 1 => n
  case _ => fib(n-1) + fib(n-2)
}
```

If Scala were purely lazy, we could imagine a definition of the Fibonacci sequence like the following and it wouldn't create an infinite loop:

```
fibonacci_sequence = for (i <- 0 to infinity) yield fib(i)
```

Scala isn't lazy by default (and there is no **infinity** value or keyword...), but the library contains a **Stream** class that supports lazy evaluation and hence it can support infinite data structures. We'll show an implementation of the Fibonacci sequence in a moment. First, here is a simpler example that uses streams to represent all positive integers, all positive odd integers, and all positive even integers:

```
// code-examples/TypeSystem/lazy/lazy-ints-script.scala

def from(n: Int): Stream[Int] = Stream.cons(n, from(n+1))

lazy val ints = from(0)
lazy val odds = ints.filter(_ % 2 == 1)
lazy val evens = ints.filter(_ % 2 == 0)

odds.take(10).print
evens.take(10).print
```

It produces this output:

```
1, 3, 5, 7, 9, 11, 13, 15, 17, 19, Stream.empty
0, 2, 4, 6, 8, 10, 12, 14, 16, 18, Stream.empty
```

The **from** method is recursive and never terminates! We use it to define the **ints** by calling **from(0)**. **Streams.cons** is an object with an **apply** method that is analogous to the **::** ("cons") method on **List**. It returns a new stream with the first argument as the head and the second argument, another stream, as the tail. The **odds** and **evens** infinite streams are computed by filtering **ints**.

Once we have defined the streams, the **take** method returns a new stream of the fixed size specified, 10 in this case. When we print this stream with the **print** method, it prints the 10 elements followed by **Stream.empty** when it hits the end of the stream.

Returning to the Fibonacci sequence, there is a famous definition using infinite, lazy sequences that exploits the **zip** operation (see, e.g., [Abelson1996]). Our discussion for Scala is adapted from [Ortiz2007]:

```
// code-examples/TypeSystem/lazy/lazy-fibonacci-script.scala

lazy val fib: Stream[Int] =
  Stream.cons(0, Stream.cons(1, fib.zip(fib.tail).map(p => p._1 + p._2)))

fib.take(10).print
```

It produces this output:

```
0, 1, 1, 2, 3, 5, 8, 13, 21, 34, Stream.empty
```

How does this work? Like our iterative definition at the start of this section, we explicitly specify the first two values, 0 and 1. The rest of the numbers are computed using **zip**, exploiting the fact that **fib(n) = fib(n-1) + fib(n-2)**, for n > 1.

The call `fib.zip(fib.tail)` creates a new stream of tuples with the elements of `fib` in the first position of the tuple, and the elements of `fib.tail` in the second position of the tuple. To get back to a single integer for each position in the stream, we map the stream of tuples to a stream of `Ints` by adding the tuple elements. Here are the tuples calculated:

(0,1), (1,1), (1,2), (2,3), (3,5), (5,8), (8,13), (13, 21), (21, 34), ...

Note that each second element is the next number in the Fibonacci sequence after the first element in the tuple. Adding them we get the following:

1, 2, 3, 5, 8, 13, 21, 34, 55, ...

Since we concatenate this stream after 0 and 1, we get the Fibonacci sequence:

0, 1, 1, 2, 3, 5, 8, 13, 21, 34, 55, ...

Another lazy Scala type, albeit a finite one, is `Range`. Typically, you write literal ranges such as `1 to 1000`. `Range` is lazy, so very large ranges don't consume too many resources. However, this feature can lead to subtle problems unless you are careful, as documented by [Smith2009b] and commenters. Using the example described there, consider this function for returning a `Seq` of three random integers:

```
// code-examples/TypeSystem/lazy/lazy-range-danger-script.scala

def mkRandomInts() = {
  val randInts = for {
    i <- 1 to 3
    val rand = i + (new scala.util.Random).nextInt
  } yield rand
  randInts
}
val ints1 = mkRandomInts

println("Calling first on ints1 Seq:")
for (i <- 1 to 3) {
  println( ints1.first)
}

val ints2 = ints1.toList
println("Calling first on List created from ints1 Seq:")
for (i <- 1 to 3) {
  println( ints2.first)
}
```

Here is the output from one run. The actual values will vary from run to run:

```
Calling first on ints1 Seq:
-1532554511
-1532939260
-1532939260
Calling first on List created from ints1 Seq:
-1537171498
-1537171498
-1537171498
```

Calling `first` on the sequence does not always return the same value! The reason is that the range at the beginning of the `for` comprehension effectively forces the whole sequence to be lazy. Hence, it is reevaluated with *each* call to `first`, and the first value in the sequence actually changes, since `Random` returns a different number each time (at least, it will if there is a sufficient time delta between calls).

However, calling `toList` on the sequence forces it to evaluate the whole range and create a *strict* list.

 Avoid using ranges in `for (...)` `yield x` constructs, while `for (...)` `{...}` alternatives are fine.

Finally, Scala version 2.8 will include a `force` method on all collections that will force them to be strict.

Recap and What's Next

It's important to remember that you don't have to master the intricacies of Scala's rich type system to use Scala effectively. As you use Scala more and more, mastering the type system will help you create powerful, sophisticated libraries that accelerate your productivity.

The [ScalaSpec2009] describes the type system in formal detail. Like any specification, it can be difficult reading. The effort is worthwhile if you want a deep understanding of the type system. There are also a multitude of papers on Scala's type system. You can find links to many of them on the official *http://scala-lang.org* website.

The next two chapters cover the pragmatics of application design and Scala's development tools and libraries.

CHAPTER 13

Application Design

In this chapter, we take a pragmatic look at developing applications in Scala. We discuss a few language and API features that we haven't covered before, examine common design patterns and idioms, and revisit *traits* with an eye toward structuring our code effectively.

Annotations

Like Java and .NET, Scala supports *annotations* for adding *metadata* to declarations. Annotations are used by a variety of tools in typical enterprise and Internet applications. For example, there are annotations that provide directives to the compiler, and some Object-Relational Mapping (ORM) frameworks use annotations on types and type members to indicate persistence mapping information. While some uses for annotations in the Java and .NET worlds can be accomplished through other means in Scala, annotations can be essential for interoperating with Java and .NET libraries that rely heavily on them. Fortunately, Java and .NET annotations can be used in Scala code.

The interpretation of Scala annotations depends on the runtime environment. In this section, we will focus on the JDK environment.

In Java, annotations are declared using special conventions, e.g., declaring annotations with the `@interface` keyword instead of the `class` or `interface` keyword. Here is the declaration of an annotation taken from a toolkit called Contract4J (see [Contract4J]) that uses annotations to support *Design by Contract* programming in Java (see also "Better Design with Design By Contract" on page 340). Some of the comments have been removed for clarity:

```
// code-examples/AppDesign/annotations/Pre.java

package org.contract4j5.contract;
import java.lang.annotation.Documented;
import java.lang.annotation.ElementType;
import java.lang.annotation.Retention;
import java.lang.annotation.RetentionPolicy;
import java.lang.annotation.Target;
```

```
@Documented
@Retention(RetentionPolicy.RUNTIME)
@Target({ElementType.PARAMETER, ElementType.METHOD, ElementType.CONSTRUCTOR})
public @interface Pre {
  /**
   * The "value" is the test expression, which must evaluate to true or false.
   * It must be a valid expression in the scripting language you are using.
   */
  String value() default "";

  /**
   * An optional message to print with the standard message when the contract
   * fails.
   */
  String message() default "";
}
```

The @Pre annotation is used to specify "preconditions" that must be satisfied when *entering* a method or constructor, or *before* using a parameter passed to a method or constructor. The conditions are specified as a string that is actually a snippet of source code that evaluates to **true** or **false**. The source *languages* supported for these snippets are scripting languages like Groovy and JRuby. The name of the variable for this string, **value**, is a conventional name for the most important field in the annotation.

The other field is an optional **message** to use when reporting failures.

The declaration has other annotations applied to it—for example, the @Retention annotation with the value RetentionPolicy.RUNTIME means that when @Pre is used, its information will be retained in the class file for runtime use.

Here is a Scala example that uses @Pre and shows several ways to specify the **value** and **message** parameters:

```
// code-examples/AppDesign/annotations/pre-example.scala

import org.contract4j5.contract._

class Person(
  @Pre( "name != null && name.length() > 0" )
  val name: String,
  @Pre{ val value = "age > 0", val message = "You're too young!" }
  val age: Int,
  @Pre( "ssn != null" )
  val ssn: SSN)

class SSN(
  @Pre( "valid(ssn)" ) { val message = "Format must be NNN-NN-NNNN." }
  val ssn: String) {

  private def valid(value: String) =
    value.matches("""^\s*\d{3}-\d{2}-\d{4}\s*$""")
}
```

In the `Person` class, the `@Pre` annotation on `name` has a simple string argument: the "precondition" that users must satisfy when passing in a name. This value can't be `null`, and it can't be of zero length. As in Java, if a single argument is given to the annotation, it is assigned to the `value` field.

A similar `@Pre` annotation is used for the third argument, the `ssn` (Social Security number). In both cases, the `message` defaults to the empty string specified in the definition of `Pre`.

The `@Pre` annotation for the age shows one way to specify values for more than one field. Instead of parentheses, curly braces are used. The syntax for each field looks like a `val` declaration, without any type information, since the types can always be inferred! This syntax allows you to use the shorthand syntax for the `value` and still specify values for other fields.

 If `Person` were a Java class, this annotation expression would look identical, except there would be no `val` keywords and parentheses would be used.

The `@Pre` annotation on the constructor parameter for the `SSN` class shows the alternative syntax for specifying values for more than one field. The `value` field is specified as before with a one-element parameter list. The `message` is initialized in a follow-on block in curly braces.

Testing this code would require the Contract4J library, build setup, etc. We won't cover those steps here. Refer to [Contract4J] for more information.

Scala annotations don't use a special declaration syntax. They are declared as normal classes. This approach eliminates a "special case" in the language, but it also means that some of the features provided by Java annotations aren't supported, as we will see. Here is an example annotation from the Scala library, `SerialVersionUID` (again with the comments removed for clarity):

```scala
package scala

class SerialVersionUID(uid: Long) extends StaticAnnotation
```

The `@SerialVersionUID` annotation is applied to a class to define a globally unique ID as a `Long`. When the annotation is used, the ID is specified as a constructor argument. This annotation serves the same purpose as a `static` field named `serialVersionUID` in a Java class. This is one example of a Scala annotation that maps to a "non-annotation" construct in Java.

The parent of `SerialVersionUID` is the trait `scala.StaticAnnotation`, which is used as the parent for all annotations that should be visible to the type checker, even across compilation units. The parent class of `scala.StaticAnnotation` is `scala.Annotation`, which is the parent of all Scala annotations.

Did you notice that there is no `val` on `uid`? Why isn't `uid` a field? The reason is that the annotation's data is not intended for use by the program. Recall that it is metadata designed for external tools to use, such as `scalac`. This also means that Scala annotations have no way to define default values in version 2.7.X, as implicit arguments don't work. However, the new default arguments feature in version 2.8.0 may work. (It is not yet implemented at the time of this writing.)

Like Java (and .NET) annotations, a Scala annotation clause applies to the definition it precedes. You can have as many annotation clauses as you want, and the order in which they appear is not significant.

Like Java annotations, Scala annotation clauses are written using the syntax `@MyAnnotation` if the annotation constructor takes no parameters, or `@MyAnnotation(arg1, .., argN)` if the constructor takes parameters. The annotation must be a subclass of `scala.Annotation`.

All the constructor parameters must be constant expressions, including strings, class literals, Java enumerations, numerical expressions and one-dimensional arrays of the same. However, the compiler also allows annotation clauses with other arguments, such as boolean values and maps, as shown in this example:

```
// code-examples/AppDesign/annotations/anno-example.scala

import scala.StaticAnnotation

class Persist(tableName: String, params: Map[String,Any])
  extends StaticAnnotation

// Doesn't compile:
//@Persist("ACCOUNTS", Map("dbms" -> "MySql", "writeAutomatically" -> true))
@Persist("ACCOUNTS", Map(("dbms", "MySql"), ("writeAutomatically", true)))
class Account(val balance: Double)
```

Curiously, if you attempt to use the standard `Map` literal syntax that is shown in the comments, you get a compilation error that the `->` method doesn't exist for `String`. The implicit conversion to `ArrowAssoc` that we discussed in "The Predef Object" on page 145 isn't invoked. Instead, you have to use a list of `Tuples`, which `Map.apply` actually expects.

Another child of `scala.Annotation` that is intended to be a parent of other annotations is the trait `scala.ClassfileAnnotation`. It is supposed to be used for annotations that should have runtime retention, i.e., the annotations should be visible in the class file so they are available at runtime. However, actually using it with the JDK version of Scala results in compiler errors like the following:

```
...: warning: implementation restriction: subclassing Classfile does not
make your annotation visible at runtime.  If that is what
you want, you must write the annotation class in Java.
...
```

Hence, if you want runtime visibility, you have to implement the annotation in Java. This works fine, since you can use any Java annotation in Scala code. The Scala library currently defines no annotations derived from `ClassfileAnnotation`, perhaps for obvious reasons.

Avoid `ClassfileAnnotation`. Implement annotations that require runtime retention in Java instead.

For Scala version 2.7.X, another important limitation to keep in mind is that annotations can't be nested. This causes problems when using JPA annotations in Scala code, for example, as discussed in [JPAScala]. However, Scala version 2.8 removes this limitation.

Annotations can only be nested in Scala version 2.8.

Tables 13-1 and 13-2 describe all the annotations defined in the Scala library (adapted and expanded from *http://www.scala-lang.org/node/106*). We start with the direct children of `Annotation`, followed by the children of `StaticAnnotation`.

Table 13-1. Scala annotations derived from Annotation

Name	Java equivalent	Description
ClassfileAnnotation	Annotate with @Retention (RetentionPolicy.RUNTIME)	The parent trait for annotations that should be retained in the class file for runtime access, but it doesn't actually work on the JDK!
BeanDescription	BeanDescriptor (class)	An annotation for *JavaBean* types or members that associates a short description (provided as the annotation argument) that will be included when generating bean information.
BeanDisplayName	BeanDescriptor (class)	An annotation for *JavaBean* types or members that associates a name (provided as the annotation argument) that will be included when generating bean information.
BeanInfo	BeanInfo (class)	A marker that indicates that a BeanInfo class should be generated for the marked Scala class. A val becomes a read-only property. A var becomes a read-write property. A def becomes a method.
BeanInfoSkip	*N.A.*	A marker that indicates that bean information should not be generated for the annotated member.
StaticAnnotation	Static fields, @Target(ElementType.TYPE)	The parent trait of annotations that should be visible across compilation units and define "static" metadata.

Name	Java equivalent	Description
TypeConstraint	*N.A.*	An annotation trait that can be applied to other annotations that define constraints on a type, relying only on information defined within the type itself, as opposed to external context information where the type is defined or used. The compiler can exploit this restriction to rewrite the constraint. There are currently no library annotations that use this trait.
unchecked	*N.A.*	A marker annotation for the selector in a match statement (e.g., the x in x match {...}) that suppresses a compiler warning if the case clauses are not "exhaustive." You can still have a runtime MatchError occur if a value of x fails to match any of the case clauses. See the upcoming example.
unsealed	*N.A.*	Deprecated, use @unchecked instead.

Table 13-2. Scala annotations derived from StaticAnnotation

Name	Java equivalent	Description
BeanProperty	*JavaBean* convention	A marker for a field (including a constructor argument with the val or var keyword) that tells the compiler to generate a JavaBean-style "getter" and "setter" method. The setter is only generated for var declarations. See the discussion in "JavaBean Properties" on page 374.
cloneable	java.lang.Cloneable (interface)	A class marker indicating that a class can be cloned.
cps	*N.A.*	(version 2.8) Generate byte code using continuation passing style.
deprecated	java.lang.Deprecated	A marker for any definition indicating that the defined "item" is obsolete. The compiler will issue a warning when the item is used.
inline	*N.A.*	A method marker telling the compiler that it should try "especially hard" to inline the method.
native	native (keyword)	A method marker indicating the method is implemented as "native" code. The method body will not be generated by the compiler, but usage of the method will be type checked.
noinline	*N.A.*	A method marker that prevents the compiler from inlining the method, even when it appears to be safe to do so.
remote	java.rmi.Remote (interface)	A class marker indicating that the class can be invoked from a remote JVM.
serializable	java.io.Serializable (interface)	A class marker indicating that the class can be serialized.
SerialVersionUID	serialVersionUID *static* field in a class	Defines a globally unique ID for serialization purposes. The annotation's constructor takes a Long argument for the UID.

Name	Java equivalent	Description
switch	N.A.	(version 2.8) An annotation to be applied to a match expression, e.g., `(x: @switch) match {...}`. When present, the compiler will verify that the match has been compiled to a table-based or lookup-based `switch` statement. If not, it will issue an error if it instead compiles into a series of conditional expressions, which are less efficient.
specialized	N.A.	(version 2.8) An annotation applied to type parameters in parameterized types and methods. It tells the compiler to generate optimized versions of the type or method for the AnyVal types corresponding to platform primitive types. Optionally, you can limit the AnyVal types for which specialized implementations will be generated. See the upcoming discussion.
tailRec	N.A.	(version 2.8) A method annotation that tells the compiler to verify that the method will be compiled with *tail-call optimization*. If it is present, the compiler will issue an error if the method cannot be optimized into a loop. This happens, for example, when the method is not `private` or `final`, when it could be overridden, and when recursive invocations are not true tail calls.
throws	throws (keyword)	Indicates which exceptions are thrown by the annotated method. See the upcoming discussion.
transient	transient (keyword)	Marks a method as "transient."
uncheckedStable	N.A.	A marker for a value that is assumed to be stable even though its type is volatile (i.e., annotated with `@volatile`).
uncheckedVariance	N.A.	A marker for a type argument that is volatile, when it is used in a parameterized type, to suppress variance checking.
volatile	volatile (keyword, for fields only)	A marker for an individual field or a whole type, which affects all fields, indicating that the field may be modified by a separate thread.

The annotations marked with "(version 2.8)" are only available in Scala version 2.8 or later. Consider `@tailrec`, as used in the following example:

```scala
import scala.annotation.tailrec

@tailrec
def fib(i: Int): Int = i match {
  case _ if i <= 1 => i
  case _ => fib(i-1) + fib(i-2)
}
println(fib(5))
```

Note that `fib`, which calculates Fibonacci numbers, is recursive, but it isn't tail-call recursive, because the call to itself is not the very last thing that happens in the second case clause. Rather, after calling itself twice, it does an addition. Hence, a tail-call optimization can't be performed on this method. When the compiler sees the `@tailrec` annotation, it throws an error if it can't apply the tail-call optimization. Attempting to run this script produces the following error:

```
... 4: error: could not optimize @tailrec annotated method
def fib(i: Int): Int = i match {
                       ^
one error found
```

We can also use the same method to demonstrate the new `@switch` annotation available in version 2.8:

```
import scala.annotation.switch

def fib(i: Int): Int = (i: @switch) match {
  case _ if i <= 1 => i
  case _ => fib(i-1) + fib(i-2)
}
println(fib(5))
```

This time we annotate the `i` in the `match` statement. This annotation causes the compiler to raise an error if it can't generate a switch construct in byte code from the cases in the match statement. Switches are generally more efficient than conditional logic. Running this script produces this output:

```
... 3: error: could not emit switch for @switch annotated match
def fib(i: Int): Int = (i: @switch) match {
                            ^
one error found
```

Conditional blocks have to be generated instead. The reason a switch can't be generated is because of the condition guard clause we put in the first case clause, `if i <= 1`.

Let's look at an example of `@unchecked` in use (adapted from the Scaladoc entry for `@unchecked`). Consider the following code fragment:

```
...
def process(x: Option[int]) = x match {
  case Some(value) => ...
}
...
```

If you compile it, you will get the following warning:

```
...: warning: does not cover case {object None}
  def f(x: Option[int]) = x match {
                          ^
one warning found
```

Normally, you would want to add a case for `None`. However, if you want to suppress the warning message in situations like this, change the method as follows:

```
...
def process(x: Option[int]) = (x: @unchecked) match {
  case Some(value) => ...
}
...
```

With the `@unchecked` annotation applied to x as shown, the warning will be suppressed. However, if x is ever `None`, then a `MatchError` will be thrown.

The `@specialized` annotation is another optimization-related annotation added in version 2.8. It is a pragmatic solution to a tradeoff between space efficiency and performance. In Java and Scala, the implementation of a parameterized type or method is generated at the point of the declaration (as we discussed in "Understanding Parameterized Types" on page 249). In contrast, in C++, a *template* is used to generate an implementation for the actual type parameters where the template is used. The C++ approach has the advantage of allowing optimized implementations to be generated for primitive types, while it has the disadvantage of resulting in code bloat from all the instantiations of templates.

In JVM-related languages, the "on-demand" generation of implementations isn't suitable, primarily because there is no "link" step as in compiled languages, where every required instantiation of a template can be determined. This creates a dilemma. By default, a Scala parameterized type or method will be translated to a single implementation assuming `Any` for the type parameters (in part due to type erasure at the byte code level). Java generics work the same way. However, if a particular use of the type or method uses one of the `AnyVal` types, say `Int`, then we get inefficient boxing and unboxing operations in the implementation.

The alternative would be to generate a separate implementation for every `AnyVal` corresponding to a primitive type, but this would lead to code bloat, especially since it would be rare that an application would use all those implementations. So, we are faced with a dilemma.

The `@specialized` annotation is a pragmatic compromise. It lets the user tell the compiler that runtime efficiency is more important than space efficiency, so the compiler will generate the separate implementations for each primitive corresponding to an `AnyVal`. Here is an example of how the annotation is used:

```
class SpecialCollection[@specialized +T](...) {
  ...
}
```

At the time of this writing, the implementation in the version 2.8 "nightly" build only supports generation of specialized implementations for `Int` and `Double`. For the final version 2.8 library, it is planned that the other `AnyVal` types will be supported. There are also plans to allow the user to specify the types for which optimized implementations are generated so that unused implementations for the other `AnyVals` are avoided. See the final 2.8 Scaladocs for details on the final feature set.

Another planned version 2.8 annotation is `@cps`, which stands for *continuation passing style*. It will be a directive interpreted by a compiler plugin that will trigger generation of continuation-based byte code for method invocation, rather than the default stack frame byte code. The annotation will have no effect unless the corresponding `scalac` plugin is used. Consult the release documentation for more information on this feature, when it becomes available.

To understand the @throws annotation, it's important to remember that Scala does not have checked exceptions, in contrast with Java. There is also no **throws** clause available for Scala method declarations. This is not a problem if a Scala method calls a Java method that is declared to throw a checked exception. The exception is treated as unchecked in Scala. However, suppose the Scala method in question doesn't catch the exception, but lets it pass through. What if this Scala method is called by other Java code?

Let's look at an example involving java.io.IOException, which is a checked exception. The following Scala class prints out the contents of a java.io.File:

```
// code-examples/AppDesign/annotations/file-printer.scala

import java.io._

class FilePrinter(val file: File) {

  @throws(classOf[IOException])
  def print() = {
    var reader: LineNumberReader = null
    try {
      reader = new LineNumberReader(new FileReader(file))
      loop(reader)
    } finally {
      if (reader != null)
        reader.close
    }
  }

  private def loop(reader: LineNumberReader): Unit = {
    val line = reader.readLine()
    if (line != null) {
      format("%3d: %s\n", reader.getLineNumber, line)
      loop(reader)
    }
  }
}
```

Note the @throws annotation applied to the **print** method. The argument to the annotation constructor is a single java.lang.Class[Any] object, in this case, classOf[IOException]. The Java IO API methods used by **print** and the private method **loop** might throw this exception.

By the way, notice that **loop** uses functional-style tail recursion, rather than a loop. No variables were mutated during the production of this output! (Well, we don't actually know what's happening inside the Java IO classes....)

Here is a Java class that uses `FilePrinter`. It provides the `main` routine:

```
// code-examples/AppDesign/annotations/FilePrinterMain.java

import java.io.*;

public class FilePrinterMain {
  public static void main(String[] args) {
    for (String fileName: args) {
      try {
        File file = new File(fileName);
        new FilePrinter(file).print();
      } catch (IOException ioe) {
        System.err.println("IOException for file " + fileName);
        System.err.println(ioe.getMessage());
      }
    }
  }
}
```

These classes compile without error. You can try them out with the following command (which assumes that `FilePrinterMain.java` is in the *annotations* directory, as in the example code distribution):

```
scala -cp build FilePrinterMain annotations/FilePrinterMain.java
```

You should get the following output:

```
 1: import java.io.*;
 2:
 3: public class FilePrinterMain {
 4:   public static void main(String[] args) {
 5:     for (String fileName: args) {
 6:       try {
 7:         File file = new File(fileName);
 8:         new FilePrinter(file).print();
 9:       } catch (IOException ioe) {
10:         System.err.println("IOException for file " + fileName);
11:         System.err.println(ioe.getMessage());
12:       }
13:     }
14:   }
15: }
```

Now, returning to the `FilePrinter` class, suppose you comment out the `@throws` line. This file will continue to compile, but when you compile `FilePrinterMain.java`, you will get the following error:

```
annotations/FilePrinterMain.java:9: exception java.io.IOException is never
thrown in body of corresponding try statement
      } catch (IOException ioe) {
        ^
1 error
```

Even though `java.io.IOException` may get thrown by `FilePrinter`, that information isn't in the byte code generated by `scalac`, so the analysis done by `javac` mistakenly concludes that `IOException` is never thrown.

So, the purpose of `@throws` is to insert the information on thrown checked exceptions into the byte code that `javac` will read.

 In a mixed Java-Scala environment, consider adding the `@throws` annotation for all your Scala methods that can throw Java checked exceptions. Eventually, some Java code will probably call one of those methods.

Enumerations Versus Pattern Matching

Enumerations are a way of defining a finite set of constant values. They are a lightweight alternative to case classes. You can reference the values directly, iterate through them, index into them with integer indices, etc.

Just as for annotations, Scala's form of enumerations are class-based, with a particular set of idioms, rather than relying on special keywords for defining them, as is used for enumerations in Java and .NET. However, you can also use enumerations defined in those languages.

Scala enumerations are defined by subclassing the abstract `scala.Enumeration` class. There are several ways to construct and use an enumeration. We'll demonstrate one idiom that most closely matches the Java and .NET forms you may already know.

Recall the HTTP methods scripts that we wrote in "Sealed Class Hierarchies" on page 151. We defined the set of HTTP 1.1 methods using a sealed case class hierarchy:

```
// code-examples/ObjectSystem/sealed/http-script.scala

sealed abstract class HttpMethod()
case class Connect(body: String) extends HttpMethod
case class Delete (body: String) extends HttpMethod
case class Get     (body: String) extends HttpMethod
case class Head    (body: String) extends HttpMethod
case class Options(body: String) extends HttpMethod
case class Post    (body: String) extends HttpMethod
case class Put     (body: String) extends HttpMethod
case class Trace   (body: String) extends HttpMethod

def handle (method: HttpMethod) = method match {
  case Connect (body) => println("connect: " + body)
  case Delete  (body) => println("delete: "  + body)
  case Get     (body) => println("get: "      + body)
  case Head    (body) => println("head: "     + body)
  case Options (body) => println("options: " + body)
  case Post    (body) => println("post: "     + body)
```

```
    case Put      (body) => println("put: "     + body)
    case Trace    (body) => println("trace: "   + body)
}

val methods = List(
  Connect("connect body..."),
  Delete ("delete body..."),
  Get    ("get body..."),
  Head   ("head body..."),
  Options("options body..."),
  Post   ("post body..."),
  Put    ("put body..."),
  Trace  ("trace body...")))

methods.foreach { method => handle(method) }
```

In that example, each method had a **body** attribute for the message body. We'll assume here that the body is handled through other means and we only care about identifying the kind of HTTP method. So, here is a Scala Enumeration class for the HTTP 1.1 methods:

```
// code-examples/AppDesign/enumerations/http-enum-script.scala

object HttpMethod extends Enumeration {
  type Method = Value
  val Connect, Delete, Get, Head, Options, Post, Put, Trace = Value
}

import HttpMethod._

def handle (method: HttpMethod.Method) = method match {
  case Connect => println("Connect: " + method.id)
  case Delete  => println("Delete: "  + method.id)
  case Get     => println("Get: "     + method.id)
  case Head    => println("Head: "    + method.id)
  case Options => println("Options: " + method.id)
  case Post    => println("Post: "    + method.id)
  case Put     => println("Put: "     + method.id)
  case Trace   => println("Trace: "   + method.id)
}

HttpMethod foreach { method => handle(method) }
println( HttpMethod )
```

This script produces the following output:

```
Connect: 0
Delete: 1
Get: 2
Head: 3
Options: 4
Post: 5
Put: 6
Trace: 7
{Main$$anon$1$HttpMethod(0), Main$$anon$1$HttpMethod(1),
Main$$anon$1$HttpMethod(2), Main$$anon$1$HttpMethod(3),
```

```
Main$$anon$1$HttpMethod(4), Main$$anon$1$HttpMethod(5),
Main$$anon$1$HttpMethod(6), Main$$anon$1$HttpMethod(7)}
```

(We wrapped the lines for the output between the {...}.) There are two uses of Value in the definition of HttpMethod. The first usage is actually a reference to an abstract class, Enumeration.Value, which encapsulates some useful operations for the "values" in the enumeration. We define a new type, Method, that functions as an alias for Value. We see it used in the type of the argument passed to the handle method, which demonstrates HttpMethod in use. HttpMethod.Method is a more meaningful name to the reader than the generic HttpMethod.Value. Note that one of the fields in Enumeration.Value is id, which we also use in handle.

The second use of Value is actually a call to a method. There is no namespace collision between these two names. The line val Connect, Delete, Get, Head, Options, Post, Put, Trace = Value defines the set of values for the enumeration. The Value method is called for each one. It creates a new Enumeration.Value for each one and adds it to the managed set of values.

In the code below the definition, we import the definitions in HttpMethod and we define a handle method that pattern matches on HttpMethod.Method objects. It simply prints a message for each value along with its id. Note that while the example has no "default" case clause (e.g. case _ ⇒ ...), none is required in this case. However, the compiler doesn't actually know that all the possible values are covered, in contrast to a sealed case class hierarchy. If you comment out one of the case statements in handle, you will get no warnings, but you will get a MatchError.

 When pattern matching on enumeration values, the compiler can't tell if the match is "exhaustive."

You might wonder why we hardcoded strings like "Connect" in the println statements in the case clauses. Can't we get the name from the HttpMethod.Method object itself? And why didn't the output of println(HttpMethod) include those names, instead of the ugly internal object names?

You are probably accustomed to using such names with Java or .NET enumerations. Unfortunately, we can't get those names from the values in the Scala enumeration, at least given the way that we declared HttpMethod. However, there are two ways we can change the implementation to get name strings. In the first approach, we pass the name to Value when creating the fields:

```
// code-examples/AppDesign/enumerations/http-enum2-script.scala

object HttpMethod extends Enumeration {
  type Method = Value
  val Connect = Value("Connect")
  val Delete  = Value("Delete")
  val Get     = Value("Get")
```

```scala
  val Head    = Value("Head")
  val Options = Value("Options")
  val Post    = Value("Post")
  val Put     = Value("Put")
  val Trace   = Value("Trace")
}

import HttpMethod._

def handle (method: HttpMethod.Method) = method match {
  case Connect => println(method + ": " + method.id)
  case Delete  => println(method + ": " + method.id)
  case Get     => println(method + ": " + method.id)
  case Head    => println(method + ": " + method.id)
  case Options => println(method + ": " + method.id)
  case Post    => println(method + ": " + method.id)
  case Put     => println(method + ": " + method.id)
  case Trace   => println(method + ": " + method.id)
}

HttpMethod foreach { method => handle(method) }
println( HttpMethod )
```

It is a bit redundant to have to use the same word twice in declarations like `val Connect = Value("Connect")`.

Running this script produces the following nicer output:

```
Connect: 0
Delete: 1
Get: 2
Head: 3
Options: 4
Post: 5
Put: 6
Trace: 7
{Connect, Delete, Get, Head, Options, Post, Put, Trace}
```

In the second approach, we pass the list of names to the `Enumeration` constructor:

```scala
// code-examples/AppDesign/enumerations/http-enum3-script.scala

object HttpMethod extends Enumeration(
    "Connect", "Delete", "Get", "Head", "Options", "Post", "Put", "Trace") {
  type Method = Value
  val Connect, Delete, Get, Head, Options, Post, Put, Trace = Value
}

import HttpMethod._

def handle (method: HttpMethod.Method) = method match {
  case Connect => println(method + ": " + method.id)
  case Delete  => println(method + ": " + method.id)
  case Get     => println(method + ": " + method.id)
  case Head    => println(method + ": " + method.id)
  case Options => println(method + ": " + method.id)
```

```
    case Post    => println(method + ": " + method.id)
    case Put     => println(method + ": " + method.id)
    case Trace   => println(method + ": " + method.id)
  }

  HttpMethod foreach { method => handle(method) }
  println( HttpMethod )
```

This script produces identical output. Note that we have a *redundant* list of name strings and names of the `vals`. *It is up to you to keep the items in the list and their order consistent with the declared values!* This version has fewer characters, but it is more error-prone. Internally, `Enumeration` pairs the strings with the corresponding `Value` instances as they are created.

The output when printing the whole `HttpMethod` object is better for either alternative implementation. When the values have names, their `toString` returns the name. In fact, our final two examples have become quite artificial because we now have identical statements for each case clause! Of course, in a real implementation, you would handle the different HTTP methods differently.

Thoughts On Annotations and Enumerations

For both annotations and enumerations, there are advantages and disadvantages to the Scala approach, where we use regular class-based mechanisms, rather than inventing custom keywords and syntax. The advantages include fewer special cases in the language. Classes and traits are used in more or less the same ways they are used for "normal" code. The disadvantages include the need to understand and use ad hoc conventions that are not always as convenient to use as the custom syntax mechanisms required in Java and .NET. Also, Scala's implementations are not as full-featured.

So, should the Scala community relent and implement ad hoc, but more full-featured mechanisms for annotations and enumerations? Maybe not. Scala is a more flexible language than most languages. Many of the features provided by Java and .NET annotations and enumerations can be implemented in Scala by other means.

Some use cases for the more advanced features of Java annotations can be implemented more elegantly with "normal" Scala code, as we will discuss in "Design Patterns" on page 325. For enumerations, sealed case classes and pattern matching provide a more flexible solution, in many cases.

Enumerations Versus Case Classes and Pattern Matching

Let's revisit the HTTP method script, which uses a sealed case class hierarchy versus the version we wrote previously that uses an `Enumeration`. Since the enumeration version doesn't handle the message body, let's write a modified version of the sealed case class version that is closer to the enumeration version, i.e., it also doesn't hold the message body and it has `name` and `id` methods:

```
// code-examples/AppDesign/enumerations/http-case-script.scala

sealed abstract class HttpMethod(val id: Int) {
  def name = getClass getSimpleName
  override def toString = name
}

case object Connect extends HttpMethod(0)
case object Delete  extends HttpMethod(1)
case object Get     extends HttpMethod(2)
case object Head    extends HttpMethod(3)
case object Options extends HttpMethod(4)
case object Post    extends HttpMethod(5)
case object Put     extends HttpMethod(6)
case object Trace   extends HttpMethod(7)

def handle (method: HttpMethod) = method match {
  case Connect => println(method + ": " + method.id)
  case Delete  => println(method + ": " + method.id)
  case Get     => println(method + ": " + method.id)
  case Head    => println(method + ": " + method.id)
  case Options => println(method + ": " + method.id)
  case Post    => println(method + ": " + method.id)
  case Put     => println(method + ": " + method.id)
  case Trace   => println(method + ": " + method.id)
}

List(Connect, Delete, Get, Head, Options, Post, Put, Trace) foreach {
  method => handle(method)
}
```

Note that we used `case object` for all the concrete subclasses, to have a true set of constants. To mimic the enumeration `id`, we added a field explicitly, but now it's up to us to pass in valid, unique values! The `handle` methods in the two implementations are nearly identical.

This script outputs the following:

```
Main$$anon$1$Connect$: 0
Main$$anon$1$Delete$: 1
Main$$anon$1$Get$: 2
Main$$anon$1$Head$: 3
Main$$anon$1$Options$: 4
Main$$anon$1$Post$: 5
Main$$anon$1$Put$: 6
Main$$anon$1$Trace$: 7
```

The object names are ugly, but we could parse the string and remove the substring we really care about.

Both approaches support the concept of a finite and fixed set of values, as long as the case class hierarchy is sealed. An additional advantage of a sealed case class hierarchy is the fact that the compiler will warn you if pattern matching statements aren't exhaustive. Try removing one of the case clauses and you'll get the usual warning. The compiler can't do this with enumerations, as we saw.

The enumeration format is more succinct, despite the name duplication we had to use, and it also supports the ability to iterate through the values. We had to do that manually in the case clause implementation.

The case class implementation naturally accommodates other fields, e.g., the **body**, as in the original implementation, while enumerations can only accommodate constant **Values** with associated names and IDs.

 For cases where you need only a simple list of constants by name or ID number, use enumerations. Be careful to follow the usage idioms. For fixed sets of more complex, constant objects, use sealed case objects.

Using Nulls Versus Options

When we introduced **Option** in "Option, Some, and None: Avoiding nulls" on page 41, we briefly discussed how it encourages avoiding **null** references in your code, which Tony Hoare, who introduced the concept of **null** in 1965, called his "billion dollar mistake" (see [Hoare2009]).

Scala has to support **null**, because **null** is supported on both the JVM and .NET and other libraries use **null**. In fact, **null** is used by some Scala libraries.

What if **null** were not available? How would that change your designs? The **Map** API offers some useful examples. Consider these two **Map** methods:

```
trait Map[A,+B] {
  ...
  def get(key: A) : Option[B]
  def getOrElse [B2 >: B](key : A, default : => B2) : B2 = ...
  ...
}
```

A map may not have a value for a particular key. Both of these methods avoid returning **null** in that case. Concrete implementations of **get** in subclasses return a **None** if no value exists for the key. Otherwise, they return a **Some** wrapping the value. The method signature tells you that a value might not exist, and it forces you to handle that situation gracefully:

```
val stateCapitals = Map("Alabama" -> "Montgomery", ...)
...

stateCapitals.get("North Hinterlandia") match {
  case None => println ("No such state!")
  case Some(x) => println(x)
}
```

Similarly, `getOrElse` forces you to design defensively. You have to specify a default value for when a key isn't in the map. Note that the default value can actually be an instance of a supertype relative to the map's value type:

```
println(stateCapitals.getOrElse("North Hinterlandia", "No such state!"))
```

A lot of Java and .NET APIs allow `null` method arguments and can return `null` values. You can write Scala wrappers around them to implement an appropriate strategy for handling `nulls`.

For example, let's revisit our previous file printing example from "Annotations" on page 289. We'll refactor our `FilePrinter` class and the Java driver into a combined script. We'll address two issues: 1) wrap `LineNumberReader.readLine` with a method that returns an `Option` instead of `null`, and 2) wrap checked `IOExceptions` in our own unchecked exception, called `ScalaIOException`:

```scala
// code-examples/AppDesign/options-nulls/file-printer-refactored-script.scala

import java.io._

class ScalaIOException(cause: Throwable) extends RuntimeException(cause)

class ScalaLineNumberReader(in: Reader) extends LineNumberReader(in) {
  def inputLine() = readLine() match {
    case null => None
    case line => Some(line)
  }
}

object ScalaLineNumberReader {
  def apply(file: File) = try {
    new ScalaLineNumberReader(new FileReader(file))
  } catch {
    case ex: IOException => throw new ScalaIOException(ex)
  }
}

class FilePrinter(val file: File) {
  def print() = {
    val reader = ScalaLineNumberReader(file)
    try {
      loop(reader)
    } finally {
      if (reader != null)
        reader.close
    }
  }

  private def loop(reader: ScalaLineNumberReader): Unit = {
    reader.inputLine() match {
      case None =>
      case Some(line) => {
        format("%3d: %s\n", reader.getLineNumber, line)
        loop(reader)
```

```
        }
      }
    }
  }

  // Process the command-line arguments (file names):
  args.foreach { fileName =>
    new FilePrinter(new File(fileName)).print();
  }
```

The ScalaLineNumberReader class defines a new method inputLine that calls
LineNumberReader.readLine and pattern matches the result. If null, then None is returned. Otherwise, the line is returned wrapped in a Some[String].

ScalaIOException is a subclass of RuntimeException, so it is unchecked. We use it to
wrap any IOExceptions thrown in ScalaLineNumberReader.apply.

The refactored FilePrinter class uses ScalaLineNumberReader.apply in its print
method. It uses ScalaLineNumberReader.inputLine in its loop method. While the original version properly handled the case of LineNumberReader.readLine returning null,
now the user of ScalaLineNumberReader has no choice but to handle a None return value.

The script ends with a loop over the input arguments, which are stored automatically
in the args variable. Each argument is treated as a file name to be printed. The script
will print itself with the following command:

```
scala file-printer-refactored-script.scala file-printer-refactored-script.scala
```

Options and for Comprehensions

There is one other benefit of using Options with for comprehensions, automatic
removal of None elements from comprehensions, under most conditions (refer to [Pol-
lak2007] and [Spiewak2009c]). Consider this first version of a script that uses
Options in a for comprehension:

```
// code-examples/AppDesign/options-nulls/option-for-comp-v1-script.scala

case class User(userName: String, name: String, email: String, bio: String)

val newUserProfiles = List(
  Map("userName" -> "twitspam", "name" -> "Twit Spam"),
  Map("userName" -> "bucktrends", "name" -> "Buck Trends",
      "email" -> "thebuck@stops.he.re", "bio" -> "World's greatest bloviator"),
  Map("userName" -> "lonelygurl", "name" -> "Lonely Gurl",
      "bio" -> "Obviously fake..."),
  Map("userName" -> "deanwampler", "name" -> "Dean Wampler",
      "email" -> "dean@....com", "bio" -> "Scala passionista"),
  Map("userName" -> "al3x", "name" -> "Alex Payne",
      "email" -> "al3x@....com", "bio" -> "Twitter API genius"))

// Version #1

var validUsers = for {
```

```
  user      <- newUserProfiles
  if (user.contains("userName") && user.contains("name") &&    // #1
      user.contains("email") && user.contains("bio"))          // #1
  userName <- user get "userName"
  name      <- user get "name"
  email    <- user get "email"
  bio      <- user get "bio" }
    yield User(userName, name, email, bio)

validUsers.foreach (user => println(user))
```

Imagine this code is used in some sort of social networking site. New users submit profile data, which is passed to this service in bulk for processing. For example, we hardcoded a list of submitted profiles, where each profile data set is a map. The map might have been copied from an HTTP session.

The service filters out incomplete profiles (missing fields), shown with the #1 comments, and creates new user objects from the complete profiles.

Running the script prints out three new users from the five submitted profiles:

```
User(bucktrends,Buck Trends,thebuck@stops.he.re,World's greatest bloviator)
User(deanwampler,Dean Wampler,dean@....com,Scala passionista)
User(al3x,Alex Payne,al3x@....com,Twitter API genius)
```

Now, delete the two lines with the #1 comment:

```
...
var validUsers = for {
  user      <- newUserProfiles
  userName <- user get "userName"
  name      <- user get "name"
  email    <- user get "email"
  bio      <- user get "bio" }
    yield User(userName, name, email, bio)

validUsers.foreach (user => println(user))
```

Before you rerun the script, what do you expect to happen? Will it print five lines with some fields empty (or containing other kinds of values)?

It prints the same thing! How did it do the filtering we wanted without the explicit conditional?

The answer lies in the way that **for** comprehensions are implemented. Here are a couple of simple for comprehensions followed by their translations (see [ScalaSpec2009]). First, we'll look at a single *generator* with a **yield**:

```
for (p1 <- e1) yield e2        // for comprehension

e1 map ( case p1 => e2 )       // translation
```

Here's the translation of a single generator followed by an arbitrary expression (which could be several expressions in braces, etc.):

```
for (p1 <- e1) e2                    // for comprehension

e1 foreach ( case p1 => e2 )         // translation
```

With more than one generator, map is replaced with flatMap in the yield expressions, but foreach is unchanged:

```
for (p1 <- e1; p2 <- e2 ...) yield eN        // for comprehension

e1 flatMap ( case p1 => for (p2 <- e2 ...) yield eN )  // translation

for (p1 <- e1; p2 <- e2 ...) eN              // for comprehension

e1 foreach ( case p1 => for (p2 <- e2 ...) eN )      // translation
```

Note that the second through the Nth generators become nested for comprehensions that need translating.

There are similar translations for conditional statements (which become calls to filter) and val assignments. We won't show them here, since our primary purpose is to describe just enough of the implementation details so you can understand how Options and for comprehensions work together. The additional details are described in [ScalaSpec2009], with examples.

If you follow this translation process on our example, you get the following expansion:

```
var validUsers = newUserProfiles flatMap {
  case user => user.get("userName") flatMap {
    case userName => user.get("name") flatMap {
      case name => user.get("email") flatMap {
        case email => user.get("bio") map {
          case bio => User(name, userName, email, bio)    // #1
        }
      }
    }
  }
}
```

Note that we have flatMap calls until the most nested case, where map is used (flatMap and map behave equivalently in this case).

Now we can understand why the big conditional was unnecessary. Recall that user is a Map and user.get("...") returns an Option, either None or Some(value). The key is the behavior of flatMap defined on Option, which lets us treat Options like other collections. Here is the definition of flatMap:

```
def flatMap[B](f: A => Option[B]): Option[B] =
  if (isEmpty) None else f(this.get)
```

If user.get("...") returns None, then flatMap simply returns None and never evaluates the function literal. Hence, the nested iterations simply stop and never get to the line marked with the comment #1, where the User is created.

The outermost flatMap is on the input List, newUserProfiles. On a multi-element collection like this, the behavior of flatMap is similar to map, but it flattens the new

---

collection and doesn't require the resulting map to have the same number of elements as the original collection, like map does.

Finally, recall from "Partial Functions" on page 183 that the case user => ... statements, for example, cause the compiler to generate a PartialFunction to pass to flatMap and map, so no corresponding foo match {...} style wrappers are necessary.

 Using Options with for comprehensions eliminate the need for most "null/empty" checks.

Exceptions and the Alternatives

If nulls are the "billion dollar mistake" as we discussed in "Option, Some, and None: Avoiding nulls" on page 41, then what about exceptions? You can argue that nulls should never occur and you can design a language and libraries that never use them. However, exceptions have a legitimate place because they *separate the concerns* of normal program flow from "exceptional" program flow. The divide isn't always clear-cut. For example, if a user mistypes his username, is that normal or exceptional?

Another question is where should the exception be caught and handled? Java's checked exceptions were designed to document for the API user what exceptions might be thrown by a method. The flaw was that it encouraged handling of the exception in ways that are often suboptimal. If one method calls another method that might throw a checked exception, the calling method is forced to either handle the exception or declare that it also throws the exception. More often than not, the calling method is the wrong place to handle the exception. It is too common for methods to simply "eat" an exception that should really be passed up the stack and handled in a more appropriate context. Otherwise, throws declarations are required up the stack of method calls. This is not only tedious, but it pollutes the intermediate contexts with exception names that often have no connection to the local context.

As we have seen, Scala doesn't have checked exceptions. Any exception can propagate to the point where it is most appropriate to handle it. However, design discipline is required to implement handlers in the appropriate places for all exceptions for which recovery is possible!

Every now and then, an argument erupts among developers in a particular language community about whether or not it's OK to use exceptions as a control-flow mechanism for normal processing. Sometimes this use of exceptions is seen as a useful longjump or non-local goto mechanism for exiting out of a deeply nested scope. One reason this debate pops up is that this use of exceptions is sometimes more efficient than a more "conventional" implementation.

For example, you might implement `Iterable.foreach` to blindly traverse a collection and stop when it catches whatever exception indicates it went past the end of the collection.

When it comes to application design, communicating *intent* is very important. Using exceptions as a `goto` mechanism breaks the *principle of least surprise*. It will be rare that the performance gain will justify the loss of clarity, so we encourage you to use exceptions only for truly "exceptional" conditions. Note that Ruby actually provides a non-local `goto`-like mechanism. In Ruby the keywords `throw` and `catch` are actually reserved for this purpose, while `raise` and `rescue` are the keywords for raising an exception and handling it.

Whatever your view on the proper use of exceptions, when you design APIs, minimizing the possibility of raising an exception will benefit your users. This is the flip side of an exception handling strategy, preventing them in the first place. `Option` can help.

Consider two methods on `Seq`, `first` and `firstOption`:

```
trait Seq[+A] {
  ...
  def first : A = ...
  def firstOption : Option[A] = ...
  ...
}
```

The `first` method throws a `Predef.UnsupportedOperationException` if the sequence is empty. Returning `null` in this case isn't an option, because the sequence could have `null` elements! In contrast, the `firstOption` method returns an `Option`, so it returns `None` if the sequence is empty, which is unambiguous.

You could argue that the `Seq` API would be more robust if it only had a "first" method that returned an `Option`. It's useful to ask yourself, "How can I prevent the user from ever failing?" When "failure" can't be prevented, use `Option` or a similar construct to document for the user that a failure mode is possible. Thinking in terms of valid state transformations, the `first` method, while convenient, isn't really valid for a sequence in an empty state. Should the "first" methods not exist for this reason? This choice is probably too draconian, but by returning `Option` from `firstOption`, the API communicates to the user that there are circumstances when the method can't satisfy the request and it's up to the user to recover gracefully. In this sense, `firstOption` treats an empty sequence as a non-exceptional situation.

Recall that we saw another example of this decision tradeoff in "Option, Some, and None: Avoiding nulls" on page 41. We discussed two methods on `Option` for retrieving the value an instance wraps (when the instance is actually a `Some`). The `get` method throws an exception if there is no value, i.e., the `Option` instance is actually `None`. The other method, `getOrElse`, takes a second argument, a default value to return if the `Option` is actually `None`. In this case, no exception is thrown.

Of course, it is impossible to avoid all exceptions. Part of the original intent of checked versus unchecked exceptions was to distinguish between potentially recoverable problems and catastrophic failures, like out-of-memory errors.

However, the alternative methods in `Seq` and `Option` show a way to "encourage" the user of an API to consider the consequences of a possible failure, like asking for the first element in an empty sequence. The user can specify the contingency in the event that a failure occurs. Minimizing the possibility of exceptions will improve the robustness of your Scala libraries and the applications that use them.

Scalable Abstractions

It has been a goal for some time in our industry to create reusable *components*. Unfortunately, there is little agreement on the meaning of the term *component*, nor on a related term, *module* (which some people consider synonymous with *component*). Proposed definitions usually start with assumptions about the platform, granularity, deployment and configuration scenarios, versioning issues, etc. (see [Szyperski1998]).

We'll avoid that discussion and use the term *component* informally to refer to a grouping of types and packages that exposes coherent abstractions (preferably just one) for the services it offers, that has minimal coupling to other components, and that is internally cohesive.

All languages offer mechanisms for defining components, at least to some degree. Objects are the primary encapsulation mechanism in object-oriented languages. However, objects alone aren't enough, because we quickly find that objects naturally cluster together into more coarse-grained aggregates, especially as our applications grow. Generally speaking, an object isn't necessarily a component, and a component may contain many objects. Scala and Java offer packages for aggregating types. Ruby modules serve a similar purpose, as do C# and C++ namespaces.

However, these packaging mechanisms still have limitations. A common problem is that they don't clearly define what is publicly visible outside the component boundary and what is internal to the component. For example, in Java, any public type or public method on a public type is visible outside the package boundary to every other component. You can make types and methods "package private," but then they are invisible to other packages encapsulated in the component. Java doesn't have a clear sense of component boundaries.

Scala provides a number of mechanisms that improve this situation. We have seen many of them already.

Fine-Grained Visibility Rules

We saw in "Visibility Rules" on page 96 that Scala provides more fine-grained visibility rules than most other languages. You can control the visibility of types and methods outside type and package boundaries.

Consider the following example of a component in package encodedstring:

```scala
// code-examples/AppDesign/abstractions/encoded-string.scala

package encodedstring {

  trait EncodedString {
    protected[encodedstring] val string: String
    val separator: EncodedString.Separator.Delimiter

    override def toString = string

    def toTokens = string.split(separator.toString).toList
  }

  object EncodedString {
    object Separator extends Enumeration {
      type Delimiter = Value
      val COMMA = Value(",")
      val TAB   = Value("\t")
    }

    def apply(s: String, sep: Separator.Delimiter) = sep match {
      case Separator.COMMA => impl.CSV(s)
      case Separator.TAB   => impl.TSV(s)
    }

    def unapply(es: EncodedString) = Some(Pair(es.string, es.separator))
  }

  package impl {
    private[encodedstring] case class CSV(override val string: String)
        extends EncodedString {
      override val separator = EncodedString.Separator.COMMA
    }

    private[encodedstring] case class TSV(override val string: String)
        extends EncodedString {
      override val separator = EncodedString.Separator.TAB
    }
  }
}
```

This example encapsulates handling of strings encoding comma-separated values (CSVs) or tab-separated values (TSVs). The encodedstring package exposes a trait EncodedString that is visible to clients. The concrete classes implementing CSVs and TSVs are declared private[encodedstring] in the encodedstring.impl package. The trait defines two abstract val fields: one to hold the encoded string, which is protected from client access, and the other to hold the **separator** (e.g., a comma). Recall from Chapter 6 that abstract fields, like abstract types and methods, must be initialized in concrete instances. In this case, **string** will be defined through a concrete constructor, and the **separator** is defined explicitly in the concrete classes, **CSV** and **TSV**.

The **toString** method on **EncodedString** prints the string as a "normal" string. By hiding the **string** value and the concrete classes, we have complete freedom in how the string is actually stored. For example, for extremely large strings, we might want to split them on the delimiter and store the tokens in a data structure. This could save space if the strings are large enough and we can share tokens between strings. Also, we might find this storage useful for various searching, sorting, and other manipulation tasks. All these implementation issues are transparent to the client.

The package also exposes an object with an **Enumeration** for the known separators, an **apply** factory method to construct new encoded strings, and an **unapply** extractor method to decompose the encoded string into its enclosed string and the delimiter. In this case, the **unapply** method looks trivial, but if we stored the strings in a different way, this method could transparently reconstitute the original string.

So, clients of this component only know about the **EncodedString** abstraction and the enumeration representing the supported types of encoded strings. All the actual implementation types and details are private to the **encodedstring** package. (We put them in the same file for convenience, but normally you would kept them separate.) Hence, the boundary is clear between the exposed abstractions and the internal implementation details.

The following script demonstrates the component in use:

```
// code-examples/AppDesign/abstractions/encoded-string-script.scala

import encodedstring._
import encodedstring.EncodedString._

def p(s: EncodedString) = {
  println("EncodedString: " + s)
  s.toTokens foreach (x => println("token: " + x))
}

val csv = EncodedString("Scala,is,great!", Separator.COMMA)
val tsv = EncodedString("Scala\tis\tgreat!", Separator.TAB)

p(csv)
p(tsv)

println( "\nExtraction:" )
List(csv, "ProgrammingScala", tsv, 3.14159) foreach {
  case EncodedString(str, delim) =>
    println( "EncodedString: \"" + str + "\", delimiter: \"" + delim + "\"" )
  case s: String => println( "String: " + s )
  case x => println( "Unknown Value: " + x )
}
```

It produces the following output:

```
EncodedString: Scala,is,great!
token: Scala
token: is
token: great!
EncodedString: Scala    is      great!
token: Scala
token: is
token: great!

Extraction:
EncodedString: "Scala,is,great!", delimiter: ","
String: ProgrammingScala
EncodedString: "Scala    is      great!", delimiter: "    "
Unknown Value: 3.14159
```

However, if we try to use the CSV class directly, for example, we get the following error:

```
scala> import encodedstring._
import encodedstring._

scala> val csv = impl.CSV("comma,separated,values")
<console>:6: error: object CSV cannot be accessed in package encodedstring.impl
       val csv = impl.CSV("comma,separated,values")
                     ^

scala>
```

In this simple example, it wasn't essential to make the concrete types private to the component. However, we have a very minimal interface to clients of the component, and we are free to modify the implementation as we see fit with little risk of forcing client code modifications. A common cause of maintenance paralysis in mature applications is the presence of too many dependencies between concrete types, which become difficult to modify since they force changes to client code. So, for larger, more sophisticated components, this clear separation of abstraction from implementation can keep the code maintainable and reusable for a long time.

Mixin Composition

We saw in Chapter 4 how traits promote mixin composition. A class can focus on its *primary domain*, and other responsibilities can be implemented separately in traits. When instances are constructed, classes and traits can be combined to compose the full range of required behaviors.

For example, in "Overriding Abstract Types" on page 120, we discussed our second version of the Observer Pattern:

```
// code-examples/AdvOOP/observer/observer2.scala

package observer

trait AbstractSubject {
```

```
  type Observer

  private var observers = List[Observer]()
  def addObserver(observer:Observer) = observers ::= observer
  def notifyObservers = observers foreach (notify(_))

  def notify(observer: Observer): Unit
}

trait SubjectForReceiveUpdateObservers extends AbstractSubject {
  type Observer = { def receiveUpdate(subject: Any) }

  def notify(observer: Observer): Unit = observer.receiveUpdate(this)
}

trait SubjectForFunctionalObservers extends AbstractSubject {
  type Observer = (AbstractSubject) => Unit

  def notify(observer: Observer): Unit = observer(this)
}
```

We used this version to observe button "clicks" in a UI. Let's revisit this implementation and resolve a few limitations, using our next tool for scalable abstractions, *self-type annotations* combined with abstract type members.

Self-Type Annotations and Abstract Type Members

There are a few things that are unsatisfying about the implementation of `Abstract Subject` in our second version of the Observer Pattern. The first occurs in `Subject ForReceiveUpdateObservers`, where the `Observer` type is defined to be the structural type `{ def receiveUpdate(subject: Any) }`. It would be nice to narrow the type of `subject` to something more specific than `Any`.

The second issue, which is really the same problem in a different form, occurs in `SubjectForFunctionalObservers`, where the `Observer` type is defined to be the type `(AbstractSubject) => Unit`. We would like the argument to the function to be something more specific than `AbstractSubject`. Perhaps this drawback wasn't so evident before, because our simple examples never needed to access `Button` state information or methods.

In fact, we expect the actual types of the subject and observer to be specialized *covariantly*. For example, when we're observing `Buttons`, we expect our observers to be specialized for `Buttons`, so they can access `Button` state and methods. This *covariant* specialization is sometimes called *family polymorphism* (see [Odersky2005]). Let's fix our design to support this covariance.

To simplify the example, let's focus on just the `receiveUpdate` form of the `Observer`, which we implemented with `SubjectForReceiveUpdateObservers` before. Here is a reworking of our pattern, loosely following an example in [Odersky2005]. (Note that the Scala syntax has changed somewhat since that paper was written.)

```
// code-examples/AppDesign/abstractions/observer3-wont-compile.scala
// WON'T COMPILE

package observer

abstract class SubjectObserver {
  type S <: Subject
  type O <: Observer

  trait Subject {
    private var observers = List[O]()
    def addObserver(observer: O) = observers ::= observer
    def notifyObservers = observers foreach (_.receiveUpdate(this)) // ERROR
  }

  trait Observer {
    def receiveUpdate(subject: S)
  }
}
```

We'll explain the error in a minute. Note how the types S and O are declared. As we saw in "Understanding Parameterized Types" on page 249, the expression type S <: Subject defines an abstract type S where the only allowed concrete types will be subtypes of Subject. The declaration of O is similar. To be clear, S and O are "placeholders" at this point, while Subject and Observer are abstract traits defined in SubjectObserver.

By the way, declaring SubjectObserver as an abstract class versus a trait is somewhat arbitrary. We'll derive concrete objects from it shortly. We need SubjectObserver primarily so we have a type to "hold" our abstract type members S and O.

However, if you attempt to compile this code as currently written, you get the following error:

```
... 10: error: type mismatch;
 found    : SubjectObserver.this.Subject
 required: SubjectObserver.this.S
       def notifyObservers = observers foreach (_.receiveUpdate(this))
                                                                ^
one error found
```

In the nested Observer trait, receiveUpdate is expecting an instance of type S, but we are passing it this, which is of type Subject. In other words, we are passing an instance of a parent type of the type expected. One solution would be to change the signature to just expect the parent type, Subject. That's undesirable. We just mentioned that our concrete observers need the more specific type, the actual concrete type we'll eventually define for S, so they can call methods on it. For example, when observing UI CheckBoxes, the observers will want to read whether or not a box is checked. We don't want to force the observers to use unsafe casts.

We looked at composition using *self-type annotations* in "Self-Type Annotations" on page 279. Let's use this feature now to solve our current compilation problem. Here is the same code again with a self-type annotation:

```
// code-examples/AppDesign/abstractions/observer3.scala

package observer

abstract class SubjectObserver {
  type S <: Subject
  type O <: Observer

  trait Subject {
    self: S =>      // #1
    private var observers = List[O]()
    def addObserver(observer: O) = observers ::= observer
    def notifyObservers = observers foreach (_.receiveUpdate(self))  // #2
  }

  trait Observer {
    def receiveUpdate(subject: S)
  }
}
```

Comment #1 shows the self-type annotation, self: S =>. We can now use self as an alias for this, but whenever it appears, the type will be assumed to be S, not Subject. It is as if we're telling Subject to impersonate another type, but in a type-safe way, as we'll see.

Actually, we could have used this instead of self in the annotation, but self is somewhat conventional. A different name also reminds us that we're working with a different type.

Are self-type annotations a safe thing to use? When an actual concrete SubjectObserver is defined, S and O will be specified and type checking will be performed to ensure that the concrete S and O are compatible with Subject and Observer. In this case, because we also defined S to be a subtype of Subject and O to be a subtype of Observer, any concrete types derived from Subject and Observer, respectively, will work.

Comment #2 shows that we pass self instead of this to receiveUpdate.

Now that we have a generic implementation of the pattern, let's specialize it for observing button clicks:

```
// code-examples/AppDesign/abstractions/button-observer3.scala

package ui
import observer._

object ButtonSubjectObserver extends SubjectObserver {
  type S = ObservableButton
  type O = ButtonObserver

  class ObservableButton(name: String) extends Button(name) with Subject {
    override def click() = {
      super.click()
      notifyObservers
```

```
      }
    }

    trait ButtonObserver extends Observer {
      def receiveUpdate(button: ObservableButton)
    }
  }
```

We declare an object `ButtonSubjectObserver` where we define S and O to be `Observable Button` and `ButtonObserver`, respectively, both of which are defined in the object. We use an `object` now so that we can refer to the nested types easily, as we'll see shortly.

`ObservableButton` is a concrete class that overrides `click` to notify observers, similar to our previous implementations in Chapter 4. However, `ButtonObserver` is still an abstract trait, because `receiveUpdate` is not defined. Notice that the argument to `receiveUpdate` is now an `ObservableButton`, the value assigned to S.

The final piece of the puzzle is to define a concrete observer. As before, we'll count button clicks. However, to emphasize the value of having the specific type of instance passed to the observer, a `Button` in this case, we'll enhance the observer to track clicks for multiple buttons using a hash map with the button labels as the keys. No type casts are required!

```
// code-examples/AppDesign/abstractions/button-click-observer3.scala

package ui
import observer._

class ButtonClickObserver extends ButtonSubjectObserver.ButtonObserver {
  val clicks = new scala.collection.mutable.HashMap[String,Int]()

  def receiveUpdate(button: ButtonSubjectObserver.ObservableButton) = {
    val count = clicks.getOrElse(button.label, 0) + 1
    clicks.update(button.label, count)
  }
}
```

Every time `ButtonClickObserver.receiveUpdate` is called, it fetches the current count for the button, if any, and updates the map with an incremented count. Note that it is now impossible to call `receiveUpdate` with a normal `Button`. We have to use an `ObservableButton`. This restriction eliminates bugs where we don't get the notifications we expected. We also have access to any "enhanced" features that `ObservableButton` may have.

Finally, here is a specification that exercises the code:

```
// code-examples/AppDesign/abstractions/button-observer3-spec.scala

package ui
import org.specs._
import observer._
```

```
object ButtonObserver3Spec extends Specification {
  "An Observer counting button clicks" should {
    "see all clicks" in {
      val button1 = new ButtonSubjectObserver.ObservableButton("button1")
      val button2 = new ButtonSubjectObserver.ObservableButton("button2")
      val button3 = new ButtonSubjectObserver.ObservableButton("button3")
      val buttonObserver = new ButtonClickObserver
      button1.addObserver(buttonObserver)
      button2.addObserver(buttonObserver)
      button3.addObserver(buttonObserver)
      clickButton(button1, 1)
      clickButton(button2, 2)
      clickButton(button3, 3)
      buttonObserver.clicks("button1") mustEqual 1
      buttonObserver.clicks("button2") mustEqual 2
      buttonObserver.clicks("button3") mustEqual 3
    }
  }

  def clickButton(button: Button, nClicks: Int) =
    for (i <- 1 to nClicks)
      button.click()
}
```

We create three buttons and one observer for all of them. We then click the buttons different numbers of times. Finally, we confirm that the clicks were properly counted for each button.

We see again how abstract types combined with self-type annotations provide a reusable abstraction that is easy to extend in a type-safe way for particular needs. Even though we defined a general protocol for observing an "event" after it happened, we were able to define subtypes specific to Buttons without resorting to unsafe casts from Subject abstractions.

The Scala compiler itself is implemented using these mechanisms (see [Odersky2005]) to make it modular in useful ways. For example, it is relatively straightforward to implement compiler plugins.

We'll revisit these idioms in "Dependency Injection in Scala: The Cake Pattern" on page 334.

Effective Design of Traits

One of the reasons that many languages (like Java) do not implement multiple inheritance is because of the problems observed with multiple inheritance in C++. One of those problems is the so-called *diamond of death*, which is illustrated in Figure 13-1.

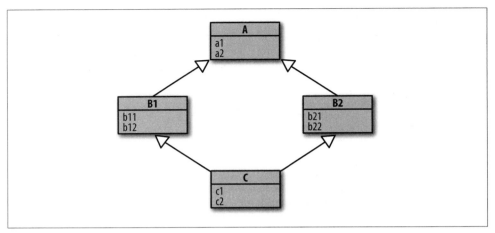

Figure 13-1. Diamond of death in languages with multiple inheritance

In C++, each constructor for C will invoke a constructor for B1 and a constructor for B2 (explicitly or implicitly). Each constructor for B1 and B2 will invoke a constructor for A. Hence, in a *naïve* implementation of multiple inheritance, the fields of A, a1 and a2, could be initialized *twice* and possibly initialized in an inconsistent way or there might be two different A "pieces" in the C instance, one for B1 and one for B2! C++ has mechanisms to clarify what should happen, but it's up to the developer to understand the details and to do the correct thing.

Scala's single inheritance and support for traits avoid these problems, while providing the most important benefit of multiple inheritance: *mixin* composition. The order of construction is unambiguous (see "Linearization of an Object's Hierarchy" on page 159). Traits can't have constructor argument lists, but Scala ensures that their fields are properly initialized when instances are created, as we saw in "Constructing Traits" on page 86 and "Overriding Abstract and Concrete Fields in Traits" on page 114. We saw another example of initializing vals in a trait in "Fine-Grained Visibility Rules" on page 314. There we defined concrete classes that overrode the definitions of the two abstract fields in the EncodedString trait.

So, Scala handles many potential issues that arise when mixing the contributions of different traits into the set of possible states of an instance. Still, it's important to consider how the contributions of different traits interact with each other.

When considering the state of an instance, it is useful to consider the instance as possessing a *state machine*, where *events* (e.g., method calls and field writes) cause transitions from one state to another. The set of all possible states form a *space*. You can think of each *field* as contributing one *dimension* to this space.

For example, recall our VetoableClicks trait in "Stackable Traits" on page 82, where button clicks were counted and additional clicks were vetoed after a certain number of clicks occurred. Our simple Button class contributed only a label dimension, while

`VetoableClicks` contributed a `count` dimension and a `maxAllowed` constant. Here is a recap of these types, collected together into a single script that also exercises the code:

```
// code-examples/AppDesign/abstractions/vetoable-clicks1-script.scala

trait Clickable {
  def click()
}

class Widget
class Button(val label: String) extends Widget with Clickable {
  def click() = println("click!")
}

trait VetoableClicks extends Clickable {
  val maxAllowed = 1
  private var count = 0
  abstract override def click() = {
    if (count < maxAllowed) {
      count += 1
      super.click()
    }
  }
}

val button1 = new Button("click me!")
println("new Button(...)")
for (i <- 1 to 3 ) button1.click()

val button2 = new Button("click me!") with VetoableClicks
println("new Button(...) with VetoableClicks")
for (i <- 1 to 3 ) button2.click()
```

This script prints the following output:

```
new Button(...)
click!
click!
click!
new Button(...) with VetoableClicks
click!
```

Note that `maxAllowed` is a constant, but it can be overridden when instantiating each instance. So, two instances could differ only by the value of `maxAllowed`. Therefore, `maxAllowed` also contributes a dimension to the state, but with only one value per instance!

So, for a button labeled "Submit," with `maxAllowed` set to 3, and which has been clicked twice (so `count` equals 2), its state can be represented by the tuple `("Submit", 2, 3)`.

In general, a single trait can either be stateless, i.e., it contributes no new dimensions of state to the instance, or it can contribute *orthogonal* state dimensions to the instance, i.e., dimensions that are independent of the state contributions from other traits and the parent class. In the script, `Clickable` is trivially stateless (ignoring the button's label), while `VetoableClicks` contributes `maxAllowed` and `count`. Traits with orthogonal state often have orthogonal methods, too. For example, the Observer Pattern traits we used in Chapter 4 contained methods for managing their lists of observers.

Independent of whether a trait contributes state dimensions, a trait can also modify the possible values for a dimension contributed by a different trait or the parent class. To see an example, let's refactor the script to move the click `count` to the `Clickable` trait:

```scala
// code-examples/AppDesign/abstractions/vetoable-clicks2-script.scala

trait Clickable {
  private var clicks = 0
  def count = clicks

  def click() = { clicks += 1 }
}

class Widget
class Button(val label: String) extends Widget with Clickable {
  override def click() = {
    super.click()
    println("click!")
  }
}

trait VetoableClicks extends Clickable {
  val maxAllowed = 1
  abstract override def click() = {
    if (count < maxAllowed)
      super.click()
  }
}

val button1 = new Button("click me!")
println("new Button(...)")
for (i <- 1 to 3 ) button1.click()

val button2 = new Button("click me!") with VetoableClicks
println("new Button(...) with VetoableClicks")
for (i <- 1 to 3 ) button2.click()
```

This script prints the same output as before. Now `Clickable` contributes one state dimension for `count` (which is now a method that returns the value of the private `clicks` field). `VetoableClicks` *modifies* this dimension by reducing the number of possible values for `count` from 0 to infinity down to just 0 and 1. Therefore, one trait affects the *behavior* of another. We might say that `VetoableClicks` is *invasive*, because it changes the behavior of other mixins.

Why is all this important? While the problems of multiple-inheritance are eliminated in Scala's model of single inheritance plus traits, care is required when mixing state and behavior contributions to create well-behaved applications. For example, if you have a test suite that `Button` passes, will a `Button with VetoableClicks` instance pass the same test suite? The suite won't pass if it assumes that you can click a button as many times as you want. There are different "specifications" for these two kinds of buttons. This difference is expressed by the *Liskov Substitution Principle* (see [Martin2003]). An instance of a `Button with VetoableClicks` won't be *substitutable* in every situation where a regular `Button` instance is used. This is a consequence of the invasive nature of `VetoableClicks`.

When a trait adds only orthogonal state and behavior, without affecting the rest of the state and behavior of the instance, it makes reuse and composition much easier, as well as reducing the potential for bugs. The Observer Pattern implementations we have seen are quite reusable. The only requirement for reuse is to provide some "glue" to adapt the generic subject and observer traits to particular circumstances.

This does not mean that invasive mixins are bad, just that they should be used wisely. The "vetoable events" pattern can be very useful.

Design Patterns

Design patterns have taken a beating lately. Critics dismiss them as workarounds for missing language features. Indeed, some of the *Gang of Four* patterns (see [GOF1995]) are not really needed in Scala, as native features provide better substitutes. Other patterns are part of the language itself, so no special coding is needed. Of course, patterns are frequently misused, but that's not the fault of the patterns themselves.

We think the criticisms often overlook an important point: the distinction between an idea and how it is implemented and used in a particular situation. Design patterns document recurring, widely useful ideas. These ideas are part of the *vocabulary* that software developers use to describe their designs.

Some common patterns are native language features in Scala, like *singleton* objects that eliminate the need for a *Singleton Pattern* ([GOF1995]) implementation like you often use in Java code.

The *Iterator Pattern* ([GOF1995]) is so pervasive in programming that most languages include iteration mechanisms for any type that can be treated like a collection. For example, in Scala you can iterate through the characters in a `String` with `foreach`:

```
"Programming Scala" foreach {c => println(c)}
```

Actually, in this case, an implicit conversion is invoked to convert the `java.lang.String` to a `RichString`, which has the `foreach` method. That's an example of the pattern called *Pimp My Library*, which we saw in "Implicit Conversions" on page 186.

Other common patterns have better alternatives in Scala. We'll discuss a better alternative to the *Visitor Pattern* ([GOF1995]) in a moment.

Finally, still other patterns can be implemented in Scala and remain very useful. For example, the *Observer Pattern* that we discussed earlier in this chapter and in Chapter 4 is a very useful pattern for many design problems. It can be implemented very elegantly using mixin composition.

We won't discuss all the well known patterns, such as those in [GOF1995]. A number of the GOF patterns are discussed at [ScalaWiki:Patterns], along with other patterns that are somewhat specific to Scala. Instead, we'll discuss a few illustrative examples. We'll start by discussing a replacement for the *Visitor Pattern* that uses functional idioms and implicit conversions. Then we'll discuss a powerful way of implementing *dependency injection* in Scala using the *Cake Pattern*.

The Visitor Pattern: A Better Alternative

The Visitor Pattern solves the problem of adding a new operation to a class hierarchy without editing the source code for the classes in the hierarchy. For a number of practical reasons, it may not be feasible or desirable to edit the hierarchy to support the new operation.

Let's look at an example of the pattern using the Shape class hierarchy we have used previously. We'll start with the case class version from "Case Classes" on page 136:

```
// code-examples/AdvOOP/shapes/shapes-case.scala

package shapes {
  case class Point(x: Double, y: Double)

  abstract class Shape() {
    def draw(): Unit
  }

  case class Circle(center: Point, radius: Double) extends Shape() {
    def draw() = println("Circle.draw: " + this)
  }

  case class Rectangle(lowerLeft: Point, height: Double, width: Double)
      extends Shape() {
    def draw() = println("Rectangle.draw: " + this)
  }

  case class Triangle(point1: Point, point2: Point, point3: Point)
      extends Shape() {
    def draw() = println("Triangle.draw: " + this)
  }
}
```

Suppose we don't want the draw method in the classes. This is a reasonable design choice, since the drawing method will be highly dependent on the particular context of use, such as details of the graphics libraries on the platforms the application will run on. For greater reusability, we would like drawing to be an operation we decouple from the shapes themselves.

First, we refactor the Shape hierarchy to support the Visitor Pattern, following the example in [GOF1995]:

```scala
// code-examples/AppDesign/patterns/shapes-visitor.scala

package shapes {
  trait ShapeVisitor {
    def visit(circle: Circle): Unit
    def visit(rect: Rectangle): Unit
    def visit(tri: Triangle): Unit
  }

  case class Point(x: Double, y: Double)

  sealed abstract class Shape() {
    def accept(visitor: ShapeVisitor): Unit
  }

  case class Circle(center: Point, radius: Double) extends Shape() {
    def accept(visitor: ShapeVisitor) = visitor.visit(this)
  }

  case class Rectangle(lowerLeft: Point, height: Double, width: Double)
      extends Shape() {
    def accept(visitor: ShapeVisitor) = visitor.visit(this)
  }

  case class Triangle(point1: Point, point2: Point, point3: Point)
      extends Shape() {
    def accept(visitor: ShapeVisitor) = visitor.visit(this)
  }
}
```

We define a ShapeVisitor trait, which has one method for each concrete class in the hierarchy, e.g., visit(circle: Circle). Each such method takes one parameter of the corresponding type to visit. Concrete derived classes will implement each method to do the appropriate operation for the particular type passed in.

The Visitor Pattern requires a one-time modification to the class hierarchy. An overridden method named accept must be added, which takes a Visitor parameter. This method must be overridden for each class. It calls the corresponding method defined on the visitor instance, passing this as the argument.

Finally, note that we declared Shape to be sealed. It won't help us prevent some bugs in the Visitor Pattern implementation, but it will prove useful shortly.

Here is a concrete visitor that supports our original draw operation:

```scala
// code-examples/AppDesign/patterns/shapes-drawing-visitor.scala

package shapes {
  class ShapeDrawingVisitor extends ShapeVisitor {
    def visit(circle: Circle): Unit =
      println("Circle.draw: " + circle)
```

```scala
    def visit(rect: Rectangle): Unit =
      println("Rectangle.draw: " + rect)

    def visit(tri: Triangle): Unit =
      println("Triangle.draw: " + tri)
  }
}
```

For each **visit** method, it "draws" the **Shape** instance appropriately. Finally, here is a script that exercises the code:

```scala
// code-examples/AppDesign/patterns/shapes-drawing-visitor-script.scala

import shapes._

val p00 = Point(0.0, 0.0)
val p10 = Point(1.0, 0.0)
val p01 = Point(0.0, 1.0)

val list = List(Circle(p00, 5.0),
                Rectangle(p00, 2.0, 3.0),
                Triangle(p00, p10, p01))

val shapesDrawer = new ShapeDrawingVisitor
list foreach { _.accept(shapesDrawer) }
```

It produces the following output:

```
Circle.draw: Circle(Point(0.0,0.0),5.0)
Rectangle.draw: Rectangle(Point(0.0,0.0),2.0,3.0)
Triangle.draw: Triangle(Point(0.0,0.0),Point(1.0,0.0),Point(0.0,1.0))
```

Visitor has been criticized for being somewhat inelegant and for breaking the *Open-Closed Principle* (OCP; see [Martin2003]), because if the hierarchy changes, you are forced to edit (and test and redeploy) *all* the visitors for that hierarchy. Note that every **ShapeVisitor** trait has methods that hardcode information about every **Shape** derived type. These kinds of changes are also error-prone.

In languages with "open types," like Ruby, an alternative to the Visitor Pattern is to create a new source file that reopens all the types in the hierarchy and inserts an appropriate method implementation in each one. No modifications to the original source code are required.

Scala does not support open types, of course, but it offers a few alternatives. The first approach we'll discuss combines pattern matching with implicit conversions. Let's begin by refactoring the **ShapeVisitor** code to remove the Visitor Pattern logic:

```scala
// code-examples/AppDesign/patterns/shapes.scala

package shapes2 {
  case class Point(x: Double, y: Double)

  sealed abstract class Shape()

  case class Circle(center: Point, radius: Double) extends Shape()
```

```
    case class Rectangle(lowerLeft: Point, height: Double, width: Double)
        extends Shape()

    case class Triangle(point1: Point, point2: Point, point3: Point)
        extends Shape()
}
```

If we would like to invoke **draw** as a method on any **Shape**, then we will have to use an implicit conversion to a wrapper class with the **draw** method:

```
// code-examples/AppDesign/patterns/shapes-drawing-implicit.scala

package shapes2 {
  class ShapeDrawer(val shape: Shape) {
    def draw = shape match {
      case c: Circle    => println("Circle.draw: " + c)
      case r: Rectangle => println("Rectangle.draw: " + r)
      case t: Triangle  => println("Triangle.draw: " + t)
    }
  }

  object ShapeDrawer {
    implicit def shape2ShapeDrawer(shape: Shape) = new ShapeDrawer(shape)
  }
}
```

Instances of **ShapeDrawer** hold a **Shape** object. When **draw** is called, the shape is pattern matched based on its type to determine the appropriate way to draw it.

A companion object declares an implicit conversion that wraps a **Shape** in a **ShapeDrawer**.

This script exercises the code:

```
// code-examples/AppDesign/patterns/shapes-drawing-implicit-script.scala

import shapes2._

val p00 = Point(0.0, 0.0)
val p10 = Point(1.0, 0.0)
val p01 = Point(0.0, 1.0)

val list = List(Circle(p00, 5.0),
                Rectangle(p00, 2.0, 3.0),
                Triangle(p00, p10, p01))

import shapes2.ShapeDrawer._

list foreach { _.draw }
```

It produces the same output as the example using the Visitor Pattern.

This implementation of **ShapeDrawer** has some similarities with the Visitor Pattern, but it is more concise, elegant, and requires no code modifications to the original **Shape** hierarchy.

Technically, the implementation has the same OCP issue as the Visitor Pattern. Changing the Shape hierarchy requires a change to the pattern matching expression. However, the required changes are isolated to one place and they are more succinct. In fact, all the logic for drawing is now contained in one place, rather than separated into **draw** methods in each Shape class and potentially scattered across different files. Note that because we **sealed** the hierarchy, a compilation error in **draw** will occur if we forget to change it when the hierarchy changes.

If we don't like the pattern matching in the draw method, we could implement a separate "drawer" class and a separate implicit conversion for each Shape class. That would allow us to keep each shape drawing operation in a separate file, for modularity, with the drawback of more code and files to manage.

If, on the other hand, we don't care about using the object-oriented **shape.draw** syntax, we could eliminate the implicit conversion and do the same pattern matching that is done in **ShapeDrawer.draw**. This approach could be simpler, especially when the extra behavior can be isolated to one place. Indeed, this approach would be a conventional functional approach, as illustrated in the following script:

```scala
// code-examples/AppDesign/patterns/shapes-drawing-pattern-script.scala

import shapes2._

val p00 = Point(0.0, 0.0)
val p10 = Point(1.0, 0.0)
val p01 = Point(0.0, 1.0)

val list = List(Circle(p00, 5.0),
                Rectangle(p00, 2.0, 3.0),
                Triangle(p00, p10, p01))

val drawText = (shape:Shape) => shape match {
  case circle: Circle =>  println("Circle.draw: " + circle)
  case rect: Rectangle => println("Rectangle.draw: " + rect)
  case tri: Triangle =>   println("Triangle.draw: " + tri)
}

def pointToXML(point: Point) =
  "<point><x>%.1f</x><y>%.1f</y></point>".format(point.x, point.y)

val drawXML = (shape:Shape) => shape match {
  case circle: Circle =>  {
    println("<circle>")
    println("  <center>" + pointToXML(circle.center) + "</center>")
    println("  <radius>" + circle.radius + "</radius>")
    println("</circle>")
  }
  case rect: Rectangle => {
    println("<rectangle>")
    println("  <lower-left>" + pointToXML(rect.lowerLeft) + "</lower-left>")
    println("  <height>" + rect.height + "</height>")
    println("  <width>" + rect.width + "</width>")
```

```
      println("</rectangle>")
    }
    case tri: Triangle => {
      println("<triangle>")
      println("  <point1>" + pointToXML(tri.point1) + "</point1>")
      println("  <point2>" + pointToXML(tri.point2) + "</point2>")
      println("  <point3>" + pointToXML(tri.point3) + "</point3>")
      println("</triangle>")
    }
  }
}

list foreach (drawText)
println("")
list foreach (drawXML)
```

We define two *function values* and assign them to variables, `drawText` and `drawXML`, respectively. Each `drawX` function takes an input `Shape`, pattern matches it to the correct type, and "draws" it appropriately. We also define a helper method to convert a Point to XML in the format we want.

Finally, we loop through the list of shapes twice. The first time, we pass `drawText` as the argument to `foreach`. The second time, we pass `drawXML`. Running this script reproduces the previous results for "text" output, followed by new XML output:

```
Circle.draw: Circle(Point(0.0,0.0),5.0)
Rectangle.draw: Rectangle(Point(0.0,0.0),2.0,3.0)
Triangle.draw: Triangle(Point(0.0,0.0),Point(1.0,0.0),Point(0.0,1.0))

<circle>
  <center><point><x>0.0</x><y>0.0</y></point></center>
  <radius>5.0</radius>
</circle>
<rectangle>
  <lower-left><point><x>0.0</x><y>0.0</y></point></lower-left>
  <height>2.0</height>
  <width>3.0</width>
</rectangle>
<triangle>
  <point1><point><x>0.0</x><y>0.0</y></point></point1>
  <point2><point><x>1.0</x><y>0.0</y></point></point2>
  <point3><point><x>0.0</x><y>1.0</y></point></point3>
</triangle>
```

Any of these idioms provides a powerful way to add additional, special-purpose functionality that may not be needed "everywhere" in the application. It's a great way to remove methods from objects that don't *absolutely have to be there*.

A drawing application should only need to know how to do input and output of shapes in one place, whether it is serializing shapes to a textual format for storage or rendering shapes to the screen. We can separate the drawing "concern" from the rest of the functionality for shapes, and we can isolate the logic for drawing, all without modifying the Shape hierarchy or any of the places where it is used in the application. The Visitor

Pattern gives us some of this separation and isolation, but we are required to add visitor implementation logic to each Shape.

Let's conclude with a discussion of one other option that may be applicable in some contexts. If you have complete control over how shapes are constructed, e.g., through a single factory, you can modify the factory to mix in traits that add new behaviors as needed:

```scala
// code-examples/AppDesign/patterns/shapes-drawing-factory.scala

package shapes2 {
  trait Drawing {
    def draw: Unit
  }

  trait CircleDrawing extends Drawing {
    def draw = println("Circle.draw " + this)
  }
  trait RectangleDrawing extends Drawing {
    def draw = println("Rectangle.draw: " + this)
  }
  trait TriangleDrawing extends Drawing {
    def draw = println("Triangle.draw: " + this)
  }

  object ShapeFactory {
    def makeShape(args: Any*) = args(0) match {
      case "circle" => {
        val center = args(1).asInstanceOf[Point]
        val radius = args(2).asInstanceOf[Double]
        new Circle(center, radius) with CircleDrawing
      }
      case "rectangle" => {
        val lowerLeft = args(1).asInstanceOf[Point]
        val height    = args(2).asInstanceOf[Double]
        val width     = args(3).asInstanceOf[Double]
        new Rectangle(lowerLeft, height, width) with RectangleDrawing
      }
      case "triangle" => {
        val p1 = args(1).asInstanceOf[Point]
        val p2 = args(2).asInstanceOf[Point]
        val p3 = args(3).asInstanceOf[Point]
        new Triangle(p1, p2, p3) with TriangleDrawing
      }
      case x => throw new IllegalArgumentException("unknown: " + x)
    }
  }
}
```

We define a Drawing trait and concrete derived traits for each Shape class. Then we define a ShapeFactory object with a makeShape factory method that takes a variable-length list of arguments. A match is done on the first argument to determine which shape to make. The trailing arguments are cast to appropriate types to construct each shape, with the corresponding drawing trait mixed in. A similar factory could be written for adding draw methods that output XML. (The variable-length list of `Any` values, heavy use of casting, and minimal error checking were done for expediency. A real implementation could minimize these "hacks.")

The following script exercises the factory:

```scala
// code-examples/AppDesign/patterns/shapes-drawing-factory-script.scala

import shapes2._

val p00 = Point(0.0, 0.0)
val p10 = Point(1.0, 0.0)
val p01 = Point(0.0, 1.0)

val list = List(
    ShapeFactory.makeShape("circle", p00, 5.0),
    ShapeFactory.makeShape("rectangle", p00, 2.0, 3.0),
    ShapeFactory.makeShape("triangle", p00, p10, p01))

list foreach { _.draw }
```

Compared to our previous scripts, the list of shapes is now constructed using the factory. When we want to draw the shapes in the `foreach` statement, we simply call `draw` on each shape. As before, the output is the following:

```
Circle.draw Circle(Point(0.0,0.0),5.0)
Rectangle.draw: Rectangle(Point(0.0,0.0),2.0,3.0)
Triangle.draw: Triangle(Point(0.0,0.0),Point(1.0,0.0),Point(0.0,1.0))
```

There is one subtlety with this approach that we should discuss. Notice that the script never assigns the result of a `ShapeFactory.makeShape` call to a `Shape` variable. If it did that, it would not be able to call `draw` on the instance!

In this script, Scala inferred a slightly different common supertype for the parameterized list. You can see that type if you use the `:load` command to load the script while inside the interactive `scala` interpreter, as in the following session:

```
$ scala -cp ...
Welcome to Scala version 2.8.0.final (Java ...).
Type in expressions to have them evaluated.
Type :help for more information.

scala> :load design-patterns/shapes-drawing-factory-script.scala
Loading design-patterns/shapes-drawing-factory-script.scala...
import shapes2._
p00: shapes2.Point = Point(0.0,0.0)
p10: shapes2.Point = Point(1.0,0.0)
p01: shapes2.Point = Point(0.0,1.0)
list: List[Product with shapes2.Shape with shapes2.Drawing] = List(...)
Circle.draw Circle(Point(0.0,0.0),5.0)
Rectangle.draw: Rectangle(Point(0.0,0.0),2.0,3.0)
Triangle.draw: Triangle(Point(0.0,0.0),Point(1.0,0.0),Point(0.0,1.0))

scala>
```

Notice the line that begins `list: List[Product with shapes2.Shape with shapes2.Drawing]`. This line was printed after the list of shapes was parsed. The inferred common supertype is `Product with shapes2.Shape with shapes2.Drawing`. `Product` is a trait mixed into all case classes, such as our concrete subclasses of `Shape`. Recall that to avoid case-class inheritance, `Shape` itself is not a case class. (See "Case Classes" on page 136 for details on why case class inheritance should be avoided.) So, our common supertype is an anonymous class that incorporates `Shape`, `Product`, and the `Drawing` trait.

If you want to assign one of these drawable shapes to a variable and still be able to invoke `draw`, use a declaration like the following (shown as a continuation of the same interactive `scala` session):

```
scala> val s: Shape with Drawing = ShapeFactory.makeShape("circle", p00, 5.0)
s: shapes2.Shape with shapes2.Drawing = Circle(Point(0.0,0.0),5.0)

scala> s.draw
Circle.draw Circle(Point(0.0,0.0),5.0)

scala>
```

Dependency Injection in Scala: The Cake Pattern

Dependency injection (DI), a form of *inversion of control* (IoC), is a powerful technique for resolving dependencies between "components" in larger applications. It supports minimizing the coupling between these components, so it is relatively easy to substitute different components for different circumstances.

It used to be that when a client object needed a database "accessor" object, for example, it would just instantiate the accessor itself. While convenient, this approach makes unit testing very difficult because you have to test with a real database. It also compromises reuse, for those alternative situations where another persistence mechanism (or none) is required. Inversion of control solves this problem by reversing responsibility for satisfying the dependency between the object and the database connection.

An example of IoC is JNDI. Instead of instantiating an accessor object, the client object asks JDNI to provide one. The client doesn't care what actual type of accessor is returned. Hence, the client object is no longer coupled to a concrete implementation of the dependency. It only depends on an appropriate *abstraction* of a persistence accessor, i.e., a Java interface or Scala trait.

Dependency injection takes IoC to its logical conclusion. Now the object does nothing to resolve the dependency. Instead, an external mechanism with system-wide knowledge "injects" the appropriate accessor object using a constructor argument or a setter method. This happens when the client is constructed. DI eliminates dependencies on IoC mechanisms in code (e.g., no more JNDI calls) and keeps objects relatively simple, with minimal coupling to other objects.

Back to unit testing, it is preferable to use a *test double* for heavyweight dependencies to minimize the overhead and other complications of testing. Our client object with a dependency on a database accessor object is a classic example. While unit testing the client, the overhead and complications of using a real database are prohibitive. Using a lightweight test double with hardcoded sample data provides simpler setup and tear down, faster execution, and predictable behavior from the data accessor dependency.

In Java, DI is usually done using an inversion of control container, like the Spring Framework ([SpringFramework]), or a Java-API equivalent like Google's Guice API (see [Guice]). These options can be used with Scala code, especially when you are introducing Scala into a mature Java environment.

However, Scala offers some unique options for implementing DI in Scala code, which are discussed by [Bonér2008b]. We'll discuss one of them, the *Cake Pattern*, which can replace or complement these other dependency injection mechanisms. We'll see that it is similar to the implementation of the Observer Pattern we discussed earlier in this chapter, in "Self-Type Annotations and Abstract Type Members" on page 317. The Cake Pattern was described by [Odersky2005], although it was given that name after that paper was published. [Bonér2008b] also discusses alternatives.

Let's build a simple component model for an overly simplified Twitter client. We want a configurable UI, a configurable local cache of past tweets, and a configurable connection to the Twitter service itself. Each of these "components" will be specified separately, along with a client component that will function as the "middleware" that ties the application together. The client component will depend on the other components. When we create a concrete client, we'll configure in the concrete pieces of the other components that we need:

```scala
// code-examples/AppDesign/dep-injection/twitter-client.scala

package twitterclient
import java.util.Date
import java.text.DateFormat

class TwitterUserProfile(val userName: String) {
  override def toString = "@" + userName
}

case class Tweet(
  val tweeter: TwitterUserProfile,
  val message: String,
  val time: Date) {

  override def toString = "(" +
    DateFormat.getDateInstance(DateFormat.FULL).format(time) + ") " +
    tweeter + ": " + message
}

trait Tweeter {
  def tweet(message: String)
}
```

```scala
trait TwitterClientUIComponent {
  val ui: TwitterClientUI

  abstract class TwitterClientUI(val client: Tweeter) {
    def sendTweet(message: String) = client.tweet(message)
    def showTweet(tweet: Tweet): Unit
  }
}

trait TwitterLocalCacheComponent {
  val localCache: TwitterLocalCache

  trait TwitterLocalCache {
    def saveTweet(tweet: Tweet): Unit
    def history: List[Tweet]
  }
}

trait TwitterServiceComponent {
  val service: TwitterService

  trait TwitterService {
    def sendTweet(tweet: Tweet): Boolean
    def history: List[Tweet]
  }
}

trait TwitterClientComponent {
  self: TwitterClientUIComponent with
        TwitterLocalCacheComponent with
        TwitterServiceComponent =>

  val client: TwitterClient

  class TwitterClient(val user: TwitterUserProfile) extends Tweeter {
    def tweet(msg: String) = {
      val twt = new Tweet(user, msg, new Date)
      if (service.sendTweet(twt)) {
        localCache.saveTweet(twt)
        ui.showTweet(twt)
      }
    }
  }
}
```

The first class, TwitterUserProfile, encapsulates a user's profile, which we limit to the username. The second class is a case class, Tweet, that encapsulates a single "tweet" (a Twitter message, limited to 140 characters by the Twitter service). Besides the message string, it encapsulates the user who sent the tweet and the date and time when it was sent. We made this class a case class for the convenient support case classes provide for creating objects and pattern matching on them. We didn't make the profile class a case class, because it is more likely to be used as the parent of more detailed profile classes.

Next is the `Tweeter` trait that declares one method, `tweet`. This trait is defined solely to eliminate a potential circular dependency between two components, `TwitterClient Component` and `TwitterClientUIComponent`. All the components are defined next in the file.

There are four components. Note that they are implemented as traits:

- `TwitterClientUIComponent`, for the UI
- `TwitterLocalCacheComponent`, for the local cache of prior tweets
- `TwitterServiceComponent`, for accessing the Twitter service
- `TwitterClientComponent`, the client that pulls the pieces together

They all have a similar structure. Each one declares a nested trait or class that encapsulates the component's behavior. Each one also declares a `val` with one instance of the nested type.

Often in Java, packages are informally associated with components. This is common in other languages, too, using their equivalent of a package, e.g., a module or a namespace. Here we define a more precise notion of a component, and a trait is the best vehicle for it, because traits are designed for mixin composition.

`TwitterClientUIComponent` declares a `val` named `ui` of the nested type `Twitter ClientUI`. This class has a `client` field that must be initialized with a `Tweeter` instance. In fact, this instance will be a `TwitterClient` (defined in `TwitterClientComponent`), which extends `Tweeter`.

`TwitterClientUI` has two methods. The first is `sendTweet`, which is defined to call the `client` object. This method would be used by the UI to call the client when the user sends a new tweet. The second method, `showTweet`, goes the other direction. It is called whenever a new tweet is to be displayed, e.g., from another user. It is abstract, pending the "decision" of the kind of UI to use.

Similarly, `TwitterLocalCacheComponent` declares `TwitterLocalCache` and an instance of it. Instances with this trait save tweets to the local persistent cache when `saveTweet` is called. You can retrieve the cached tweets with `history`.

`TwitterServiceComponent` is very similar. Its nested type has a method, `sendTweet`, that sends a new tweet to Twitter. It also has a `history` method that retrieves all the tweets for the current user.

Finally, `TwitterClientComponent` contains a concrete class, `TwitterClient`, that integrates the components. Its one `tweet` method sends new tweets to the Twitter service. If successful, it sends the tweet back to the UI and to the local persistent cache.

`TwitterClientComponent` also has the following *self-type annotation*:

```
self: TwitterClientUIComponent with
      TwitterLocalCacheComponent with
      TwitterServiceComponent =>
```

The effect of this declaration is to say that any concrete `TwitterClientComponent` must also behave like these other three components, thereby composing all the components into one client application instance. This composition will be realized by mixing in these components, which are traits, when we create concrete clients, as we will see shortly.

The self-type annotation also means we can reference the `vals` declared in these components. Notice how `TwitterClient.tweet` references the `service`, `localCache`, and the `ui` as if they are variables in the scope of this method. In fact, they *are* in scope, because of the self-type annotation.

Notice also that all the methods that call other components are concrete. Those intercomponent relationships are fully specified. The abstractions are directed "outward," toward the graphical user interface, a caching mechanism, etc.

Let's now define a concrete Twitter client that uses a textual (command-line) UI, an in-memory local cache, and fakes the interaction with the Twitter service:

```scala
// code-examples/AppDesign/dep-injection/twitter-text-client.scala

package twitterclient

class TextClient(userProfile: TwitterUserProfile)
    extends TwitterClientComponent
    with TwitterClientUIComponent
    with TwitterLocalCacheComponent
    with TwitterServiceComponent {

  // From TwitterClientComponent:

  val client = new TwitterClient(userProfile)

  // From TwitterClientUIComponent:

  val ui = new TwitterClientUI(client) {
    def showTweet(tweet: Tweet) = println(tweet)
  }

  // From TwitterLocalCacheComponent:

  val localCache = new TwitterLocalCache {
    private var tweets: List[Tweet] = Nil

    def saveTweet(tweet: Tweet) = tweets ::= tweet

    def history = tweets
  }

  // From TwitterServiceComponent

  val service = new TwitterService() {
    def sendTweet(tweet: Tweet) = {
      println("Sending tweet to Twitter HQ")
```

```
        true
    }
    def history = List[Tweet]()
  }
}
```

Our TextClient concrete class extends TwitterClientComponent and mixes in the three other components. By mixing in the other components, we satisfy the self-type annotations in TwitterClientComponent. In other words, TextClient *is* also a TwitterClientUIComponent, a TwitterLocalCacheComponent, and a TwitterServiceComponent, in addition to being a TwitterClientComponent.

The TextClient constructor takes one argument, a user profile, which will be passed onto the nested client class.

TextClient has to define four vals, one from TwitterClientComponent and three from the other mixins. For the client, it simply creates a new TwitterClient, passing it the userProfile.

For the ui, it instantiates an anonymous class derived from TwitterClientUI. It defines showTweet to print out the tweet.

For the localCache, it instantiates an anonymous class derived from TwitterLocalCache. It keeps the history of tweets in a List.

Finally, for the service, it instantiates an anonymous class derived from TwitterService. This "fake" defines sendTweet to print out a message and to return an empty list for the history.

Let's try our client with the following script:

```
// code-examples/AppDesign/dep-injection/twitter-text-client-script.scala

import twitterclient._

val client = new TextClient(new TwitterUserProfile("BuckTrends"))
client.ui.sendTweet("My First Tweet. How's this thing work?")
client.ui.sendTweet("Is this thing on?")
client.ui.sendTweet("Heading to the bathroom...")
println("Chat history:")
client.localCache.history.foreach {t => println(t)}
```

We instantiate a TextClient for the user "BuckTrends." Old Buck sends three insightful tweets through the UI. We finish by reprinting the history of tweets, in reverse order, that are cached locally. Running this script yields output like the following:

```
Sending tweet to Twitter HQ
(Sunday, May 3, 2009) @BuckTrends: My First Tweet. How's this thing work?
Sending tweet to Twitter HQ
(Sunday, May 3, 2009) @BuckTrends: Is this thing on?
Sending tweet to Twitter HQ
(Sunday, May 3, 2009) @BuckTrends: Heading to the bathroom...
Chat history:
(Sunday, May 3, 2009) @BuckTrends: Heading to the bathroom...
```

```
(Sunday, May 3, 2009) @BuckTrends: Is this thing on?
(Sunday, May 3, 2009) @BuckTrends: My First Tweet. How's this thing work?
```

Your date will vary, of course. Recall that the `Sending tweet to Twitter HQ` line is printed by the fake service.

To recap, each major component in the Twitter client was declared in its own trait, with a nested type for the component's fields and methods. The client component declared its dependencies on the other components through a self-type annotation. The concrete client class mixed in those components and defined each component `val` to be an appropriate subtype of the corresponding abstract classes and traits that were declared in the components.

We get type-safe "wiring" together of components, a flexible component model, and we did it all in Scala code! There are alternatives to the Cake Pattern for implementing dependency injection in Scala. See [Bonér2008b] for other examples.

Better Design with Design By Contract

We'll conclude this chapter with a look at an approach to programming called *Design by Contract* ([DesignByContract]), which was developed by Bertrand Meyer for the Eiffel language (see [Eiffel], [Hunt2000], and Chapter 4). Design by Contract has been around for about 20 years. It has fallen somewhat out of favor, but it is still very useful for thinking about design.

When considering the "contract" of a module, you can specify three types of conditions. First, you can specify the required inputs for a module to successfully perform a service (e.g., when a method is called). These constraints are called *preconditions*. They can also include system requirements, e.g., global data (which you should normally avoid, of course).

You can also specify the results the module guarantees to deliver, the *postconditions*, if the preconditions were satisfied.

Finally, you can specify *invariants* that must be true before and after an invocation of a service.

The specific addition that Design by Contract brings is the idea that these contractual constraints should be specified as executable code, so they can be enforced automatically at runtime, but usually only during testing.

A constraint failure should terminate execution immediately, forcing you to fix the bug. Otherwise, it is very easy to ignore these bugs.

Scala doesn't provide explicit support for Design by Contract, but there are several methods in `Predef` that can be used for this purpose. The following example shows how to use `require` and `assume` for contract enforcement:

```
// code-examples/AppDesign/design-by-contract/bank-account.scala

class BankAccount(val balance: Double) {
  require(balance >= 0.0)
  def debit(amount: Double) = {
    require(amount > 0.0, "The debit amount must be > 0.0")
    assume(balance - amount > 0.0, "Overdrafts are not permitted")
    new BankAccount(balance - amount)
  }
  def credit(amount: Double) = {
    require(amount > 0.0, "The credit amount must be > 0.0")
    new BankAccount(balance + amount)
  }
}
```

The class BankAccount uses require to ensure that a non-negative balance is specified for the constructor. Similarly, the debit and credit methods use require to ensure that a positive amount is specified.

The specification in Example 13-1 confirms that the "contract" is obeyed.

Example 13-1. design-by-contract/bank-account-spec.scala: Testing the contract

```
// code-examples/AppDesign/design-by-contract/bank-account-spec.scala

import org.specs._

object BankAccountSpec extends Specification {
  "Creating an account with a negative balance" should {
    "fail because the initial balance must be positive." in {
      new BankAccount(-100.0) must throwAn[IllegalArgumentException]
    }
  }

  "Debiting an account" should {
    "fail if the debit amount is < 0" in {
      val account = new BankAccount(100.0)
      (account.debit(-10.0)) must throwAn[IllegalArgumentException]
    }
  }

  "Debiting an account" should {
    "fail if the debit amount is > the balance" in {
      val account = new BankAccount(100.0)
      (account.debit(110.0)) must throwAn[AssertionError]
    }
  }
}
```

If we attempt to create a BankAccount with a negative balance, an IllegalArgumentExcep tion is thrown. Similarly, the same kind of exception is thrown if the debit amount is less than zero. Both conditions are enforced using require, which throws an IllegalArgumentException when the condition specified is false.

The `assume` method, which is used to ensure that overdrafts don't occur, is functionally almost identical to `require`. It throws an `AssertionError` instead of an `IllegalArgumentException`.

Both `require` and `assume` come in two forms: one that takes just a boolean condition, and the other that also takes an error message string.

There is also an `assert` pair of methods that behave identically to `assume`, except for a slight change in the generated failure message. Pick `assert` or `assume` depending on which of these "names" provides a better conceptual fit in a given context.

`Predef` also defines an `Ensuring` class that can be used to generalize the capabilities of these methods. `Ensuring` has one overloaded method, `ensure`, some versions of which take a function literal as a "predicate."

A drawback of using these methods and `Ensuring` is that you can't disable these checks in production. It may *not* be acceptable to terminate abruptly if a condition fails, although if the system is allowed to "limp along," it might crash later and the problem would be harder to debug. The performance overhead may be another reason to disable contract checks at runtime.

These days, the goals of Design by Contract are largely met by Test-Driven Development (TDD). However, thinking in terms of Design by Contract will complement the design benefits of TDD. If you decide to use Design by Contract in your code, consider creating a custom module that lets you disable the tests for production code.

Recap and What's Next

We learned a number of pragmatic techniques, patterns, and idioms for effective application development using Scala.

Good tools and libraries are important for building applications in any language. The next chapter provides more details about Scala's command-line tools, describes the state of Scala IDE support, and introduces you to some important Scala libraries.

CHAPTER 14

Scala Tools, Libraries, and IDE Support

In the previous chapter, Chapter 13, we looked at how to design scalable applications in Scala. In this chapter, we discuss tools and libraries that are essential for Scala application developers.

We briefly introduced you to the Scala command-line tools in Chapter 1. Now we explore these tools in greater detail and learn about other tools that are essential for the Scala developer. We'll discuss language-aware plugins for editors and IDEs, testing tools, and various libraries and frameworks. We won't cover these topics in exhaustive detail, but we will tell you where to look for more information.

Command-Line Tools

Even if you do most of your work with IDEs, understanding how the command-line tools work gives you additional flexibility, as well as a fallback should the graphical tools fail you. In this chapter, we'll give you some practical advice for interacting with these tools. However, we won't describe each and every command-line option. For those gory details, we recommend downloading and consulting the tool documentation package `scala-devel-docs`, as described in "For More Information" on page 10 and also in "The sbaz Command-Line Tool" on page 352.

All the command-line tools are installed in the *scala-home/bin* directory (see "Installing Scala" on page 8).

scalac Command-Line Tool

The `scalac` command compiles Scala source files, generating JVM class files. In contrast with Java requirements, the source file name doesn't have to match the public class name in the file. In fact, you can define as many public classes in the file as you want. You can also use arbitrary package declarations without putting the files in corresponding directories.

However, in order to conform to JVM requirements, a separate class file will be generated for each type with a name that corresponds to the type's name (sometimes encoded, e.g., for nested type definitions). Also, the class files will be written to directories corresponding to the package declarations. We'll see an example of the types of class files generated in the next section, when we discuss the `scala` command.

The `scalac` command is just a shell-script wrapper around the `java` command, passing it the name of the Scala compiler's `Main` object. It adds Scala JAR files to the `CLASSPATH` and it defines several Scala-related system properties. You invoke the command as follows:

```
scalac [options ...] [source-files]
```

For example, we used the following `scalac` invocation command in "A Taste of Scala" on page 10, where we created a simple command-line tool to convert input strings to uppercase:

```
scalac upper3.scala
```

Table 14-1 shows the list of the `scalac` *options*, as reported by `scalac -help`.

Table 14-1. The scalac command options

Option	Description
-X	Print a synopsis of advanced options.
-bootclasspath *path*	Override location of bootstrap class files.
-classpath *path*	Specify where to find user class files.
-d *directory*	Specify where to place generated class files.
-dependencyfile *file*	Specify the file in which dependencies are tracked. (version 2.8)
-deprecation	Output source locations where deprecated APIs are used.
-encoding *encoding*	Specify character encoding used by source files.
-explaintypes	Explain type errors in more detail.
-extdirs *dirs*	Override location of installed compiler extensions.
-g:*level*	Specify *level* of generated debugging info: none, source, line, vars, notailcalls.
-help	Print a synopsis of standard options.
-make:*strategy*	Specify recompilation detection strategy: all, changed, immediate, transitive. (version 2.8)
-nowarn	Generate no warnings.
-optimise	Generate faster byte code by applying optimizations to the program.
-print	Print program with all Scala-specific features removed.
-sourcepath *path*	Specify where to find input source files.
-target:*target*	Specify for which target JVM object files should be built: jvm-1.5, jvm-1.4, msil.
-unchecked	Enable detailed unchecked warnings.
-uniqid	Print identifiers with unique names for debugging.

Option	Description
-verbose	Output messages about what the compiler is doing.
-version	Print product version and exit.
@*file*	A text file containing compiler arguments (options and source files).

 We recommend routine use of the -deprecation and -unchecked options. They help prevent some bugs and encourage you to eliminate use of obsolete libraries.

The advanced -X options control verbose output, fine-tune the compiler behavior, including use of experimental extensions and plugins, etc. We'll discuss the -Xscript option when we discuss the scala command in the next section.

A few other advanced options, -Xfuture and -Xcheckinit, are useful for the val override issue described in "Overriding Abstract and Concrete Fields in Traits" on page 114 that affects Scala version 2.7.X. Similarly, the -Xexperimental option enables experimental changes and issues warnings for potentially risky behavior changes. See "Overriding Abstract and Concrete Fields in Traits" on page 114 for details.

An important feature of scalac is its plugin architecture, which has been significantly enhanced in version 2.8. Compiler plugins can be inserted in all phases of the compilation, enabling code transformations, analysis, etc. For example, version 2.8 will include a continuations plugin that developers can use to generate byte code that uses a continuation-passing style (CPS), rather than a stack-based style. Other plugins that are under development include an "effects" analyzer, useful for determining whether functions are truly side-effect-free, whether or not variables are modified, etc. Finally, the preliminary sxr documentation tool (see [SXR]) uses a compiler plugin to generate hyperlinked documentation of Scala code.

You can read more information about scalac in the developer tools documentation that you can install with the sbaz command, discussed later in "The sbaz Command-Line Tool" on page 352. In particular, Table 14-4 shows an example sbaz command that installs the scala-devel-docs documentation.

 Scala version 2.8 compiled byte code will not be fully compatible with version 2.7.5 byte code. Source compatibility will be preserved in most cases. If you have your own collections implementations, they may require changes.

The scala Command-Line Tool

The scala command is also a shell-script wrapper around the java command. It adds Scala JAR files to the CLASSPATH, and it defines several Scala-related system properties. You invoke the command as follows:

```
scala [options ...] [script-or-object] [arguments]
```

For example, after compiling our *upper3.scala* file in "A Taste of Scala" on page 10, which we revisited in the previous discussion of `scalac`, we can execute the "application" as follows:

```
scala -cp . Upper Hello World!
```

The `-cp .` option adds the current working directory to the class path. `Upper` is the class name with a `main` method to run. `Hello World` are arguments passed to `Upper`. This command produces the following output:

```
HELLO WORLD!
```

The command decides what to do based on the *script-or-object* specified. If you don't specify a script or object, `scala` runs as an interactive interpreter. You type in code that is evaluated on the fly, a setup sometimes referred to as a REPL (Read, Evaluate, Print, Loop). There are a few special commands available in the interactive mode. Type `:help` to see a list of them.

 The version 2.8 REPL adds many enhancements, including code completion.

Our `Upper` example demonstrates the case where you specify a fully qualified `object` name (or Java `class` name). In this case, `scala` behaves just like the `java` command; it searches the `CLASSPATH` for the corresponding code. It will expect to find a `main` method in the type. Recall that for Scala types, you have to define `main` methods in `objects`. Any *arguments* are passed as arguments to the `main` method.

If you specify a Scala source file for *script-or-object*, `scala` interprets the file as a script (i.e., compiles and runs it). Many of the examples in the book are invoked this way. Any *arguments* are made available to the script in the `args` array. Here is an example script that implements the same "upper" feature:

```
// code-examples/ToolsLibs/upper-script.scala

args.map(_.toUpperCase()).foreach(printf("%s ",_))
println("")
```

If we run this script with the following command, `scala upper.scala Hello World`, we get the same output we got before, `HELLO WORLD`.

Finally, if you invoke `scala` without a script file or object name argument, `scala` runs in interpreted mode. Here is an example interactive session:

```
$ scala
Welcome to Scala version 2.8.0.final (Java ...).
Type in expressions to have them evaluated.
Type :help for more information.
```

```
scala> "Programming Scala" foreach { c => println(c) }
P
r
o
g
...
```

The scala command accepts all the options that scalac accepts (see Table 14-1), plus the options listed in Table 14-2.

Table 14-2. The scala command options (in addition to the scalac options)

Option	Description
-howtorun script	Explicitly interpret *script-or-object* as a script file.
-howtorun object	Explicitly interpret *script-or-object* as a compiled object.
-howtorun guess	Guess what *script-or-object* is (default).
-i *file*	Preload *file*. It is only meaningful for interactive shells.
-e *argument*	Parse *argument* as Scala code.
-savecompiled	Save the compiled script for future use.
-nocompdaemon	Don't use fsc, the offline compiler. (See "The fsc Command-Line Tool" on page 353.)
-D*property=value*	Set a Java system *property* to *value*.

Use the -i *file* option in the interactive mode when you want to preload a file before typing commands. Once in the shell, you can also load a file using the command :load *filename*. Table 14-3 lists the special :X commands available within the interactive mode.

Table 14-3. Commands available within the scala interactive mode

Option	Description
:help	Prints a help message about these commands.
:load	Followed by a file name, loads a Scala file.
:replay	Resets execution and replays all previous commands.
:quit	Exits the interpreter.
:power	Enables power user mode. (version 2.8)

The new "power user mode" adds additional commands for viewing in-memory data, such as the abstract syntax tree and interpreter properties, and for doing other operations.

For *batch-mode* invocation, use the -e *argument* option to specify Scala code to interpret. If you are using command shells that support I/O redirection (e.g., the Bourne shell, the C shell, or their descendants) and you need to build up lines of code dynamically, you can also pipe the code into scala, as shown in the following somewhat contrived *bash* script example:

```
#!/usr/bin/env bash
# code-examples/ToolsLibs/pipe-example.sh

h=Hello
w=World
function commands {
cat <<-EOF
println("$h")
println("$w")
EOF
}

commands | scala
```

Invoking scripts with scala is tedious when you use these scripts frequently. On Windows and Unix-like systems, you can create standalone Scala scripts that don't require you to use the scala *script-file-name* invocation.

For Unix-like systems, the following example demonstrates how to make an executable script. Remember that you have to make the permissions executable, e.g., chmod +x secho:

```
#!/bin/sh
exec scala "$0" "$@"
!#
print("You entered: ")
argv.toList foreach { s => format("%s ", s) }
println
```

Here is how you might use it:

```
$ secho Hello World
You entered: Hello World
```

Similarly, here is an example Windows .bat command:

```
::#!
@echo off
call scala %0 %*
goto :eof
::!#
print("You entered: ")
argv.toList foreach { s => format("%s ", s) }
println
```

See the scala man page in the developer documentation package scala-devel-docs to find out more about all the command-line options for scala,

Limitations of scala versus scalac

There are some limitations when running a source file with scala versus compiling it with scalac.

Any scripts executed with scala are wrapped in an anonymous object that looks more or less like the following example:

```
// code-examples/ToolsLibs/script-wrapper.scala

object Script {
  def main(args: Array[String]): Unit = {
    new AnyRef {
      // Your script code is inserted here.
    }
  }
}
```

As of this writing, Scala objects cannot embed package declarations, and as such you can't declare packages in scripts. This is why the examples in this book that declare packages must be compiled and executed separately, such as this example from Chapter 2:

```
// code-examples/TypeLessDoMore/package-example1.scala

package com.example.mypkg

class MyClass {
  // ...
}
```

Conversely, there are valid scripts that can't be compiled with scalac, unless a special -X option is used. For example, function definitions and function invocations outside of types are not allowed. The following example runs fine with scala:

```
// code-examples/ToolsLibs/example-script.scala

case class Message(name: String)

def printMessage(msg: Message) = {
  println(msg)
}

printMessage(new Message(
    "Must compile this script with scalac -Xscript <name>!"))
```

Running this script with scala produces the following expected output:

```
Message(Must compile this script with scalac -Xscript <name>!)
```

However, if you try to compile the script with scalac (without the -Xscript option), you get the following errors:

```
example-script.scala:3: error: expected class or object definition
def printMessage(msg: Message) = {
^
example-script.scala:7: error: expected class or object definition
printMessage(new Message("Must compile this script with scalac -Xscript <name>!"))
^
two errors found
```

The script itself describes the solution; to compile this script with `scalac` you must add the option `-Xscript` *name*, where *name* is the name you want to give the compiled class file. For example, using `MessagePrinter` for *name* will result in the creation of several class files with the name prefix `MessagePrinter`:

```
scalac -Xscript MessagePrinter example-script.scala
```

You can now run the compiled code with the command:

```
scala -classpath . MessagePrinter
```

The current directory will contain the following class files:

```
MessagePrinter$$anon$1$Message$.class
MessagePrinter$$anon$1$Message.class
MessagePrinter$$anon$1.class
MessagePrinter$.class
MessagePrinter.class
```

What are all those files? `MessagePrinter` and `MessagePrinter$` are wrappers generated by `scalac` to provide the entry point for the script as an "application." Recall that we specified `MessagePrinter` as the *name* argument for `-Xscript`. `MessagePrinter` has the `static main` method we need.

`MessagePrinter$$anon$1` is a generated class that wraps the whole script. The `printMessage` method in the script is a method in this class. `MessagePrinter$$anon$1$Message` and `MessagePrinter$$anon$1$Message$` are the `Message` class and companion object, respectively, that are declared in the script. They are nested inside the generated class `MessagePrinter$$anon$1` for the whole script. If you want to see what's inside these class files, use one of the decompilers, which we describe next.

The scalap, javap, and jad Command-Line Tools

When you are learning Scala and you want to understand how Scala constructs are mapped to the runtime, there are several decompilers that are very useful. They are especially useful when you need to invoke Scala code from Java and you want to know how Scala names are *mangled* into JVM-compatible names, or you want to understand how the scala compiler translates Scala features into valid byte code.

Let's discuss three decompilers and the benefits they offer. Since the class files generated by `scalac` contain valid JVM byte codes, you can use Java decompilers tools:

- `scalap` is included with the Scala distribution. It outputs declarations as they would appear in Scala source code.
- `javap` is included with the JDK. It outputs declarations as they would appear in Java source code. Therefore, running `javap` on Scala-generated class files is a good way to see how Scala definitions are mapped to valid byte code.

- jad is an open source command-line tool (see [JAD]). It attempts to reconstruct an entire Java source file from the class file, including method definitions, as well as the declarations.

MessagePrinter.class is one of the class files generated from the example script in the previous section. Let's run scalap -classpath . MessagePrinter. We get the following output:

```
package MessagePrinter;
final class MessagePrinter extends scala.AnyRef {
}
object MessagePrinter {
  def main(scala.Array[java.lang.String]): scala.Unit;
  def $tag(): scala.Int;
    throws java.rmi.RemoteException
}
```

Note that the first method inside object MessagePrinter is the main method. The $tag method is part of Scala's internal implementation. It is an abstract method defined by ScalaObject. The compiler automatically generates implementations for concrete types. The $tag method was originally introduced to optimize pattern matching, but it is now deprecated and it may be removed in a forthcoming release of Scala.

Let's compare the scalap output to what we get when we run javap -classpath . MessagePrinter:

```
Compiled from "(virtual file)"
public final class MessagePrinter extends java.lang.Object{
  public static final void main(java.lang.String[]);
  public static final int $tag()        throws java.rmi.RemoteException;
}
```

Now we see the declaration of main as we would typically see it in a Java source file.

Finally, to use jad, you simply give it the file name of the class file. It generates a corresponding output file with the *.jad* extension. If you run jad MessagePrinter.class, you get a long file named *MessagePrinter.jad*. You will also get several warnings that jad could not fully decompile some methods. We won't reproduce the output here, but the *.jad* file will print normal Java statements interspersed with several sections of JVM byte code instructions, where it could not decompile the byte code.

All these tools have command-line help:

- scalap -help
- javap -help
- jad --help

The Scala developer documentation contains documentation for scalap. Similar documentation comes with the JDK for javap. The jad distribution includes a *README* file with documentation. The Mac and Linux distributions also include a man page.

Finally, as an exercise, compile the following very simple `Complex` class, representing complex numbers. Then run `scalap`, `javap`, and `jad` on the resulting class files:

```
// code-examples/ToolsLibs/complex.scala

case class Complex(real: Double, imaginary: Double) {
  def +(that: Complex) =
    new Complex(real + that.real, imaginary + that.imaginary)
  def -(that: Complex) =
    new Complex(real - that.real, imaginary - that.imaginary)
}
```

How are the + and - methods encoded? What are the names of the reader methods for the `real` and `imaginary` fields? What Java types are used for the fields?

The scaladoc Command-Line Tool

The `scaladoc` command is analogous to `javadoc`. It is used to generate documentation from Scala source files, called Scaladocs. The `scaladoc` parser supports the same @ annotations that `javadoc` supports, such as `@author`, `@param`, etc.

If you use `scaladoc` for your documentation, you might want to investigate `vscaladoc`, an improved `scaladoc` tool that is available at *http://code.google.com/p/vscaladoc/*. You can also find documentation on `vscaladoc` at [ScalaTools].

The sbaz Command-Line Tool

The Scala Bazaar System (`sbaz`) is a packaging system that helps automate maintenance of a Scala installation. It is analogous to the *gem* packaging system for Ruby, *CPAN* for Perl, etc.

There is a nice summary of how to use `sbaz` on the scala-lang.org website (*http://www .scala-lang.org/node/93*). All command-line options are described in the developer documentation. Table 14-4 summarizes the most useful options.

Table 14-4. The most useful sbaz command options

Command	Description
sbaz showuniverse	Show the current "universe" (remote repository). Defaults to *http://scala-we bapps.epfl.ch/sbaz/scala-dev*.
sbaz setuniverse *univ*	Points to a new "universe" *univ*.
sbaz installed	What's already installed locally?
sbaz available	What goodness awaits on the Interwebs?
sbaz install scala-devel-docs	Install the invaluable `scala-devel-docs` package (for example).
sbaz upgrade	Upgrade all installed packages to the latest and greatest.

Note that a remote repository used by `sbaz` is called a "universe."

The fsc Command-Line Tool

The *fast (offline) scala compiler* runs as a daemon process to enable faster invocations of the compiler, mostly by eliminating the startup overhead. It is particularly useful when running scripts repeatedly (for example, when re-running a test suite until a bug can be reproduced). In fact, fsc is invoked automatically by the scala command. You can also invoke it directly.

Build Tools

Scala plugins have been implemented for several, commonly used build tools, including *Ant (http://ant.apache.org/)*, *Maven (http://maven.apache.org/)*, and *Buildr (http://buildr .apache.org/)*. There are also several build tools written in Scala and aimed specifically at Scala development. Perhaps the best known example of these tools is SBT (simple build tool—see [SBT]).

These plugins and tools are documented very well on their respective websites, so we refer you to those sites for details.

The Scala distribution includes Ant tasks for scalac, fsc, and scaladoc. They are used very much like the corresponding Java Ant tasks. They are described at *http://scala-lang .org/node/98*.

A Scala Maven plugin is available at *http://scala-tools.org/mvnsites/maven-scala-plu gin/*. It does not require Scala to be installed, as it will download Scala for you. Several third-party Scala projects, such as Lift (see "Lift" on page 367), use Maven.

Buildr is an Apache project available at *http://buildr.apache.org/*. It is aimed at JVM applications written in any language, with built-in support for Scala and Groovy as well as Java. It is compatible with Maven repositories and project layouts. Since build scripts are written in Ruby, they tend to be much more succinct than corresponding Maven files. Buildr is also useful for testing JVM applications with Ruby testing tools, like *RSpec (http://rspec.info)* and Cucumber (*http://cukes.info*), if you use JRuby (*http://jruby .codehaus.org/*) to run your builds.

The Scala-oriented SBT, available at *http://code.google.com/p/simple-build-tool/*, has some similarities to Buildr. It is also compatible with Maven, but it uses Scala as the language for writing build scripts. It also has built-in support for generating Scaladocs and for testing with ScalaTest, Specs, and ScalaCheck.

Integration with IDEs

If you come from a Java background, you are probably a little bit spoiled by the rich features of today's Java IDEs. Scala IDE support is not yet as good, but it is evolving rapidly in Eclipse, IntelliJ IDEA, and NetBeans. At the time of this writing, all the Scala plugins for these IDEs support syntax highlighting, project management, limited support for automated refactorings, etc. While each of the plugins has particular advantages over the others, they are all close enough in functionality that you will probably find it acceptable to adopt the plugin for the IDE that you already prefer.

This section describes how to use the Scala support available in Eclipse, IntelliJ IDEA, and NetBeans. We assume you already know how to use each IDE for development in other languages, like Java.

Eclipse

For details on the Eclipse Scala plugin, start at this web page, *http://www.scala-lang .org/node/94*. If you are interested in contributing to the development of the plugin, see this web page, *http://lampsvn.epfl.ch/trac/scala/wiki/EclipsePlugin*.

Installing the Scala plugin

The plugin requires JDK 5 or higher (JDK 6 is recommended) and Eclipse 3.3 or higher (Eclipse 3.4 is recommended). The plugin installs the Scala SDK itself. To install the plugin, invoke the "Software Updates" command in the Help menu.

Click the Available Software tab and click the "Add Site..." button on the righthand side. You will see the dialog shown in Figure 14-1.

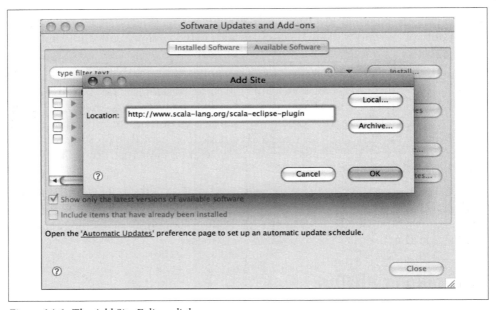

Figure 14-1. The Add Site Eclipse dialog

Enter the URL that is shown in the figure, *http://www.scala-lang.org/scala-eclipse-plugin*. Some people prefer to work with the *nightly* releases, *http://www.scala-lang.org/scala-eclipse-plugin-nightly*, but you should be aware that there is no guarantee they will work!

Select the checkbox next to the newly added update site and click the Install button, as indicated in Figure 14-2. *Don't* click the "default" Close button!

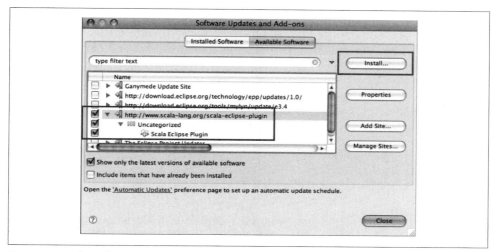

Figure 14-2. The Software Updates and Add-ons dialog

 It is easy to be confused by the poor usability of the Software Updates dialog.

After finding the plugin on the update site, an Install dialog is presented. Click through the sequence of screens to complete the installation. You will be asked to restart Eclipse when the installation completes.

Developing Scala applications

Once the plugin is installed, you can create Scala projects using the File → New → Other... menu item. You will find a *Scala Wizards* folder that contains a wizard called Scala Project. This wizard works just like the familiar Java Project Wizard.

You can work with your Scala project using most of the same commands you would use with a typical Java project. For example, you can create a new Scala `trait`, `class`, or `object` using the context menu.

The Eclipse Scala plugin still has some rough edges, but Scala developers using Eclipse should find it acceptable for their daily needs.

IntelliJ

The IntelliJ *IDEA* team provides a *beta*-quality Scala plugin. Start here for details: *http://www.jetbrains.net/confluence/display/SCA/Scala+Plugin+for+IntelliJ+IDEA*.

Installing the Scala plugins

To use the plugin, you must use IntelliJ 8.0.X or later. Consider using the most recent "EAP" build for the latest feature updates.

To install the Scala plugin, start IDEA. Open the Settings panel, e.g., using the File → Settings menu item. On the lefthand side, scroll down to and click the Plugins item, as shown in Figure 14-3.

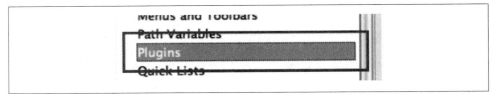

Figure 14-3. IntelliJ IDEA Settings → Plugins

Select the Available tab on the righthand side. Scroll down to the Scala plugin, as shown in Figure 14-4.

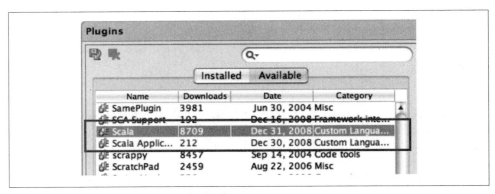

Figure 14-4. Available IntelliJ IDEA Scala plugins

Right-click the Scala plugin name and select "Download and Install" from the menu. Repeat for the Scala Application plugin. You will have to restart IDEA for the plugins to be enabled.

After IDEA restarts, confirm that the two plugins were installed correctly by reopening the Plugin Manager. Click the Installed tab and scroll down to find the two Scala plugins. They should be listed with a black font, and the checkboxes next to them should be checked, as seen in Figure 14-5.

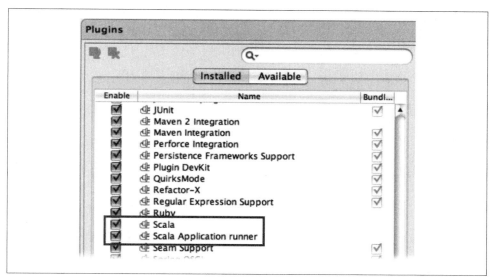

Figure 14-5. Installed IntelliJ IDEA Scala plugins

If the font is red or the checkboxes are not checked, refer to the Scala plugin web page above for debugging help.

Developing Scala applications

To create an IDEA Scala project, start by selecting the File → New Project menu item. In the dialog, select the appropriate radio button for your situation, e.g., "Create New Project from Scratch."

On the next screen, select "Java Module" and fill in the usual project information. An example is shown in Figure 14-6.

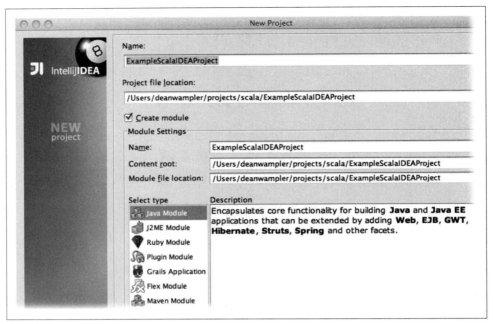

Figure 14-6. Specifying IntelliJ IDEA Scala project details

Click through to the screen titled "Please Select Desired Technology." Check the "Scala" checkbox, and check the "New Scala SDK" checkbox. Click the button labeled "..." to navigate to the location of your Scala SDK installation, as shown in Figure 14-7. You will only need to specify the SDK the first time you create a project or when you install a new SDK in a different location.

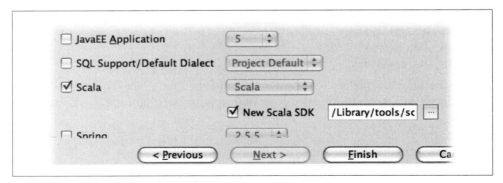

Figure 14-7. Adding Scala to the IntelliJ IDEA project

Click Finish. You will be prompted to create either a project or an application. Select "Application" if you want to share this project with other Scala projects on the same machine.

Now you can work with your Scala project using most of the same commands you would use with a typical Java project. For example, you can create a new Scala `trait`, `object`, or `class` using the context menu, as for Java projects.

The IntelliJ IDEA Scala plugin is still *beta*-quality, but Scala developers using IDEA should find it acceptable for their daily needs.

NetBeans

NetBeans has *beta*-quality Scala plugins. Start at this web page for details, *http://wiki .netbeans.org/Scala*. NetBeans 6.5 or a more recent nightly build is required. The Scala plugin contains a version of the Scala SDK. The wiki page provides instructions for using a different SDK, when desired.

Installing the Scala plugins

To install the plugin, download the plugins ZIP file from *http://sourceforge.net/project/ showfiles.php?group_id=192439&package_id=256544*. Unzip the file in a convenient directory.

Start NetBeans and invoke the Tools → Plugins menu item. Select the Downloaded tab and click the "Add Plugins..." button. Choose the directory where the Scala plugins are unzipped, and select all the listed *.nbm* files, as shown in Figure 14-8. Click Open.

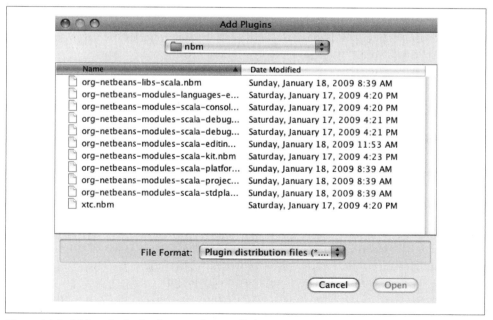

Figure 14-8. Adding the Scala plugins to be installed

Back in the Plugins dialog, make sure the checkboxes for all the new plugins are checked. Click Install.

Click through the installation dialog and restart NetBeans when finished.

Developing Scala applications

To create a NetBeans Scala Project, start by selecting the File → New Project menu item or clicking the New Project button. In the pop-up dialog, select "Scala" under Categories and "Scala Application" under Projects, as shown in Figure 14-9. Click Next.

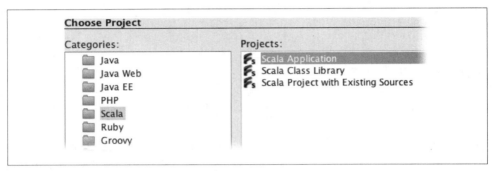

Figure 14-9. Creating a new NetBeans Scala project

Fill in the project name, location, etc., and click Finish.

Once the project is created, you can work with it using most of the same commands you would use with a typical Java project. There are some differences. For example, when you invoke the New item in the context menu, the submenu does not show items for creating new Scala types. Instead, you have invoke the Other... menu item and work through a dialog. This will be changed in a future release.

Despite some minor issues like this, the NetBeans Scala plugin is mature enough for regular use.

Text Editors

The sbaz tool manages the scala-tool-support package that includes Scala plugins for several editors, including Emacs, Vim, TextMate and others. Like sbaz, the scala-tool-support package is also included with the language installation. See the directories in *scala-home/misc/scala-tool-support* for the supported editors. Most of the editor-specific directories contain instructions for installing the plugin. In other cases, consult your editor's instructions for installing third-party plugins.

Some of the packages are fairly immature. If you want to contribute to the Scala community, please consider improving the quality of the existing plugins or contributing new plugins.

At the time of this writing, there are several variations of a Scala "bundle" for the TextMate editor, which is a popular text editor for Mac OS X. These bundles are currently being managed by Paul Phillips on the GitHub website (*http://github.com/paulp/scala-textmate/tree/master*). Hopefully, the best features of each bundle will be unified into an "authoritative" bundle and integrated back into the `scala-tool-support` package.

Test-Driven Development in Scala

One of the most important developer practices introduced in the last decade is *Test-Driven Development* (TDD). The Scala community has created several tools to support TDD.

If you work in a "pure" Java shop, consider introducing one or more of these Scala testing tools to test-drive your Java code. This approach is a low-risk way to introduce Scala to your environment, so you can gain experience with it before making the commitment to Scala as your production code language. In particular, you might experiment with ScalaTest (see "ScalaTest" next), which can be used with JUnit ([JUnit]) and TestNG ([TestNG]). You might also consider ScalaCheck or Reductio (see "Scala-Check" on page 365), which offer innovations that may not be available in Java testing frameworks. All of the tools we describe here integrate with Java testing and build tools, like JUnit, TestNG, various mocking libraries, Ant ([Ant]), and Maven ([Maven]). All of them also offer convenient Scala DSLs for testing.

ScalaTest

Scala's version of the venerable XUnit tool is ScalaTest, available at *http://www.artima .com/scalatest/*.

You can drive your tests using the built-in `Runner` or use the provided integration with JUnit or TestNG. ScalaTest also comes with an Ant task and it works with the Scala-Check testing tool (described later).

Besides supporting the traditional XUnit-style syntax with test methods and assertions, ScalaTest provides a *Behavior-Driven Development* ([BDD]) syntax that is becoming increasingly popular. The *ScalaTest* website (*http://www.artima.com/scalatest/*) provides examples for these and other options.

Here is an example ScalaTest test for the simple `Complex` class we used in "The scalap, javap, and jad Command-Line Tools" on page 350:

```
// code-examples/ToolsLibs/complex-test.scala

import org.scalatest.FunSuite

class ComplexSuite extends FunSuite {
```

```
    val c1 = Complex(1.2, 3.4)
    val c2 = Complex(5.6, 7.8)

    test("addition with (0, 0)") {
      assert(c1 + Complex(0.0, 0.0) === c1)
    }

    test("subtraction with (0, 0)") {
      assert(c1 - Complex(0.0, 0.0) === c1)
    }

    test("addition") {
      assert((c1 + c2).real === (c1.real + c2.real))
      assert((c1 + c2).imaginary === (c1.imaginary + c2.imaginary))
    }

    test("subtraction") {
      assert((c1 - c2).real === (c1.real - c2.real))
      assert((c1 - c2).imaginary === (c1.imaginary - c2.imaginary))
    }
  }
```

This particular example uses the "function value" syntax for each test that is provided by the FunSuite parent trait. Each call to **test** receives as arguments a descriptive string and a *function literal* with the actual test code.

The following commands compile *complex.scala* and *complex-test.scala*, putting the class files in a *build* directory, and then run the tests. Note that we assume that *scalatest-0.9.5.jar* (the latest release at the time of this writing) is in the *../lib* directory. The downloadable distribution of the code examples is organized this way:

```
scalac -classpath ../lib/scalatest-0.9.5.jar -d build complex.scala complex-test.scala
scala -classpath build:../lib/scalatest-0.9.5.jar org.scalatest.tools.Runner \
  -p build -o -s ComplexSuite
```

(We used a \ to continue the long command on a second line.) The output is the following:

```
Run starting. Expected test count is: 4
Suite Starting - ComplexSuite: The execute method of a nested suite is \
  about to be invoked.
Test Starting - ComplexSuite: addition with (0, 0)
Test Succeeded - ComplexSuite: addition with (0, 0)
Test Starting - ComplexSuite: subtraction with (0, 0)
Test Succeeded - ComplexSuite: subtraction with (0, 0)
Test Starting - ComplexSuite: addition
Test Succeeded - ComplexSuite: addition
Test Starting - ComplexSuite: subtraction
Test Succeeded - ComplexSuite: subtraction
Suite Completed - ComplexSuite: The execute method of a nested suite \
  returned normally.
Run completed. Total number of tests run was: 4
All tests passed.
```

Again, we wrapped the long output lines with a \.

Specs

The Specs library ([ScalaSpecsTool]) is a Behavior-Driven Development ([BDD]) testing tool for Scala. It is inspired by Ruby's RSpec ([RSpec]). In a nutshell, the goal of BDD is to recast traditional test syntax into a form that better emphasizes the role of TDD as a process that drives *design*, which in turn should implement the *requirements* "specification." The syntax of traditional TDD tools, like the XUnit frameworks, tend to emphasize the *testing* role of TDD. With the syntax realigned, it is believed that the developer will be more likely to stay focused on the *primary* role of TDD: driving application design.

You can also find documentation on Specs at [ScalaTools].

We have already used Specs in several examples in the book, e.g., `ButtonObserverSpec` in "Traits As Mixins" on page 76. Here is another example for the simple `Complex` class we showed previously:

```scala
// code-examples/ToolsLibs/complex-spec.scala

import org.specs._

object ComplexSpec extends Specification {
  "Complex addition with (0.0, 0.0)" should {
    "return a number N' that is identical to original number N" in {
      val c1 = Complex(1.2, 3.4)
      (c1 + Complex(0.0, 0.0)) mustEqual c1
    }
  }
  "Complex subtraction with (0.0, 0.0)" should {
    "return a number N' that is identical to original number N" in {
      val c1 = Complex(1.2, 3.4)
      (c1 - Complex(0.0, 0.0)) mustEqual c1
    }
  }
  "Complex addition" should {
    """return a new number where
    the real and imaginary parts are the sums of the
    input values' real and imaginary parts, respectively.""" in {
      val c1 = Complex(1.2, 3.4)
      val c2 = Complex(5.6, 7.8)
      (c1 + c2).real mustEqual (c1.real + c2.real)
      (c1 + c2).imaginary mustEqual (c1.imaginary + c2.imaginary)
    }
  }
  "Complex subtraction" should {
    """return a new number where
    the real and imaginary parts are the differences of the
    input values' real and imaginary parts, respectively.""" in {
      val c1 = Complex(1.2, 3.4)
      val c2 = Complex(5.6, 7.8)
```

```
        (c1 - c2).real mustEqual (c1.real - c2.real)
        (c1 - c2).imaginary mustEqual (c1.imaginary - c2.imaginary)
      }
    }
  }
```

An object that extends Specification is the analog of a test suite. The next level of grouping, e.g., the clause "Complex addition with (0.0, 0.0)" should {...}, encapsulates the information at the level of the type being tested, or perhaps a "cluster" of behaviors that go together for the type.

The next level clause, e.g., the clause "return a number N' that is identical to original number N" in {...}, is called an "example" in BDD terminology. It is analogous to a single test. Like typical XUnit frameworks, the testing is done using "representative examples," rather than by doing an exhaustive exploration of the entire "space" of possible states. Hence, the term "example." (However, see the discussion of ScalaCheck next.)

Statements like (c1 + Complex(0.0, 0.0)) mustEqual c1 are called "expectations." They do the actual verifications that conditions are satisfied. Hence, expectations are analogous to assertions in XUnit tools.

There are several ways to run your specs. After compiling *complex-spec.scala* earlier, we can run the specs as follows:

```
scala -classpath ../lib/specs-1.4.3.jar:build ComplexSpec
```

Here, as before, we assume the *Specs* JAR is in the *../lib* directory and we assume the compiled class files are in the *build* directory. We get the following output:

```
Specification "ComplexSpec"
  Complex addition with (0.0, 0.0) should
  + return a number N' that is identical to original number N

  Total for SUT "Complex addition with (0.0, 0.0)":
  Finished in 0 second, 0 ms
  1 example, 1 expectation, 0 failure, 0 error

  Complex subtraction with (0.0, 0.0) should
  + return a number N' that is identical to original number N

  Total for SUT "Complex subtraction with (0.0, 0.0)":
  Finished in 0 second, 0 ms
  1 example, 1 expectation, 0 failure, 0 error

  Complex addition should
  + return a new number where
        the real and imaginary parts are the sums of the
        input values real and imaginary parts, respectively.

  Total for SUT "Complex addition":
  Finished in 0 second, 0 ms
  1 example, 2 expectations, 0 failure, 0 error
```

```
Complex subtraction should
+ return a new number where
      the real and imaginary parts are the differences of the
      input values real and imaginary parts, respectively.

Total for SUT "Complex subtraction":
Finished in 0 second, 0 ms
1 example, 2 expectations, 0 failure, 0 error

Total for specification "ComplexSpec":
Finished in 0 second, 37 ms
4 examples, 6 expectations, 0 failure, 0 error
```

Note that the strings in the specification are written in a form that reads somewhat like a requirements specification:

```
...
Complex addition with (0.0, 0.0) should
+ return a number N' that is identical to original number N
...
```

There are many ways to run specifications, including using an Ant task or using the built-in integration with ScalaTest or JUnit. JUnit is the best approach for running specifications in some IDEs. These and other options are described in the User's Guide at *http://code.google.com/p/specs/wiki/RunningSpecs*.

ScalaCheck

ScalaCheck ([ScalaCheckTool] is a Scala port of the innovative Haskell QuickCheck ([QuickCheck]) tool that supports *Automated Specification-Based Testing*, sometimes called *type-based "property" testing* in the Haskell literature (e.g., [O'Sullivan2009]).

ScalaCheck can be installed using sbaz, i.e., sbaz install scalacheck.

Using ScalaCheck (or QuickCheck for Haskell), conditions for a type are specified that should be true for any instances of the type. The tool tries the conditions using automatically generated instances of the type and verifies that the conditions are satisfied.

Here is a ScalaCheck test for Complex:

```
// code-examples/ToolsLibs/complex-check-script.scala

import org.scalacheck._
import org.scalacheck.Prop._

def toD(i: Int) = i * .1

implicit def arbitraryComplex: Arbitrary[Complex] = Arbitrary {
  Gen.sized {s =>
    for {
      r <- Gen.choose(-toD(s), toD(s))
      i <- Gen.choose(-toD(s), toD(s))
    } yield Complex(r, i)
  }
}
```

```
  }

  object ComplexSpecification extends Properties("Complex") {
    def additionTest(a: Complex, b: Complex) =
      (a + b).real.equals(a.real + b.real) &&
      (a + b).imaginary.equals(a.imaginary + b.imaginary)

    def subtractionTest(a: Complex, b: Complex) =
      (a - b).real.equals(a.real - b.real) &&
      (a - b).imaginary.equals(a.imaginary - b.imaginary)

    val zero = Complex(0.0, 0.0)

    specify("addition with (0,0)", (a: Complex)  => additionTest(a, zero))
    specify("subtraction with (0,0)", (a: Complex)  => subtractionTest(a, zero))

    specify("addition", (a: Complex, b: Complex) => additionTest(a,b))
    specify("subtraction", (a: Complex, b: Complex) => subtractionTest(a,b))
  }
  ComplexSpecification.check
```

The toD function just converts an Int to a Double by dividing by 0.1. It's useful to convert an Int index provided by ScalaCheck into Double values that we will use to construct Complex instances.

We also need an implicit conversion visible in the scope of the test that generates new Complex values. The arbitraryComplex function provides this generator. An Arbitrary[Complex] object (part of the ScalaCheck API) is returned by this method. ScalaCheck invokes another API method, Gen[Complex].sized. We provide a *function literal* that assigns a passed-in Int value to a variable s. We then use a for comprehension to return Complex numbers with real and imaginary parts that range from -toD(s) to toD(s) (i.e., -(s * .1) to (s * .1)). Fortunately, you don't have to define implicit conversions or generators for most of the commonly used Scala and Java types.

The most interesting part is the definition and use of ComplexSpecification. This object defines a few helper methods, additionTest and subtractionTest, that each return true if the conditions they define are true. For additionTest, if a new Complex number is the sum of two other Complex numbers, then its real part must equal the sum of the real parts of the two original numbers. Likewise, a similar condition must hold for the imaginary part of the numbers. For subtractionTest, the same conditions must hold with subtraction substituted for addition.

Next, two specify clauses assert that the addition and subtraction conditions should hold for any Complex number when Complex(0.0, 0.0) is added to it or subtracted from it, respectively. Two more specify classes assert that the conditions should also hold for any pair of Complex numbers.

Finally, when ComplexSpecification.check is called, test runs are made with different values of Complex numbers, verifying that the properties specified are valid for each combination of numbers passed to the helper methods.

We can run the check using the following command (once again assuming that Complex is already compiled into the *build* directory):

```
scala -classpath ../lib/scalacheck.jar:build complex-check-script.scala
```

It produces the following output:

```
+ Complex.addition with (0,0): OK, passed 100 tests.
+ Complex.addition: OK, passed 100 tests.
+ Complex.subtraction with (0,0): OK, passed 100 tests.
+ Complex.subtraction: OK, passed 100 tests.
```

Note that ScalaCheck tried each specify case with 100 different inputs.

It's important to understand the value that ScalaCheck delivers. Rather than going through the process of writing enough "example" test cases with representative data, which is tedious and error-prone, we define reusable "generators," like the arbitrary Complex function, to produce an appropriate range of instances of the type under test. Then we write property specifications that should hold for any instances. ScalaCheck does the work of testing the properties against a random sample of the instances produced by the generators.

You can find more examples of ScalaCheck usage in the online code examples. Some of the types used in the payroll example in "Internal DSLs" on page 218 were tested with ScalaCheck. These tests were not shown in "Internal DSLs" on page 218.

Finally, note that there is another port of QuickCheck called *Reductio*. It is part of the *Functional Java* project ([FunctionalJava]). *Reductio* is less widely used than Scala-Check, but it offers a "native" Java API as well as a Scala API, so it would be more convenient for "pure" Java teams.

Other Notable Scala Libraries and Tools

While Scala benefits from the rich legacy of Java and .NET libraries, there is a growing collection of libraries written specifically for Scala. Here we discuss some of the more notable ones.

Lift

Lift (http://liftweb.net/) is the leading web application framework written in Scala. It recently reached "1.0" status. Lift has been used for a number of commercial websites. You can also find documentation on the Lift website.

Other web frameworks include Sweet (*http://code.google.com/p/sweetscala/*), Pinky (*http://bitbucket.org/pk11/pinky/wiki/Home*), and Slinky (*http://code.google.com/p/slinky2/*).

Scalaz

Scalaz (http://code.google.com/p/scalaz/) is a library that fills in gaps in the standard library. Among its features are enhancements to several core Scala types, such as `Boolean`, `Unit`, `String`, and `Option`, plus support for functional *control* abstractions, such as `FoldLeft`, `FoldRight`, and `Monad`, that expand upon what is available in the standard library.

Scalax

Scalax (http://scalax.scalaforge.org/) is another third-party library effort to supplement the Scala core library.

MetaScala

MetaScala (http://www.assembla.com/wiki/show/metascala) is an experimental meta-programming library for Scala. Metaprogramming features tend to be weaker in statically typed languages than in dynamically typed languages. Also, the JVM and .NET CLR impose their own constraints on metaprogramming.

Many of the features of Scala obviate the need for metaprogramming, compared to languages like Ruby, but sometimes metaprogramming is still useful. MetaScala attempts to address those needs more fully than Scala's built-in reflection support.

JavaRebel

JavaRebel (http://www.zeroturnaround.com/javarebel/) is a commercial tool that permits dynamic reloading of classes in a running JVM (written in any language), beyond the limited support provided natively by the "HotSwap" feature of the JVM. JavaRebel is designed to offer the developer faster turnaround for changes, providing an experience more like the rapid turnaround that users of dynamic languages enjoy. JavaRebel can be used with Scala code as well.

Miscellaneous Smaller Libraries

Finally, Table 14-5 is a list of several Scala-specific libraries you might find useful for your applications.

Table 14-5. Miscellaneous Scala libraries

Name	Description and URL
Kestrel	A tiny, very fast queue system (*http://github.com/robey/kestrel/tree/master*).
ScalaModules	Scala DSL to ease OSGi development (*http://code.google.com/p/scalamodules/*).
Configgy	Managing configuration files and logging for "daemons" written in Scala (*http://www.lag.net/configgy/*).

Name	Description and URL
scouchdb	Scala interface to CouchDB (*http://code.google.com/p/scouchdb/*).
Akka	A project to implement a platform for building fault-tolerant, distributed applications based on REST, Actors, etc. (*http://akkasource.org/*).
scala-query	A type-safe database query API for Scala (*http://github.com/szeiger/scala-query/tree/master*).

We'll discuss using Scala with several well-known Java libraries after we discuss Java interoperability, next.

Java Interoperability

Of all the alternative JVM languages, Scala's interoperability with Java source code is among the most seamless. This section begins with a discussion of interoperability with code written in Java. Once you understand the details, they can be generalized to address interoperability with other JVM languages, such as JRuby or Groovy. For example, if you already know how to use JRuby and Java together, and you know how to use Java and Scala together, then you can generalize to using JRuby and Scala together.

Because Scala syntax is primarily a superset of Java syntax, invoking Java code from Scala is usually straightforward. Going the other direction requires that you understand how some Scala features are encoded in ways that satisfy the JVM specification. We discuss several of the interoperability issues here. [Spiewak2009a] and [Odersky2008] provide additional information.

Java and Scala Generics

We have seen many examples of Scala code that uses Java types, such as `java.lang.String` and various java collection classes. Instantiating Java generic types is straightforward in Scala (since Scala version 2.7.0). Consider the following very simple Java generic class, `JStack`:

```java
// code-examples/ToolsLibs/JStack.java

import java.util.*;

public class JStack<T> {
  private List<T> stack = new ArrayList<T>();
  public void push(T t) {
    stack.add(t);
  }
  public T pop() {
    return stack.remove(stack.size() - 1);
  }
}
```

We can instantiate it from Scala, specifying the type parameter, as shown in Example 14-1.

Example 14-1. A Scala "spec" to test the simple Java stack

```scala
// code-examples/ToolsLibs/JStack-spec.scala

import org.specs._

object JStackSpec extends Specification {
  "Calling a Java generic type from Scala" should {
    "Support parameterization" in {
      val js = new JStack[String]
      js must notBe(null)  // Dummy check...
    }
    "Support invoking the the type's methods" in {
      val js = new JStack[String]
      js.push("one")
      js.push("two")
      js.pop() mustEqual "two"
      js.pop() mustEqual "one"
    }
  }
}
```

Since Scala version 2.7.2, you can also use Scala generics from Java. Consider the following JUnit 4 test, which shows some of the idiosyncrasies you might encounter:

```java
// code-examples/ToolsLibs/SMapTest.java

import org.junit.*;
import static org.junit.Assert.*;
import scala.*;
import scala.collection.mutable.LinkedHashMap;

public class SMapTest {
  static class Name {
    public String firstName;
    public String lastName;

    public Name(String firstName, String lastName) {
      this.firstName = firstName;
      this.lastName  = lastName;
    }
  }

  LinkedHashMap<Integer, Name> map;

  @Before
  public void setup() {
    map = new LinkedHashMap<Integer, Name>();
    map.update(1, new Name("Dean", "Wampler"));
    map.update(2, new Name("Alex", "Payne"));
  }

  @Test
  public void usingMapGetWithWarnings() {
    assertEquals(2, map.size());
    Option<Name> n1 = map.get(1);  // warning
```

```
    Option<Name> n2 = map.get(2);  // warning
    assertTrue(n1.isDefined());
    assertTrue(n2.isDefined());
    assertEquals("Dean", n1.get().firstName);
    assertEquals("Alex", n2.get().firstName);
  }

  @Test
  public void usingMapGetWithoutWarnings() {
    assertEquals(2, map.size());
    Option<?> n1 = map.get(1);
    Option<?> n2 = map.get(2);
    assertTrue(n1.isDefined());
    assertTrue(n2.isDefined());
    assertEquals("Dean", ((Name) n1.get()).firstName);
    assertEquals("Alex", ((Name) n2.get()).firstName);
  }
}
```

On Unix-like systems, it is compiled with the following command line:

```
javac -Xlint:unchecked \
  -cp $SCALA_HOME/lib/scala-library.jar:$JUNIT_HOME/junit-4.4.jar SMapTest.java
```

(Again, we wrapped the long line with \.) *SCALA_HOME* and *JUNIT_HOME* are the installation directories of Scala and JUnit, respectively.

The SMapTest class defines a nested Name class that is used as the "value" type in a scala.collection.mutable.LinkedHashMap. For simplicity, Name has public firstName and lastName fields and a constructor.

The setup method creates a new LinkedHashMap<Integer,Name> and inserts two key-value pairs. The two tests, usingMapGetWithWarnings and usingMapGetWithoutWarnings, exercise the Java-Scala interoperability the same way. However, the first test has two compile-time warnings, indicated by the // warning comments, while the second test compiles without warnings:

```
SMapTest.java:29: warning: [unchecked] unchecked conversion
found    : scala.Option
required: scala.Option<SMapTest.Name>
    Option<Name> n1 = map.get(1);  // warning
                             ^
SMapTest.java:30: warning: [unchecked] unchecked conversion
found    : scala.Option
required: scala.Option<SMapTest.Name>
    Option<Name> n2 = map.get(2);  // warning
                             ^

2 warnings
```

The warnings occur because of type erasure. In the compiled Scala library, the return type of Map.get is Option with no type parameter, or effectively Option<Object>. So we get warnings for the conversion to Option<Name>.

The second test, `usingMapGetWithoutWarnings`, has no warnings, because we assign the values returned by `Map.get` to `Option<?>` and then do an explicit cast to `Name` when we call `Option.get` in the final two assertions.

Using Scala Functions in Java

Continuing with our previous `SMapTest` example, we can explore invoking Scala code from Java where Scala functions are required:

```java
// code-examples/ToolsLibs/SMapTestWithFunctions.java

import org.junit.*;
import static org.junit.Assert.*;
import scala.*;
import scala.collection.mutable.LinkedHashMap;
import static scala.collection.Map.Projection;

public class SMapTestWithFunctions {
  static class Name {
    public String firstName;
    public String lastName;

    public Name(String firstName, String lastName) {
      this.firstName = firstName;
      this.lastName  = lastName;
    }

    public static Name emptyName = new Name("","");

    public static Function0<Name> empty = new Function0<Name>() {
      public Name apply() { return emptyName; }

      public int $tag() { return 0; }
    };
  }

  LinkedHashMap<Integer, Name> map;

  @Before
  public void setup() {
    map = new LinkedHashMap<Integer, Name>();
    map.update(1, new Name("Dean", "Wampler"));
    map.update(2, new Name("Alex", "Payne"));
  }

  @Test
  public void usingMapGetOrElse() {
    assertEquals(2, map.size());
    assertEquals("Dean", ((Name) map.getOrElse(1, Name.empty)).firstName);
    assertEquals("Alex", ((Name) map.getOrElse(2, Name.empty)).firstName);
  }

  Function1<Integer, Boolean> filter = new Function1<Integer, Boolean>() {
    public Boolean apply(Integer i) { return i.intValue() <= 1; }
```

```
  public <A> Function1<A,Boolean> compose(Function1<A,Integer> g) {
    return Function1$class.compose(this, g);
  }

  public <A> Function1<Integer,A> andThen(Function1<Boolean,A> g) {
    return Function1$class.andThen(this, g);
  }

  public int $tag() { return 0; }
};

@Test
public void usingFilterKeys() {
  assertEquals(2, map.size());
  Projection<Integer, Name> filteredMap =
      (Projection<Integer, Name>) map.filterKeys(filter);
  assertEquals(1, filteredMap.size());
  assertEquals("Dean", filteredMap.getOrElse(1, Name.empty).firstName);
  assertEquals("",     filteredMap.getOrElse(2, Name.empty).firstName);
}
}
```

The SMapTestWithFunctions class has its own Name class that adds a static emptyName object and a static scala.Function0 object empty, which defines apply to return emptyName. Note that it is also necessary to define the $tag method that was discussed previously in "The scalap, javap, and jad Command-Line Tools" on page 350.

The empty function object is needed when we use Map.getOrElse in the test method, usingMapGetOrElse. The signature of getOrElse is the following:

```
def getOrElse[B2 >: B](key : A, default : => B2) : B2
```

Where A is the key type parameter, B is the value type parameter, and B2 is a supertype of B or the same as B. The second default argument is a *by-name parameter*, which we discussed in Chapter 8. Note that by-name parameters are implemented as scala.Func tion0 objects. So, we can't simply pass in the static object emptyName.

The second test, usingFilterKeys, requires a Function1 object, which has an apply method that takes one argument. We use this Function1 object as a filter passed to Map.filterKeys.

We define the filter before the test. The Java code here is considerably more involved than the equivalent Scala code would be! Not only do we have to define the apply and $tag methods, we must also define methods used for function composition, compose and andThen. Fortunately, we can delegate to objects that are already in the Scala library, as shown. Note that other FunctionN types, for N equals 2 to 22, have other methods that would have to be implemented using similar "boilerplate." For example, these types each have a curry method.

Finally, recall that in "Companion Objects and Java Static Methods" on page 133, we discussed that methods defined in companion objects are not visible as static methods to Java code. For example, `main` methods defined in companion objects can't be used to run the application. Instead, you should define such methods in *singleton* objects.

So, using Scala function objects from Java can be challenging. If you find it necessary to use them frequently, you could define Java utility classes that handle the boilerplate for all the methods except `apply`.

JavaBean Properties

We saw in Chapter 5 that Scala does not follow the JavaBeans ([JavaBeansSpec]) conventions for field reader and writer methods, for reasons described in "When Accessor Methods and Fields Are Indistinguishable: The Uniform Access Principle" on page 123. However, there are times when you need JavaBeans accessor methods. For example, you need them when you want your Scala instances to be configurable by a *dependency injection* mechanism, like the one provided by the Spring Framework ([SpringFramework]). You may also need JavaBeans accessor methods for some IDEs that do bean "introspection."

Scala solves this problem with an annotation that you can apply to a field, `@scala.reflect.BeanProperty`, which tells the compiler to generate JavaBeans-style getter and setter methods. We introduced this annotation in "Annotations" on page 289.

Recall the `Complex` class we saw previously. Now we add the annotation to each constructor argument, which is a field in the `case` class:

```
// code-examples/ToolsLibs/complex-javabean.scala

case class ComplexBean(
  @scala.reflect.BeanProperty real: Double,
  @scala.reflect.BeanProperty imaginary: Double) {

  def +(that: ComplexBean) =
    new ComplexBean(real + that.real, imaginary + that.imaginary)
  def -(that: ComplexBean) =
    new ComplexBean(real - that.real, imaginary - that.imaginary)
}
```

If you compile this class, then decompile it with `javap -classpath ... ComplexBean`, you get the following output:

```
public class ComplexBean extends java.lang.Object
  implements scala.ScalaObject,scala.Product,java.io.Serializable{
  public ComplexBean(double, double);
  public java.lang.Object productElement(int);
  public int productArity();
  public java.lang.String productPrefix();
  public boolean equals(java.lang.Object);
  public java.lang.String toString();
  public int hashCode();
  public int $tag();
  public ComplexBean $minus(ComplexBean);
```

```
    public ComplexBean $plus(ComplexBean);
    public double imaginary();
    public double real();
    public double getImaginary();
    public double getReal();
}
```

Now compare this output with the result of decompiling the original *Complex.class* file:

```
public class Complex extends java.lang.Object
    implements scala.ScalaObject,scala.Product,java.io.Serializable{
    public Complex(double, double);
    public java.lang.Object productElement(int);
    public int productArity();
    public java.lang.String productPrefix();
    public boolean equals(java.lang.Object);
    public java.lang.String toString();
    public int hashCode();
    public int $tag();
    public Complex $minus(Complex);
    public Complex $plus(Complex);
    public double imaginary();
    public double real();
}
```

The order of the methods shown may be different when you run `javap` on these files. We reordered them so the two listings would match as closely as possible. Note that the only differences are the names of the classes and the presence of `getImaginary` and `getReal` methods in the `ComplexBean` case. We would also have corresponding setter methods if the `real` and `imaginary` fields were declared as `vars` instead of `vals`.

 The Scaladoc page for `@BeanProperty` (version 2.7) says that you can't call the bean setter methods from Scala. You can call them, but as the Scaladoc page goes on to say, you should use the Scala-style writer (and reader) methods instead.

AnyVal Types and Java Primitives

Notice also in the previous `Complex` example that the `Doubles` were converted to Java primitive `doubles`. All the `AnyVal` types are converted to their corresponding Java primitives. We showed the mapping in Table 7-3. In particular, note that `Unit` is mapped to `void`.

Scala Names in Java Code

As we discussed in Chapter 3, Scala allows more flexible identifiers, e.g., *operator characters* like *, <, etc. These characters are encoded (or "mangled," if you prefer) to satisfy the tighter constraints of the JVM specification. They are translated as shown in Table 14-6 (adapted from [Spiewak2009a]).

Table 14-6. Encoding of operator characters

Operator	Encoding
=	$eq
>	$greater
<	$less
+	$plus
-	$minus
*	$times
/	$div
\	$bslash
|	$bar
!	$bang
?	$qmark
:	$colon
%	$percent
^	$up
&	$amp
@	$at
#	$hash
~	$tilde

You can see this at work in the following contrived trait, where each character is used to declare an abstract method that takes no arguments and returns Unit:

```
// code-examples/ToolsLibs/all-op-chars.scala

trait AllOpChars {
  def == : Unit    // $eq$eq
  def >  : Unit    // $greater
  def <  : Unit    // $less
  def +  : Unit    // $plus
  def -  : Unit    // $minus
  def *  : Unit    // $times
  def /  : Unit    // $div
  def \  : Unit    // $bslash
  def |  : Unit    // $bar
  def !  : Unit    // $bang
  def ?  : Unit    // $qmark
  def :: : Unit    // $colon$colon
  def %  : Unit    // $percent
  def ^  : Unit    // $up
  def &  : Unit    // $amp
  def @@ : Unit    // $at$at
  def ## : Unit    // $hash$hash
```

```
    def ~  : Unit    // $tilde
  }
```

Note that we doubled up some of the characters to get them to compile as method names, where using single characters would have been ambiguous. Compiling this file and decompiling the resulting class file with `javap AllOpChars` yields the following Java interface. (We have rearranged the output order of the methods to match the order in the original Scala file.)

```
Compiled from "all-op-chars.scala"
public interface AllOpChars{
  public abstract void $eq$eq();
  public abstract void $greater();
  public abstract void $less();
  public abstract void $plus();
  public abstract void $minus();
  public abstract void $times();
  public abstract void $div();
  public abstract void $bslash();
  public abstract void $bar();
  public abstract void $bang();
  public abstract void $qmark();
  public abstract void $colon$colon();
  public abstract void $percent();
  public abstract void $up();
  public abstract void $amp();
  public abstract void $at$at();
  public abstract void $hash$hash();
  public abstract void $tilde();
}
```

To conclude, interoperability between Java and Scala works very well, but there are a few things you must remember when invoking Scala code from Java. If you're uncertain about how a Scala identifier is encoded or a Scala method is translated to valid byte code, use `javap` to find out.

Java Library Interoperability

This section specifically considers interoperability with several important Java frameworks: AspectJ, the Spring Framework, Terracotta, and Hadoop. Because they are widely used in "enterprise" and Internet Java applications, successful interoperability with Scala is important.

AspectJ

AspectJ ([AspectJ]) is an extension of Java that supports *aspect-oriented programming* (AOP), also known as *aspect-oriented software development* ([AOSD]). The goal of AOP is to enable systemic changes of the same kind across many modules, while avoiding copying and pasting the same code over and over into each location. Avoiding this duplication not only improves productivity, it greatly reduces bugs.

For example, if you want all field changes to all "domain model" objects to be persisted automatically after the changes occur, you can write an aspect that observes those changes and triggers a persistence write after each change.

AspectJ supports AOP by providing a *pointcut language* for specifying in a declarative way all the "execution points" in a program for which a particular behavior modification (called *advice*) is required. In AspectJ parlance, each execution point is called a *join point*, and a particular query over join points is a *pointcut*. Hence the *pointcut language* is a query language, of sorts. For a given pointcut, AspectJ incorporates the desired behavior modifications into each join point. Manual insertion of these changes is not required. An *aspect* encapsulates pointcuts and advices, much the way a class encapsulates member fields and methods.

For a detailed introduction to AspectJ with many practical examples, refer to [Laddad2009].

There are two issues that must be considered when using AspectJ with Scala. The first issue is how to reference Scala execution points using AspectJ's pointcut language, e.g., Scala types and methods. The second issue is how to invoke Scala code as *advice*.

Let's look at an aspect that logs method calls to the `Complex` class we used previously in this chapter. We'll add a package declaration this time to provide some scope:

```scala
// code-examples/ToolsLibs/aspectj/complex.scala

package example.aspectj

case class Complex(real: Double, imaginary: Double) {
  def +(that: Complex) =
    new Complex(real + that.real, imaginary + that.imaginary)
  def -(that: Complex) =
    new Complex(real - that.real, imaginary - that.imaginary)
}
```

Here is an `object` that uses `Complex`:

```scala
// code-examples/ToolsLibs/aspectj/complex-main.scala

package example.aspectj

object ComplexMain {
  def main(args: Array[String]) {
    val c1 = Complex(1.0, 2.0)
    val c2 = Complex(3.0, 4.0)
    val c12 = c1 + c2
    println(c12)
  }
}
```

Next, here is an AspectJ aspect that defines one *pointcut* for the creation of `Complex` instances and another pointcut for invocations of the + method:

```
// code-examples/ToolsLibs/aspectj/LogComplex.aj

package example.aspectj;

public aspect LogComplex {
  public pointcut newInstances(double real, double imag):
    execution(Complex.new(..)) && args(real, imag);

  public pointcut plusInvocations(Complex self, Complex other):
    execution(Complex Complex.$plus(Complex)) && this(self) && args(other);

  before(double real, double imag): newInstances(real, imag) {
    System.out.println("new Complex(" + real + "," + imag + ") called.");
  }

  before(Complex self, Complex other): plusInvocations(self, other) {
    System.out.println("Calling " + self + ".+(" + other + ")");
  }

  after(Complex self, Complex other) returning(Complex c):
    plusInvocations(self, other) {
    System.out.println("Complex.+ returned " + c);
  }
}
```

We won't explain all the details of AspectJ syntax here. See the AspectJ document at [AspectJ] and [Laddad2009] for those details. We'll limit ourselves to a "conceptual" overview of this aspect.

The first pointcut, newInstances, matches on executions of the constructor calls, using the syntax Complex.new to refer to the constructor. We expect double arguments to the constructor call. As we saw previously, scala.Double occurrences are converted to Java primitive doubles when generating byte code. The args clause "binds" the values of the arguments passed in, so we can refer to them in *advice*.

The second pointcut, plusInvocations, matches on "executions" of the + method, which is actually $plus in the byte code. The self and other parameters are bound to the object on which the + method is invoked (using the this clause) and the argument to it (using the args clause), respectively.

The first before advice is executed for the newInstances pointcut, that is, before we actually enter the constructor. We "log" the call, displaying the actual real and imaginary values passed in.

The next before advice is executed for the plusInvocations pointcut, that is, before the + method is executed. We log the value of self (i.e., this instance) and the other number.

Finally, an after returning advice is also executed for the plusInvocations pointcut, that is, after the + method returns. We capture the return value in the variable c and we log it.

If you have AspectJ installed in an *aspectj-home* directory, you can compile this file as follows:

```
ajc -classpath .:aspectj-home/lib/aspectjrt.jar:../lib/scala-library.jar \
  aspectj/LogComplex.aj
```

This is one line; we used the \ to indicate a line wrap. To run this code with the `LogComplex` aspect, we use *load-time weaving (http://www.eclipse.org/aspectj/doc/re leased/devguide/ltw.html)*. We'll invoke Java with an *agent* that "weaves" the advice from `LogComplex` into `Complex`. To use load-time weaving, we also need the following configuration file, `META-INF/aop.xml`:

```
<!-- code-examples/ToolsLibs/META-INF/aop.xml -->

<aspectj>
  <aspects>
    <aspect name="example.aspectj.LogComplex" />
    <include within="example.aspectj.*" />
  </aspects>

  <weaver options="-verbose">
    <dump within="example.aspectj.*" beforeandafter="true">
      <include within="example.aspectj.*" />
    </dump>
  </weaver>
</aspectj>
```

(The *META-INF* directory should be on the class path; we'll assume it's in the current working directory.) This file tells the weaver which aspects to use (the `aspect` tag) and which classes to target for weaving (the `include` tag), and it also enables verbose output, which is useful for debugging purposes. Finally, we can run the application with the following command:

```
java -classpath .:aspectj-home/lib/aspectjrt.jar:../lib/scala-library.jar \
  -javaagent:aspectj-home/lib/aspectjweaver.jar example.aspectj.ComplexMain
```

You get several lines of messages logging the weaving process. The output ends with these lines:

```
new Complex(1.0,2.0) called.
new Complex(3.0,4.0) called.
Calling Complex(1.0,2.0).+(Complex(3.0,4.0))
new Complex(4.0,6.0) called.
Complex.+ returned Complex(4.0,6.0)
Complex(4.0,6.0)
```

All but the last line were output by `LogComplex`. We added this additional behavior without manually inserting these statements in `Complex` itself!

Recall we said that the second issue you might encounter when using AspectJ is how to invoke Scala code from *advice*. In our `LogComplex` aspect, the statements inside our different `before` and `after` advices are really just Java code. Therefore, we can just as easily invoke Scala code, applying the same lessons we have already learned for invoking Scala from Java.

Scala traits *almost* replace aspects. We saw in Chapters 4 and 13 how you can construct traits that modify the behavior of other traits, then mix the behaviors together when you create new classes or instances. This powerful technique lets you implement a form of aspect advice. However, Scala doesn't have a pointcut language, like AspectJ. When you need to affect a set of join points that don't share a common supertype, you'll need the capabilities of AspectJ. However, if you find yourself in that situation, you should consider if you can refactor your code to extract a common trait that provides the "hooks" you need for advice implemented using traits.

The Spring Framework

The Spring Framework (see [SpringFramework]) is an open source, modular Java enterprise framework that provides a "pure" Java AOP API, integrated support for AspectJ, a *dependency injection* (DI) container, uniform and well-designed APIs for invoking a variety of other Java third-party APIs, and additional components for security, web development, etc.

Here we focus on dependency injection, as interoperability issues with the other parts of the Spring Framework boil down to either Java or AspectJ issues, which we covered earlier.

We discussed the concept of DI in "Dependency Injection in Scala: The Cake Pattern" on page 334, where we showed elegant patterns for injecting dependencies using Scala itself. However, if you are in a mixed Java/Scala environment, it might be necessary to use a DI framework like the one provided by Spring to manage dependencies.

In Spring DI, dependencies are specified using a combination of XML configuration files and source-code annotations. The Spring API resolves these dependencies as classes are instantiated. Spring expects these classes to follow JavaBean conventions (see [JavaBeansSpec]). Well-designed classes will only depend on abstractions, i.e., Java interfaces or Scala traits, and the concrete instances satisfying those dependencies will be given to the bean through constructor arguments or through JavaBean setter methods. Hence, if you use Spring DI with Scala classes, you will need to use the `@scala.reflect.BeanProperty` annotation when you use setter injection. The annotation is not needed when you use constructor injection.

 Prefer constructor injection, when possible. Not only does this choice eliminate the need to use the `@BeanProperty` annotation, it leaves each instances in a known good state when the construction process is finished.

However, if you inject dependencies into Scala `objects`, you must use setter injection, as you have no way to define constructor parameters and you have no control over the construction process.

One other point; remember that Spring will expect Java-compatible names, so you must use *encoded* names for methods and `objects`, as needed.

Here is an example that illustrates "wiring together" objects with Spring:

```scala
// code-examples/ToolsLibs/spring/object-bean.scala

package example.spring

case class NamedObject(name: String)

trait Factory {
  @scala.reflect.BeanProperty
  var nameOfFactory = "unknown"

  def make(name: String): AnyRef
}
object NamedObjectFactory extends Factory {
  def make(name: String) = NamedObject(name)
}

case class FactoryUsingBean(factory: Factory)
```

The case class `FactoryUsingBean` is a simple type with a dependency on a `Factory` abstraction that we want to inject using constructor injection.

The trait `Factory` defines the factory abstraction. It has a `make` method to create instances of some kind. To demonstrate setter injection on `objects`, we also give it a `nameOf Factory` field. This will demonstrate `object` dependency injection because the concrete subtype we will actually use, `NamedObjectFactory`, is an `object`.

Scala requires us to initialize `nameOfFactory` with a value, but we will use Spring to set the real value. We have to use the `@BeanProperty` annotation to generate the `setNameOf Factory` method Spring will expect to find.

The concrete `make` method in `NamedObjectFactory` creates a new `NamedObject`. It is a simple case class with a `name` field.

Note that none of these types depend on the Spring API. You can compile this file without any Spring JAR files.

Next, we define the dependency "wiring" using a standard Spring XML configuration file:

```xml
<!-- code-examples/ToolsLibs/spring/scala-spring.xml -->

<beans xmlns="http://www.springframework.org/schema/beans"
       xmlns:xsi="http://www.w3.org/2001/XMLSchema-instance"
       xsi:schemaLocation="http://www.springframework.org/schema/beans
```

```
        http://www.springframework.org/schema/beans/spring-beans-2.5.xsd">

    <bean id="factory" class="example.spring.NamedObjectFactory$">
      <property name="nameOfFactory" value="Factory for Named Objects" />
    </bean>

    <bean id="factoryUsingBean" class="example.spring.FactoryUsingBean">
      <constructor-arg ref="factory" />
    </bean>
  </beans>
```

We define two **beans**. Our factory is given the ID `factory`. The "class" is actually the object `NamedObjectFactory`. Note that we have to append a $ to the end of the name, the actual name of the `object` in the byte code.

The `property` tag sets the value of `nameOfFactory`. We can't control instantiation of `objects`, so we have to inject the correct dependency after construction completes.

The second bean is our simple `FactoryUsingBean`. Since this is a `class`, we can use constructor injection. The `constructor` tag specifies that the `factory` bean is used to satisfy the dependency at construction time.

Finally, here is a script that uses these types to demonstrate Spring DI with Scala:

```
// code-examples/ToolsLibs/spring/object-bean-script.scala

import example.spring._
import org.springframework.context.support._

val context = new ClassPathXmlApplicationContext("spring/scala-spring.xml");

val bean = context.getBean("factoryUsingBean").asInstanceOf[FactoryUsingBean]
println("Factory Name: " + bean.factory.nameOfFactory)

val obj  = bean.factory.make("Dean Wampler")
println("Object: " + obj)
```

We create an instance of `ClassPathXmlApplicationContext`, specifying our XML file. This context object is our gateway to the DI container. We ask it for our `factoryUsingBean`. We have to cast the returned `AnyRef` (i.e., Java `Object`) to the correct type. We print out the factory's name, to see if it is correct.

Next, we ask the bean's factory to make "something" with the string `"Dean Wampler"`. When we print the returned object, it should be a `NamedObject`.

If you have Spring installed in a *spring-home* directory, you can run this script with the following command:

```
scala -cp \
  spring-home/dist/spring.jar:spring-home/.../commons-logging.jar:. \
  spring/object-bean-script.scala
```

(The current working directory ".." is needed in the classpath to find the XML file.) There are many lines of logging output. The last two lines are what we care about:

```
...
Factory Name: Factory for Named Objects
Object: NamedObject(Dean Wampler)
```

This example required a number of files and configuration details to get working. For a moderately large Java application, the effort is justified. However, Scala gives you new and simpler ways to implement dependency injection in Scala code without configuration files and a DI container.

Terracotta

Terracotta (see [Terracotta]) is an open source clustering product that distributes an application over several servers by clustering JVMs upon which the application executes. For efficiency, not all of the application's heap objects are distributed. Instead, the programmer specifies which data structures to distribute through configuration files. A benefit of Terracotta is that the application does not require code changes to support this clustering (at least in principle; some limited customization can be useful for performance reasons). Instead, the byte code is instrumented to provide the clustering. Terracotta is an alternative to distributed caches that require code changes.

[Bonér2008a] provides a detailed write-up of how to use Terracotta with Scala Actors. A Scala-specific Terracotta Integration Module (TIM) must be installed. When configuring which objects to distribute, you have to use the encoded names for companion objects, method names, etc., as they exist at the byte code level. We discussed these encodings in "Scala Names in Java Code" on page 375. Finally, you have to add some more parameters to the java invocation command inside the scala script. Otherwise, clustering Scala applications with Terracotta works just like it does for Java applications.

Hadoop

MapReduce is a divide-and-conquer programming model for processing large data sets in parallel. In the "map" phase, a data set is divided into N subsets of approximately equal size, where N is chosen to optimize the amount of work that can be done in parallel. For example, N might be close to the total number of processor cores available. (A few cores might be left idle as "backups" or for doing other processing.) The desired computation is performed on each subset. The "reduce" phase combines the results of the subset calculations into a final result.

Note that mapping and reducing are essentially functional operations. Therefore, a functional language like Scala is ideally suited for writing MapReduce applications.

MapReduce frameworks provide tools for mapping and reducing data sets, managing all phases of the computation, including the processing nodes, restarting operations that fail for some reason, etc. The user of a MapReduce framework only has to write the algorithms for mapping (subdividing) the input data, the computations with the data subsets, and reducing the results. See [MapReduceTutorial] for a succinct overview and [MapReduce] for a description of Google's MapReduce framework. The name of the Google framework has become a de facto standard for these frameworks.

Hadoop (see [Hadoop]) is an open source MapReduce framework created and maintained by Yahoo!. There are two Scala wrappers around the Hadoop API: *SHadoop* (see [SHadoop]) and *SMR* (see [SMRa] and ([SMRb]). Both examples demonstrate the great reduction in code size when using Scala. [SMRa] attributes this code reduction to Scala's support for higher-order and anonymous functions, its sophisticated type system and type inference, and the ability of **for** comprehensions to generate maps in an elegant and succinct way.

Recap and What's Next

This chapter filled in the details of the Scala command-line tools that you will use every day. We also surveyed the available support for Scala in various text editors and IDEs. We discussed a number of important libraries, such as testing APIs. Finally, we discussed interoperability between Scala and other JVM languages and libraries.

This completes our survey of the world of Scala programming. The next chapter is a list of references for further exploration, followed by a glossary of terms that we have used throughout the book.

References

[Abelson1996] Harold Abelson, Gerald Jay Sussman, and Julie Sussman, *Structure and Interpretation of Computer Programs*, The MIT Press, 1996.

[Agha1987] Gul Agha, *Actors*, The MIT Press, 1987.

[Akka] Akka: RESTful Distributed Persistent Transactional Actors, *http://akkasource .org*.

[Ant] *The Apache Ant Project, http://ant.apache.org/*.

[Antlr] *Antlr, http://www.antlr.org/*.

[AOSD] *Aspect-Oriented Software Development, http://aosd.net/*.

[AspectJ] *The AspectJ Project, http://www.eclipse.org/aspectj/*.

[BDD] *Behavior-Driven Development, http://behaviour-driven.org/*.

[Bloch2008] Joshua Bloch, *Effective Java* (Second Edition), Addison-Wesley, 2008.

[Bonér2008a] Jonas Bonér, *Clustering Scala Actors with Terracotta, http://jonasboner .com/2008/01/25/clustering-scala-actors-with-terracotta.html*.

[Bonér2008b] Jonas Bonér, *Real-World Scala: Dependency Injection (DI), http://jonasb oner.com/2008/10/06/real-world-scala-dependency-injection-di.html*.

[Bruce1998] Kim Bruce, Martin Odersky, and Philip Wadler, *A Statically Safe Alternative to Virtual Types*, Proc. ECOOP '98, E. Jul (Ed.), LNCS 1445, pp. 523–549, Springer-Verlag, 1998.

[Buildr] *Buildr, http://buildr.apache.org/*.

[Contract4J] *Contract4J: Design by Contract for Java, http://contract4j.org/*.

[Cucumber] *Cucumber - Making BDD Fun, http://cukes.info*.

[DesignByContract] *Building bug-free O-O software: An introduction to Design by Contract™, http://archive.eiffel.com/doc/manuals/technology/contract/*.

[Deursen] Arie van Deursen, Paul Klint, and Joost Visser, *Domain-Specific Languages: An Annotated Bibliography*, *http://homepages.cwi.nl/~arie/papers/dslbib/*.

[EBNF] *Extended Backus-Naur Form*, *http://en.wikipedia.org/wiki/Extended_Backus–Naur_Form*.

[Eiffel] *Eiffel Software*, *http://eiffel.com*.

[Ford] Bryan Ford, *The Packrat Parsing and Parsing Expression Grammars Page*, *http://pdos.csail.mit.edu/~baford/packrat/*.

[Ford2009] Neal Ford, *Advanced DSLs in Ruby*, *http://github.com/nealford/presentations/tree/master*.

[Fowler2009] Martin Fowler, *Domain Specific Languages* (forthcoming), *http://martinfowler.com/dslwip/*.

[FunctionalJava] *Functional Java*, *http://functionaljava.org*.

[Ghosh2008a] Debasish Ghosh, *External DSLs made easy with Scala Parser Combinators*, *http://debasishg.blogspot.com/2008/04/external-dsls-made-easy-with-scala.html*.

[Ghosh2008b] Debasish Ghosh, *Designing Internal DSLs in Scala*, *http://debasishg.blogspot.com/2008/05/designing-internal-dsls-in-scala.html*.

[GOF1995] Erich Gamma, Richard Helm, Ralph Johnson, and John Vlissides ("Gang of Four"), *Design Patterns: Elements of Reusable Object-Oriented Software*, Addison-Wesley, 1995.

[Guice] *Guice*, *http://code.google.com/p/google-guice/*.

[Hadoop] *Hadoop*, *http://hadoop.apache.org*.

[Haller2007] Philipp Haller and Martin Odersky, *Actors That Unify Threads and Events*, *http://lamp.epfl.ch/~phaller/doc/haller07coord.pdf*.

[Hewitt1973] Carl Hewitt, Peter Bishop, and Richard Steiger, *A Universal Modular Actor Formalism for Artificial Intelligence*, *http://dli.iiit.ac.in/ijcai/IJCAI-73/PDF/027B.pdf*, 1973.

[Hoare2009] Tony Hoare, *Null References: The Billion Dollar Mistake*, *http://qconlondon.com/london-2009/speaker/Tony+Hoare*.

[Hofer2008] Christian Hofer, Klaus Ostermann, Tillmann Rendel, and Adriaan Moors, *Polymorphic Embedding of DSLs*, GPCE '08, October 19–23, 2008, Nashville, Tennessee, *http://www.daimi.au.dk/~ko/papers/gpce50_hofer.pdf*.

[HTTP11] *Hypertext Transfer Protocol — HTTP/1.1*, *http://www.w3.org/Protocols/rfc2616/rfc2616.html*.

[Hunt2000] Andrew Hunt and Dave Thomas, *The Pragmatic Programmer*, Addison-Wesley, 2000.

[JAD] *JAva Decompiler (JAD)*, *http://www.varaneckas.com/jad*.

[Java6API] *Java Platform SE 6 API*, *http://java.sun.com/javase/6/docs/api/*.

[JavaBeansSpec] *JavaBeans Specification*, *http://java.sun.com/javase/technologies/desk top/javabeans/docs/spec.html*.

[JPAScala] *Using JPA with Scala*, *http://www.hars.de/2009/03/jpa-with-scala.html*.

[JRuby] *JRuby*, *http://jruby.codehaus.org/*.

[JUnit] *JUnit*, *http://junit.org*.

[Laddad2009] Ramnivas Laddad, *AspectJ in Action* (Second Edition), Manning Press, 2009.

[Mailslot] *Mailslot*, *http://github.com/stevej/mailslot/*.

[MapReduce] *MapReduce*, *http://labs.google.com/papers/mapreduce.html*.

[MapReduceTutorial] *Introduction to Parallel Programming and MapReduce*, *http:// code.google.com/edu/parallel/mapreduce-tutorial.html*.

[Martin2003] Robert C. Martin, *Agile Software Development: Principles, Patterns, and Practices*, Prentice Hall, 2003.

[Maven] *The Apache Maven Project*, *http://maven.apache.org/*.

[McBeath] Jim McBeath, *Scala Syntax Primer*, *http://jim-mcbeath.blogspot.com/2008/ 09/scala-syntax-primer.html*.

[McIver2009] David R. MacIver, *Scala trivia of the day: Traits can extend classes*, *http: //www.drmaciver.com/2009/04/scala-trivia-of-the-day-traits-can-extend-classes/*.

[Meyer1997] Bertrand Meyer, *Object-Oriented Software Construction* (Second Edition), Prentice Hall, 1997.

[MINA] *Apache MINA*, *http://mina.apache.org/*.

[MoneyInJava] Thomas Paul, *Working with Money in Java*, *http://www.javaranch.com/ journal/2003/07/MoneyInJava.html*.

[Naftalin2006] Maurice Naftalin and Philip Wadler, *Java Generics and Collections*, O'Reilly Media, 2006.

[Naggati] *Naggati*, *http://github.com/robey/naggati/*.

[Odersky2005] Martin Odersky and Matthias Zenger, *Scalable Component Abstractions*, OOPSLA '05, October 16–20, 2005, San Diego, California, USA.

[Odersky2006] Martin Odersky, *Pimp My Library*, *http://www.artima.com/weblogs/ viewpost.jsp?thread=179766*.

[Odersky2008] Martin Odersky, Lex Spoon, and Bill Venners, *Programming in Scala*, Artima Press, 2008.

[Odersky2009] Martin Odersky, Lex Spoon, and Bill Venners, *How to Write an Equality Method in Java*, *http://www.artima.com/lejava/articles/equality.html*.

[Okasaki1998] Chris Okasaki, *Purely Functional Data Structures*, Cambridge University Press, 1998.

[Ortiz2007] Jorge Ortiz, *Fun with Project Euler and Scala*, *http://scala-blogs.org/2007/12/project-euler-fun-in-scala.html*.

[Ortiz2008] Jorge Ortiz, *Manifests: Reified Types*, *http://scala-blogs.org/2008/10/manifests-reified-types.html*.

[OSullivan2009] Bryan O'Sullivan, John Goerzen, and Don Steward, *Real World Haskell*, O'Reilly Media, 2009.

[PEG] *Parsing Expression Grammar*, *http://en.wikipedia.org/wiki/Parsing_expression_grammar*.

[Pierce2002] Benjamin C. Pierce, *Types and Programming Languages*, The MIT Press, 2002.

[Pollak2007] David Pollak, *The Scala Option class and how lift uses it*, *http://blog.lostlake.org/index.php?/archives/50-The-Scala-Option-class-and-how-lift-uses-it.html*.

[QuickCheck] *QuickCheck, Automated Specification-Based Testing*, *http://www.cs.chalmers.se/~rjmh/QuickCheck/*.

[Rabhi1999] Fethi Rabhi and Guy Lapalme, *Algorithms: A Functional Programming Approach*, Addison-Wesley, 1999.

[RSpec] *RSpec*, *http://rspec.info/*.

[SBT] *Simple Build Tool*, *http://code.google.com/p/simple-build-tool/*.

[Scala] *The Scala Programming Language*, *http://www.scala-lang.org/*.

[ScalaAPI2008] *The Scala Library*, *http://www.scala-lang.org/docu/files/api/index.html*.

[ScalaCheckTool] *ScalaCheck*, *http://code.google.com/p/scalacheck/*.

[ScalaSpec2009] *The Scala Language Specification*, *http://www.scala-lang.org/sites/default/files/linuxsoft_archives/docu/files/ScalaReference.pdf*.

[ScalaSpecsTool] *Specs*, *http://code.google.com/p/specs/*.

[ScalaTestTool] *ScalaTest*, *http://www.artima.com/scalatest/*.

[ScalaTips] *Scala Tips Blog*, *http://scalatips.tumblr.com/*.

[ScalaTools] *Scala Tools*, *http://www.scala-tools.org/*.

[ScalaWiki] *Scala Wiki*, *http://scala.sygneca.com/*.

[ScalaWikiPatterns] *Scala Wiki: Scala Design Patterns*, *http://scala.sygneca.com/patterns/start*.

[ScalaZ] *Scalaz*, *http://code.google.com/p/scalaz/*.

[SHadoop] Jonhnny Weslley (sic), *SHadoop: What is Scala and Hadoop?*, *http://jonhnny -weslley.blogspot.com/2008/05/shadoop.html*.

[SleepingBarberProblem] *Sleeping barber problem*, *http://en.wikipedia.org/wiki/Sleep ing_barber_problem*.

[SMRa] David Hall, *A Scalable Language, and a Scalable Framework*, *http://scala-blogs .org/2008/09/scalable-language-and-scalable.html*.

[SMRb] *Scala Map Reduce*, *http://github.com/dlwh/smr/*.

[Smith2009a] Eishay Smith, *Beware of Scala's Type Inference*, *http://www.eishay.com/ 2009/05/beware-of-scalas-type-inference.html*.

[Smith2009b] Eishay Smith, *Unexpected repeated execution in Scala*, *http://www.eishay .com/2009/06/unexpected-repeated-execution-in-scala.html*.

[Spiewak2008] Daniel Spiewak, *What is Hindley-Milner? (and why is it cool?)*, *http:// www.codecommit.com/blog/scala/what-is-hindley-milner-and-why-is-it-cool*.

[Spiewak2009a] Daniel Spiewak, *Interop Between Java and Scala*, *http://www.codecom mit.com/blog/java/interop-between-java-and-scala*.

[Spiewak2009b] Daniel Spiewak, *The Magic Behind Parser Combinators*, *http://www .codecommit.com/blog/scala/the-magic-behind-parser-combinators*.

[Spiewak2009c] Daniel Spiewak, *Practically Functional*, talk at the Chicago-Area Scala Enthusiasts, May 21, 2009.

[SpringFramework] *The Spring Framework*, *http://springframework.org*.

[SXR] *A Scala source code browser*, *http://github.com/harrah/browse/tree/master*.

[Szyperski1998] Clemens Szyperski, *Component Software: Beyond Object-Oriented Programming*, Addison-Wesley Longman Limited, 1998.

[TDD] *Test-Driven Development*, *http://en.wikipedia.org/wiki/Test-driven_develop ment*.

[Terracotta] *Terracotta*, *http://terracotta.org/*.

[TestNG] *TestNG*, *http://testng.org/*.

[Turbak2008] Franklyn Turbak, David Gifford, and Mark A. Sheldon, *Design Concepts of Programming Languages*, The MIT Press, 2008.

[TypeInference] *Type inference*, *http://en.wikipedia.org/wiki/Type_inference*.

[VanRoy2004] Peter Van Roy and Seif Haridi, *Concepts, Techniques, and Models of Computer Programming*, The MIT Press, 2004.

[Wampler2008] Dean Wampler, *Traits vs. Aspects in Scala*, *http://blog.objectmentor .com/articles/2008/09/27/traits-vs-aspects-in-scala*.

[WirfsBrock2003] Rebecca Wirfs-Brock and Alan McKean, *Object Design: Responsibilities, and Collaborations*, Pearson Education, 2003.

Glossary

$tag

A method declared by the `ScalaObject` trait and used internally by Scala. It takes no arguments and returns an integer. It is currently used to optimize pattern matching, but it may be removed in a future release of Scala. While normally invisible to Scala code (it is generated automatically by the compiler), Java code that extends some Scala traits and classes may need to implement this method.

Abstraction

The outwardly visible state, state transformations, and other operations supported by a type. This is separate from the *encapsulated* implementation (fields and methods) of the abstraction. Scala *traits* and *abstract classes* are often used to define abstractions and optionally implement them. *Concrete types* provide complete implementations.

Abstract Type

i. A *class* or *trait* with one or more methods, fields, or types declared, but undefined. Abstract types can't be instantiated. Contrast with *concrete types*.

ii. A `type` declaration within an *class* or *trait* that is abstract.

Actor

An autonomous sender and receiver of messages in the *Actor model of concurrency*.

Actor Model of Concurrency

A concurrency model where autonomous *Actors* coordinate work by exchanging messages. An Actor's messages are stored in a *mailbox* until the Actor processes them.

Annotated Type

Any type that has one or more @ annotations applied to it.

Annotation

A way of attaching "metadata" to a declaration that can be exploited by the compiler and other tools for code generation, verification and validation, etc. In Scala (and Java), an annotation is a class. When used, it is prefixed with the @ character.

Any explicit type declarations are also called *type annotations*.

One or more additions to a type declaration that specify behaviors like variance under inheritance, bounds, and views.

Application

In Scala, any `object` with a `main` routine that is invoked by the JVM or .NET CLR at the start of a new process.

Arity

The number of arguments to a function.

Aspect-Oriented Programming

(Sometimes called *aspect-oriented software development*.) An approach to *cross-cutting concerns*, where the concerns are designed and implemented in a "modular" way (that is, with appropriate encapsulation, lack of duplication, etc.), then integrated into all the relevant execution points in a succinct and robust way, e.g., through declarative or programmatic means. In AOP terms, the execution points are called *join points*; a particular set of them is called a *pointcut*; and the new behavior that is executed before, after, or "around" a join point is called *advice*. *AspectJ* is the best known AOP toolkit. Scala *traits* can be used to implement some aspect-like functionality.

AspectJ

An extension of Java that supports *Aspect-Oriented Programming*. AspectJ ([AspectJ]) supports two forms of syntax: an extended Java-based syntax, and a "pure" Java syntax that uses Java annotations to indicate the *pointcuts* and *advices* of an aspect. The aspect behaviors (advices) can be incorporated into the target code at compile time, as a post-compile "weaving" step, or at load time.

Attribute

Another name for a *field*, used by convention in many object-oriented programming languages. Scala follows Java's convention of preferring the term *field* over *attribute*.

Auxiliary Constructor

A secondary constructor of a class, declared as a method named `this` with no return type. An auxiliary constructor must invoke the *primary constructor* or a previously defined *auxiliary constructor* as the first or only statement in its method body.

Base Type

A synonym for *parent type*.

Behavior-Driven Development

A style of *Test-Driven Development* (TDD) that emphasizes TDD's role in driving the understanding of requirements for the code. You follow the same process as in TDD, where the "tests" are written before the code. The difference is that the automated tests are written in a format that looks more like a requirements (or behavioral) specifi-

cation and less like a test of the code's conformance to the requirements. However, the specification format is still executable and it still provides the verification, validation, and regression testing service that TDD tests provide.

Bound Variable

A *variable* that is declared as an argument to a *function literal*. It is "bound" to a value when the *closure* created from the function literal is invoked.

By-Name Parameter

A *by-name parameter* looks like a function value that takes no parameters, but rather than being declared with the signature `p: ()` $\Rightarrow$ R, where R is the return type, it is declared with the signature `p:` $\Rightarrow$ R. By-name parameters are evaluated every time they are referenced in the function, rather than being evaluated *once* just before the function call, like a *by-value parameter*. For example, they are useful for a function that is designed to look like a control construct that takes a "block," not a function with explicit parameter arguments (think of how `while` loops look, for example). The function argument that has block-like behavior would be a by-name parameter.

By-Value Parameter

A *by-value parameter* is the usual kind of method parameter that is evaluated before it is passed to the method. Contrast with *by-name parameter*.

Call By Name

See *by-name parameter*.

Call By Value

See *by-value parameter*.

Call Site

See *declaration site*.

Case

The keyword used in *pattern matching* expressions for testing an object against an *extractor*, type check, etc.

Case Class

A class declared with the keyword `case`. The Scala compiler automatically defines `equals`, `hashCode` and `toString` methods for the class and creates a *companion object* with an `apply` factory method and an `unapply` extractor method. Case classes are particularly convenient for use with *pattern matching* (*case*) expressions.

Child Type

A class or trait that inherits from a `parent` class or trait. Sometimes called a *subtype* or *derived type*. See *inheritance*.

Client

An informal term used throughout the book to indicate a section of software that uses another as an API, etc.

Class

A template for *instances* that will have the same fields, representing state values, and the same methods. Scala classes support single *inheritance* and zero or more *mixin* traits. Contrast with *type*.

Closure

In Scala, an instance that has been created from a *function literal* with all the *free variables* referenced in the function literal bound to variables of the same name in the enclosing scope where the function literal was defined. In other words, the instance is "closed" in the sense that the free variables are bound. Because they are instances, closures are *first-class* values. They can be passed to other functions to customize their behavior. For example, `List.foreach` takes a closure that is applied to each element in the list. See also *bound variables* and *function literals*.

Comments

Scala follows the same comment conventions as Java, C#, C++, etc. A `// comment` goes to the end of a line, while a `/* comment */` can cross line boundaries.

Companion Class

A `class` declared with the same name as an object and defined in the same source file. See also *companion object*.

Companion Object

An `object` declared with the same name as a class (called its *companion class*) and defined in the same source file. Companion objects are where methods and fields are defined that would be statics in Java classes, such as factory methods, `apply` and `unapply` for pattern matching, etc.

Component

For our purposes, an aggregation of cohesive types that expose services through well-defined abstractions, while encapsulating implementation details and minimizing coupling to other components. (There is a wide-range of definitions for *component* in computer science and industry.)

Compound Type

The actual type of a declaration of the form `T1 extends T2 with T3 with ... TN { R }`, where R is the *refinement* (body). Definitions in R affect the type.

Concrete Type

A *class*, *trait*, or *object* with all methods, fields, and types defined. *Instances* can be created from concrete types. Contrast with *abstract types*.

Contract

The protocol and requirements that exist between a module (e.g., class, trait, object, or even function or method) and clients of the module. More specifically, see *Design by Contract*.

Context-Free Grammar

A kind of language grammar for which each *nonterminal* can be specified as a *production* without reference to additional context information. That is, each nonterminal can appear by itself on the lefthand side of the production the specifies it.

Contravariance or Contravariant

In the context of the variance behavior of *parameterized types* under inheritance, if a parameter A is *contravariant* in a parameterized type T[-A], then the - is the *variance annotation*, and a type T[B] is a *supertype* of T[A] if B is a *subtype* of A. See also *covariance* and *invariance*.

Covariance or Covariant

In the context of the variance behavior of *parameterized types* under inheritance, if a parameter A is *covariant* in a parameterized type T[+A], then the + is the *variance annotation*, and a type T[B] is a *subtype* of T[A] if B is a *subtype* of A. See also *contravariance* and *invariance*.

Cross-Cutting Concerns

"Concerns" (kinds of requirements, design or coding issues) that don't fit in the same boundaries as the primary modularity decomposition. The same behaviors must be invoked consistently at specific execution points over a range of objects and functions. For example, the same ORM (Object-Relational Mapping) persistence strategy needs to be used consistently for a set of classes, not just a single class. Hence, such concerns are said to be cross-cutting. Supporting these concerns should not involve duplication of code, etc. See also *aspect-oriented programming*.

Currying

Converting an N argument function into a sequence of N functions of one argument, where each function except for the last returns a new function that takes a single argument that returns a new function, etc., until the last function that takes a single argument and returns a value.

Declaration Site

In reference to how the *variance* behavior of parameterized types is specified, in Scala, this is done when types are *declared*, i.e., at the *declaration site*. In Java, it is done when types are *called* (that is, used), i.e., at the *call site*.

Declarative Programming

The quality of many *functional* programs and *Domain-Specific Languages* where the code consists of statements that declare relationships between values and types, rather than directing the system to take a particular sequence of action. Contrast with *imperative programming*.

Default Argument Value

(Scala version 2.8.) The ability to define a default value for a method argument that will be used if the caller does not specify a value. See also *implicit argument* and *named argument*.

Dependency Injection

A form of *inversion of control* where an object's external dependencies are given to it, either programmatically or through a DI framework that is driven by configuration information. Hence, the object remains "passive," rather than taking an active role in resolving dependencies. The injection mechanism uses constructor arguments or field setters provided by the object. DI minimizes the coupling of objects; they only need to know about the abstractions of their dependencies.

Derived Type

A synonym for *child type*.

Design By Contract

An approach to class and module design invented by Bertrand Meyer for the Eiffel language. For each entry point, valid inputs are specified in a programmatic way, so they can be validated during testing. These specifications are called *preconditions*. Similarly, assuming the preconditions are specified, specifications on the guaranteed results are called *postconditions* and are also specified in an executable way. *Invariants* can also be specified that should be true on entry and on exit.

Design Pattern

A solution to a problem in a context. A code idiom or design structure that satisfies the needs of a frequently occurring problem, constraint, requirement, etc.

Domain-Specific Language

A custom programming language that resembles the terms, idioms, and expressions of a particular domain. An *internal* DSL is an idiomatic form of a general-purpose programming language. That is, no special-purpose parser is created for the language. Instead, DSL code is written in the general-purpose language and parsed just like any other code. An *external* DSL is a language with its own grammar and parser.

Duck Typing

A term used in languages with *dynamic typing* for the way method resolution works. As long as an object accepts a method call (message send), the runtime is satisfied. "If it walks like a duck and talks like a duck, it's a duck." Contrast with the use of *structural types* in some *statically typed* languages like Scala.

Dynamic Typing

Loosely speaking, late binding of type information, sometimes referred to as binding to the value a reference is assigned to, rather than to the reference itself. Contrast with *static typing*.

Encapsulation

Restricting the visibility of members of a type so they are not visible to clients of the type when they shouldn't be. This is a way of exposing only the *abstraction* supported by the type, while hiding implementation details, which prevents unwanted access to them from clients and keeps the *abstraction* exposed by the type consistent and minimal.

Event

The notification of a state change in *event-based concurrency*.

Event-Based Concurrency

A high-performance form of concurrency where events are used to signal important state changes and handlers are used to respond to the events.

Existential Types

A way of expressing the presence of a type without knowing its concrete value, sometimes, because it can't be known. It is used primarily to support aspects of Java's type system within Scala's type system, including *type erasure*, "raw" types (e.g., pre-Java 5 collections), and *call site type variance*.

Extractor

An `unapply` method defined in a *companion object* that is used to extract the constituent values for fields in an object. They are most commonly used in *pattern matching* expressions.

Field

A `val` or `var` in a type that represents part, if not all, of the state of a corresponding instance of the type.

Final

Keyword for declarations. For types, `final` prevents users from subclassing the type. For type members, `final` prevents users from overriding the members.

First Class

An adjective indicating that the applicable "thing" is a first-class value in the language, meaning you can assign instances to variables, pass them as function parameters, and return them from functions. Often used to refer to *functions*, which are first-class values in Scala and other *functional programming* languages.

For Comprehension

Another name for Scala's `for` expression.

Formal Parameter

Another name for a function argument, used in the context of binding the *free variables* in the function.

Free Variable

A *variable* that is referenced in a *function literal* but is not passed in as an argument. Therefore, it must be "bound" to a defined variable of the same name in the context where the function literal is defined, to form a *closure*.

Function

In Scala, the term *function* is used for a function that is not tied to a particular object or class. Contrast with *method*. Functions are instances of `FunctionN` types, where `N` is the *arity* of the function.

Function Literal

Scala's term for an anonymous *function* expression, from which *closures* are created.

Function Type

In Scala, all functions are instances of `FunctionN[-T1, T2, ..., TN, +R]` types, where `N` is the number of arguments (0 through 22 are supported). The type signature syntax `(T1, T2, ..., TN)` ⇒ `R` is used for declaring concrete instances, i.e., function literals.

Functional Programming

A form of programming that mimics the way mathematical functions and variables work. Mathematical functions are *side-effect-free*, and they are composable from other functions. Variables are assigned once. Functions can be assigned to variables and returned from other functions.

Generator

Expressions like `i <- listOfInts` in `for` expressions. Each pass through the loop *generates* a new `val i` taken from the list `listOfInts`, in this example.

Generics

Another term for *parameterized types*, used more often in Java than Scala.

Higher-Order Functions

Functions that take other functions as arguments or return a function value.

Immutable Value

A value that can't be changed after it has been initialized. Contrast with *mutable value*.

Imperative Programming

The quality of many *object-oriented* and "procedural" programs where the code consists of statements directing the system to take a particular sequence of actions. Contrast with *declarative programming*.

Implicit

A Scala keyword used to mark a method or function value as eligible for use as an *implicit type conversion*. The keyword is also used to mark an *implicit argument*.

Implicit Type Conversion

A method or function value that is marked with the *implicit* keyword, marking it as eligible for use as an *implicit type conversion*, whenever it is in scope and conversion is needed (e.g., for the *Pimp My Library* pattern).

Implicit Argument

Method arguments that are optional for the user to specify and indicated with the `implicit` keyword. If the user does not specify a value for the argument, a default value is used instead, which is either an in-scope value of the same type or the result of calling an in-scope, no-argument method that returns an instance of the same type. See also *default argument value*.

Infinite Data Structure

A data structure that represents a nonterminating collection of values, but which is capable of doing so without exhausting system resources. The values are not computed until the data structure is asked to produce them. As long as only a finite subset of the values are requested, resource exhaustion is avoided.

Infix Notation

A syntax supported by the compiler for methods with one argument. The method can be invoked without the period between the object and the method name and without the parentheses around the argument. When used for methods named with *operator characters*, the syntax provides a form of *operator overloading*. Sometimes also called *operator notation*. See also *postfix notation*.

Infix Type

When a parameterized type of the form `Op[A,B]` is used to instantiate a type, it can also be written as `A Op B`. For example, `Or[Throwable,Boolean]` can be written `Throwable Or Boolean`.

Inheritance

A strong relationship between one class or trait and another class or trait. The inheriting (*derived*) class or trait incorporates the members of the *parent* class or trait, as if they were defined within the derivative. The derivative may override inherited members (in most cases). Instances of a derivative are *substitutable* for instances of the parent.

Instance or Instantiate

An *object* created by invoking a *class* constructor. The word *object* is synonymous in most object-oriented languages, but we use the term *object* to refer to an explicitly declared Scala *object*, and we use the term *instance* (and the verb *instantiate*) for the more general case.

Instantiation can also refer to creating a *concrete type* from a *parameterized type* by specifying concrete types for the parameters.

Invariance and Invariant

In the context of the variance behavior of *parameterized types* under inheritance, if a parameter `A` is *invariant* in a parameterized type `T[A]`, then there is no *variance annotation*, and a type `T[B]` is a *subtype* of `T[A]` if and only if `B` equals `A`. That is, the type can't be changed. See also *covariance* and *contravariance*.

In the context of *Design by Contract*, an assertion that should be true before and after a method is executed.

Inversion of Control

The idea that an object should not instantiate its own copies of external dependencies, but rather rely on other mechanisms to supply those dependencies. IoC promotes better decoupling and testability, as the object only knows about the abstractions of its dependencies, not specific concrete implementers of them. A weak form of IoC is when an object calls a factory, service locator, etc., to obtain the dependents. Hence, the object still has an active role and it has a dependency on the "provider." The strongest form of IoC is *dependency injection*, where the object remains "passive."

Lazy

Immutable variables (`vals`) can be declared `lazy`, meaning they will only be evaluated when they are read. This feature is useful for expensive evaluations that may not be needed.

Lazy data structures can also be used to define infinite data structures that won't exhaust system resources as long as only a finite subset of the structure is evaluated. The `Stream` and `Range` classes are both lazy. Contrast with *strict*.

Linearization

The algorithm used for a type to resolve member lookup, such as overridden methods, including calls to `super`.

Literal

Used to refer to "literal" value expressions, such as numbers (e.g., `1`, `3.14`), strings (e.g., "Hello Scala!"), tuples (e.g., `(1, 2, 3)`), and *function literals* (e.g., `(x) => x + x`).

Lower Type Bounds

See *type bounds*.

Mailbox

The queue where an *Actor's* messages are stored until the Actor processes them in the *Actor model of concurrency*.

Main

The entry function for an application that is invoked by the runtime is called `main`. The name dates back to the C language. In Scala, a `main` *method* must be defined in an `object`. Java, by way of contrast, requires a `main` method to be defined as a static method of a `class`.

MapReduce

A divide-and-conquer strategy for processing large data sets in parallel. In the "map" phase, the data sets are subdivided. The desired computation is performed on each subset. The "reduce" phase combines the results of the subset calculations into a final result. MapReduce frameworks handle the details of managing the operations and the nodes they run on, including restarting operations that fail for some reason. The user of the framework only has to write the algorithms for mapping and reducing the data sets and computing with the subsets.

Member

A generic term for a *type*, *field*, or *method* declared in a *class* or *trait*.

Memoization

A form of caching that optimizes function invocations. The results from a function's invocations are saved so that when repeated invocations with the same inputs are made, the cached results can be returned instead of reinvoking the function.

Message

In the *Actor model of concurrency*, messages are exchanged between Actors to coordinate their work.

In object-oriented programming, method invocation is sometimes referred to as "sending a message to an object," especially in certain languages, like Smalltalk and, to some extent, Ruby.

Method

A *function* that is associated exclusively with an instance, either defined in a *class*, *trait*, or *object* definition. Methods can only be invoked using the `object.method` syntax.

Mixin

A narrowly focused encapsulation of state and behavior that is more useful as an adjunct to another object's state and behavior, rather than standing on its own. Mixins in Scala are implemented using *traits*.

Multiple Inheritance

In some languages, but not Scala, a type can extend more than one parent class. Compare to *single inheritance*.

Mutable Value

A value that can be changed after it has been initialized. Contrast with *immutable value*.

Named Argument

(Scala version 2.8.) The ability to refer to a method argument by name when calling the method. It is useful in combination with *default argument values* for minimizing the number of arguments that have to be specified by the caller.

Nonterminal

An item in a grammar that requires further decomposition into one or more *nonterminals* (including possibly a recursive reference to itself) and *terminals*.

Object

A cohesive unit with a particular state, possible state transitions, and behaviors. In Scala, the keyword `object` is used to declare a *singleton* explicitly, using the same syntax as *class* declarations, except for the lack of constructor parameters and auxiliary parameters (because `objects` are instantiated by the Scala runtime, not by user code). To avoid confusion with `objects`, we use the term *instance* to refer to *instances* of *classes* and `objects` generically.

Object-Oriented Programming

A form of programming that encapsulates state values and operations on that state, exposing a cohesive abstraction to clients of the object while hiding internal implementation details. OOP also supports subtyping to define specializations and "family" relationships between types.

Operator Characters

Characters like <, *, etc. that are not letters, nor digits, nor reserved characters, like left and right parentheses, curly braces, square brackets, the semicolon, colon, or comma. These characters can be used in method names to implement a form of *operator overloading.*

Operator Notation

See *infix notation.*

Operator Overloading

The feature in some languages where standard mathematical operators, like *, /, <, etc., can be defined by users for custom types. In Scala, a form of operator overloading is supported by allowing operator characters to be used as normal method names and by allowing methods with one argument to be invoked with *infix notation.* The "operator precedence" for these methods is determined by the first character, e.g., method *< will have higher precedence than method +<.

Overloaded Functions

Two or more functions defined in the same scope (e.g., as methods in a type or as "bare" functions) that have the same name but different *signatures.*

Package Objects

A special kind of object declaration that declares members that should be visible at the scope of the named package. For example, for the declaration `package object math { type Complex = ... }`, the `Complex` type can be referenced as `math.Complex`. (Scala version 2.8.)

Packrat Parsers

Parsers for *parsing expression grammars* (PEGs; see [Ford]). They have several benefits, such as lack of ambiguity and good performance characteristics. The forthcoming Scala version 2.8 parser combinator library will add support for creating packrat parsers.

Parameterized Types

Scala's analog of *generics* in Java. Parameterized types are defined with placeholder parameters for types they use. When an instance of a parameterized type is created, specific types must be specified to replace all the type parameters. See also *type constructor.*

Parent Type

A class or trait from which another class or trait is *derived.* Also called a *supertype* or *base type.* See *inheritance.*

Parsing expression grammars (PEGs)

An alternative to *context-free grammars* that provide guaranteed linear-time parsing using *memoization* and unambiguous grammars ([PEG]).

Partial Application

Associated with *currying,* where a subset of a curried function's arguments are applied, yielding a new function that takes the remaining arguments.

Partial Function

A function that is not valid over the whole range of its arguments. Pattern matching expressions can be converted to partial functions by the compiler in some contexts.

Path-Dependent Type

A nested type T is unique based on its "path," the hierarchical, period-delimited list of the enclosing packages, the enclosing types, and finally the type T itself. Instances of T can have different, incompatible types. For example, if T is nested in a trait and the trait appears in the *linearizations* of different types, then the instances in those Ts will have different types.

Pattern Matching

Case expressions, usually in a match expression, that compare an object against possible types, type extractors, regular expressions, etc., to determine the appropriate handling.

Pimp My Library

The name of a design pattern that appears to add new methods to a type. It uses an *implicit type conversion* to automatically wrap the type in a wrapper type, where the wrapper type has the desired methods.

Precondition

An assertion that should be true on entry to a method or other entry point. See *Design by Contract.*

Postcondition

An assertion that should be true on exit from a method or other boundary point. See *Design by Contract*.

Postfix Notation

A syntax supported by the compiler for methods with no argument, sometimes called *nullary* methods. The method can be invoked without the period between the object and the method name. See also *infix notation*.

Primary Constructor

The main constructor of a class, consisting of the class body with the parameter list specified after the name of the class. See also *auxiliary constructor*.

Primitive Type

A non-object type on the underlying runtime platform (e.g., JVM and .NET). Scala does not have primitive types at the source code level. Rather, it uses *value types*, which are subclasses of `AnyVal`, to wrap runtime primitives, providing object semantics at the code level, while using boxing and unboxing of primitives at the byte code level to optimize performance.

Production

A term used for each part of a grammar that decomposes a specific *nonterminal* into other nonterminals (perhaps including a recursive reference to the original nonterminal) and *terminals*.

Pure

Used in the context of functions to mean that they are *side-effect-free*. See also *referential transparency*.

Recursion

When a function calls itself as part of its computation. A termination condition is required to prevent an infinite recursion. See also *tail-call recursion*.

Reference Type

A type whose instances are implemented as objects on the runtime platform. All reference types subtype `AnyRef`.

Referential Transparency

The property of an expression, such as a function, where it can be replaced with its value without changing the behavior of the code. This can be done with *side-effect-free* functions when the inputs are the same. The primary benefit of referential transparency is that it is easy to reason about the behavior of a function, without having to understand the context in which it is invoked. That makes the function easier to test, refactor, and reuse.

Refinement

The term used for adding or overriding members in a type body for a *compound type*.

Reified Types

Where the specific types used when instantiating a generic type are retained in the byte code, so the information is available at runtime. This is a property of .NET byte code, but not JVM byte code, which uses *type erasure*. To minimize incompatibilities, both the Java and .NET Scala versions use *type erasure*.

REPL

A name given to interactive language interpreters, like the `scala` command in interpreter mode. REPL is an acronym for *Read, Evaluate, Print, Loop*.

Scaladocs

The API documentation generated from Scala source code using the `scaladoc` tool, analogous to Java's Javadocs.

Scope

A defined boundary of *visibility*, constraining what types and their members are visible within it.

Sealed

Keyword for parent classes when *all* the direct subclasses allowed are defined in the same source *file*.

Self-Type Annotation

A declaration in a trait or class that changes its type, sometimes with an alias for `this` defined (`self` is conventional). A self type can be used to indicate dependencies on other traits that will have to be mixed into a concrete instance to resolve the dependency. In some cases, these dependencies are used to ensure that an instance of the current type can be used as an instance of a dependent type in certain contexts (e.g., as used in the Observer Pattern in "Self-Type Annotations and Abstract Type Members" on page 317).

Side-Effect-Free

Functions or expressions that have no side effects, meaning they modify no global or "object" state.

Signature

For a function: the name, parameter list types, and return value. For a *method*: also includes the type that defines the method.

Single Inheritance

A class, object, or trait can extend one parent class. Compare to *multiple inheritance*.

Singleton

A class that has only one instance. In Scala, singletons are declared using the keyword `object` instead of `class`.

Singleton Types

The unique type designator that excludes path dependencies. If `p1` and `p2` are two different path-dependent types, their singleton types are `p1.type` and `p2.type`, which may be the same. Contrast with *singleton* objects. Singleton types are not specifically the types of singleton objects, but singleton objects do have singleton types.

Stable Types

Used in the context of *path-dependent types*, all but the last elements in the path must be *stable*, which roughly means that they are either packages, singleton objects, or type declarations that alias the same.

State

As in, "the state of an object," where it informally means the set of all the current values of an object's *fields*.

Static Typing

Loosely speaking, early binding of type information, sometimes referred to as binding to a reference, rather than the value to which the reference is assigned.

Strict

Used to refer to data structures that are not *lazy*, i.e., they are defined "eagerly" by the expressions used to construct them.

Structural Type

A *structural type* is like an anonymous type, where only the "structure" a candidate type must support is specified, such as *members* that must be present. Structural types do not name the candidate types that can match, nor do any matching types need to share a common *parent trait* or *class* with the structural type. Hence, structural types are a type-safe analog to *duck typing* in dynamically typed languages, like Ruby.

Subtype

A synonym for *derived type*.

Supertype

A synonym for *parent type*.

Symbol

An interned string. Literal symbols are written starting with a single "right quote," e.g., `'name`.

Tail-Call Recursion

A form of recursion where a function calls itself as the *last* thing it does, i.e., it does no additional computations with the result of the recursive call. The Scala compiler will optimize *tail-call* recursions into a loop.

Test-Driven Development

A development discipline where no new functionality is implemented until a test has been written that will pass once the functionality is implemented. See also *Behavior-Driven Development*.

Terminal

A token in a grammar, such as a keyword, that requires no further decomposition. See also *nonterminal*.

Test Double

When testing the behavior of one object, a test double is another object that satisfies a dependency in the object under test. The test double may assist in the testing process, provide controlled test data and behaviors, and modify the interaction between the object under test and the test double. Specific types of test doubles include "fakes," "mocks," and "stubs."

Trait

A class-like encapsulation of state (fields) and behavior (methods) that is used for *mixin* composition. Zero or more traits can be mixed into class declarations or when creating instances directly, effectively creating an anonymous class.

Trampoline

A loop that iterates through a list of functions, invoking each in turn. The metaphor of bouncing the functions off a trampoline is the source of the name. It can be used to rewrite a form of recursion where a function doesn't call itself, but rather calls a different function that invokes the original function, and so forth, back and forth. There is a proposal for the Scala version 2.8 compiler to include a trampoline implementation.

Tuple

A grouping of two or more items of arbitrary types into a "Cartesian product," without first defining a class to hold them. Literal tuple values are written in parentheses and separated by commas, e.g., (x1, x2, ...). They are *first-class* values, so you can assign them to variables, pass them as values, and return them from functions. Tuples are represented by TupleN classes, for N between 2 and 22, inclusive.

Type

A categorization of allowed states and operations on those states, including transformations from one state to another. The type of an instance is the combination of its declared *class* (explicitly named or anonymous), mixed-in *traits*, and the specific types used to resolve any parameters if the class or traits are *parameterized types*. In Scala, **type** is also a keyword. When indicated in the text, we sometimes use the term type to refer to a *class*, *object*, or *trait* generically.

Type Annotation

An explicit declaration of the type of a value, e.g., count: Int, where Int is the *type annotation*. A type annotation is required when *type inference* can't be used. In Scala, function parameters require type annotations, and annotations are required in some other contexts where the type can't be inferred, e.g., for return values of some functions.

Type Bounds

Constraints on the allowed types that can be used for a parameter in a *parameterized type* or assigned to an *abstract type*. In Scala, the expression A <: B defines an *upper bound* on A; it must be a *subtype* or the same as B. The expression A >: B defines a *lower bound* on A; it must be a *supertype* or the same as B.

Type Constructor

Informally, a *parameterized type* is sometimes called a type constructor, although a "non-parameterized" type is really a type constructor too, just with zero parameters! The analogy with an instance constructor is that you specify specific concrete types for the parameters to create a new concrete type, just as you specify values to an instance constructor to create an instance.

Type Designators

The conventional type IDs commonly used, e.g., class Person, object O { type t }. They are actually a shorthand syntax for *type projections*.

Type Erasure

A property of the generics type model on the JVM. When a type is created from a generic, the information about the specific types substituted for the type parameters is not stored in the byte code and is therefore not available at runtime. Scala must follow the same model. So, for example, instances of

List[String] and List[Int] are indistinguishable. Contrast with *reified types*.

Type Inference

Inferring the type of a value based on the context in which it is used, rather than relying on explicit type *annotations*. Sometimes called *implicit typing*.

Type Projections

A way to refer to a type nested within another type. For example, if a type t is declared in a class C, then the type projection for t is C#t.

Type Variance

When a *parameterized type* is declared, the variance behavior under inheritance of each type parameter can be specified using a *type variance annotation* on the type symbol.

Type Variance Annotation

On a type parameter in a parameterized types, a + prefixed to the type symbol is used to indicate *covariance*. A - prefix on the type symbol is used to indicate *contravariance*. No variance annotation is used to indicate *invariance* (the default).

Upper Type Bounds

See *type bounds*.

Value

The actual state of an instance, usually in the context of a variable that refers to the instance. See also *value type*.

Value Object

An immutable instance or object.

Value Type

A subclass of AnyVal that wraps a corresponding non-object "primitive" type on the runtime platform (e.g., JVM and .NET). The value types are Boolean, Char, Byte, Double, Float, Long, Int, and Short. (Unit is also a value type.) All are declared abstract final so they can't be used in new V expressions. Instead, programs specify literal values, e.g., 3.14 for a Double or use methods that return new values. The Scala runtime

handles instantiation. All the instances of value types are immutable *value objects*.

The term *value type* is also used to mean the categories of types for instances. That is, the type of every instance must fall into one of several categories: *annotated types*, *compound types*, *function types*, *infix types*, *parameterized types*, *tuples*, *type designators*, *type projections*, and *singleton types*.

Variable

A named reference to a value. If the variable is declared with the val keyword, a new value can't be assigned to the variable. If the variable is declared with the var keyword, a new value can be assigned to the variable. The value a variable references must be type-compatible with the declared or inferred type of the variable.

View

An implicit value of function type that converts a type A to B. The function has the type A => B or (=> A) => B. (In the later case, the (=> A) is a *by-name parameter*.) An in-scope *implicit type conversion* method with the same signature can also be used as a view.

View Bounds

A type specification of the form A <% B, which says that any type can be used for A as long as an in-scope *view* exists that can convert an A to a B.

Visibility

The *scope* in which a declared *type* or type *member* is visible to other types and members.

Index

Symbols

! (exclamation point)
    ! method, sending messages to Actors, 21, 55, 196
    !! method, sending messages to Actors, 202
    != (not equal) method, 143
    != (not equal) operator, 63
    encoding in Java identifiers, 375
    operator precedence, 56
" " (quotation marks, double)
    enclosing string literals, 39
    escaping in character literals, 38
    triples of double quotes, bounding multi-line string literals, 39
(pound sign)
    encoding in Java identifiers, 375
    use in type projections, 51
$ (dollar sign) in identifiers, 54
% (percent sign)
    encoding in Java identifiers, 375
    operator precedence, 56
& (ampersand)
    && (and) operator, 63
    encoding in Java identifiers, 375
    operator precedence, 56
' ' (quotation marks, single)
    enclosing character literals, 38
    in symbol literals, 39
( ) (parentheses)
    capture groups in regular expressions, 69
    in method invocations, dropping, 53
    omitting for by-name function parameter, 189
    omitting in method definitions, 124

    omitting in method invocations, 55
    substituting curly braces for in method call, 19
* (asterisk)
    multiplication operator, encoding in Java identifiers, 375
    operator precedence, 56
    zero or more repetitions in production rule, 233
+ (plus sign)
    ++ method, appending to lists, 57
    encoding in Java identifiers, 375
    operator precedence, 56
    specifying at least one repetition in production rule, 233
    variance annotations, 251, 254
- (minus sign)
    encoding in Java identifiers, 375
    operator precedence, 56
    variance annotations, 251, 254
-> (right arrow) operator, 41
. (dot)
    infix operator notation, 223
    omitting in method calls, 53, 55
    period-delimited path expressions, 274
/ (slash)
    /* */ in multi-line comments, 11
    // in single-line comments, 11
    division operator, encoding in Java identifiers, 375
    operator precedence, 56
: (colon)
    :: (constructor) method
        extracting head and tail of list, 65
        prepending to a list, 57

We'd like to hear your suggestions for improving our indexes. Send email to *index@oreilly.com*.

:: class, 263

:\ (foldRight) and :/ (foldLeft), 180

    encoding in Java identifiers, 375

    methods ending in, right-associative invocation, 57

    operator precedence, 56

    separator between identifiers and type annotations, 12, 51

; (semicolon)

    ending production rule definitions, 232

    ending statements in Scala code, 23

    separators in for expression, 60

< > (angle brackets)

    < (less than) operator, 63

        encoding in Java identifiers, 375

    <% indicating view bound in type declaration, 51, 264

    <- (left-arrow) operator, generators, 51, 60, 62

    <:, use in parameterized and abstract type declarations, 51

    > (greater than) operator, 63

        encoding in Java identifiers, 375

    >:, constraining allowed types in parameterized and abstract type declarations, 51

    in method names, 13

    operator precedence, 56

= (equals sign)

    == (equals) method, 143

    == (equals) operator, 63, 138

    => in function literals, 51

    assignment operator, 51

    encoding in Java identifiers, 375

    in method definitions, 13, 26

        missing, 35

    operator precedence, 56

? (question mark)

    encoding in Java identifiers, 375

@ (at sign)

    encoding in Java identifiers, 375

    extracting value of XML attributes, 213

    marking annotations, 51

[ ] (square brackets)

    enclosing optional items in parser grammar, 233

    use with parameterized types, 13, 29, 47

\ (backslash)

    in character escape sequences, 38

    encoding in Java identifiers, 375

    escaping double quotes in string literals, 39

    projection functions, 212

    \ and \\ operators for document structures, 55

^ (caret)

    encoding in Java identifiers, 375

    operator precedence, 56

_ (underscore)

    in identifiers, 54

    method chaining and function-literal shorthands, 16

    placeholder in imports, function literals, etc., 15, 51

    reserved word, 54

    wildcard character in Scala, 19, 45, 64

`` (back quotes) in literals, 54

{ } (curly braces)

    enclosing class body, 12

    enclosing for expressions, 60

    in method declarations, 26

    substituting for parentheses in method call, 19

    { indicating more code on next line, 24

| (vertical bar)

    encoding in Java identifiers, 375

    operator precedence, 56

    or case in parser grammar, 235

    || (or) operator, 63

~ (tilde)

    case class defined by Parsers trait, 238

    encoding in Java identifiers, 375

    ~, ~>, and <~ combinator operators, 234

A

abstract classes, 18

abstract keyword, 83

abstract type members, 6, 111

    overriding abstract methods, 113

abstract types, 47, 267–272

    combined with self-type annotations, 317

    defined, 393

    overriding, 120–123

    parameterized types versus, 270

abstraction, 393

access modifier keywords, 97

Actors, 5, 194–203

    in abstract, 194

    Actor class, 194

Actor class and object, 19
Actor model of concurrency, 393
    defined, 393
    effective use of, 202
    example, 17–21
    example using sleeping barber problem,
        197–202
    factory method for creating, 194
    mailbox, 196
    methods, listed, 202
    sending messages to, 195
    shortcut operators used with, 55
    using with MINA NIO and Naggati library
        for SMTP server, 205–210
actors.maxPoolSize system property, 208
advice (in AOP), 378
alternative composition, 232
and operator (&&), 63
annotated types, 275, 393
Annotation class, 291
    Scala annotations derived from, 293
annotations, 289–300
    advantages and disadvantages of, 304
    available only in Scala version 2.8 or later,
        295
    defined, 393
    nesting, 293
    Scala annotations derived from Annotation,
        293
    Scala annotations derived from
        StaticAnnotation, 294
    @scala.reflect.BeanProperty, 374, 381
anonymous classes
    creating, 82
Ant, Scala plugin for, 353
Any class, 91
    != (not equal) method, 143
    == (equals) method, 143
Any object, 155
AnyRef class
    == (equals) method, 143
    eq and ne methods, 143
AnyRef object, 155
    direct and indirect subtypes, 156
    reflection methods, 248
AnyVal object, 155
    direct subtypes, 156
AnyVal types, conversion to Java primitives,
    375

AOP (see aspect-oriented programming)
Apache MINA, 205
application design, 289–342
    annotations, 289–300
    Design by Contract, 340
    design patterns, 325–340
    effective trait design, 321–325
    enumerations versus case classes and
        pattern matching, 304
    enumerations versus pattern matching,
        300–304
    exceptions and alternatives, 311
    nulls versus Options, 306
    scalable abstractions, 313
applications, 393
apply method, 127–129
    for collections, 132
    objects with, considered as functions, 277
arity, 393
Array class
    apply method, 129
    sameElements method, 143
Array object, apply method overloaded for
        AnyVal and AnyRef types, 259
ArrayBuffer object, 176
arrays, comparing for equality, 143
arrow operator (<-), 60, 62
ArrowAssoc class, 146
aspect-oriented programming (AOP), 76, 377
    defined, 394
AspectJ library, 377–381, 394
AtomFeed class (example), 215
attributes, 90, 394
auxiliary constructors, 92, 394

B

bang method (see ! (exclamation point), under
        Symbols)
base classes, 91
base type, 394
BDD (Behavior-Driven Development), 57
    BDD syntax provided by ScalaTest, 361
    defined, 394
    specification exercising combined Button
        and Subject types, 80
    Specs library, 363–365
BigDecimal class, 221
blogging system (example), 215–216
    AtomFeed class, 215

methods defined in, visibility to Java code, 374

Pair object for Pair class, 146

unapply method, 129–131

compiled, command-line tool, converting script to, 15

compiler (see scalac compiler)

compiling versus interpreting, 12

component model, functional programming and, 192

components

defined, 313, 395

fine-grained visibility rules in Scala, 314

implementing as traits, 337

compound types, 276

defined, 395

comprehensions, 59

concrete types, 395

concurrency, 16–21

Actor model of, 393

event-based, 397

Java and, 2

problems of shared, synchronized state, 193

traditional, using threading and events, 203–210

events, 205–210

one-off threads, 203

using java.util.concurrent, 204

using Actors, 194–203

Actors in abstract, 194

Actors in Scala, 194–203

conditional operators, 63

Console.println( ) method, 14

constant identifiers, 54

constants

default argument values, 27

defining, 149

constructors, 18, 92–95

case class, 138

constraints on, advantages and disadvantage of, 94

parent class constructors, calling, 94

context-free grammars, 230, 395

contract, 254

defined, 395

contractual constraints in Design by Contract, 340

contravariance or contravariant, 396

contravariant subclassing, 252

covariance or covariant, 396

covariant specialization, 317

covariant subclassing, 252

@cps (continual passing style) annotation, 298

cross-cutting concerns, 396

cross-platform installer (lzPack), 8

curried functions, 184, 278

currying, 396

D

data types, 247–288

abstract, 47, 267

parameterized types versus, 270

AnyVal types, conversion to Java primitives, 375

defined, 404

documentation for Scala type system, 288

existential types, 284

importing types and their members, 45

inferring type information, 29–36

infinite data structures and lazy vals, 285

Nothing and Null, 267

parameterized types, 47, 249

path-dependent types, 272

pattern matching on type, 65

reflection, 248

Scala's sophisticated type system, 6

self-type annotations, 279–283

static versus dynamic typing, 2

structural types, 77, 283

type bounds, 259–267

type hierarchy in Scala, 155

value types, 275–279

variance under inheritance, 251

variance in Scala versus Java, 256–259

variance of mutable types, 255

decimal integer literals, 36

declaration site, 251, 396

declarations

annotations in, 289–300

order of declaration, traits and, 86

visibility modifiers in, 97

declarative composition of traits, 86

declarative programming, 396

decompilers (scalap, javap, and jad), 350

deep matching, 67

def keyword, 12, 26

external DSLs, 218, 230
  (see also DSLs)
  internal DSLs versus, 244
extractors, 397
  translating regular expression capture
      groups to, 69
  unapply methods, 129
  use in pattern matching case statements,
      138

F

factory methods, apply method as, 127
family polymorphism, 317
Fibonacci sequence, calculating, 285
fields, 90
  comparison to Java class-level, 148
  defined, 397
  indistinguishable from accessor methods,
      overriding, 123–126
  mutable, 18
  order of initialization, using lazy vals, 190
  overriding abstract and concrete fields, 114
  overriding abstract and concrete fields in
      classes, 119
  overriding abstract and concrete fields in
      traits, 114–119
  referencing object field, 149
  visibility and access to, 97
filtering
  in for expressions, 60
  in functional programming, 178
final declarations, attempting to override, 112
final keyword, 397
finishing problem (in DSL design), 229
first class, 397
floating-point literals, 37
fluent interface, 226
folding data structures, 179–181
for comprehensions, 59–61
  expanded variable scope, 61
  filters in, 60
  simple example, 59
  using Options with, 308
  yielding collections, 60
  yielding successive blocks of dynamically
      formatted XML, 216
foreach method, 79
  traversal operations in functional
      programming, 175

formal parameters, 397
FP (see functional programming)
free variables, 397
fsc (fast scala compiler) tool, 353
function literals, 78
  closures and, 169
  defined, 13, 398
  passing to foreach, 16
  passing to method for pattern matching, 19
function types, 277
  defined, 398
Function.curried method, 185
Functional Java project, 367
functional programming, 165–192, 398
  call by name and call by value, 189
  component model and, 192
  currying, 184
  data structures, 172
    lists, 173
    maps, 173
  definition of, 166
  filtering operations, 178
  folding and reducing operations, 179–181
  functions in mathematics, 166
  implicit conversions, 186
  implicit function parameters, 188
  implicits, caution with, 189
  lazy vals, 190
  mapping operations, 175
  mixed paradigm in Scala, 5
  Options object, 181
  partial functions, 183
  pattern matching, 182
  recursion, 170
  in Scala, 167–170
    function literals and closures, 169
    tail calls and tail-call optimization, 171
  traversal of data structures, 175
  variables, immutable values of, 166
FunctionN object, 159
  defining traits for, 277
  variance under inheritance, 252
functions, 165
  (see also functional programming)
  defined, 398
  higher order, 166, 398
  overloaded, 401
  Scala, using in Java, 372
futures, 202

G

Gang of Four (GOF) patterns, 325
generator expressions, 62
generators
    <- (left-arrow) operator, 60
    defined, 398
    in for comprehensions, 309
generics, 6, 369–372
    defined, 398
    Java, 47
        using from Scala, 369
    Scala, using from Java, 370
    variance under inheritance, differences
        between Java and Scala, 251
grammars
    context-free, 395
    EBNF notation for external payroll DSL
        grammar, 231
    parsing expression grammars (PEGs), 401
guards, pattern matching on, 67

H

Hadoop library, 384
Haskell, QuickCheck tool, 365
hexadecimal integer literals, 36
higher-order functions, 166, 398

I

I/O (input/output)
    automatic importation of methods by Scala,
        15
    NIO (non-blocking I/O), 205
identifiers, characters allowed in, 54
IDEs (integrated development environments),
    354–360
    Eclipse
        developing Scala applications, 355
        installing Scala plugin, 354
    IntelliJ
        developing Scala applications, 357
        installing Scala plugins, 356
    NetBeans
        developing Scala applications, 360
        installing Scala plugins, 359
    text editors, 360
if statements, 58
immutable values, 398
immutable variables, 5

declaring, 24
imperative languages, 20
imperative programming, 398
implicit arguments, 398
implicit conversions
    caution with, 189
    defined, 398
    defining custom object and conversion
        method, 187
    in functional programming, 186
    in internal DSL payroll implementation,
        223
    Int into RichInt, 62
    Predef.any2ArrowAssoc method, 147
    rules for compiler to find and use conversion
        methods, 187
implicit function parameters, 188
    caution with, 189
implicit keyword, 186
    defined, 398
implicit typing, 405
import statements, 19
    importing Java types and their members,
        45
    relative path used in, 46
infinite data structures, 398
    laziness and, 285
    using lazy vals to manage, 191
infix notation, 53
    defined, 398
infix operator notation, 223
infix types, 276, 399
inheritance
    case class, 140
    defined, 399
    definition, 87
    linearization of object hierarchy, 159–163
    multiple, problems with, 321
    single inheritance plus traits in Scala, 322
    variance under, 251–259
instance, 89, 399
instantiate, 399
integer literals, 36
IntelliJ IDEA
    developing Scala applications, 357
    installing Scala plugins, 356
interactive mode, scala command, 10
@interface keyword (Java), 289
internal DSLs, 218, 229

NetBeans
developing Scala applications, 360
installing Scala plugins, 359
new operator, 14
Nil case object, 267
NIO (non-blocking I/O), 205
NioSocketAcceptor object, 208
NodeSeq class, \ and \\ methods, 55
NodeSeq object, 212
None class, 41
nonterminals, 232, 400
Nothing type, 259, 267
Null object, 267
nulls
avoiding using Option, Some, and None classes, 41–43
Options versus, 306

0

object system (Scala), 145–164
classes and objects, 148
package objects, 150
linearization of object hierarchy, 159–163
Predef object, 145
sealed class hierarchies, 151–155
type hierarchy, 155
object-oriented programming (OOP), 89
case classes, 136–142
classes and objects, basics of, 89
companion objects, 126–136
constructors, 92–95
defined, 400
equality of objects, 142
mixed paradigm in Scala, 4
nested classes, 95
overriding members of classes and traits, 111–126
parent classes, 91
reusable software components and, 192
visibility rules, 96–110
objects
basics of, 89
deep matching on contents, 67
defined, 400
instantiation in Scala, 149
in Scala, 5
versus class-level members, 14
ObservableClicks trait (example), 83

working with VetoableClicks trait (example), 85
Observer Pattern, 77, 326
trait implementing, 77
octal integer literals, 36
Odersky, Martin, 7
Open-Closed Principle (OCP), 153
violation by Visitor Pattern, 328
operator characters, 54
defined, 401
encoding in Java identifiers, 375
in identifiers, 54
operator notation, 398
infix operator notation, 53, 223
operator overloading, 401
operator precedence, 56
operators, 53
conditional, 63
Option class, 41–43
alternatives to exceptions, 312
functional operations on, 181
nulls versus, 306
using with for comprehensions, 308
or operator (||), 63
overloaded functions, 401
overloaded methods, 90
explicit return type requirement, 32
override keyword, 18, 79, 111
overriding class and trait members, 111–126
abstract and concrete fields, 114
in classes, 119
in traits, 114–119
abstract and concrete methods, 112
abstract types, 120–123
accessor methods indistinguishable from fields, 123–126
final declarations, 112

P

package objects, 150, 401
packages, 44
defining using nested package syntax in Scala, 44
root package for Scala library classes, 45
packrat parsers, 245, 401
Pair class, 146
apply method, 127
Pair object, 146
parameterized methods, 251

Q

QuickCheck (Haskell), 365

R

Range object, 287
Range.Inclusive class, 62
raw strings in regular expression pattern
    matching, 69
recursion, 28, 402
    explicit return type annotation, 30, 31
    in functional programming, 170
    tail-call, 171
        foldLeft and reduceLeft, 181
reducing data structures, 179–181
Reductio tool, 367
reference types, 91, 402
    linearization algorithm for, 160, 161
    listed, 156
    parent of, AnyRef, 155
    testing equality, 143
referential transparency, 402
refinement in compound type declarations,
    276
    defined, 402
reflection, 248
Regex class, 69
regular expressions
    matching on, 68
    use in parsing, 235
reified types, 402
relative imports, 46
REPL (Read, Evaluate, Print, Loop), 402
Request case class, 207
requirements specification, 363
reserved words
    listing of reserved words in Scala, 49
    not allowed in identifiers, 54
@Retention annotation, 290
@return annotation, 241
return keyword, 13, 31
return type for methods, 30–36
    required explicit declarations of, 31
    using Option, Some, and None types, 41
RichInt class, 62
RichString class, 186
right-associative method invocations, 57
Ruby
    dynamic typing, 2

exceptions, 312
method resolution in, 283

S

sbaz tool, 10, 352
    installing ScalaCheck, 365
SBT (simple build tool), 353
Scala
    benefits of, 7
    code examples, 10–16
    combining with other languages, 8
    installing, 8
    introduction to, 4
    official website, 8
    resources for more information, 10
scala command, 10, 12, 345–350
    -cp option, 16, 346
    commands available in scala interactive
        mode, 347
    documentation, 348
    interactive mode, 10
    invoking scripts, 348
    limitations of, versus scalac, 348
    options, 347
    running in interpreted mode, 346
    script or object specified for, 346
scala-tool-support package, 360
scala.actors.Actor class, 194
@scala.reflect.BeanProperty annotation, 374,
    381
scalability, Scala support for, 6
scalable abstractions (see components)
scalable language (Scala), 7
scalac compiler, 10, 343
    -X options, 345
    -Xscript option, 349
    command options, 344
    compiling code into JVM .class file, 16
    plugin architecture, 345
    scala command versus, 348
ScalaCheck, 365
scaladoc tool, 10, 352
Scaladocs, 402
ScalaObject class, 157
    $tag method, 351, 393
scalap tool, 350
ScalaTest, 361
Scalax library, 368
Scalaz library, 368

About the Authors

Dean Wampler is a consultant, trainer, and mentor with Object Mentor, Inc. He specializes in Scala, Java, and Ruby, and works with clients on application design strategies that combine object-oriented programming, functional programming, and aspect-oriented programming. He also consults on Agile methods, such as Lean and XP. Dean is a frequent speaker at industry and academic conferences on these topics. He has a Ph.D. in physics from the University of Washington.

Alex Payne is Platform Lead at Twitter, Inc., where he develops services that enable programmers to build atop the popular social messaging service. Alex has previously built web applications for political campaigns, non-profits, and early-stage startups, and supported information security efforts for military and intelligence customers. In his free time, Alex studies, speaks, and writes about the history, present use, and evolution of programming languages, as well as minimalist art and design.

Colophon

The animal on the cover of *Programming Scala* is a Malayan tapir (*Tapirus indicus*), also called an Asian tapir. It is a black-and-white hoofed mammal with a round, stocky body similar to that of a pig. At 6–8 feet long and 550–700 pounds, the Malayan is the largest of the four tapir species. It lives in tropical rain forests in Southeast Asia.

The Malayan tapir's appearance is striking: its front half and hind legs are solid black, and its midsection is marked with a white saddle. This pattern provides perfect camouflage for the tapir in a moonlit jungle. Other physical characteristics include a thick hide, a stumpy tail, and a short, flexible snout. Despite its body shape, the Malayan tapir is an agile climber and a fast runner.

The tapir is a solitary and mainly nocturnal animal. It tends to have very poor vision, so it relies on smell and hearing as it roams large territories in search of food, tracking other tapirs' scents and communicating via high-pitched whistles. The Malayan tapir's predators are tigers, leopards, and humans, and it is considered endangered due to habitat destruction and overhunting.

The cover image is from the Dover Pictorial Archive. The cover font is Adobe ITC Garamond. The text font is Linotype Birka; the heading font is Adobe Myriad Condensed; and the code font is LucasFont's TheSansMonoCondensed.

Get even more for your money.

Join the O'Reilly Community, and register the O'Reilly books you own.It's free, and you'll get:

- 40% upgrade offer on O'Reilly books
- Membership discounts on books and events
- Free lifetime updates to electronic formats of books
- Multiple ebook formats, DRM FREE
- Participation in the O'Reilly community
- Newsletters
- Account management
- 100% Satisfaction Guarantee

Signing up is easy:

1. **Go to: oreilly.com/go/register**
2. **Create an O'Reilly login.**
3. **Provide your address.**
4. **Register your books.**

Note: English-language books only

To order books online:

oreilly.com/order_new

For questions about products or an order:

orders@oreilly.com

To sign up to get topic-specific email announcements and/or news about upcoming books, conferences, special offers, and new technologies:

elists@oreilly.com

For technical questions about book content:

booktech@oreilly.com

To submit new book proposals to our editors:

proposals@oreilly.com

Many O'Reilly books are available in PDF and several ebook formats. For more information:

oreilly.com/ebooks

Spreading the knowledge of innovators   www.oreilly.com

©2009 O'Reilly Media, Inc. O'Reilly logo is a registered trademark of O'Reilly Media, Inc. 00000

Buy this book and get access to the online edition for 45 days—for free!

Programming Scala
By Dean Wampler & Alex Payne
September 2009, $44.99
ISBN 9780596155957

With Safari Books Online, you can:

Access the contents of thousands of technology and business books

- Quickly search over 7000 books and certification guides
- Download whole books or chapters in PDF format, at no extra cost, to print or read on the go
- Copy and paste code
- Save up to 35% on O'Reilly print books
- **New!** Access mobile-friendly books directly from cell phones and mobile devices

Stay up-to-date on emerging topics before the books are published

- Get on-demand access to evolving manuscripts.
- Interact directly with authors of upcoming books

Explore thousands of hours of video on technology and design topics

- Learn from expert video tutorials
- Watch and replay recorded conference sessions

To try out Safari and the online edition of this book FREE for 45 days,
go to *www.oreilly.com/go/safarienabled* and enter the coupon code PPOZYBI.
To see the complete Safari Library, visit safari.oreilly.com.

Spreading the knowledge of innovators   safari.oreilly.com

©2009 O'Reilly Media, Inc. O'Reilly logo is a registered trademark of O'Reilly Media, Inc. 00000